FUNDAMENTALISM

Studies in Comparative Religion
Frederick M. Denny, Series Editor

FUNDAMENTALISM

Perspectives on a Contested History

::

Edited by

Simon A. Wood and David Harrington Watt

The University of South Carolina Press

Published by the University of South Carolina Press
Columbia, South Carolina 29208

www.sc.edu/uscpress

Manufactured in the United States of America

23 22 21 20 19 18 17 16 15 14 10 9 8 7 6 5 4 3 2 1

Library of Congress Cataloging-in-Publication Data

Fundamentalism : perspectives on a contested history / edited by Simon A. Wood and David Harrington Watt.
pages cm.—(Studies in comparative religion)
Includes bibliographical references and index.
ISBN 978-1-61117-354-3 (hardbound : alk. paper)—ISBN 978-1-61117-355-0 (ebook)
1. Religious fundamentalism—History. I. Wood, Simon A. II. Watt, David Harrington.

BL238.F825 2014 200—dc23 2013042689

This book was printed on a recycled paper with 30 percent postconsumer waste content.

Contents

Series Editor's Preface

As series editor of Studies in Comparative Religion and as a religious studies professor who has addressed "fundamentalism" for many years in courses and discussions with students and colleagues, I am confident that this book will take the extensive, diverse, and often passionate discourses on fundamentalism to a newer and higher level as we think of the concept globally and comparatively. As editors Wood and Watt remarked early in discussing their proposal with the press: "Originally embedded in American Protestantism, fundamentalism was subsequently applied to Islam and thence to Judaism and world religions generally. Here Islam is the critical pivot in the development of a genuinely global concept and hence the attention paid to it. Audience was also a consideration, seminars on Islam being one of the course categories for which our book is designed."

I am pleased to add that this book will in itself be valued as a major "study in comparative religion," not only with respect to theories and methods but equally with respect to deeper understandings of actual "brand name" religious traditions in their own spaces and times. I am confident that the book will be received as a solid contribution to advanced scholarship as well as an accessible guide for college- and graduate-level students in a variety of humanities and social science courses beyond religious studies as well as thoughtful readers outside academe generally and in a wide range of religious traditions and organizations.

Frederick M. Denny

Acknowledgments

We are very grateful for the generous support we have received from the Harris Center for Judaic Studies at the University of Nebraska–Lincoln. The University of Nebraska–Lincoln, the American Academy of Religion, the Midwestern Political Science Association, Columbia University, and Monash University all gave us opportunities to try out our ideas about fundamentalism before intelligent, generous, and critical audiences. We are grateful to them.

We would also like express our gratitude to the many scholars and others who have helped propel this project along. Jim Denton, Mahmoud Ayoub, Laura Levitt, Sidnie Crawford, Julia Keown, G. Antony Wood, Marco Abel, Deborah Ruigh, Joel Carpenter, Jennifer Hammer, and Matthew Brittingham deserve special mention. We are particularly indebted to them for all the help that they have given us. Finally, thanks go to our three anonymous readers for their extremely helpful comments.

Introduction

Simon A. Wood and David Harrington Watt

This book explores the ways in which the concept of fundamentalism does and does not illuminate developments in modern Christianity, Judaism, and Islam. For reasons elaborated below, Asian religions are not examined in detail. At issue is whether the word *fundamentalism* captures something important that is not captured—or not as well—by some other word. Readers will quickly discover that in exploring this issue, as Gordon D. Newby observes in the conclusion, the book is "at war with itself." This is intentional. We have self-consciously created a book in which there is a range of voices. This is reflective of a spectrum of views that scholars have offered on the topic. This includes the views of those who find the concept not merely helpful but important as well, those who have concerns about it but do not reject it, those who find that it has been misapplied in critical instances, and those who simply find it unhelpful. While there are, then, many more than two perspectives on the topic, one may identify two very broad groups of scholars, one at each end of the spectrum: those who find the concept illuminating and those who do not. We take the latter position but have not privileged that here, as the selection of essays and the conclusion reflect.

It would be a considerable understatement to characterize the literature on fundamentalism as extensive. The production of books and articles grew exponentially during the last two decades of the previous century and continues at a prolific rate. In view of this circumstance, one might speculate whether there can be any ground left to explore that has not been thoroughly covered already.[1] Yet the rubric of fundamentalism clearly continues to provide a venue for important discussions about the nature of religion in the modern world. The essays in this book do not survey all of these discussions, but they do engage a variety of works arguing for and against the claim that fundamentalism is a helpful term. Taking the literature as a whole, scholarly and popular, the affirmative position is ascendant. Within the humanities the picture is less clear, with dissenting voices both numerous and prominent. The most prominent scholars arguing that use of the word *fundamentalism* facilitates our understanding of religion in the modern world are probably Martin Marty and R. Scott Appleby, who edited the well-known multivolume Fundamentalism Project (University of Chicago Press, 1991–1995). With various refinements, Marty and Appleby have continued to advance this argument in a variety of venues, scholarly and nonscholarly. Among various publications, one may cite Appleby's 2003 book, coauthored by Gabriel A. Almond and Emmanuel Sivan, *Strong Religion: The Rise of Fundamentalisms around the World*,[2] which is the final installment in the Fundamentalism Project, his encyclopedia article,[3] and Marty's foreword to *The Fundamentalist Mindset: Psychological Perspectives on Religion, Violence, and History*.[4]

Many others who have argued for the usefulness and importance of the term include Bruce Lawrence, Youssef M. Choueiri, Malise Ruthven, Karen Armstrong, Richard Antoun, Brenda Brasher, Laurence J. Silberstein, and Ian Lustick. Lawrence's *Defenders of God: The Fundamentalist Revolt against the Modern Age* is a seminal work on the topic. Choueiri's *Islamic Fundamentalism: The Story of Islamist Movements* is now in its third edition. Ruthven's *Fundamentalism: A Very Short Introduction* is a telling indication of the extent to which many find that the term has taken hold. His very short introduction is published in an Oxford University Press series alongside scores of introductions to topics such as humanism, capitalism, socialism, communism, nationalism, and fascism. The inclusion of fundamentalism here might be taken as evidence that the argument for the usefulness of the term has been won. While Armstrong does not write in the same vein of academic scholarship as the other writers mentioned, she has made an important contribution to the discussion. Her book *The Battle for God: A History of Fundamentalism* is a *New York Times* best seller and has been an assigned textbook in numerous university courses in the English-speaking world. Thousands of undergraduate students have been influenced by her interpretation of fundamentalism, one that draws on the work of Marty and Appleby.[5]

How, in a nutshell, do these scholars see the word *fundamentalism* as illuminating? They find that, in Charles B. Strozier's representative wording, "something important" has been happening in the world during the last several decades that is not captured by words such as *traditionalism, conservatism,* and *orthodoxy*.[6] The word *fundamentalism* captures this "important something," and nothing is to be gained by using an alternative term. Indeed, alternative terms are likely to be more misleading than *fundamentalism,* if not simply inaccurate.[7] The important something is real: it exists. It is reasonably well known that the word *fundamentalists* was coined by Curtis Lee Laws, a Baptist journalist, in 1920, to designate a movement within American Protestantism whose emergence was clearly evident at that year's annual meeting of the Northern Baptist Convention, held in Buffalo, New York. This movement can be referred to as historic fundamentalism. It was a movement of conservative Protestants who felt that modernist Protestants

(Harry E. Fosdick, for example) had jettisoned core doctrines—"fundamentals"—of the Christian faith. No formal consensus was ever reached as to which specific doctrines were fundamentals, but the following were emphasized: the Trinity, the inerrancy of the Christian scriptures, the virgin birth, Christ's substitutionary atonement for mankind's sins, the physical resurrection of Christ, and the imminent return of Christ to earth to inaugurate a thousand-year reign of peace.

During the 1920s fundamentalists received a great deal of attention. Newspapers and magazines reported on fundamentalists' efforts to make sure that modernists did not exercise undue influence on America's leading seminaries and largest denominations and on fundamentalists' campaigns to prevent evolution from being taught in the nation's public schools. During the 1930s fundamentalists attracted less press attention than they had in the 1920s. But fundamentalists were clearly quite active throughout the 1930s; during that decade fundamentalists' schools, publishing houses, magazines, and radio shows displayed considerable vitality. In the 1940s, 1950s, and 1960s people who called themselves fundamentalists did not play an especially prominent role in American culture. But with the rise in the 1970s of the new Christian Right—a movement whose leaders included men such as Jerry Falwell, who wore the fundamentalist label with pride—fundamentalism once again became a phenomenon in which Americans were deeply interested.

Over the last few decades the term has become, in Lynda Clarke's wording, "unanchored" from American Protestant contexts. While there are some instances of Muslims being labeled fundamentalists in the period from the 1920s to the 1970s (e.g., by H.A.R. Gibb), works published during this period mainly examine fundamentalism as a Protestant movement. But many works published since then treat it as a worldwide phenomenon. Hence it is helpful to distinguish "global fundamentalism" from "historic fundamentalism," which is specific to American Protestantism. This dramatic shift was primarily triggered by the so-called Islamic revival of the 1970s and the Iranian Revolution in 1979. A Google book search for "Islamic Fundamentalism" from 1920 to 2000 produces a graph with a striking hockey stick image: a horizontal straight line near zero for several decades that shoots skyward in the late 1970s. Tellingly, searches for "Jewish Fundamentalism," "Hindu Fundamentalism," and "Buddhist Fundamentalism" produce almost identical images, but with the dramatic upward turn occurring a few years later. These graphs indicate that by the 1980s many writers had determined that the word *fundamentalism* captured something important that had arisen not only within Protestantism but also within other religions. Further, these graphs point to the pivotal role of Islam: *fundamentalism* was first applied to Protestantism, second to Islam, and third to world religions generally. An important article reflecting this shift is Martin Marty's seminal "Fundamentalism Reborn: Faith and Fanaticism."[8] Marty described fundamentalism as a "sociopsychological" reaction against modernity that could be found within Roman Catholicism, Hinduism, Judaism, and

Islam. The article was illustrated with a photograph of Falwell juxtaposed to one of Ayatollah Khomeini. Clearly, whatever global fundamentalism was for writers like Marty, it had something important to do with Khomeini.

Khomeini's Islamic revolution, then, is critical. While some found the ayatollah resembling Latin American revolutionaries who had been influenced by liberation theology, that idea never swayed a majority of scholars or other observers. Rather, his movement came to be seen by many as a particularly dramatic illustration of an apparent global revitalization of religion. If Khomeini's revitalization of Islam resembled Falwell's revitalization of Protestantism—as Marty suggested—then both could be labeled with the same word, *fundamentalism.* In this connection Khomeini is, almost literally, fundamentalism's poster child. His capture of a substantial state and establishment of an Islamic government had dramatically caught Western observers—academic, media, governmental—off guard. Shortly before the revolution, one U.S. intelligence report had predicted that the shah would remain in power for ten more years. Within academic circles, prevailing theories about religion's station in the modern world, largely informed by secularization theory, did not very well equip observers to understand and explain events in Iran. Hence, per Marty's suggestion, the turn to the concept of fundamentalism, unanchored from its original context, as a means to capture those events, and, subsequently, events in other parts of the Middle East, India, Israel, and elsewhere. The catalytic role played by the ayatollah has subsequently been emphasized by numerous scholars. For instance, in his review of the Fundamentalism Project, Earle H. Waugh referred to Khomeini's movement as having forced the hand of the academic establishment and as a harbinger of revisionism.[9] More recently Marranci's *Understanding Muslim Identity: Rethinking Fundamentalism* (2009) has been introduced by Palgrave Macmillan with the observation that, "since 1979, the year of the Iranian Revolution, scholars have tried to understand what has been called Islamic fundamentalism."

How then, unanchored from Protestantism, does the term capture developments in Iran and elsewhere? For many of those who find it useful, it captures a form of religiously motivated resistance to certain features of modern secularism that, ironically or paradoxically, also incorporates certain ideological and material aspects of the modern age. The more interesting analyses note that fundamentalism is something more complex than mere anachronism. It is not a medieval theocratic relic or a regressive effort to "turn back the clock" to a premodern paradigm, notwithstanding that it is sometimes described in such terms. Fundamentalism, then, is not primitivism, restorationism, or an isolationist ultraconservatism. Further, this combination of resistance and incorporation follows a "discernible pattern," or reflects a "family resemblance." Hence, so long as they can be seen or shown to be broadly representative of this pattern, movements do not need to resemble American Protestant movements in all respects to be reasonably called examples of fundamentalism. Thus, one may speak of *fundamentalisms*—Islamic,

Jewish, and even Hindu and Buddhist—rather than fundamentalism. To be sure, one must certainly allow for differences, such as those between colonized and uncolonized or colonizing peoples and cultures. Yet differences notwithstanding, Christian, Islamic, Jewish, and Hindu movements representing the "something important" are sufficiently similar to justify using the same word, *fundamentalism,* to label them: they belong to the same family. For many scholars fundamentalism has thus become a "comparative construct" or "umbrella term" comparable to older such terms including *capitalism, socialism,* and *nationalism.*

The rubric of global fundamentalism took hold. In the 1990s the Library of Congress created a new subject heading in its catalog: Religious Fundamentalism. That heading was the one under which were filed works on "militant or radical religious groups" who were "opposed to modernity and secularism" and who sought "a revival of orthodox or conservative religious beliefs and practices." Quite deliberately, the description of religious fundamentalism was written in a way that made it possible to think of Jews, Muslims, and Hindus as fundamentalists. The Library of Congress began cataloging books that treated religious fundamentalism under BL 238. It retained an older subject heading, BT 82.2, for books on Protestant fundamentalism. By the time the Library of Congress established its new subject heading, scholars had been arguing for at least a decade that fundamentalism was a phenomenon that could be found not just in Christianity but in Islam and other religions as well. Many scholars have found that argument convincing. Many university libraries now contain scores of books that are cataloged under BL 238. For many scholars the existence of religious fundamentalism is an established fact. The most important work currently cataloged under BL 238 is the multivolume series the Fundamentalism Project. The books by Ruthven, Antoun, and Armstrong mentioned above are a few of many works that more or less explicitly build upon the Fundamentalism Project, generally adopting the notion of family resemblances and/or the suggestion that fundamentalism is a useful broad umbrella term.

Other works on the topic, however, give voice to an entirely different take, one articulated by scholars such as Daniel Varisco, Gabriele Marranci, Ervand Abrahamian, Jay M. Harris, Bruce Lincoln, Susan Harding, Saba Mahmood, Bobby S. Sayyid, Juan Campo, Alvin Plantinga, Laurence R. Iannocone, David Harrington Watt, and Simon A. Wood.[10] These scholars have largely concluded that the concept is unhelpful or that it obscures more than it clarifies. Some have found that, "unanchoring" notwithstanding, it remains too tied up with specifically Christian tropes to be meaningfully applied to other religions. David Harrington Watt has suggested that labeling Jews or Muslims fundamentalists is somewhat akin to labeling Christians Sunnis or Shiites or labeling Muslims Methodists. Additionally, it has been suggested that the word is far too vague to be helpful. Harris points out that so many diverse and often disparate forms of Judaism have been labeled fundamentalist that the entire exercise of applying the word to Jewish groups is of dubious utility. Varisco states in plain terms that the term is unhelpful. Lincoln finds that *maximalism* better captures what is at stake in the discourse on religion and modernity than does *fundamentalism.* Some have suggested that certain non-Christian movements that have been labeled fundamentalism are better captured by another word. For instance, Abrahamian finds that Khomeinism is better understood as an Iranian instantiation of populism than as an Islamic instantiation of fundamentalism. Vanessa Martin characterizes Khomeinism as Islamist and with a variety of other terms. But she firmly rejects the notion that Khomeinism is accurately described as fundamentalist.

A theme common to several critiques of the concept is neatly encapsulated by Marranci's suggestion that the "important something," is not a thing at all but rather an idea of a thing: the "discernible pattern" or "family resemblance" exists more in the minds of those who write about fundamentalism than it does in the phenomena they are writing about.[11] Those who take this view disagree with the claim that there are sufficiently important similarities between, for instance, certain Christian and Islamic movements to justify using the same word to label them. The word *fundamentalism,* then, does not identify a pattern or family. Rather, it unreasonably homogenizes difference or is insufficiently attentive of it. To be sure, those who find the term useful have allowed for differences, such as the differing trajectories of Christian, Jewish, and Islamic encounters with and responses to modern secularism. But critics find that the implications of such differences have been insufficiently theorized. For critics, fundamentalism is not a phenomenon that can be identified or whose existence can be proven but a construction that is unhelpful for two reasons. First, it simply is not well made: the "analogs" on which it rests are not analogous. Second, some find that the construction is more ideological than critical. It may enable labeling of "things of which I disapprove," but since there is little agreement, scholarly or otherwise, about what is deserving of disapproval it does little to help us understand the world in which we live. For critics of the concept the upshot is probably not that the word *fundamentalism* does not mean anything—it is, after all, in the dictionary —but that it does not mean anything useful.

Many of those who have found the concept helpful have acknowledged and grappled with some of the criticisms noted above. But they have determined that the concept is sound enough to withstand them. Proponents have largely found that critics have adopted an overly narrow, or, perhaps what is more pertinent, inflexible understanding of the word. Vis-à-vis the need to define *fundamentalism* in precise terms they find that critics have set the bar unreasonably and unrealistically high. They further set forth what might be described as an argument for patience: given the term's relative newness—for instance, in comparison to such older words as *capitalism* and *socialism*—a certain amount of imprecision at this juncture is inevitable. In their introduction to *Strong Religion: The Rise of Fundamentalisms around the World,* Almond, Appleby, and Sivan stress some of these points, laying out and then rebutting some of the major criticisms of the concept. Additionally, proponents of the term find that it is plainly too late in the conversation to replace or eliminate it, as indicated by the Library of Congress categorization, whose importance Gordon D. Newby emphasizes in this book's conclusion. Critics, however, remain unpersuaded. For instance, the argument for persevering with the term simply because it presently has a certain currency is rejected by Varisco, who notes that the same rationale would apply to a word such as *Mohammedanism,* a once-popular term that has largely fallen into disuse. A similar argument could be made for *primitive religion,* another rubric that is now largely discredited and that has been removed from the Library of Congress Classifications List. The disagreement between proponents and critics is not settled in this book, nor is it likely to be settled any time soon. And while we do not imagine that the following twelve essays resolve the multitude of thorny issues associated with fundamentalism, we do feel that they present some of the best current thinking on both sides of the debate. If this volume provides readers with a sense of the current state of the discourse it will have achieved its aim.

In "Fundamentalists of the 1920s and 1930s," David Harrington Watt explores the nature of historic fundamentalism. Fundamentalism ought to be understood, Watt asserts, as a popular religious movement that began to coalesce in the early twentieth century and which was given the name by which it is now known in 1920. Watt argues that historic fundamentalism was more than a diffuse sense that traditional religious ideas are better than modern ones. Nor was fundamentalism simply an aggregation of all of the Protestant groups in the United States who did not embrace theological modernism. Fundamentalism had its own set of theological emphases (the absolute authority of the Christian scriptures and the imminent premillennial Second Coming of Christ, for example), and it drew its strength from a specific and identifiable network of schools, colleges, publishing houses, magazines, and radio programs. Fundamentalism was a distinct form of conservative Protestantism and also, in some respects, a somewhat narrow and idiosyncratic one. The fundamentalist movement never won the loyalty, for example, of the leaders of the Assemblies of God, the Church of the Nazarene, the Southern Baptist Convention, or the Missouri Synod of the Lutheran Church. Watt implies that it is misleading to talk as if those conservative Protestants who declined to attach themselves to the fundamentalist movement were nevertheless Christian fundamentalists. Indirectly at least, Watt's essay seems to raise doubts about the usefulness of the concept of global fundamentalism. If it is misleading to speak as though all conservative Protestants in the United States were fundamentalists, why is it helpful to speak of Jewish settlers in the occupied territories or Muslim religious leaders in Iran as though they were fundamentalists?

Militancy is often said to be one of the defining characteristics of fundamentalism. In "The Idea of Militancy in American Fundamentalism," Dan D. Crawford explores the various meanings of *militancy* and suggests that focusing on the issue of militancy can get in the way of understanding American fundamentalism. Crawford notes that militancy can refer to a willingness to use violence (exploding a bomb) or a willingness to use combative rhetoric (saying that one's adversaries are heretics) or confrontational tactics (attempting to have one's adversaries expelled from a seminary) to achieve one's goals. Crawford argues that American fundamentalists' militancy was almost exclusively limited to matters of rhetoric and tactics and almost never included a resort to physical violence. Having made that point, Crawford goes on to argue that after the volatile 1920s, a new generation of youth leaders, evangelists, and Bible teachers, who consciously eschewed combativeness and negative attacks, came on the scene and gradually came to represent the main body of the movement, displacing the loud voices of extremists such as John R. Rice, Bob Jones Sr., and Carl MacIntire. Crawford suggests that some of the most influential historians of American fundamentalism (Joel A. Carpenter and George M. Marsden, for example) tend to pay too much attention to fundamentalist extremists and too little attention to moderate fundamentalism. Extremism, Crawford says, is not necessarily one of the hallmarks of Protestant fundamentalism. Extremism is rather a tendency exhibited by some, but by no means all, fundamentalists.

Near the beginning of "Fundamentalism and Christianity," Margaret Bendroth says that she believes that there can be no doubt that "the cross-cultural interpretation of fundamentalism is a helpful way of understanding how religion 'works' in the world today." But Bendroth then goes on to present an analysis of Christian fundamentalism and the role it has played in shaping American Christianity and world Christianity that emphasizes the difficulties that arise when scholars use the concept of fundamentalism to explore the role that religion plays in the contemporary world. In Bendroth's analysis Christian fundamentalism in the United States is an exceedingly complex phenomenon in and of it itself. It does not provide a simple, straightforward, or stable platform from which to begin thinking about religion in the contemporary world. And fundamentalism's role in shaping American Christianity is, Bendroth argues, easy to overstate. One could make a good case for seeing the fundamentalist–modernist controversies that took place in the 1920s as a relatively minor episode in the history of Christianity in the United States. Bendroth goes on to argue that fundamentalism's role in shaping world Christianity in the twentieth and twenty-first centuries is easily exaggerated. That role, especially when compared to the influence exercised by Pentecostal and charismatic movements, was actually quite limited. Pentecostal and charismatic forms of Christianity have a history that can be traced back to the famous Azusa Street Revival that broke in Los Angeles, California, in 1906, and, in every decade from 1906 to the present, Pentecostal and charismatic forms of Christianity have experienced extraordinary growth. Nearly one-third of all the church members in the world today, Bendroth estimates, practice some form of charismatic or Pentecostal Christianity. Clearly, Pentecostal and charismatic Christians have much in common with Christian fundamentalists. But there are also important differences between them and fundamentalists. And some of the differences—those that concern matters such as sacred texts, religious experience, rationality, and the legacy of the European Enlightenment, for example—have important implications for the way that Christians relate to the modern world. Bendroth's essay raises the possibility that Pentecostal and charismatic forms of Christianity might well provide us with a more interesting starting point for comparing religious traditions in the contemporary world than does Christian fundamentalism.

Shaul Magid's essays under the title "'America Is No Different,' 'America Is Different'—Is There an American Jewish Fundamentalism?" focus on two groups of ultra-Orthodox Jews: Habad and Satmar. As Magid's pieces make clear, there are many differences between the two groups. Their understandings of the Messiah, Zionism, and the importance of mystical experience are, for example, quite distinct. But Magid's essays (both of which provide readers with a wealth of empirical information about groups whose influence has been much discussed but little understood) make a strong case for seeing both Habad and Satmar as two disparate expressions of a single phenomenon—Jewish fundamentalism in the United States of America. Magid distinguishes between these groups in the United States and their Israeli counterparts as well as their prewar European antecedents. He suggests that the American context of disestablishment and religious freedom creates distinctive conditions for these ultra-Orthodox groups to develop an American Orthodox fundamentalism. He takes very seriously the roots of fundamentalism as an American (Christian) phenomenon and divides the phenomenon into the two operative categories of pre- and postmillennialism that are common in scholarship on American fundamentalism. He argues that while Habad and Satmar are not directly influenced by Christian fundamentalists they have absorbed the American ethos such that a distinctive form of that American phenomenon has emerged in these two groups. He brings numerous examples, both in terms of metaphysical assumptions (gleaned from kabbalistic sources) and social realities, to illustrate why he thinks these groups are American religious communities, America being not simply a geographic location but an ideational one as well. He shows how both groups use secular society to their fundamentalist advantage, in one case (Habad) as a forum for postmillennial missionary activism and in a second case (Satmar) as a social system that can, or perhaps must, support the cultivation of a premillennial enclave society. In both cases he argues that America is not simply the next stage of the diaspora but serves as well as the social framework for the cultivation of real messianic politics; in the case of Habad through the Noahide Law campaign and in the case of Satmar through a full-out expression of separatism that was not even possible in the prewar European context.

In these cases, then, Magid finds the term *fundamentalist* more appropriate than a culturally neutral term such as *maximalism*. The latter may capture forms of extremism across diverse cultural and political divides but it often does not capture the ways in which these movements constitute amalgamations of Old-World traditions and ideologies and contemporary concerns and absorb features from outside their own systems. Magid thus has a different take from Harris and others who are leery of speaking of Jewish fundamentalisms.

Jean Axelrad Cahan's essay "The Jewish Settler Movement and the Concept of Fundamentalism" focuses on a group of people who are often seen as the embodiment of Jewish fundamentalism: the Jewish settlers who live in Hebron. Cahan argues that the settlers, when carefully considered, simply cannot be shoehorned into the category of fundamentalists as that concept is usually understood. Many of the characteristics said to constitute the hallmarks of fundamentalists simply do not apply to them. Cahan goes on to argue that the tendency to see the settlers as an example of the dangers of fundamentalism obscures our understanding of the issues at stake in the fate of the occupied territories. Cahan acknowledges that it might be comforting to assume that Jewish settlers on the West Bank who are religious fundamentalists pose the greatest obstacle to obtaining a peace agreement between Israelis and Palestinians. But such an assumption would be, Cahan argues, mistaken. The fundamental obstacles to peace would not, she says, disappear if Jewish fundamentalism somehow vanished from the face of the earth. The obstacles are more fundamental than that. Turning Jewish fundamentalists into scapegoats whose existence explains all that has gone wrong in the relations between Israelis and Palestinians is not helpful. And dismissing the settlers as irrational fundamentalists is simplistic. Such a dismissal is polemic masquerading as analysis.

Simon A. Wood's essay "The Concept of Global Fundamentalism: A Short Critique" interrogates the notions of fundamentalist "family resemblances" and *fundamentalism* as an "umbrella term." He briefly surveys the move from historic to global fundamentalism and the latter's particular association with Islam. In view of this association Wood finds that for global fundamentalism to be a useful concept, what has been called Islamic fundamentalism must be seen or shown to exhibit fundamentalist family resemblances. One must be able to see or show that the proposed analog is, in fact, analogous. To be sure, describing Islamic cases as fundamentalist need not be contingent upon their complete alignment with the paradigms associated with the Protestants and identified by Curtis Lee Laws in 1920. But, Wood finds, this description would require their alignment with the broad definition of global fundamentalism delineated in Almond, Appleby and Sivan's final installment in the Fundamentalism Project and numerous other works conceived in a similar vein. If fundamentalism is defined as X, Islamic varieties must be shown to resemble X. If they do not, it would be preferable to call them something else.

Wood finds the argument for family resemblances unpersuasive. He finds that it is too preoccupied with similarity and insufficiently allows for difference. He illustrates his case by discussing Mawlana Abul-Ala Mawdudi and Ruhollah Khomeini. He argues that these figures' worldviews and agendas are better comprehended in terms of local conditions (a suggestion made in broader terms by Khalid Yahya Blankinship) than in terms of a global fundamentalist phenomenon. He finds that there are several important instances in which Mawdudi and Khomeini are not reasonably labeled fundamentalists, Khomeini's "rule of the jurist" being a case in point. Wood acknowledges that *fundamentalism* is a broad rubric whose proponents have stressed the need for flexible application. But for Wood the list of exceptions is simply too long: the term's application involves something considerably looser than what "flexible use" would allow.

Wood disagrees with the claim that nothing is to be gained by using different words in place of *fundamentalism.* As *fundamentalism* does not successfully capture a global phenomenon (or, to quote Strozier et al., "something"), it should not simply be replaced with another single term. His answer to the "What would you call it?" question is: "There is no it here." Depending on the example under discussion terms such as *Islamism, political Islam, populism, communalism,* and *maximalism* better capture what is at issue. To be sure, these terms bring their own sets of advantages and disadvantages. In the case of Islamism, these have been examined in detail.[12] While one must reckon with the difficulties associated with any term, Wood finds alternatives clearly preferable to *fundamentalism.* For instance, if in certain Islamic cases *fundamentalism* effectively means a politicized form of the religion, why not call it *political Islam*? That term may not work as well with cross-cultural comparisons as *fundamentalism* does, but in some instances that is a price worth paying, as when the cases examined are more different than similar. For Wood, those who argue that *fundamentalism* works effectively as a broad comparative construct or umbrella term have not made a persuasive case.

Of the essays in this book Khalid Yahya Blankinship's "Muslim 'Fundamentalism,' Salafism, Sufism, and Other Trends" is perhaps the most forthrightly critical of the concept of fundamentalism. Blankinship finds that it has no merit whatsoever. For him, the word *fundamentalism* has an "utter lack of specificity." He marshals a range of points, examples, and sources to support this contention. First, he finds unsatisfactory that Marty, Strozier, and others use a word to label millions of people while simultaneously—in the case of Strozier et al. within the space of a single paragraph—relieving themselves of the burden of defining the word. The act of labeling, Blankinship finds, carries an obligation to define the label. For Blankinship, comments such as the introductory ones in *The Fundamentalist Mindset: Psychological Perspectives on Religion, Violence, and History* by Strozier et al., which argue against concrete definition and even speak of "benefits of ambiguity," reflect a questionable exercise in seeking to "have it both ways."

Blankinship then offers a critique of Choueiri's *Islamic Fundamentalism: The Story of Islamist Movements,* which effectively also stands for numerous books conceived along similar lines. Blankinship finds that Choueiri effectively renders almost all forms of Muslim activism—a stunningly wide geographical and chronological range—fundamentalist. That is, Choureiri stretches the conceptual umbrella so wide that there is very little in the world of modern Islam that is not underneath it. Blankinship's critique is informed by the notion that it would only be helpful to speak of something called fundamentalism if it were distinguishable from something that is not fundamentalism. It would only help us to call some Muslims fundamentalists if we thereby could distinguish them from Muslims who are not fundamentalists. But, for Blankinship, Choueiri's discussion leaves us without a payoff because it fails to make these distinctions sufficiently. While Choueiri does not render everything within the world of modern Islam as fundamentalism, Blankinship finds that he comes close enough to doing so that the term is rendered hopelessly vague.

Blankinship then examines *fundamentalism* in relation to two other critical terms for the discussion: *Salafism* and *Sufism.* Regarding the former, he rebuts the notion that Salafist Islam conforms to the definition of Islamic fundamentalism. On topics such as belief, practice, and political leadership he shows that Salafist texts replicate standard classical positions in a largely unremarkable fashion. Unless, then, one would also want to label the like of Ibn Khaldun (d. 1406) a fundamentalist, Salafist treatments of these topics cannot reasonably be characterized as fundamentalist. Further, they simply do not point to the kinds of activism associated with fundamentalism. Elsewhere, Salafist discourse involves arcane intra-Muslim debates over creed that would be remote and irrelevant to most non-Muslims. Blankinship's critique here raises the important question of where, within any of this, one might identify a family resemblance indicative of a global trend. Blankinship also suggests that Salafist stances characterized as fundamentalist—for instance, exclusivism or shunning of other Muslims—are also characteristic of Sufism. Yet Sufis are very rarely called fundamentalists, and Sufism, almost by definition, is not fundamentalism. In other words Blankinship finds untenable the suggestion that fundamentalism could be understood as typified by Salafism and nonfundamentalism as typified by Sufism.

Finally, Blankinship shows that what is called fundamentalism sometimes effectively appears to be exclusivism. Why not simply call it exclusivism? The same point applies to separatism. Why not call separatists separatists? What is to be gained by calling them fundamentalists? *Exclusivism* and *separatism* may not be perfect terms, but they may be less problematical than *fundamentalism.* Readers may not find Blankinship's take persuasive, yet it is by our reading one of the more powerful critiques of the term's applicability to Islam offered to date.

Contra Blankinship, Watt, and Wood, Lynda Clarke argues that the concept of fundamentalism is helpful. She finds it illuminating differences between Sunni and Shii patterns of activism and pointing toward the influence of a particular Sunni sensibility upon Shiism. Her first essay, "Fundamentalism and Shiism," considers why Shiism does not generally lend itself to fundamentalism. In her second essay, "Fundamentalism, Khomeinism, and the Islamic Republic of Iran," Clarke argues that as a Shii fundamentalism Khomeinism is an exceptional case enabled by the distinctive features of the Iranian context that needs to be examined separately from Shiism elsewhere.

For Clarke, fundamentalism captures reconfigurations of Islam that subjugate religion to politics. She refers to three waves of Islamic fundamentalism represented first by Hasan al-Banna (d. 1949), second by Mawlana Mawdudi (d. 1979) and Sayyid Qutb (d. 1966), and third by extremist groups such as al-Qaeda. Contra Watt and along similar lines to Magid, Clarke rejects the suggestion that fundamentalism is too implicated with the Christian tradition to be imported into another religion. She treats its applicability to Sunni Islam as firmly established. She then turns her attention to Shiism and delineates four features that largely occlude the emergence of Shii fundamentalism: minority status, quietism, clerical authority, and lack of scripturalism (surely a more helpful term in this connection than *literalism*). Here, her discussion provides a double payoff: in addition to fundamentalism, we learn a great deal about Shiism.

Clarke's second essay examines Khomeinism and the Islamic Republic of Iran. Contra Wood, she argues that Khomeinism is fundamentalist. Given that Shiism's qualitative nature generally precludes fundamentalism, this makes it highly exceptional. Clarke sees Khomeini's fundamentalism as derivative of the second wave of Sunni fundamentalism, that of Mawdudi and Qutb, characterized by a totalizing agenda and the subjugation of religion to politics. By and large, the disagreement between Clarke and Wood is a disagreement about fundamentalism, not a disagreement about Khomeini or Mawdudi. That is, the object of the differing takes on whether or not Khomeini embodies X is X, not Khomeini. Both stress Khomeinism's political character, its lack of precedent in Shii tradition, its populist, Third Worldist or Iranian character, and a disconnect between ideals—Khomeini's "utopian scheme" (Clarke) or "rhetorical flourish" (Wood)—and "facts on the ground." For Clarke, these four features, particularly the first two, point toward fundamentalism, while for Wood they do not. As Clarke notes, there has been considerable disagreement about whether or not Khomeinism is fundamentalist. Clarke's discussion is partially informed by the work of Marty and Appleby, whose definitions of fundamentalism she finds illustrated by Khomeini's movement. Wood is more influenced by Abrahamian and Martin, who find that the word *fundamentalism* fails to capture Khomeinism's critical dynamics.

Florian Pohl's essay "Islamic Education and the Limitations of Fundamentalism as an Analytical Category" helpfully expands the global reach of this book's investigation by examining institutions of Islamic education in contemporary Indonesia. Through this case study, he explores the heuristic value of the term *fundamentalism* as a category for cross-cultural analysis, especially when applied to public expressions of Islam such as Islamic education. He argues that the term lacks critical purchase because it is premised on an Enlightenment understanding of religion, of what it is or what it should be: namely, a distinct sphere of life kept separate from other spheres such as politics, economy, law, and education. Pohl's discussion here is informed by the notion that this understanding is a cultural product, not a universal value. He is here influenced by scholars such as Talal Asad who have problematized what many find to be an underlying assumption of the Fundamentalism Project and like works. This is the assumption that there is something inherently natural and even apposite about the post-Enlightenment paradigm. But why, Pohl asks, should we assume that religious institutions in Indonesia conform—or ought to conform—to this paradigm? That assumption undermines our ability to distinguish between different ways in which religion can be public, and heightens, perhaps unnecessarily, suspicion of religious formations that transgress the boundaries between private and public spheres. His discussion may be seen together with those of Blankinship and others who are unsatisfied with scholarship that appears to evaluate developments in the Muslim majority world on the basis of their deviation from what is too easily regarded as normal or apposite. Pohl simply does not accept that Western history provides a universally applicable paradigm for what is normal or apposite.

David L. Johnston in his essay on Islamic environmentalism, "Fundamentalism Diluted: From Enclave to Globalism in Conservative Muslim Ecological Discourse," argues that among the three most common traits that scholars associate with religious "fundamentalism" only the "enclave reflex" is a strong candidate for a dependable, useful, and widely applicable characteristic. Militancy and an antimodern stance are either incoherent, or false, or simply too vague to be meaningful. Following Olivier Roy, he points out that globalization, "as the acceleration of population, capital and commodity flows, and its accompanying westernization process," has created a vacuum for people who, once detached from their original cultural context, throw themselves headlong into a new community of "true believers." For him, this "us versus the world" mentality represents the most serviceable aspect of Almond, Appleby and Sivan's thesis in *Strong Religion.*

Yet that fortress mentality, so characteristic of all traditional religious communities, including postglobalization born-again movements (Roy's "neofundamentalists"), is exactly what is being eroded, and indeed "diluted," by the discovery of the much wider horizon of solidarity advocated by the environmentalist movement. Johnston argues that this strong ethic of caring for the common planet shared by all of humankind and "otherkind" is what drives these Muslims to come to the Quran and Sunnah from a new perspective. In essence, however, this is what people of faith in every tradition do from generation to generation—they are "doing theology." They come to the sacred texts with the questions raised by the burning issues of their day; and, inevitably, the answers that come are different from those that came to believers from other times and places. And in this case, interfaith activism on behalf of a troubled earth will in fact dilute any kind of enclave reflex.

Scholars routinely use terms that originated in the Western world to analyze other parts of the world or terms that originated within one cultural tradition to analyze other traditions. Together with *fundamentalism,* numerous other terms including *secularism, socialism, capitalism,* and *humanism* have been migrated from their original contexts. These moves are a natural consequence of efforts to identify and capture structural similarities observed in different global contexts. The essays included here interrogate whether or not in the case of one term, *fundamentalism,* this move is a helpful one. This book does not rigorously interrogate what might be termed "sister categories" to fundamentalism such as secularism, humanism, and socialism, and it certainly does not claim that the practice of migrating terms from Western to non-Western or Christian to non-Christian contexts is always illegitimate. But we do think that most contemporary scholars acknowledge that that practice can sometimes be unhelpful or more confusing than clarifying. In the essays offered here, a group of scholars who work in the humanities offer differing takes on whether or not this applies to fundamentalism.

In exploring this theme, we focus on Abrahamic religions. While Hinduism and Buddhism are mentioned on occasion, the book does not rigorously investigate how *fundamentalism* does or does not apply to Asian religions. Two main considerations inform this focus. The first is pragmatic: an investigation with an already ambitious scope would struggle to retain cohesion if it incorporated Asia. The second is our feeling that the most interesting arguments for and against discussing religious phenomena in terms of fundamentalism focus mainly on Abrahamic religions. In our view efforts to apply the rubric of fundamentalism to Asian contexts have not provided as much of a payoff. In short, we have not found suggestions that Hinduism, Buddhism, and other Asian religions take fundamentalist forms very stimulating.

Further, some of those who are most committed to the term have, at minimum, raised the possibility that *fundamentalism* does not apply to Asian contexts, if they have not said so explicitly. Appleby has suggested that "Hinduism and Buddhism do not readily lend themselves to the political dynamics of fundamentalism,"[13] while scholars such as Karen Armstrong and Richard Antoun have focused their discussions on monotheism. Almond, Appleby, and Sivan strive to incorporate Asia in their discussion of global fundamentalism, yet the primary object is again monotheism. Their effort to understand, for instance, certain Hindu groups in terms of "ethno-nationalist fundamentalism" may be a stretch too far. After all, by definition, nationalism is not fundamentalism. Neither do we find a great deal to engage in the suggestion that a distinctively fundamentalist form of

Buddhism is found, for instance, in Sri Lanka. Overall we feel that scholars and others can disagree on whether, for instance, Khomeinism or certain elaborations of Orthodox Judaism are fundamentalism while acknowledging that there is merit on both sides of the argument. Discussions of Hindu, Buddhist, and other Asian fundamentalisms appear less fruitful.

We appreciate that this book's analysis of the Christian, Jewish, and Muslim groups who have been labeled fundamentalist is far from exhaustive. But this book is not intended to be a survey of all the movements that have been labeled fundamentalist, much less the last word on the topic. It is intended, rather, to be an introduction to some noteworthy current thinking about the concept of fundamentalism. If this book accomplishes that it will have achieved its aims.

Notes

1. See, for instance, the disclaimer with which Gabriele Marranci introduces his book on fundamentalism. Marranci notes that since 2001 more than 100 books and 5,600 articles have been published on Islamic fundamentalism. Gabriele Marranci, *Understanding Muslim Identity: Rethinking Fundamentalism* (New York: Palgrave Macmillan, 2009), 1.

2. Gabriel A. Almond, R. Scott Appleby, and Emmanuel Sivan, *Strong Religion: The Rise of Fundamentalisms around the World* (Chicago: University of Chicago Press, 2003).

3. R. Scott Appleby, "Fundamentalism," in *Encyclopedia of Politics and Religion*, 2nd ed., ed. Robert Wuthnow (Washington, D.C.: CQ Press, 2007).

4. Charles B. Strozier, David M. Terman, and James W. Jones, with Katherine A. Boyd, *The Fundamentalist Mindset: Psychological Perspectives on Religion, Violence, and History* (Oxford: Oxford University Press, 2010).

5. Bruce B. Lawrence *Defenders of God: The Fundamentalist Revolt against the Modern Age* (San Francisco: Harper & Row, 1989); Youssef M. Choueiri, *Islamic Fundamentalism: The Story of Islamist Movements*, 3rd ed. (London: Continuum, 2010). Malise Ruthven, *Fundamentalism: A Very Short Introduction* (New York: Oxford University Press, 2007); Karen Armstrong, *The Battle for God: A History of Fundamentalism* (New York: Ballantine Books, 2001).

6. Strozier et al., *The Fundamentalist Mindset*, 11.

7. On this point see, for instance, Almond et al., *Strong Religion*, 14–17, and Mansoor Moaddel and Karam Talattof, eds. *Modernist and Fundamentalist Debates in Islam: A Reader* (New York: Palgrave Macmillian, 2000), 2–3. On the issue of whether for Islamic cases *Islamism* is a preferable term to *fundamentalism*, also see Richard C. Martin and Abbas Barzegar, eds., *Islamism: Contested Perspectives on Political Islam* (Stanford: Stanford University Press, 2010).

8. Martin E. Marty, "Fundamentalism Reborn: Faith and Fanaticism," *Saturday Review* 7 (May 1980): 37–42.

9. Earle H. Waugh, "Fundamentalism: Harbinger of Academic Revisionism," *Journal of the American Academy of Religion* 65 (Spring 1997): 161–68.

10. Ervand Abrahamian, *Khomeinism: Essays on the Islamic Republic* (Berkeley: University of California Press, 1993), 13–38; Juan Eduardo Campo, "Hegemonic Discourse and the Islamic Question in Egypt," *Contention* 4 (Spring 1995): 167–94; Susan Friend Harding, *The Book of Jerry Falwell: Fundamentalist Language and Politics* (Princeton: Princeton University Press, 2000); Jay Michael Harris, "'Fundamentalism': Objections from a Modern Jewish Historian," in *Fundamentalism and Gender*, ed. John Stratton Hawley (New York: Oxford University Press, 1994): 137–73; Laurence R. Iannaccone, "Toward an Economic Theory of 'Fundamentalism,'" *Journal of Institutional and Theoretical Economics* 153 (March 1997): 100–116; Bruce Lincoln, *Holy Terrors: Thinking about Religion after September 11* (Chicago: University of Chicago Press,

2003), 5; Saba Mahmood, "Islamism and Fundamentalism," *Middle East Report* 24 (November–December 1994): 29–30; Gabriele Marranci, *Understanding Muslim Identity: Rethinking Fundamentalism* (New York: Palgrave Macmillan, 2009); Alvin Plantinga, *Warranted Christian Belief* (New York: Oxford University Press, 2000); Bobby S. Sayyid, *A Fundamental Fear: Eurocentrism and the Emergence of Islamism*, 2nd ed. (London: Zed Books, 2003); Daniel Varisco, "The Tragedy of a Comic: Fundamentalists Crusading against Fundamentalists," *Contemporary Islam* 1 (October 2007): 207–30 (see especially 212n11); David Harrington Watt, "What's In a Name?: The Meaning of 'Muslim Fundamentalist,'" *Origins* 1 (June 2008): 1–5; Watt, "Meaning and End of Fundamentalism," *Religious Studies Review* 30 (October 2004): 271–74; Simon A. Wood, *Christian Criticisms, Islamic Proofs: Rashid Rida's Modernist Defense of Islam* (Oxford: Oneworld, 2008), 48–64; Wood, "Rethinking Fundamentalism: Ruhollah Khomeini, Mawlana Mawdudi, and the Fundamentalist Model," *Journal for Cultural and Religious Theory* 11 (Spring 2011): 171–98.

11. Marranci, *Understanding Muslim Identity.*

12. See Martin and Barzegar's *Islamism: Contested Perspectives on Political Islam.*

13. Appleby, "Fundamentalism," 325.

Fundamentalists of the 1920s and 1930s

David Harrington Watt

The term *fundamentalists* was invented in 1920 in order to talk about a specific group of Protestants. Nearly everyone agrees that calling those Protestants fundamentalists is a perfectly legitimate thing to do; almost everyone agrees, too, that a proper definition of *fundamentalists* has to be structured in a way that includes them. And many people would go on to say that the validity of describing other sorts of people—Muslims who have been inspired by the ideas of Sayyid Qutb, for example—as fundamentalists depends in part on how much those people have in common with the group of Protestants to whom the term was first applied. The more similarities we see between the two groups of people, the more likely it is that we will conclude that it makes sense to assign them the same classification.

In order to make an informed judgment about that, we have to know something about the Protestant fundamentalists of the 1920s and 1930s. We need to understand who they were, what they believed, and how they acted. We also need to understand what it was that set them apart from other sorts of Protestant Christians. Those questions are explored in this essay, paying special attention to matters connected to modernity, literalism, militancy, and politicization. There is a simple reason for this focus. When scholars are discussing the defining characteristics of global fundamentalism, they frequently talk about such matters as a determination to resist modernity, a tendency to read texts literally, a predilection for getting involved in politics, and a proclivity for militant rhetoric and action. So it makes sense, then, to reflect on the degree to which the Protestant fundamentalists of the 1920s and 1930s displayed those particular characteristics.

Inventing Fundamentalism

The fundamentalist movement took its name from a set of booklets called *The Fundamentals: A Testimony to the Truth.* Those pamphlets were based on the conviction that a sizeable portion of Christendom had fallen into grievous error. *The Fundamentals,* which were published from 1910 to 1915, were edited by three evangelists: A. C. Dixon, Louis Meyer, and Reuben Torrey. Much of the money to pay for the production and distribution of *The Fundamentals* came from a pious and influential oil tycoon named Lyman Stewart. In keeping with Stewart's wishes, the essays in *The Fundamentals* admonished Christians to reject heretical ideas, cling to the truths that were set forth in the Bible, and dedicate themselves to disseminating those truths thoughout the world. The authors who contributed essays to *The Fundamentals* believed that they were living in age when many people within the church had an "uneasy and distrustful feeling" about the Bible. The authors assured their readers that there was no reason in the world why Protestant Christians should feel that way: God had revealed himself to his people, "the Bible is the record of that revelation, and that revelation shines in its light from the beginning to the end of it."[1] According to the conservative Protestants who wrote *The Fundamentals,* the Christian Bible is *absolutely* trustworthy; it contains no errors whatsoever. They viewed the Bible as God's definitive revelation of himself to man. To them, the claim that subsequent texts—such as *Science and Health,* the *Book of Mormon,* and the *Quran*—were somehow a continuation of the ongoing work revelation was simply absurd.

In 1919, four years after the final volume of *The Fundamentals* was published, six thousand people assembled in Philadelphia to take part in the creation of the World's Christian Fundamentals Association (WCFA). Membership in the association was open to anyone who was willing to pay annual dues—associate members paid one dollar, full members paid five—and to sign the doctrinal statement upon which the WCFA was founded.[2] That statement affirmed the doctrine of the Trinity, the inerrancy of the Christian scriptures, the virgin birth, Christ's substitutionary atonement for humankind's sins, the physical resurrection of Christ, and the imminent return of Christ to earth to inaugurate a thousand-year reign of peace.[3] Those were the sorts of the fundamentals whose importance the leaders of the WCFA wanted to reassert. The leaders of the WCFA believed that many of America's denominations included ministers and seminary professors who had rejected the fundamental doctrines of the Christian faith. They hoped that the WCFA could protect Christians against the baneful influence of such men. Nominal Christians who had rejected the fundamental truths of biblical Christianity and yet went on insisting that they had the right to occupy positions of authority within the church were, the leaders of the WCFA believed, a terrible threat to the cause of Christ.[4]

Although the people who founded the WCFA were wholeheartedly committed to defending the fundamentals of the Christian faith, we can be certain that when those men and women gathered together in Philadelphia in 1919 they did *not* think of themselves as "fundamentalists" or as proponents of "fundamentalism." Neither of those words entered the English language until the 1920s. The word *fundamentalists* was invented the year after the WCFA was launched. Curtis Lee Laws, a pastor and journalist, coined the term while writing about the events that had taken place during that year's meeting of the Northern Baptist Convention. Laws used the word to refer to those Protestants who were firmly committed to "the great fundamentals" of the Christian faith and who were willing to "do battle royal" on behalf of Christian orthodoxy.[5] The text in which Laws suggested that resolute defenders of orthodoxy call themselves fundamentalists was called "Convention Sidelights." It was not a long article and most of it was concerned with matters other than what the opponents of theological liberalism ought to call themselves. Given how much influence it has had on the nomenclature we use to describe religious conservatives, "Convention Sidelights" said surprising little about what it was that the fundamentalists were trying to conserve. The article did not specify what Laws thought the fundamentals of the Christian faith actually were, and it did not describe the theological errors that fundamentalists ought to fight against. "Convention Sidelights" did not try to predict when and where the battles between the fundamentalists and their adversaries would take place. And the article said nothing about which social classes, which regions of the country, and which denominations could be counted on to support the fundamentalist cause. It did not try to specify which institutions and publications could be counted on to back the fundamentalist cause, and it did not say to whom the fundamentalists should turn to for leadership and guidance. On those topics—and many others besides—Laws's "Convention Sidelights" was silent.

There is, however, nothing inherently mysterious about those sorts of topics. From our present vantage point they can be addressed with considerable certitude. In the 1970s a group of gifted historians began to focus their attention on the fundamentalist movements of the 1920s and 1930s. Historical investigations of those movements have continued until the present day. Those investigations have not, of course, produced a set of objective, universally agreed upon generalizations about the true nature of fundamentalism that are destined to last until the end of time. Inevitably, historians' understanding of the nature of fundamentalism will be somewhat different in 2035 than it is right now. And it is not accurate to say that the investigations of fundamentalism that historians have undertaken from 1970 to the present have produced analyses of fundamentalism that are superior, in every single respect, to those analyses of fundamentalism that were produced in earlier decades. Older works (such as Norman Furniss's *The Fundamentalist Controversy, 1918–1931*, and Richard Hofstadter's *Anti-Intellectualism in American Life*) can still be read with profit.[6] But the analyses of fundamentalism that historians have produced in the last four decades are generally less tendentious, more fine-grained, and more sophisticated than the older interpretation of fundamentalism. They are also based on a greater familiarity with the primary sources that illuminate the history of the fundamentalist movement. These more recent analyses provide us with depictions of the fundamentalist movement of the 1920s and 1930s in which the fundamentalists are portrayed as imperfect human beings rather than as villainous monsters or saintly servants of God. Recent historical investigation has shown us a fundamentalism with a human face.[7]

Fundamentalism was a popular religious movement that won the allegiance of Protestant Christians from every region of the United States. Fundamentalism had its own distinctive institutions, publications, leaders, networks of influence, and doctrinal emphases that differentiated it from other forms of conservative Protestantism. Fundamentalists knew that they had much in common with other conservative Protestants, but their relations with conservative Protestants who were not a part of the fundamentalist movement were sometimes cool rather than warm.[8]

Fundamentalists never created an organization whose membership roles included all the fundamentalists in the United States, and they never drew up a creedal statement that all of them recognized as authoritative.[9] But a fundamentalist, almost by definition, believed in the virgin birth of Christ, Christ's divinity, and the reality of the miracles recorded in the Bible. And a great many fundamentalists put tremendous emphasis on the doctrine of biblical inerrancy and on what they called the "blessed hope"—by which they meant "the personal, premillennial and imminent return" of Christ to earth.[10] Fundamentalists believed that they were living in an age when many powerful men and women disregarded the fundamentals of the Christian faith. Fundamentalists strove to live their lives in accord with the truths revealed in the Bible, and they endeavored to convince others that ignoring those truths was a dangerous thing to do. They strove to give people throughout the world an opportunity to hear and accept the truths of the Bible. It seemed certain to them that God had graciously revealed a set of eternal truths to them, and they were sure that God called them to teach those truths to others. So fundamentalism was, in part, a sort of educational crusade.[11]

Fundamentalists believed that many of the colleges and universities in the United States were run by people who had rejected the fundamentals of the Christian faith. But they had confidence in schools such as the Bible Institute of Los Angeles, Bob Jones College, Moody Bible Institute, Northwestern Bible and Missionary Training School, Philadelphia School of the Bible, and Wheaton College. Fundamentalists believed that if they sent their sons and daughters to those schools, or schools like them, then they could be certain that their offspring would receive a godly education.[12]

Fundamentalists listened devotedly to radio programs such as *Radio Bible Class, Bible Study Hour,* and *Old Fashioned Revival Hour.* They filled their bookshelves with texts such as *In His Image, The Conflict of the Ages, The Menace of Modernism,* and the *Scofield Reference Bible* and subscribed to magazines such as the *Fundamentalist,* the *King's Business, Moody Bible Institute Monthly, Our Hope,* the *Presbyterian, Revelation, Sunday School Times, Sword of the Lord,* and the *Watchman-Examiner.*[13] Fundamentalists looked to men such as Bob Jones Sr., Charles E. Fuller, William Jennings Bryan, A. C. Gaebelein, James M. Gray, J. Gresham Machen, Clarence Macartney, J. C. Massee, Carl McIntire, G. Campbell Morgan, J. Frank Norris, John R. Rice, William Bell Riley, Wilbur Smith, John Roach Straton, and Reuben Torrey for guidance and leadership.[14]

In retrospect it seems clear that the movement that eventually came to be known as fundamentalism began to coalesce around the turn of the twentieth century. The movement gathered force during World War I and rose to national prominence in the 1920s. During that decade fundamentalists threw themselves wholeheartedly into two distinct but related campaigns. The goal of the first campaign was to make certain that America's most important denominations were controlled by conservative Protestants rather than by modernists. The goal of the second was to deter teachers in the nation's public schools from teaching their students the scientific theories developed by Charles Darwin.

Neither campaign was completely successful. Fundamentalists scored a few victories in the denominational battles of the 1920s, but they certainly did not succeed in driving their opponents out of the denominations. When the decade ended a number of the nation's denominations were still what they were when the decade began: complex aggregations whose membership included modernists as well as moderates and conservatives. Fundamentalists and their allies did succeed in making it difficult for teachers in many of the nation's public schools to discuss Darwinian evolution.[15] But when the 1920s ended many of the nation's public schools were continuing to expose their students to what the fundamentalists saw as the absurd scientific theories of a dangerous man. And the way that fundamentalists conducted themselves during the anti-evolution campaigns made them appear foolish in the eyes of many well-educated Americans: when the 1920s ended it was quite clear that fundamentalists were viewed as less than respectable in many circles. Many observers had come to believe that the fundamentalists had been exiled to the margins of American culture and that their years in exile would never come to an end.

But the defeats they suffered during the 1920s did not in fact plunge the fundamentalists into catatonic despair. During the 1930s fundamentalists exhibited great zeal and dedication. They flocked to summer conferences at which the fundamentals of the Christian faith were set forth with great conviction. Fundamentalists also poured a tremendous amount of energy into strengthening their congregations, Bible institutes, and colleges. And they expended much time and money in evangelistic campaigns in the United States and in missionary work in places such as China and Africa. By the time the United States entered World War II there were many indications that the fundamentalist movement was flourishing rather than declining.

The fundamentalist movement began to break apart in the early 1940s. The breakup stemmed in large part from a disagreement over whether or not changed social and cultural conditions necessitated a rethinking of fundamentalists' traditional emphasis on bellicose opposition to theological error. Men such as Bob Jones Sr. and Carl McIntire thought that no change was necessary. Others, including Billy Graham and Harold Ockenga, came to believe that Bible-believing Christians should adopt a new set of tactics to advance the cause of Christ: they thought that it made sense to adopt a more irenic approach to defending the fundamentals of the Christian faith. The debates over this issue were sometimes quite heated. Sometimes McIntire seemed to spend more time berating people like Graham than he did condemning modernism. But the splintering of fundamentalism did not by any means put an end to fundamentalism's influence. Men who had grown up in the fundamentalist movement and who had been decisively shaped by their involvement in that movement played an important role in shaping the revival that occurred in the aftermath of World War II.[16]

Demography

It is sometimes assumed that the great majority of fundamentalists lived in the American South. That assumption is unfounded. Many fundamentalists did live there and important leaders of the fundamentalist movement—Bob Jones Sr. and J. Frank Norris, for example—were southerners. Fundamentalists could, however, be found in every region of the United States, and many of the fundamentalist movement's most prominent leaders lived in cities in the North, the Midwest, or the West.[17] Clarence Macartney lived in Pittsburgh; J. Gresham Machen lived in Philadelphia; John Roach Straton lived in New York; and Minneapolis was William Bell Riley's home. Minneapolis, Los Angeles, and Boston were all places in which fundamentalists were particularly active, and Chicago was, arguably, the most important fundamentalist stronghold in the nation.[18] To a much greater degree than is often realized, fundamentalism was a northern movement that appealed to men and women who lived in cities.

Although many fundamentalists lived in cities that had many African American residents, the vast majority of the people who were a part of the fundamentalist movement were native-born white Americans.[19] The leadership of the fundamentalist movement was lily-white.[20] From time to time an African American student would matriculate at a fundamentalist institution such as the Moody Bible Institute or Wheaton College, but such matriculations seem to have been uncommon.[21] And though many African Americans were deeply suspicious of Darwin's ideas, few African Americans threw themselves fully into the fundamentalists' campaign to keep evolution from being taught in the nation's public schools. Indeed, some African Americans came to believe that the leaders of the crusade to keep Darwinism out of the schools were dangerous fools.[22]

The leaders of the fundamentalist movement who gained the most notoriety and the most fame were men. But fundamentalism was not, by any means, a movement made up exclusively of men. Indeed there is some reason to suppose that most of the rank-and-file members of the movement were women. Throughout all of American history most congregations have had more women than men on their membership rolls; there is little reason to believe that fundamentalist churches deviated from the general pattern. Indeed we know for certain that most of the members of some of the most important fundamentalist congregations were women. During the 1920s, for example, women made up nearly 70 percent of the membership of Boston's Park Street Church.[23] We also know that even when fundamentalist leaders made a determined effort to convince men to come hear them preach, they still ended up addressing audiences in which women outnumbered men by a ratio of three to one.[24] It is also clear that many of the teachers in fundamentalist congregations and schools were women and that women made up a large proportion of the missionaries that fundamentalists sent to foreign lands. Women also seem to have exercised a good deal of behind-the-scenes leadership in some fundamentalist organizations. It is difficult to gauge just how much covert influence women fundamentalists were actually able to exercise, but it is possible that their influence was considerable. It is certainly the case that male fundamentalists complained bitterly that Christian churches in United States had been overly influenced by the values and outlooks of women.[25]

Relatively few of the women and men who actively participated in the fundamentalist movement possessed great fortunes. But the fundamentalist movement did win the allegiance of a few rich Christians, and some wealthy fundamentalists —Robert G. Letourneau, Henry Parsons Crowell, John M. Studebaker, and Milton and Lyman Stewart, for example—used their riches to advance the cause of fundamentalism. Their generosity was one of the keys to the movement's strength. The fundamentalist movement was not, of course, a capitalist plot; but it was a movement that enjoyed some support from wealthy capitalists. Fundamentalism also drew support from people who were poor and from people who were a part of the working class. But the proportion of fundamentalists who made their living through manual labor and the proportion who were impoverished can easily be exaggerated. The fundamentalist movement seems to have appealed especially to people from the lower-middle class, the middle class, and upper-middle class. Many fundamentalists made their livings working as semiskilled craftsmen, tradesmen, teachers, or ministers. Some of them made their livings as lawyers or physicians. A good many fundamentalists were small businessmen. There is some reason to believe that the fundamentalist movement included a large number of men and women who were upwardly mobile.[26] Indeed in some instances aligning oneself with the fundamentalist movement was, in and of itself, a form of upwardly mobility. Subscribing to a fundamentalist journal and reading it regularly could make one more learned. Mastering the intricacies of the dispensationalist scheme could sharpen one's mind. Attending a fundamentalist Bible institute gave one a set of skills that could be used to live a life with wide horizons rather than narrow ones.

Religion and Morality

Although there is good reason to believe that a good many fundamentalists were upwardly mobile, there is little evidence to show that most fundamentalists were obsessed with making money. But many fundamentalists were obsessed with deepening their relationship with God and with living lives that glorified God. The range of activities in which they engaged in an attempt to do that was breathtaking. Fundamentalists participated in prayer groups in which they asked God to meet the physical and spiritual needs of others and of themselves. They sang hymns that glorified God and gave personal testimonies designed to demonstrate God's power and might. Fundamentalists attended classes in which they learned about God and his ways. Fundamentalists read religious newspapers, magazines, and books that taught them how to live their lives in accord with God's will. They listened to sermons that exhorted and inspired them to do so.[27]

The sermons that fundamentalists heard were full of language and imagery drawn from the Bible. So were the testimonies they gave, the hymns they sang, and the supplications they made. The newspapers, magazines, and books that fundamentalists read focused on the truths to be found in the Bible and on how Christians could apply those truths to their own lives. For fundamentalists the Bible served as something rather like a talisman. For them the Bible was quite literally a gift from God. It was holy in the fullest sense of that word. It told them what God was like; it taught them the true nature of the universe that God had created.

Fundamentalists believed that a large proportion of the world's population had never embraced the truths to be found in the Bible. They believed that those men and women—both nominal Christians and those that were not Christians at all—were headed toward eternal torment.[28] Fundamentalists were determined to save as many people as they could from that fate and to point them instead toward a walk with God. That determination pushed them to send missionary expeditions throughout the world and to launch evangelistic crusades throughout the United States. But a fundamentalist did not, of course, have to become a missionary or an evangelist in order to win the lost to Christ. Fundamentalist preachers could—and did—make sure that their sermons ended with invitations for non-Christians to come to Christ. Fundamentalist laypeople could—and did—continually look for opportunities to ask their acquaintances, coworkers, neighbors, and friends to become Christians.[29] Once converted, new Christians were expected to live their lives in accord with the truths to be found in the Bible. Living their lives in accord with those truths would enable converts to look forward to spending eternity with God, and it would also enable the Lord to make use of them in the here and now. As their understanding of biblical truths deepened, new Christians could encourage non-Christians to embrace those truths. Whatever else it was—and it was certainly many other things—the fundamentalist movement was also a zealous campaign to get people throughout the world to read the Bible, to interpret it properly, and then live out the truths it contained.

Fundamentalists often asserted that in order to understand the truths to be found in the scriptures, one had to interpret the Bible literally. They claimed that they relied on literal interpretations of the sacred text and that their modernist opponents relied instead on less trustworthy interpretations of the scriptures. Those claims were certainly not preposterous. (Fundamentalists really did believe that many passages in the Bible that modernists tended to say were true spiritually rather than literally—those that said Mary was a virgin when Jesus was conceived, for instance—were in fact literal declarations about clear facts.) It is worth nothing, however, that fundamentalists did not always read the Bible "literally" in the fullest sense of that word. When fundamentalists read the fifteenth chapter of the Gospel of John—a chapter in which Jesus declares that he is "the true vine"—they did not come away thinking that Jesus was a herbaceous plant. And though there are a great many passages in the Bible that refer to God's hand, fundamentalists did not believe that the Lord possessed a literal hand. Nor did they believe that Jesus' advice about what a Christian ought to do if he discovers that his right eye is leading him into sin—gouge out that eye—ought to be taken literally. If fundamentalists had interpreted that advice literally, then presumably the fundamentalist movement would have included a very large number of one-eyed Christians. In fact it did not. In practice, fundamentalists read the Bible in ways that suggest that they knew that the Bible included a great many tropes. And though they seldom emphasized that point in their public pronouncements, fundamentalists did sometimes acknowledge that it was a mistake to interpret all the passages in the Bible in a literal fashion. Some fundamentalists said for instance that it was wrong to say that God had to have created the universe in six twenty-four hour days. It might well, they suggested, make more sense to assume that the days in the first chapter of Genesis were figurative days rather than literal ones.[30]

In general, fundamentalists seemed to have been far more interested in biblical hermeneutics than in politics. Most of them were more interested in making sense of the book of Daniel than they were in trying to influence the outcome of elections. And even when fundamentalists did turn their attention to political events, they often seemed less interested in those events' social and economic effects than they were in those events' implications concerning Christ's second advent. When they examined those events, fundamentalists focused their attention on how they dovetailed with the Bible's prophecies concerning the rapture, the tribulation, the rise of the Antichrist, and the battle of Armageddon.[31] So those interpretations of the fundamentalist movement that present it as a political phenomenon rather than a religious one simply cannot be brought into accord with the evidence to be found in the primary sources.[32] But to say that the fundamentalist movement was a religious phenomenon is not, of course, to say that it was not a political one. Politics is not just about who gets elected to office. It is also about how power is distributed, about the ways in which power can be utilized, and about to which ends power ought to be used. Those sorts of questions were of great interest to the fundamentalists. Even those fundamentalists who were least interested in politics in the narrowest sense of that term certainly were concerned with matters—whether or not women ought to work outside the home, for example—that are, when considered from certain points of view, as political as political can be.

One of the political issues in which fundamentalists took a special interest had to do with the Roman Catholic Church. Fundamentalists tended to believe that Catholics had gained too much power in American society and that Catholics' political potency constituted a grave threat to American democracy. Fundamentalists were, therefore, frequently on the lookout for opportunities to reduce Catholics' influence on the United States government. As George M. Marsden has noted, many fundamentalists assumed that the "United States was a Protestant nation founded upon Biblical principles" and that fundamentalists had a duty to try to return the nation to its roots.[33] Those fundamentalists wanted the American government to embrace Protestant norms fully and to take steps to cultivate virtue and to suppress sin. So fundamentalists often tried to get the government to prevent ungodly ideas from being taught in the nation's public schools. They also worked to get the government to do all that it could to limit the consumption of alcohol. And fundamentalists also attempted to convince the government to curb fornication, adultery, and divorce.

Although fundamentalists wanted the U.S. government to do what it could to improve the nation's moral tenor, most of them seemed to have thought that it was unwise for the government to take direct action to try to solve economic problems such as poverty and homelessness. Such problems, they believed, were best addressed by spiritual revival and by individual effort. Most fundamentalists had sympathy for the tenets of laissez-faire liberalism. They tended to assume that aside from encouraging its citizens to act morally the government should play a relatively small role in shaping American society. They seemed to have believed that in many respects the government that governed least was the one that governed the best.[34] Although many fundamentalists who lived in the South routinely supported the Democratic Party, fundamentalists seldom displayed enthusiasm for the New Deal. From time to time they denounced it with great vigor. Fundamentalists often worried that the U.S. government had grown too large and too powerful. They believed that the government had placed too many restrictions on entrepreneurs. The contention that government has a duty to limit the power of businessmen and to support the rights of labor—a contention that a fair number of modernists were inclined to accept—was one that many fundamentalists rejected out of hand.[35]

Polemics

Fundamentalists were not categorically opposed to *all* the phenomena that we associate with the coming of modernity. They made skillful use of some modern inventions—the radio, for instance—to advance their cause. And fundamentalists adopted some of the attitudes associated with modern commercial enterprise—such as a tremendous confidence in the power of marketing and advertising—with great avidity. Indeed some of the fundamentalists came to think of their evangelical endeavors as something very closely akin to a modern business venture. One fundamentalist leader, Mel Trotter, went so far as to calculate precisely how much money it took for his organization to save a soul. Each soul cost, Trotter concluded, $1.60.[36]

Despite their great respect for the achievements of modern commerce, fundamentalists certainly did find some aspects of the modern age repellent. They tended to see the modern era as a time of darkness rather than of light and as an epoch of wickedness rather than of progress. In their eyes the modern age was a time of lawlessness, sexual licentiousness, and cultural decline. Fundamentalists had little good to say about modern literature or modern art, and they enumerated the shortcomings of modern intellectuals such as Karl Marx and Charles Darwin with great zeal. Fundamentalists often believed that novel religious ideas were inferior to traditional ones; they were convinced that theological modernism was a collection of erroneous and dangerous hypotheses.

Protestant modernism was a complicated and multifaceted phenomenon.[37] Some of the men associated with the fundamentalist movement—J. Gresham Machen, for example—had a firm grasp of what the modernists wanted to do and what it was that they believed. Others did not. But even those fundamentalists who knew relatively little about modernism were sure that they knew enough about that movement to understand that it was a terrible threat to true Christianity. Fundamentalists believed that modernists occupied positions of power within many of the large denominations and that they used that power to harass laymen and ministers who remained true to the fundamentals of Christianity.[38] Some fundamentalists, A. C. Gaebelein, for example, believed that the modernists who were tormenting them were dangerous apostates.[39] Other fundamentalists, including Machen, adopted a more extreme position: they argued that modernists were adherents of a recently invented religion that was completely at odds with the Christian faith.

Machen was born in 1881 in Baltimore, Maryland. His mother and his father were both well educated, accomplished, and well-to-do. His mother gave him a deep grounding in the fundamentals of the Christian faith as they had been traditionally understood by Presbyterians. Machen studied at Johns Hopkins University, Princeton Seminary, and Princeton University and then went to Germany to pursue more advanced work at the University of Marburg and the University of Göttingen. From 1906 to 1929 Machen taught New Testament at Princeton Seminary; he taught at Westminster Seminary from 1929 to 1937. During the course of his life Machen published several scholarly books—*The Origins of Paul's Religion* and *The Virgin Birth of Christ,* for example—and also some popular ones such as the *Christian Faith in the Modern World,* a book that was based on a series of talks that Machen delivered on a radio station in Philadelphia. Machen's best-known book, *Christianity and Liberalism,* was published in 1923. It was enthusiastically received by many Christian theologians and by some secular intellectuals. (Both H. L. Menken and Walter Lippmann admired *Christianity and Liberalism.*) Machen was reluctant to label himself a fundamentalist; he thought of himself, rather, as simply a Christian. Nevertheless during the 1920s and 1930s Machen was generally thought of as one of fundamentalism's most important spokesmen.[40]

Machen argued that it was a mistake to view the religious controversies of the 1920s as a set of battles between Christians who adhered to fundamentalism and Christians who embraced modernism. The people who were commonly thought to be defending fundamentalism were, he said, actually trying to defend Christianity itself. The opponents of the fundamentalists did not, Machen said, subscribe to a sophisticated forward-looking version of Christianity, or even a perverse form of Christianity.[41] They subscribed rather to an entirely different religion—a religion whose doctrines were on "almost every conceivable point" the opposite of those of Christianity. When both religions were carefully analyzed, it became obvious that one could not simultaneously give one's loyalty to both liberalism and Christianity. The two religions were "mutually exclusive."[42] Liberalism emphasized human goodness. Christianity focused on divine grace. Christianity was a supernatural faith; liberalism was rooted in a set of assumptions that were thoroughly naturalistic.[43]

Machen believed that modern liberals systematically downplayed the differences between liberalism and Christianity. Liberals made use of reassuring traditional terms such as the atonement and the deity of Christ, but they *radically* reinterpreted the meaning of those words.[44] Machen noted that men who had embraced liberalism generally refused to withdraw from the church and that such men believed that they had a perfect right to exercise power within Christian institutions. To Machen, that belief was simply ludicrous. It seemed obvious to him that people who did not accept the fundamental doctrines of the Christian church should not try to serve as ministers in that church. Instead they should make their way into voluntary associations that were explicitly devoted to the doctrines of the religion of liberalism. If the liberals would join such organizations then they could give them unfeigned loyalty. And after the liberals emigrated, the church would be left firmly under the authority of men who were committed to the core doctrines of the Christian faith.[45]

Machen had a knack for presenting his arguments in an irenic manner, and he sometimes leaned over backwards to be respectful of persons with whom he disagreed.[46] He made a point of saying that he had no intention of questioning the sincerity of the liberals' beliefs. And Machen assured his readers that he did not believe that liberals' inability to embrace the doctrines of Christian faith demonstrated that they were bad people. Socrates, he noted, did not embrace those doctrines either, and he clearly towered "immeasurably above the common run of men."[47] Machen also said that he was not in a position to say whether or not any particular individual was or was not going to spend eternity in heaven. It was possible, Machen emphasized, that there were some liberals who were unable to accept the fundamental doctrines of the Christian religion who nevertheless maintained an attitude toward Christ that constituted "a saving faith."[48]

In spite of the gentlemanly manner in which Machen presented his analysis of what was really at stake in the religious controversies of the 1920s, many modernists found Machen's arguments exasperating.[49] That is entirely understandable. Machen made no real effort to give a sympathetic portrayal of modernists' understanding of Christianity; he had much less to say about what liberals stood for than he did about what they were against. And though Machen *said* he did not mean to give offense when he asserted that a good many people who thought of themselves as adherents of the Christian religion were in fact no such thing, it is not hard to see how such a claim could be deeply offensive. That claim was, after all, somewhat analogous to arguing that a group of men and women who thought of themselves as loyal citizens of the United States of America were, in fact, subjects of the Empire of Japan. Moreover, the categories Machen used to analyze the controversies between people he called liberals and the ones he called Christians were remarkably brittle. Those categories consisted, in large part, of stark binaries that left little room for complexity or nuance. And, of course, there was nothing in Machen's analysis of the differences between liberals and Christians to indicate that the Christians might be mistaken. Machen wanted his readers to realize that on every single one of the issues about which liberals and Christians differed, the liberals were simply wrong. The liberals had misperceived the nature of the universe. Machen and his cobelligerents had got it right. Christians embraced the true religion; liberals had given their loyalty to a false one.

Even when it was presented as politely as Machen presented it, the message "we're completely right and you're completely wrong" could sound a little arrogant. And fundamentalist polemicists often spoke and wrote as though they had no intention of trying to be polite. Sometimes they seemed to go out of their way to be insulting. J. Frank Norris, a prominent Texas fundamentalist, declared that modernists were "lepers" and "Judases."[50] Arno Clemens Gaebelein said that modernists were leading the world toward atheism, communism, and ruin.[51] He also insisted that they lacked virility. W. B. Riley agreed: modernists, he said, were womanly.[52] Riley argued, too, that college professors who had embraced modernism posed a terrible threat to both democracy and Christianity.[53]

Fundamentalists' rhetoric was studded with metaphors drawn from warfare: they tended to speak of their encounters with modernists as skirmishes, battles, crusades, and battle royals. But the contests between fundamentalists and their opponents almost never involved actual physical violence.[54] The so-called theological battles of the 1920s were fought with sermons, books, and votes, not with knives, guns, and grenades. During the hard-fought contests for control of Princeton Seminary, for example, angry words were exchanged but no shots. And when the men who were trying to protect the fundamentals of the faith lost control of Princeton, those men accepted their defeat with a certain equanimity and then established a new institution—Westminster Seminary—which was firmly under their control and which was located about forty miles to the south and west of Princeton. Fundamentalists' actions were far less violent than their words.

Definitions, Boundaries, and Specificity

This brings us back, of course, to the matter raised in the introduction to this essay: the defining characteristics of fundamentalism. From my perspective it seems clear that focusing on topics such as militancy, literalism, political involvement, and opposition to modernity does not really help us understand the distinctive characteristics of the fundamentalist movement of the 1920s and 1930s. From time to time fundamentalists did display some signs of militancy as that term is commonly understood. And they did sometimes read texts literally, exhibit an interest in politics, and express a certain amount of hostility to the modern world. But the militancy of the Protestant fundamentalists of the 1920s and 1930s can easily be overstated. Fundamentalists' interpretations of the Bible were not always literal. Their interest in politics was somewhat sporadic. Their resistance to modernity was inconsistent and sometimes half-hearted.

The scholarly literature on Protestant fundamentalism in the 1920s and 1930s suggests that fundamentalism was not simply a heterogeneous assortment of combative men and women who did not approve of the modern world. Fundamentalism was an organized religious movement that possessed its own institutions, leaders, concerns, and doctrinal emphases. The men and women who attached themselves to the fundamentalist movement had much in common with other conservative Protestants. But the fundamentalists were also, in several respects, somewhat atypical. In the 1920s and 1930s all fundamentalists were conservative Protestants, but many conservative Protestants were decidedly *not* fundamentalists. The fundamentalists certainly did not speak for all conservative Protestants. Most members of the Assemblies of God, the Church of the Nazarene, the National Baptist Convention, the Southern Baptist Convention, the Churches of Christ, and the Missouri Synod of the Lutheran Church were not a part of the fundamentalist coalition. In the 1920s and 1930s fundamentalism was only one of the many tiles to be found in the conservative Protestant mosaic. And it was probably not the largest or most important of the tiles.

There can be no doubt then that when we are talking about the United States in the 1920s and 1930s it is inappropriate to use the term *fundamentalism* as a synonym for *conservative Protestantism.* Within the context of American religious history, fundamentalism is a concept that is most valuable when it used with precision and specificity; in that context, at least, the more elastic the concept becomes, the less useful it is.

Perhaps we should not try to stretch the concept of fundamentalism to make it large enough to cover Jews and Muslims. If it is misleading to use *fundamentalism* as a synonym for *conservative Protestantism* in the United States, there is some reason to suppose that it is also misleading to use it to describe all the Jewish, Christian, and Muslim movements in the world that are said to be making militant attempts to resist modernity. It is not at all clear that we really need a single fixed category into which to sort all those movements. If we do, then it seems unlikely that the proper label to affix to that category is *fundamentalism.*

Notes

1. James Orr, "Holy Scripture and Modern Negations," in *The Fundamentals: A Testimony to the Truth,* ed. George M. Marsden (New York: Garland, 1988), 3:31 and 45; first edition published 1910–1915.

2. C. Allyn Russell, *Voices of American Fundamentalism: Seven Biographical Studies* (Philadelphia: Westminster, 1976), 98.

3. World Conference on Christian Fundamentals, *God Hath Spoken: Twenty-Five Addresses Delivered at the World Conference on Christian Fundamentals, May 25-June 1, 1919,* ed. Joel A. Carpenter (New York: Garland, 1988), 11–12; first published 1919.

4. W. B. Riley, "The Menace of Modernism," in *Conservative Call to Arms,* ed. Joel A. Carpenter (New York: Garland, 1988), 35; first published 1917. Riley was the driving force behind the creation of the WCFA.

5. Curtis Lee Laws, "Convention Side Lights," *Watchman-Examiner* 8, July 1, 1920, 834.

6. Norman F. Furniss, *The Fundamentalist Controversy, 1918–1931* (New Haven: Yale University Press, 1954), and Richard Hofstadter, *Anti-Intellectualism in American Life* (New York: Knopf, 1963).

7. Particularly helpful analyses of fundamentalism can be found in: Douglas Carl Abrams, *Selling the Old-Time Religion: American Fundamentalists and Mass Culture, 1920–1940* (Athens: University of Georgia Press, 2001); Margaret Lamberts Bendroth, *Fundamentalists in the City: Conflict and Division in Boston's Churches, 1885–1950* (New York: Oxford University Press, 2005); Virginia Lieson Brereton, *Training God's Army: The American Bible School, 1880–1940* (Bloomington: Indiana University Press, 1990); Joel A. Carpenter, *Revive Us Again:*

The Reawakening of American Fundamentalism (New York: Oxford University Press, 1997); Betty A. DeBerg, *Ungodly Women: Gender and the First Wave of American Fundamentalism* (Minneapolis: Fortress, 1990); D. G. Hart, *Defending the Faith: J. Gresham Machen and the Crisis of Conservative Protestantism in Modern America* (Baltimore: Johns Hopkins University Press, 1994); George M. Marsden, *Fundamentalism and American Culture: The Shaping of Twentieth-Century Evangelicalism, 1870–1925*, 2nd ed. (New York: Oxford University Press, 2006); William Vance Trollinger, *God's Empire: William Bell Riley and Midwestern Fundamentalism* (Madison: University of Wisconsin Press, 1990); and Timothy P. Weber, *Living in the Shadow of the Second Coming: American Premillennialism, 1875–1925* (New York: Oxford University Press, 1979). Fundamentalism is also analyzed in David Harrington Watt, *A Transforming Faith: Explorations of Twentieth-Century American Evangelicalism* (New Brunswick: Rutgers University Press, 1991).

8. American fundamentalists had a number of connections to conservative Protestants in Great Britain, but fundamentalism proper was firmly rooted in North America. And though there were fundamentalists in Canada, fundamentalism's center of gravity, unquestionably, rested in the United States. For a particularly lucid analysis of this question, see Marsden, *Fundamentalism and American Culture*, 179–80, 221–28.

9. William R. Hutchison, *Religious Pluralism in America: The Contentious History of a Founding Ideal* (New Haven: Yale University Press, 2003), 148, notes that some lists of the fundamentals contained five points and that others listed as many as fourteen. Such discrepancies, Hutchison notes, gave some observers the impression that fundamentalists could not agree on exactly what it was that they believed to be fundamental.

10. World Conference on Christian Fundamentals, *God Hath Spoken*, 12.

11. Brereton, *Training God's Army*, xiii–xix.

12. A fine analysis of the role that Bible institutes played in shaping the fundamentalist movement can be found in Brereton, *Training God's Army.*

13. Carpenter, *Revive Us Again*, 25–28.

14. Although many fundamentalists looked to him for intellectual leadership, Machen did not like to call himself a fundamentalist. Machen acknowledged that he was, according to some definitions of the term, a fundamentalist. But he generally avoided using that term to describe himself, and he declined an invitation to join the WFCA. J. Gresham Machen to R. S. Kellerman, October 7, 1924, Machen Archives, Westminster Theological Seminary. Hart, *Defending the Faith*, 61–65.

15. Edward J. Larson, *Summer for the Gods: The Scopes Trial and America's Continuing Debate over Science and Religion* (New York: Basic Books, 1997), 230–31.

16. Carpenter, *Revive Us Again*, 236–46.

17. Robert Elwood Wenger, "Social Thought in American Fundamentalism, 1918–1933" (Ph.D. dissertation, University of Nebraska, 1973).

18. Bendroth, *Fundamentalists in the City*; Trollinger *God's Empire*; and Carpenter, *Revive Us Again*, 16–31.

19. Brereton, *Training God's Army*, 29.

20. Jeffrey P. Moran, "The Scopes Trial and Southern Fundamentalism in Black and White: Race, Region, and Religion," *Journal of Southern History* 70 (February 2004): 115.

21. Barbara Dianne Savage, *Your Spirits Walk Beside Us: The Politics of Black Religion* (Cambridge: Harvard University Press, 2008), 124. Carl Abrams, e-mail message to the author, October 11, 2009.

22. Moran, "The Scopes Trial and Southern Fundamentalism," 118–20; Jeffrey P. Moran, "Reading Race into the Scopes Trial: African American Elites, Science, and Fundamentalism," *Journal of American History* 90 (December 2003): 896–99.

23. Ann Braude, "Women's History *Is* American Religious History," in *Retelling U.S. Religious History*, ed. Thomas A. Tweed (Berkeley: University of California Press, 1997), 87–107; Bendroth, *Fundamentalists in the City*, 166.

24. Margaret Lamberts Bendroth, "The New Evangelical History" (paper presented at the annual meeting of the American Academy of Religion, Montreal Canada, November 9, 2009).

25. Bendroth, *Fundamentalism and Gender*, 81–89.

26. Brereton, *Training God's Army*, 26–29. Brereton notes that advertisements that appeared in fundamentalist magazines suggest that many fundamentalists wanted to improve their command of the English language in order to improve their social standing and their economic condition.

27. For a discussion of fundamentalists' willingness to pour their energy into serving God, see Brereton, *Training God's Army*, 114–15.

28. A chart, drawn by one of the fundamentalists' spiritual ancestors, that illustrates this point is reproduced in Marsden, *Fundamentalism and American Culture*, 69.

29. Carpenter, *Revive Us Again*, 76–80.

30. Larson, *Summer for the Gods*, 188–89.

31. Carpenter, *Revive Us Again*, 89–109.

32. Brereton, *Training God's Army*, 29; Carpenter, *Revive Us Again*, 63–64, 107.

33. George M. Marsden, "Fundamentalism," *Encyclopedia of the American Religious Experience*, ed. Charles H. Lippy and Peter W. Williams (New York: Scribner, 1988), 2: 956.

34. Ibid., 949.

35. Ibid.

36. Abrams, *Selling*, 21.

37. A clear statement of the modernists' own understanding of who they were and what they stood for can be found in Shailer Mathews, *The Faith of Modernism* (New York: Macmillan, 1924), 15–36 and 169–82. The classic analysis of the history of Protestant modernism is William R. Hutchison, *The Modernist Impulse in American Protestantism* (Cambridge: Harvard University Press, 1976).

38. Elizabeth Knauss, *The Conflict: A Narrative Based on the Fundamentalist Movement* (Los Angeles: Bible Institute of Los Angeles, 1923).

39. Arno Clemens Gaebelein, *The Conflict of the Ages* (New York: Our Hope, 1933), 150.

40. Machen was, moreover, willing to say that according to some definitions of the term, he was indeed a fundamentalist. J. Gresham Machen to R. S. Kellerman, October 7, 1924; Machen Archives, Westminster Theological Seminary. The best analysis of Machen's life and thought is Hart, *Defending the Faith*.

41. J. Gresham Machen, *Christianity and Liberalism* (New York: Macmillan, 1924), 52.

42. J. Gresham Machen, *What Is Faith?* (New York: Macmillan, 1925), 102.

43. Hart, *Defending the Faith*, 69–71.

44. Machen, *Christianity and Liberalism*, 110 and 117.

45. Ibid., 157–80. Machen did not argue, however, that church membership should be limited to people who were wholeheartedly committed to the central doctrines of the Christian faith. He wanted there to be room in the church for laypeople who were beset by doubt but who were also engaged in an honest search for truth. (On this point, see pages 163 and 164 of *Christianity and Liberalism*.)

46. The Machen Archives at Westminster Theological Seminary include letters in which Machen respectfully addresses people with whom he had deep disagreements. See, for example, J. Gresham Machen to John W. Milton, May 27, 1923; J. Gresham Machen to Arthur E. Whatham, January 14, 1924; and J. Gresham Machen to Charles J. Wood, December 31, 1924.

47. Machen, *Christianity and Liberalism*, 8.

48. Ibid., 160.

49. Hutchison, *Modernist Impulse*, 264 and 267.

50. Russell, *Voices*, 65–66.

51. Gabelein, *Conflict of the Ages*, 135.

52. Bendroth, *Fundamentalism and Gender*, 66.

53. W. B. Riley, *Inspiration or Evolution*, 2nd ed. (Cleveland, Ohio: Union Gospel Press, 1926), 5.

54. For an analysis of a struggle that did involve actual violence, see Barry Hankins, *God's Rascal: J. Frank Norris and the Beginnings of Southern Fundamentalism* (Lexington: University Press of Kentucky, 1996), 118–20.

The Idea of Militancy in American Fundamentalism

Dan D. Crawford

By the time Curtis Lee Laws, the editor of the conservative Baptist magazine *Watchman-Examiner,* proposed that the "men among us . . . who still cling to the great fundamentals and who mean to do battle royal for the fundamentals shall be called 'fundamentalists'" (in 1920), the terms *fundamental* and *fundamentals* had already been widely used in evangelical circles. It was first put into active service as the title of a twelve-volume series, *The Fundamentals: A Testimony to the Truth,* published from 1910 to 1915, an interdenominational effort of moderate and conservative authors aimed at reaffirming the basic doctrines of American evangelicalism and thwarting the criticisms coming from modern science and modern scholarship that threatened to undermine biblical faith. The term was used again at a hugely successful Philadelphia conference in 1919, when a series of "Bible and Prophecy" conferences that had been held intermittently since 1878 changed its name to the World Conference on Christian Fundamentals and shifted in emphasis from prophecy to defining and defending the fundamentals of the faith. One of the principal architects of the gathering movement, William Bell Riley, who had delivered two of the twenty-five addresses at the conference, used the occasion to form the World's Christian Fundamentals Association, which aided in giving the new movement some organizational structure. And Laws's editorial was prompted by the gathering of three thousand conservative Baptists who met before the 1920 Northern Baptist Convention for a preconvention "Conference on Fundamentals of our Baptist Faith." Laws counted himself among the conservative group he was naming and continued to champion the fundamentalist cause; in an editorial written a year later, following the 1921 Baptist Convention, he captured the spirit of the "aggressive conservative movement" that he represented in his own denomination with this rallying cry: "The movement itself will never die, because always there will be men brave enough to contend earnestly for the faith delivered once for all to the saints. And it is this condition—sharp, vigorous, insistent—that is so distasteful to men without convictions."[1]

More recently, the designator *fundamentalist* has been detached from the particular movement that formed in North America in the late 1910s and has acquired a generalized use in which it refers to religious groups that may be loosely defined as ones that rigidly adhere to a set of traditional beliefs and practices that are antimodern or antiworldly. Joel A. Carpenter articulates the current usage in even more generic terms: "Fundamentalism has become a generic label for militant religious and cultural conservatism worldwide. It has been used to identify Mormons, Roman Catholics, Jews, Muslims, and Hindus who share some basic traits with the [original] party within American Protestantism."[2] We can add to Carpenter's analysis by noting that since 9/11, 2001, the sense of *militant* in the definition has been stretched to include the terrorist actions of suicide attackers, so that the element of employing violent means (to further a cause) has come to the fore in the public mind, while other elements have receded.

Carpenter warns that it "can create havoc" when the term *fundamentalism* is used "as an easy tag for a variety of 'conservative' religious movements and traditions." He notes that when groups such as Pentecostals, Mennonites, Seventh-day Adventists, Missouri Synod Lutherans, Jehovah's Witnesses, Churches of Christ, black Baptists, Mormons, Southern Baptists, and holiness Wesleyans are labeled fundamentalist, it "belittles their great diversity and violates their unique identities." He maintains that historians of American religion have a right "to define fundamentalism narrowly, for in their field of study the more generic usage obscures more than illumines."[3] In his path-breaking book, *Revive Us Again* (1997), Carpenter takes on the task of defining the term more narrowly and laying out, chapter by chapter, the specific traits and commitments of the original movement, focusing primarily on the critical formative period—the 1930s and 1940s—when it developed into a "thriving popular movement." While he does discard some elements of the current usage in his narrower definition, nevertheless, as we will see, he retains the notion of militancy as one of the basic traits that the first fundamentalists share with their modern counterparts.

My aim in this essay is to look back at the fundamentalist movement that emerged within the evangelical tradition, particularly in its early and middle phases (from 1917 to the post–World War II era) and explore some of the traits it may have in common with latter-day fundamentalisms, paying particular attention to how the idea of militancy is applicable to that indigenous American movement. Why was this one group singled out to be the model or prototype of a kind of religious group that now includes among its denotation extremist terrorist groups bent on the violent destruction of their enemies? We have named these extremist groups "fundamentalist" or "fundamentalisms," not "mennonite," "mormon," "catholic," "adventist," or "baha'i"; what was it about fundamentalists' particular beliefs and the way in which they practiced their faith that led to their being branded by their surrounding culture in this derogatory fashion?

Two Senses of *Militant*

The term *militant* is an elusive and ambiguous term, badly in need of clarification. The first and central meaning of *militant* (in my dictionary) is *warring or fighting*. Indeed the term is most often used to refer to insurgent groups or resistance movements that are engaged in armed conflict with an established government or occupying power. When these militant groups are motivated by religious and/or political ideals and ideologies, they are often referred to by scholars and in the media as "fundamentalisms." Let us say then that in the first sense of the word *militant*, it implies the use of fighting or warring tactics (in a military sense) and hence physical violence in the service of a cause.

A slightly weaker or extended sense of this first usage implies the use of tactics that employ something less than overt physical force but nonetheless imply the *coercion* of the opponent in the propagation of a cause or set of beliefs. There are many forms of coercion—physical and psychological—that might be described as militant and that involve the imposition of a set of beliefs or practices on another party, usually backed by some form of punishment or the threat of punishment. In religious contexts one thinks of the *militant church* of the medieval and Reformation periods and the forced conversion of individuals or whole peoples. One might also think of the brainwashing tactics used on children and adults, as illustrated forcefully in the documentary film *Jesus Camp*, or the bully pulpit and the use of harsh rhetoric and the threat of eternal damnation to win converts as forms of militancy.

The second dictionary sense of *militant* does not imply the use of violence or force but refers to the style or manner employed in maintaining or propagating some cause or ideal: *having a combative character; aggressive, especially in the service of a* cause; the illustrative example given is: *militant political activist.* Another source gives as an example *militant feminist.* Groups and movements that are militant in this weaker sense, secular or religious, do not employ or advocate physical force to further their cause, and, moreover, they usually work within the legal system of their state or government. However, their actions are analogous to militant actions in the first sense insofar as they are taking the offensive, engaging with their opponent, and using aggressive means to achieve their goals—for example, marketing techniques, grassroots organizing, lobbying, protest marches, boycotts, or lawsuits.[4] The most common (offensive and defensive) weapon used by militants in this second sense, however, is argument and rhetoric. Militant individuals or groups are those that are combative, argumentative, and contentious in defending and advancing their cause or beliefs.

It often happens that these militant-combative groups spawn an extremist wing or subgroup that does advocate strategies that employ physical (violent) means against authorities, thus giving rise to a militant-violent group, as, for example, when the Black Panthers emerged from the Civil Rights movement, Earth First from the environmental movement, and the Animal Liberation Front from the animal rights movement. This is an ever-present danger for these groups, especially if their cause is ideological. But when it does occur, we should resist the temptation to conflate the two meanings of *militant,* that is, to view the combative techniques employed by the original group as inherently violent. Such groups may be, and often are, strongly opposed to violence in any form, and even to coercive measures.

Another aspect of fundamentalists' militant-combative attitude should be noted, namely the *dogmatism* that goes hand in hand with it but is distinguishable from it. Here I refer to a type of uncompromising attitude and a refusal to admit even the possibility that the group might be wrong or that there might be some truth in the opposing view. This rigid mind-set is a reflection of fundamentalists' absolute certainty that they possess the truth as spoken by God and recorded without error in scripture. Dogmatism in this sense does not necessarily imply militancy. One can be dogmatic and unyielding in argument (as for example "dogmatic theologians" are wont to be, or philosophers or scientists who are wedded to a theory or worldview) without being combative and attacking one's opponent. Admittedly there is a fine line here in that dogmatism normally implies contentiousness. But there is a difference: dogmatism is essentially a defensive posture, whereas militancy implies taking the offensive, exhibiting combative tactics and maneuvers, adopting an action program and aggressively pursuing it.

It is the secondary sense of *militant-combative-contentious* that is directly applicable to American fundamentalists. This style of defending their faith against what they perceived to be the corrosive effects of liberal theology and modern biblical-critical methods was characteristic of the movement primarily in the 1920s, when the "fundamentalist-modernist controversies" raged. The vitriolic exchanges, bitter accusations, and defensive posturing that took place during this early period stamped fundamentalism with an indelible negative image in the public mind. However, a second phase of the movement, beginning in the early 1930s, saw the rise of a new generation of fundamentalists—evangelists, youth leaders, and Bible teachers—that consciously eschewed the contentious, negative tactics of their forebears and made it their business to repair the bad reputation the movement had incurred. While a few outspoken leaders of the movement continued to use the old controversialist strategies and tactics in the 1930s, 1940s, and 1950s, these extremists were gradually marginalized within the movement, losing their power and influence over the main body of fundamentalists. The more moderate fundamentalists that displaced them were indeed uncompromising and zealous defenders of what they saw to be the essential elements of the biblical gospel message, and they were aggressive in their efforts to save lost souls and promote worldwide evangelism; but they were nonmilitant in all of the above senses, and it was largely due to their strenuous efforts that fundamentalism was transformed from a beleaguered and socially alienated "oppressed" minority into a flourishing popular movement in the 1930s and 1940s.

Moreover, there appears to be no clear justification for passing from militancy in the sense of combative and contentious to militancy in the sense of promoting violent means. Many critics of fundamentalism have assumed too easily, and without argument, that the combination of fundamentalist beliefs (usually centering on the *premillennialist* doctrine) and militant rhetoric and tactics produced a mixture that was (is) volatile and inherently violent or prone to violence. These critics (and the historians among them) have failed to justify this inference, in large part as a result of their uncritical assimilation of the two senses of militant distinguished above. The fact that fundamentalist conservative views have attracted unstable or psychotic individuals who do commit violent acts does not warrant the inference that the whole movement, or its views, are violent or conducive to violence.

The Uses of *Militant*

When and how did the idea of militancy enter the discourse relating to the fundamentalist movement? How has the term been used in the historiography of the movement? And do these uses of the term give a fair and accurate description of what the fundamentalists were thinking and doing?

We can begin to answer these questions by noting that fundamentalists themselves rarely used the term *militant* to describe their own conduct;[5] rather it was used almost exclusively in the metalinguistic narratives constructed by historians and commentators to describe fundamentalists' actual attitudes and actions. Fundamentalists did, however, often use the near-synonym *aggressive* in describing the strategies they employed in defending the faith and in their evangelistic efforts.[6] And, not surprisingly, at a time when the country was engaged in a world war, they began to adopt the war metaphor and use military imagery in describing their opposition to modernism.

It is useful to examine the role that militancy played in the historical interpretations of fundamentalism offered by several key historians—Norman F. Furniss, C. Allyn Russell, George M. Marsden, and Joel A. Carpenter. Furniss's 1954 book, *The Fundamentalist Controversy, 1918–1931,* was arguably the first to introduce the idea of militancy in a robust sense into the historiography of the movement. He points to "the outbreak of militant fundamentalism after 1918,"[7] and sees the postwar mentality as a contributing cause, as in this passage:

> Another phenomenon of World War days, the unreasoning hatred of ideas and men became one more force behind the rise of the fundamentalist movement. Having learned well that intolerance was justified when the nation was

> combatting foreign enemies, the Fundamentalists in the subsequent years of peace found themselves no longer able to meet domestic crises, especially a serious challenge to their faith, with Galilean charity. Whereas in 1912 and 1913 the religious conservatives attempted to overcome heretical tendencies primarily by reasoned argument, after 1918 the Fundamentalists sought forcibly to expel the modernist traffickers from the various denominations and to impose rigid creeds upon all who remained. . . . Violence in action and language had now become characteristic of the Fundamentalists.[8]

For Furniss, the rise of militancy is explained in part by the leaders adopting an attitude of "intolerance" and "unreasoning hatred" toward modernist ideas and individuals and also by their use of *force,* namely, coercive tactics in trying to "expel" liberals from their denominations and "impose" their creeds on the larger church body. Furniss and other historians have given ample documentation of the infighting that occurred between liberals and conservatives in the (Northern) Baptist and Presbyterian denominations and the political maneuvering that went on as each side tried to gain the upper hand. But Furniss's account is one-sided and later historians' accounts of these events (as we will see) should cause us to ask whether the attitudes and rhetoric of these early fundamentalists were any more uncivil and intolerant, and their tactics any more devious, than those of their liberal opponents. As it turned out, the only important difference between these two warring camps was that the fundamentalists lost the war, and the liberals were successful in taking control of their denominations and driving out (or censuring) those who identified with the fundamentalist cause.

We should also note Furniss's casual description of the words and actions employed by fundamentalists as forms of *violence.* Since he surely does not mean by *violent* the use of physical force, he must mean some lesser form of injury or insult to the persons addressed; however, he does not specify what that injury is. But whether or not *violent* is an appropriate description of the "action and language" of these antagonists, there seems to be little difference in this regard between the two parties, at least in these early struggles. In any case later historians eventually toned down Furniss's rhetoric: while they retained the idea of militancy as characteristic of fundamentalism, they dropped completely any implication of force or violence.

In his classic work, *Voices of American Fundamentalism: Seven Biographical Studies* (1976), C. Allyn Russell recognizes the importance of an attitudinal complex in understanding what is distinctive about fundamentalism. Russell examines seven representative leaders of the fundamentalist movement that were active during the fundamentalist-modernist controversies in the 1920s, when the struggle was at its height: J. Frank Norris, John Roach Straton, William Bell Riley, J. C. Massee, J. Gresham Machen, William Jennings Bryan, and Clarence E. Macartney.

Employing what he calls a "biographical method," Russell emphasizes the attitudes, temperament, and lifestyle of these men as well as the particular fundamentalist doctrines that each of them espoused. He notes that what was "typical and distinguishing" of fundamentalists, more than any of the doctrines that they embraced, was their "characteristic attitude," which he describes as "harsh," "arrogant," "aggressive," "acrimonious." He notes that when fundamentalists criticized the sins and shortcomings of secular society, "what irritated people, however, was not so much the correctness or incorrectness of the views of the fundamentalists in these areas as it was their dogmatic, absolutist, haughty insistence that they and they alone were right."[9]

How is it then with militancy in his analysis? Russell recognizes that the aggressive-dogmatic style he describes did become militant-combative in several of his voices. He uses the term *militant* infrequently and almost exclusively to refer to the crusaders Norris, Straton, and Riley; but it hardly applies to two of the leaders, Massee and Macartney. Russell's seven voices are arranged on a spectrum that runs from moderate to extreme. J. Frank Norris (whom Russell labels in his chapter title "Violent Fundamentalist") is the most extreme (and the most militant) in his actions and temperament, having actually killed a man who accosted him in his office.[10] At the other end of the spectrum is Clarence Macartney, the "preacher fundamentalist," whom Russell calls a "gentlemanly force among the fundamentalists, light-years removed from the shenanigans of such men as John Roach Straton or J. Frank Norris."[11] Macartney was a forceful defender of the faith against modernist "unbelief" (as he called it), but was consistently civil and fair-minded in his preaching and writing, and as Moderator of the Presbyterian Church in the U.S.A. (1924–25). What makes him a fundamentalist attitudinally, for Russell, was his "intransigence": "He would not be moved from his immutable theological, social, or ecclesiastical positions, whatever the cost or whatever the seeming validity of new interpretations."[12] But this sort of dogmatic, traditionalist stance, that we have distinguished from militancy, was certainly not unique to fundamentalists.

Russell describes J. C. Massee as the "moderate fundamentalist" who gradually went through a kind of conversion away from fundamentalism. Initially Massee led the charge as "general of the fundamentalist forces" in the 1920 Northern Baptist Convention against liberal tendencies in the Baptist schools and seminaries, calling for an investigation into "the attitudes of faculty members and trustees concerning the cardinal doctrines of the faith."[13] But as early as 1923 he was splitting from the extremists in his conservative party—notably Riley, Straton, and T. T. Shields—thus forming a third (middle) faction between liberals and ultraconservatives. By 1926 Massee had led the more numerous moderate fundamentalist group in a decisive break with the extremists, declaring, "I do not believe in the wisdom or the righteousness of denunciation, misinterpretation, the imputing of motives and the widespread directing of suspicion toward men who declare their conservatism and their faithful adherence to the Word and to the Christ of God."[14] The specific set of qualities that keeps Massee in the fundamentalist camp for Russell were his lifelong struggle to counter the eroding tide of modernism in his denomination, his anti-intellectualism, his passion for evangelism, his strong emphasis on a strict, pietistic morality, and his opposition to a social gospel interpretation of the New Testament—indicating that Russell is able to select from many other distinguishing fundamentalist traits relating to doctrine and style after contentiousness and negative attacks are removed.

Militancy then is a part of the general profile of the fundamentalist mind or attitude that Russell sets out, but it is not the dominant characteristic, which seems to be captured more by terms such as *obstinate, arrogant, haughty.* Moreover, militancy is not an *essential* or *definitional* trait of fundamentalism since several of his champions lack it and yet are still definitely fundamentalists. Russell's portrayal of the fundamentalist mind-set consists of a family of traits, many of which are not even possessed by its leading representatives. And so it is not at all clear that he has identified traits that distinguish fundamentalists from other religious and secular groups. Moreover, Russell can be faulted for suggesting an easy connection between fundamentalism and violence by taking Norris, the "violent fundamentalist," as representing one style of fundamentalism. Although he concludes that Norris's "problems . . . were more psychological than theological, rooted in the deprivations of his own unfortunate childhood," in placing Norris on a continuum of expressions of the characteristic attitude of fundamentalism he gives the impression that fundamentalist beliefs-plus-characteristic-attitude naturally lead to extremism and violence when put into practice by unstable and highly temperamental individuals. But like Furniss, Russell does not specify what it is about this mix of ideas and attitudes that makes one any more prone to violent behaviors than do the beliefs-cum-attitudes of any other religion or ideology.

It was George M. Marsden who first gave the idea of militancy a systematic application to fundamentalism by arguing that a militant style or attitude was an essential or *defining* characteristic of the movement.[15] In his monumental 1980 work, *Fundamentalism and American Culture: The Shaping of Twentieth-Century Evangelicalism, 1870–1925,* Marsden fully incorporates the idea of militancy (and the war metaphor) into his analysis of the development of fundamentalism. He describes what he calls "a dramatic transformation" that occurred among conservative evangelicals from 1917 to the early 1920s post–World War I period. Until 1917 these conservatives "operated within the same denominations and interdenominational agencies [as their liberal opponents], and at times still cooperated." But "after 1920 conservative evangelical councils were dominated by 'fundamentalists' engaged in holy warfare to drive the scourge of modernism out of church and culture." Marsden goes on to explain "this remarkable shift from moderation to militancy" as a response to cultural changes on two "fronts": 1) it was initially a response to attacks against fundamentalists, after America's entrance into the war, made by "aggressive and radical forms of theological liberalism"; and 2) it was the result of a "cultural crisis" following the Great War with all its barbarism and atrocities, that was marked by a moral decline and cynicism that seemed to these conservatives "startlingly alien" to the image of a Christian America.[16]

On the first front Marsden gives a revealing account of an exchange that took place during the war years between conservatives (soon to be called fundamentalists) and several liberal theologians at the University of Chicago Divinity School—notably its dean, Shailer Mathews, and his colleague in early church history, Shirley Jackson Case—who launched "a fierce assault" on premillennialism and its tendency to foster pacifism and indifference to the war effort.[17] "The American nation [wrote Case in an article titled "The Premillennial Menace"] is engaged in a gigantic effort to make the world safe for democracy." Hence "it would be almost traitorous negligence to ignore the detrimental character of premillennial propaganda." Case also told reporters that there was a "strong suspicion" that the large sum of money used to propagate the premillennial doctrine "emanates from German sources," and that "the fund would be a profitable field for governmental investigation."[18]

Marsden views Case's remarks (and the fundamentalist response) as expressions of the "wartime paranoia" that was prevalent in the nation: "Such acrimony indicated the extent to which the war fanned the smoldering coals of theological debate. For premillennialists and other doctrinal militants, of course, it did not take much provocation to unleash fierce controversy." Indeed it did not, for the liberal attacks had opened up a clear line of counterattack. Fundamentalists responded by pointing to what they believed to be a direct link between German militarism and brutality and German biblical theology.

It was, to be sure, a "fierce controversy." There were conflicting theologies at issue, as well as factual disagreements, but there was little in the way of real debate in the true sense of one side offering criticism of the other's viewpoint and the other responding to that criticism. The militant aspect of the exchange lies mainly in its bitter and accusatory tone. It can be noted, however, that while this exchange does illustrate the beginnings of the adoption of a militant-combative and controversialist stance by the fundamentalists, it is significant that their militant response was provoked by the aggressive attacks of the liberals. The conservatives were in this case drawn into the battle (from their own pacifist position regarding the war) to counter the charges made against them and to defend one of their central doctrines.

On the second front that explains fundamentalists' shift from cooperation to militant opposition—the "cultural crisis" that followed World War I—Marsden points to the anti-evolution crusade spearheaded by Riley and his World's Christian Fundamentals Association, which made common cause with William Jennings Bryan's separate campaign and fought vigorously against the teaching of evolution in the schools and universities. Not unlike the suffrage and temperance crusaders, the fundamentalists expressed their militancy outwardly in their aggressive campaigns against evolution and in their attempts to promote legislation that would prohibit the teaching of evolution in public institutions. However, as historians have noted, Riley's attempt to make evolution the dominant issue for the growing movement collapsed for lack of support, and by the end of the 1920s the anti-evolution crusade was essentially finished; other ways of meeting the cultural crisis, such as a renewed emphasis on evangelism, came to the fore.[19]

Joel A. Carpenter accepts Marsden's setting of the problem facing the historian of American fundamentalism—to explain the transition from moderation to militancy in the post–World War I period—and gives a fuller explanation of the causes of this shift, building on Marsden's account. Moreover, Carpenter is in complete accord with Marsden in regarding militancy as a distinguishing mark of fundamentalism: "Militancy was the mark of fundamentalism, and ideological militancy especially. Fundamentalists were, in other words, a contentious lot, and they held up confrontation as one of their principal duties."[20]

Carpenter identifies an exchange that took place in 1917—between liberal theologian Shailer Mathews and Reuben Torrey, at that time dean of the Bible Institute of Los Angeles—as a turning point in the fundamentalists' attitude toward modernists.[21] Mathews had published a pamphlet entitled *Will Christ Come Again?* which denied the literal second coming of Christ, and Torrey wrote a vituperative response that denounced Mathews the man and accused him of duplicitous motives. For Carpenter, this exchange "shows the breakdown of serious dialogue between liberals and conservatives by [1917]"; that is to say, the level of discussion had by this time degenerated into personal, ad hominem attacks and accusations. In addition, Carpenter notes, the tract reveals a "growing distrust of liberal Protestants' basic honesty," as when Torrey exclaims that he could not recall ever reading a work, "even by the bitterest infidel, that was more evidently, egregiously, deliberately, intentionally unfair" than the pamphlet by Shailer Mathews.[22]

But Carpenter finds a more profound meaning in Torrey's dismissal of Mathews relating to Torrey's premillennialist theological belief. He comments that Mathews's attack on a literal second coming was for Torrey "clear evidence of the apostasy of the church, a sign of the end times that he and his fellow dispensationalists had been predicting." [23] Torrey cites 2 Peter 3:3: "In the last days mockers shall come with mockery, walking after their own lust, and saying, 'Where is the promise of His coming?'" and Carpenter comments: "Once equated with the dreaded apostasy of the end times, liberals no longer warranted the civility commonly granted to worthy opponents." Torrey's militant attitude is here expressed in his uncivil behavior that disrespects his opponent and refuses to take his argument seriously.[24]

To sum up, Marsden and Carpenter, the chief advocates of militant fundamentalism, use the term *militant* to describe *militant-combative* behavior along the lines of Laws's original idea. The primary sense of the term has to do with the aggressive manner in which fundamentalists defended their beliefs, mainly in argumentation, and the negative tactics and rhetoric used against their opponents. They took the offensive, always ready and willing to contend for the faith and do battle with their foes, whether in the modernist churches, in the secular world, or, as time went on, within their own ranks. They made fierce attacks against their opponents, accusing and condemning them in vehement tones.

Further, militancy was expressed in an action program that involved the writing of polemical tracts, books, and publications; the forming of associations with radical goals, such as the World's Christian Fundamentals Association and the General Association of Regular Baptists (whose primary goal was to aid churches in withdrawing from the Northern Baptist Convention); and in conducting outright crusades aimed at social or political reform (namely, the anti-evolution crusades of Riley and Bryan).

Moderate Fundamentalism

Carpenter and Marsden are certainly right that militancy was characteristic of fundamentalism in its formative period (1917–1926). One thinks here of the founders and early leaders of the movement: Riley, Torrey, A. C. Dixon, I. M. Haldeman, Shields, Norris, Straton, W. H. Griffith Thomas, Charles Trumbull, T. C. Horton, Robert (Fighting Bob) Shuler, and their ally at Princeton Seminary, the New Testament scholar John Gresham Machen. These men, coming from different strands of the evangelical tradition, were largely shaped and defined by the liberal, modernist challenge that was taking hold in the established denominations and the prestigious seminaries. And they met this challenge by reaffirming the fundamentals and adopting a militant stance against their foes.

Moreover, this spirit of contentiousness was carried on in the 1930s and 1940s by younger fundamentalists, such as Donald Grey Barnhouse, Robert (Fighting Bob) Ketcham, Oliver Buswell, Harold Laird, John R. Rice, Bob Jones Sr., and Carl McIntire, following in their elders' footsteps. The militancy of these men was directed chiefly at the established Protestant denominations and their several agencies, such as the Federal Council of Christian Churches. Many of them were active separatists or "come-outers" who bore a deep resentment against the denominations that had forced them out or that they had left because of the church's apostasy. Barnhouse, pastor of the prestigious Tenth Presbyterian Church in Philadelphia, who was put on trial for violating "the spirit of Christian comity" by holding meetings outside his church but who nevertheless remained in the church, expressed this sentiment: "As the church is in the world but not of the world, I can truly say before God that we, though in the church organization, are not of it in spirit as it is at present organized and believe that what we are seeing is a part of the prophetic tendency so clearly pictured in the Word of God that shows us all church organization running into the confusion of Babylon the Great, the Mother of Harlots."[25]

Carl McIntire, editor of the influential *Christian Beacon* magazine, was another one of this band of men who perpetuated the combative-condemning spirit of the 1920s into the 1930s, 40s, and 50s. A militant separatist who in 1938 lost his court battle with the Presbyterian Church of the U.S.A. to keep his historic Collingswood Presbyterian Church, he conducted a lifelong campaign against his former denomination and those who remained in it (including Barnhouse). In his 1944 book, *Twentieth-Century Reformation,* McIntire made a broadside attack on the Federal Council of Churches, coming down hard on those "so-called fundamentalists" who were members: "How can a man be truly a defender of the faith and a proclaimer of the good news of redemption through the precious blood of Jesus Christ and at the same time make common cause with those who count the blood of the covenant an unholy thing? This is the compromise—deadly, soul-crushing compromise—that is the sin of all those who knowingly or unknowingly work with or permit themselves to count for the Federal Council's ministry."[26]

In his concluding chapter McIntire issues a rallying cry that has about it a tone of desperation and defeat: "The fundamentalists are coming back, organized, with their feet on solid ground. The arsenals of the historic faith are being freshly stocked, and with a full dependence on the King of kings, the Leader of the battle, they believe that their efforts shall not be in vain. Yes, it is the age-long battle in which we are now engaged, right inside the church—it is light versus darkness."[27]

But these men of controversy represented a radical wing of the fundamentalist movement that was on its way out, for there were many more fundamentalist leaders of this younger, second generation who had an entirely different outlook. These were reformers who never had a strong loyalty to the established churches and consequently did not experience a painful separation from them. They were influenced more by a network of independent organizations that had been built up over the previous half century consisting of nondenominational churches and missions, organizations such as the YMCA, Bible conferences, the Bible institutes, and prestigious Wheaton College. And although this new wave of fundamentalist leaders was convinced that the Protestant churches had gone over to the modernists, they did not harbor the same bitter and vindictive feelings toward them as did their separatist brethren.

This new wave comprised a group of young evangelists, Bible teachers, and youth workers that emerged in the early 1930s who saw that the fundamentalist–modernist controversies of the 1920s had weakened the movement and diverted its energies from the primary task of winning souls. These "young men on fire" (as Mel Larson described them in his firsthand chronicle of this phase of the movement[28]) took the fundamentalist creed as a given, no longer in need of defense against an enemy that had been defined and neutralized. They took up the cause of evangelism with renewed vigor, carrying the simple gospel message to "a lost world." They realized that the Billy Sunday–type of evangelism had brought the "sacred calling" of evangelism into ill repute, and they were determined to return to a "sane" and reasonable approach that downplayed sensationalism and emotionalism. They were wary of the extremist wing of the movement—led by Carl McIntire, John R. Rice, and Bob Jones Sr.—whom they saw as stirring up controversy over matters of doctrine and practice that were not essential to the biblical gospel message. They consciously refrained from negative attacks against their opponents and particularly avoided attacking their fellow fundamentalists. They spoke mainly to the youth whom they saw as moving away from the churches that had nurtured them and falling into reckless living and cynicism. Many of them were the pioneer radio (and later television) evangelists who saw the potential of these new media to reach millions with the gospel if they moved beyond narrow sectarianism and crafted a message with a wider popular appeal. These were the workers, laboring in the fields, who reenergized the movement when it was languishing and marginalized in American life and helped it to regain a measure of respect and legitimacy.

What is important for our discussion is that these evangelists and Bible teachers consciously eschewed militancy and contentiousness in their preaching style and general manner. Nonetheless, they were true-blue fundamentalists—antimodernist, uncompromising in upholding the fundamentals of the faith but more interested in presenting the gospel in a positive light than in "tearing down" those with whom they disagreed.

During the 1930s and 1940s the extreme conservative wing of the movement was gradually marginalized and the balance of power shifted to these moderates. This shift was due in large part to what Carpenter calls the "separatist impulse" of the extremists, which led them to fracture into smaller and smaller, more isolated subunits. As this happened, prominent voices such as Riley, Rice, McIntire, Trumbull, and Bob Jones, Sr. were spending as much time and energy being watchdogs over their own fundamentalist flocks as they were battling against their worldly opponents, although increasingly their crusades became more an expression of their own belligerent personalities than of the spirit of the movement as a whole. In each instance in which the conservative forces narrowed their conception of faith, ousted one of their fellows for heretical modernist tendencies, or tightened their definition of the "higher Christian life," they lost key supporters and weakened their cause while at the same time becoming more defensive and strident in their rhetoric—more militant.

George W. Dollar illustrates this logic of the narrowing boundaries of the faithful remnant in his 1973 account of the history of fundamentalism in America.[29] Dollar makes militancy and a strict separatism essential properties of fundamentalism (in its "genuine, historic" meaning). To qualify as a militant fundamentalist, an individual (or institution) must not only adhere to and expound the truths of the Bible literally interpreted but also be militant in the "exposure of error and of all compromise with error."[30] Dollar looks back to the first phase of the movement to locate the true exemplars of this kind of militant faith and singles out Shields,

Riley, Straton, and Norris. "Those were days as never before and probably never again, when giants strode across the land, locked in fiercest debates, none giving quarter, and all dedicated to their positions until the death."[31] But since that time only a handful of those who profess to be fundamentalists have held true to that high standard. Among the second-generation fundamentalist leaders, he has praise for Carl McIntire (who through his expanding "Fundamentalist empire . . . continues to expose and attack"), Charles Woodbridge (for whom "any connection, even remotely, with anything new-evangelical is a 'sinister error'"), and Bob Jones Jr. (to whom "it is clear that the Bible commands separation from those who aid and encourage any kind of compromise with infidelity").[32] In sum, by defining fundamentalism in terms of militancy in the strong sense of exposing error and applying a strict standard of separatism, Dollar ends up equating fundamentalism with a tiny minority of extremists at the edge of the movement and their devoted followers.

Carpenter is certainly sensitive to the influence of the more moderate fundamentalist forces that we have identified, working to reform and revive the movement from within. Indeed, one needs to look to his seminal work *Revive Us Again* to understand how American fundamentalism flourished in these years and the role the moderates played in this resurgence. In each chapter of his book he brings into vivid relief several of the less conspicuous figures (alongside the better known ones) who made significant positive contributions to the movement's success: Lloyd Bryant, Clarence Jones, J. Elwin Wright, Percy Crawford, Bob Cook, Torrey Johnson, Will Houghton, William Ward Ayer, Howard Ferrin, Grace Woods, Charles Erdman, Merv Rosell, Bob Pierce, Edwin Orr, Henrietta Mears, and many others. Hundreds more could be added to Carpenter's list.

But Carpenter's commitment to militancy as a defining trait of fundamentalism prevents him from giving full recognition to the committed moderates of this transitional period. And when he does acknowledge these individuals, he treats them as if they were exceptions to the rule when in fact they made up the majority. Another reason for this misrepresentation is that he puts his emphasis on other moderate elements and trends within the movement. In full agreement with Marsden's analysis in this respect, he sees the trajectory of fundamentalism as moving toward the formation of a "coalition" of moderate forces—the so-called new evangelicals—who emerged in the late 1940s and consciously repudiated the old fundamentalists and their sectarian and militant ways. Hence he accentuates earlier developments that anticipated the formation of this new party of progressives.

Carpenter traces the beginning of this new coalition to the vision and determination of J. Elwin Wright of the New England Fellowship and Harold Ockenga, pastor of Park Street Church in Boston, to organize a "united front" for evangelicals, which led to the founding of the National Association of Evangelicals (NAE) in 1942. A fault line that had been forming opened up between the moderate NAE and the extremist separatist wing of the party when Wright refused to join with Carl McIntire's American Council of Christian Churches, formed in the previous year in direct opposition to the Federal Council of Churches. Wright and his associates viewed McIntire's group as too exclusive because it gave voting membership only to separatist denominations, whereas the NAE welcomed mainline churches and evangelical leaders that were members of the Federal Council, as well as Pentecostal and Holiness churches. In addition, Wright wanted the NAE to foster a more irenic and cooperative spirit. But although Wright succeeded in molding the NAE into an effective organization, Carpenter notes that he was not successful in bringing the main body of the movement under his umbrella organization.[33]

It was not until the late 1940s, in Carpenter's analysis, that the coalition of new evangelicals would achieve an identity distinct from the militant separatists and mount a real challenge with which fundamentalists had to reckon. This occurred when a group of reform-minded fundamentalists, led by Harold Ockenga and educators Wilbur Smith and Carl Henry, joined evangelist Charles Fuller in founding Fuller Seminary in 1947. The goal of these reformers was to reclaim intellectual respectability for their conservative faith by engaging more with the scholarly community and by making fundamentalism more socially relevant. They accepted fundamentalist theology but criticized its "spirit of lovelessness and strife."[34] Ockenga struck this note in his address at the opening of Fuller Seminary, proclaiming that Fuller graduates would have no time for the "kind of negativism" that existed "to attack others, and to derogate others, and to drag them down, and to besmirch them."[35] This account is in accord with what Marsden claimed in an earlier brief analysis of the history of fundamentalism (1975)—that the "new evangelicalism" that emerged in the 1940s had modified its fundamentalist heritage in that its constituents had "dropped militancy as a primary aspect of their identity."[36]

Continuing with this narrative, the coalition was greatly strengthened by gaining the support of evangelist Billy Graham who shared with these progressives a strong desire for reform. First, he agreed with the new evangelicals' goal of shedding the anti-intellectual image of fundamentalism and of becoming more socially aware.[37] Further, Graham had been steadily moving toward a greater inclusiveness by allowing the mainline denominations to participate in his crusades. And equally important for our discussion was Graham's desire to stop "the fighting, feuding and controversies among God's people." Both Carpenter and Marsden view Graham as aligning himself with the new evangelicals to form the coalition of moderates who self-consciously broke from the original fundamentalist tradition, thus splitting it into "two major movements"—evangelicalism and the fundamentalists who were "marked by continued militant separatism."[38]

But this sharp division between the nonmilitant, more moderate, intellectually oriented new evangelicals and the militant separatist fundamentalists does not make a natural cut in the way the movement developed. To begin with, the main body of nonmilitant fundamentalists of the 1930s and 1940s that we have distinguished are practically invisible, while the extreme wing of the movement occupies center stage. Those more moderate fundamentalist leaders and workers had dropped militancy long before the new evangelicals emerged in the late 1940s and had kept their distance from extremists such as Rice, McIntire, and Bob Jones Sr.[39]

Moreover, even though most of these mainstream fundamentalists and their organizations were independent of the mainline churches, they did not think of themselves as "separatists" or "come-outers"—terms that usually carried with them the connotation of actively denouncing the apostate churches and organizations from which they had departed and encouraging others to do the same. As Torrey Johnson said about his pastorate at the Midwest Bible Church in Chicago during the 1930s, "I was neither a come-outer nor a go-inner. I was just a worker."[40]

But neither did these moderates unite with the new evangelicals. They resisted the label *neo-evangelical*, with its sense of reform and critique of the old fundamentalism, because they did not think their movement needed reform. Their main interest was always to win souls and bring revival to America, and they were satisfied with the progress they were making toward that goal. As a consequence they came to occupy a place in the middle and continued to identify with fundamentalism (even if they were increasingly unwilling to call themselves by that name because of its negative connotations). This included Graham, who wanted to stop the fighting and feuding but did not want to change the basic theology or the main objective of fundamentalism. When Graham finally made a decisive break with the separatists, precipitated by his allowing the mainline Protestant churches to sponsor his 1957 New York crusade, he kept the moderate majority of fundamentalists with him, even though some, like Rice, thought he had swung too far toward the modernists and repudiated him for it.[41] But his adherence to the essentials of the faith, his zeal for evangelism, his basic message of sin and salvation, his forthright and sincere style, and his positive, hopeful tone made him the chosen leader of the movement and the true representative of what it stood for. Throughout the 1960s and 1970s it was the main body of fundamentalists with Graham at the head that gradually assimilated the new evangelicals and absorbed the more intellectual emphasis of Carl Henry and the faculty at Fuller, and not the other way round. Beyond that, the influence of the new evangelicals on the amorphous mass of fundamentalists was minimal.

Marsden's and Carpenter's failure to assign Graham his proper place in the fundamentalist movement by linking him so closely with the new evangelicals is part and parcel of their failure to acknowledge the importance of the moderate fundamentalists who preceded Graham and who provided the main impetus for the growth and appeal of the movement at a critical juncture in its history. And their neglect of this group is a direct result of their holding firmly to the idea of militancy as a defining trait of fundamentalism. In taking militancy to be central, their narratives bring to the foreground the most controversial and vociferous elements of the movement, thus reinforcing the common stereotype of fundamentalists as militant extremists, and put into the shadows the moderate middle majority of the movement that drove it and accounted for its success.[42]

Notes

1. *Watchman-Examiner* 9, no. 31, August 4, 1921, 974.

2. Joel A. Carpenter, *Revive Us Again: The Reawakening of American Fundamentalism* (New York: Oxford University Press, 1997), 4.

3. Ibid.

4. Margaret Lamberts Bendroth locates the origins of the militant spirit of fundamentalism as it emerged in the city of Boston in the suffrage and temperance campaigns of the late-nineteenth and early-twentieth centuries and notes the role of women in these movements: Boston's Protestant women "excelled at provoking conflict: at every turn in the story of rising religious confrontation, they were at the forefront." See chapter 4, "Militant Protestants," *Fundamentalists in the City: Conflict and Division in Boston's Churches, 1885–1950* (New York: Oxford University Press, 2005); quotation on p. 58.

5. I find only two instances in Carpenter's *Revive Us Again* of fundamentalists using the term *militant* to describe their own actions (pp. 47, 63)—the exceptions that prove the rule.

6. The terms *aggressive* and *aggression* (like their cousin *militant*) are closely tied to the idea of physical force, usually as the outward expression of inner feelings of anger, hatred, or resentment. But *aggressive* also has a more general meaning that encompasses a wider range of behavior than does *militant*: exhibiting driving, forceful energy or initiative, without implying belligerence or combativeness.

7. Norman F. Furniss, *The Fundamentalist Controversy, 1918–1931* (New Haven: Yale University Press, 1954), 26.

8. Ibid., 24–25.

9. C. Allyn Russell, *Voices of American Fundamentalism: Seven Biographical Studies* (Philadelphia: Westminster, 1976), 214–15.

10. In 1926 Norris shot and killed an unarmed man, D. E. Chipps, who, Norris claimed, entered Norris's office intoxicated and threatened him. Norris was indicted for murder, tried, and acquitted.

11. Russell, *Voices*, 211.

12. Ibid.

13. Ibid., 120.

14. Letter to James M. Gray, June 29, 1926. Massee papers. (Cited in *Voices*, 127.)

15. "Defining Fundamentalism," *Christian Scholar's Review* 1 (Winter, 1971).

16. George M. Marsden, *Fundamentalism and American Culture: The Shaping of Twentieth-Century Evangelicalism: 1870–1925*, 2nd ed. (New York: Oxford University Press, 2006), 141.

17. Ibid., 145.

18. Ibid., 147.

19. See Ernest R. Sandeen, *The Roots of Fundamentalism: British and American Millennarianism, 1800–1930* (Chicago: University of Chicago Press, 1970), 247, 266–68; William Vance Trollinger, *God's Empire: William Bell Riley and Midwestern Fundamentalism* (Madison: University of Wisconsin Press, 1990), 44–51.

20. Carpenter, *Revive Us Again*, 64.

21. Carpenter, introduction, in Carpenter, ed., *The Fundamentalist–Modernist Conflict: Opposing Views on Three Major Issues* (New York: Garland, 1988), no pagination.

22. Reuben Torrey, "Will Christ Come Again? An Exposure of the Foolishness, Fallacies and Falsehoods of Shailer Mathews," in Carpenter, *The Fundamentalist–Modernist Conflict*, 21.

23. The dispensationalist theological view, propagated in the United States by the Irish clergyman John Nelson Darby in the 1870s, held that human history was divided into seven ages or dispensations and that God operated differently in each age. According to Darby's interpretation of scripture, the current age, the Age of the Church, was coming to an end with the church in ruins, and human history was passing into the final millennial age.

24. Carpenter, introduction to *The Fundamentalist–Modernist Conflict*, no pagination.

25. Letter from Barnhouse to Carl McIntire, February 6, 1937, cited in Allen C. Guelzo, "Barnhouse," in *Making God's Word Plain: One Hundred and Fifty Years in the History of Tenth Presbyterian Church of Philadelphia*, ed. James M. Boice (Philadelphia: Tenth Presbyterian Church, 1979), 77–78.

26. Carl McIntire, *Twentieth Century Reformation*, 2nd ed. (Collingswood, N.J.: Christian Beacon Press, 1945), 56.

27. Ibid., 212.

28. Mel Larson, *Youth for Christ* (Grand Rapids: Zondervan, 1947).

29. George W. Dollar, *A History of Fundamentalism in America* (Greenville, S.C.: Bob Jones University Press, 1973; repr., Orlando: Daniels Publishing Company, 1983). Citations are from the 1983 edition.

30. Ibid., 283.

31. Ibid., 85.

32. Ibid., 240, 280, 281.

33. Carpenter, *Revive Us Again*, 146, 148, 159.

34. Carl Henry, "Dare We Renew the Controversy?" *Christianity Today* (June 24, 1957): 26. Cited in George M. Marsden, *Reforming Fundamentalism: Fuller Seminary and the New Evangelicalism* (Grand Rapids: Eerdmans, 1987), 165.

35. Carpenter, *Revive Us Again*, 204.

36. George M. Marsden, "From Fundamentalism to Evangelicalism: A Historical Analysis," in *The Evangelicals*, ed. David F. Wells and John D. Woodbridge (New York: Abingdon, 1975), 128–29.

37. Graham gave his support to Fuller Seminary and later, in 1956, to the creation of a new magazine, *Christianity Today*, with Carl Henry as editor, that would raise the scholarly level of fundamentalist concerns.

38. Marsden, "From Fundamentalism to Evangelicalism," 128.

39. For an account of the nonmilitant approach of one of these moderates, see my *A Thirst for Souls: The Life of Evangelist Percy B. Crawford (1902–1960)* (Selinsgrove, Penn.: Susquehanna University Press, 2010).

40. Cited in Carpenter, *Revive Us Again*, 56.

41. Andrew Himes, *The Sword of the Lord: The Roots of Fundamentalism in an American Family* (Seattle: Chiara Press, 2011), 242–48.

42. In a more recent essay, "Fundamentalism and American Evangelicalism," in *The Variety of American Evangelicalism*, ed. Donald Dayton and Robert K. Johnston (Downers Grove, Ill.: InterVarsity Press, 1991), 22–35, Marsden continues to view militancy as definitional of fundamentalism, but with a new twist. He traces fundamentalism to two sources in the broader evangelical tradition—"positively in the aggressive soul-saving tradition of American evangelical revivalism, negatively militant in defense of literal interpretations of the Bible" (25). Later in the essay, in the formulation of a fuller definition of fundamentalism, these

two strains are lumped together into one, and what had been called "aggressive soul-saving" is now referred to as "militant" soul-saving: "Fundamentalism thus can be traced on two tracks, one a broad militancy for soul-saving, Bible-believing evangelicalism, and the other a more explicitly organized coalition of such militants" (26). But Marsden does not explain why aggressive evangelism should be called militant or what it has in common with militant defenses of the faith. It certainly looks as if Marsden is here trying to shore up his definition of fundamentalism as militant by broadening the term to include another related (but very different) aspect of fundamentalist faith, namely the drive to save lost souls. But the effect of this extended use of militant is to weaken its meaning so that it applies to any activity that is vigorously pursued.

Fundamentalism and Christianity

Margaret Bendroth

Fundamentalism is a Christian word, at least in its original incarnation. It came into play in the early twentieth century to describe a series of complex disputes among white, mostly American Protestants concerned about the state of society and of the churches. Their disagreements covered a range of thorny issues, from the timing of Christ's Second Coming to tenure at Princeton Theological Seminary, but they boiled down to a single complaint against the secular drift of modern culture. The historian George M. Marsden's seminal book, *Fundamentalism and American Culture* (1980), put it succinctly: the heart of the movement was "militant opposition to modernism."[1]

No discussion of fundamentalism stays simple for long, however. During the 1980s and 1990s the global resurgence of conservative religious movements from Iran to the United States brought many more scholars to the table. The very power and persistence of militant faith in the technologically advanced scientific and secular world of the twentieth century suggested something important about religion's capacity for survival in modern society. Even more, understanding fundamentalism seemed key to critical questions about rising political conflicts tying faith to violence.

That task meant moving beyond the geographic and theological boundaries of American Protestantism, and even Christianity itself. Efforts such as the Fundamentalism Project, involving a large and sophisticated community of scholars from a wide range of disciplines, took a comparative view, searching out "family resemblances" among militants in all the major faiths—Islamic, Jewish, Hindu, Buddhist, and Christian. The commonalities were startlingly clear: all of them shared a radical commitment to doctrinal purity, moral absolutes, cultural separatism, and a vision of a redeemed future time—and all of them have selectively embraced and rejected the habits and values of western culture.[2]

Without doubt, the cross-cultural interpretation of fundamentalism is a helpful way of understanding how religion "works" in the world today. As the many essays generated by the Fundamentalism Project made clear, what may look like conservative traditional faith is actually deeply modern. Though fundamentalists insist that they are upholding orthodox belief and behavior, "they do so by crafting new methods, formulating new ideologies, and adopting the latest processes and organizational structures." They are, in other words, creatures of the very same modernity they denounce, employing satellite television and Internet resources to proclaim eternally unchanging truths.[3] Fundamentalists are "moderns, but not modernists," Bruce Lawrence wrote in 1989, "at once the consequence of modernity and the antithesis of modernism."[4]

If the commonalities are clear, applying the concept to different groups is surprisingly complex. *Fundamentalism* is a word with a complicated history of its own, one that has often obscured as much as it has explained. Not surprisingly, the cross-cultural parallels made many scholars nervous, especially those from outside the Christian tradition.[5] Using an American Protestant word to classify believers from diverse religious and cultural backgrounds, they argued, veered dangerously close to ethnocentrism. As the other essays in this collection amply document, problems with the fundamentalist label still generate considerable scholarly controversy.

We might also ask whether or not *fundamentalism* is a word that really elucidates what is most important about contemporary Christianity, both inside and outside the United States. Moving for a moment from the cross-cultural problem to a more pragmatic one, the question is whether fundamentalism is even the right topic for one interested in understanding the role of religion in the modern world.

Certainly, when scholars first began to study militant faiths in the 1970s and 1980s, American culture itself was taking on an increasingly combative tone. *Fundamentalism* seemed to be a word particularly geared to describe the precipitous rise of the Religious Right and an escalating culture war both at home and abroad. But now, several decades later, those crystal-clear polarities look a lot muddier and the general picture far more complicated.

Indeed, the world itself has become a much different place, and Christianity a different faith over the course of the past several decades. Since 1980 the statistical majority of the world's Christians is no longer living in the Northern Hemisphere, but in the south; the geographical center is no longer Europe or the United States but Africa, Asia, and South America. The largest churches, the most influential evangelists, and an entire new generation of theologians and church leaders are now coming from such places as South Korea, the Philippines, Brazil, and South

Africa. Given this deep seismic shift in the makeup of Christian churches, another round of discussion about fundamentalism seems long overdue.

Evaluating fundamentalism in its larger Christian context also leads back to questions about religion in the United States, which will be taken up in the second part of this essay. If the significance of the word has changed in the wider world, what about in the country where it originated? American Christianity is not an isolated phenomenon; over the past several hundred years it has been continually fed and shaped by immigrants, first from Europe and now from Asia, Africa, and Central America. Even as the Christian world has shifted south, the United States has remained an integral part of the emerging new Christendom. And it has been changing too: recent right-wing protests against mosque-building, government health insurance, and social spending of the past several years do not look as religious as they did in the 1980s, when evangelical voters swept Ronald Reagan into power. Many signs indicate that evangelicals are returning to their traditional wariness of national politics, especially as the Republican Party becomes increasingly libertarian in tone—an insupportable position for advocates of moral legislation concerning abortion and gay marriage.[6]

Some are even moving to the left. According to a *Newsweek* poll, one-third of white evangelicals from age eighteen to twenty-nine supported Barack Obama in the 2008 election—up from 16 percent who supported John Kerry in 2004. Nor do Protestant churches fall as easily into conservative and liberal boxes as they once did. The lines between progressive evangelicals and mainline Protestants, on matters both spiritual and political, are much more blurred than they once were.[7] All of this suggests that abstract polarities have a tendency to break down rapidly in American religious culture.

But they do persist in perceptions about American religion. At issue, therefore, is where *ideas* about fundamentalism come from—how they reflect changing Christian conceptions of faith, secularity, and the modern world. In the early twentieth century the widespread understanding of fundamentalism as something reactionary and backward rested on the prevailing assumption that faith and reason did not overlap, that the world itself was locked in a contest between religious and secular forces, with enlightenment and progress securely on the side of the latter. In more recent decades the dynamism of global religion has made the picture much muddier. Instead of simple dualisms, we see religion and secularity in a variety of guises, often with no clear line between the two.

The broad scope of this essay and the brief and impressionistic picture of global Christianity that follows—I am far more a consumer than a producer of books on this subject—provides an opportunity, to sketch out the history of *fundamentalism* as an explanatory term. More than simply a straightforward description of reality, it is in some ways a symbol itself, pointing to larger understandings of divine and secular in a rapidly changing world.

The Next Christendom

The past century, and the past several decades in particular, have been some of the most dynamic in the history of Christianity. The absolute percentage of Christians in the world has not changed substantially—since 1900 it has hovered around one-third—but the demographic profile has altered radically. In 1910 only about 1.5 percent of the world's Christians lived in Africa, and 66 percent lived in Europe; by century's end Africa accounted for 17 percent of the total, and Europe had fallen to 27 percent. Over the course of the next twenty-five years the percentages are expected to shift even more, with nearly half of the Christian world in Africa and Latin America, and only one-fifth remaining in Europe. In terms of geographic scale and cultural diversity, Christianity remains a powerful presence in the modern world.[8]

Generalizations about this new Christian population are difficult, but most observers agree that its dominant form is Pentecostal and charismatic, not fundamentalist. The modern Pentecostal movement began in a series of late-nineteenth-century revivals in the American South and lower Midwest, culminating in the great Azuza Street meeting in Los Angeles in 1906. That was the moment when, as later accounts would read, the Holy Spirit descended on a small multiracial prayer meeting in a poor section of the city. Men and women, black, white, Mexican, and Chinese, received the gift of tongues, the sudden ability to converse in other languages. As the movement spread, other believers received gifts of prophecy and healing and a fervent desire to spread the message of baptism by the Holy Spirit. Since 1906 the American Pentecostal movement has never stopped garnering new converts. In the 1960s a new wave of prophecy, healing, and tongue-speaking spread outside Pentecostalism into Roman Catholic and white Protestant churches, where it became known as the charismatic movement.[9]

A century after Azuza Street, Pentecostal and charismatic believers account for almost one-third of all members in Christian churches worldwide—some 523 million people in many thousands of independent and denominational organizations. This growth reflects aggressive evangelism as well as the changing dynamics of the world's population. Most Pentecostal/charismatics are nonwhite (71 percent), poor (87 percent), young, urban, and female. Though the movement is often stereotyped as a rural phenomenon, the great majority of these new churches are in the world's largest cities: Lagos, Seoul, Rio de Janeiro, and Manila.[10]

To an outsider, Pentecostals and charismatics may look a lot like fundamentalists. Indeed in their classic form both groups insist on the absolute authority of the Bible and the universality of divine truth. They are both generally pessimistic about the future of secular society and believe that history is heading into a downward spiral. Historically neither group has placed great hope in the work of liberal social reformers or government programs to eradicate poverty or inequality; this is a task that God will complete at the end of time, with the inauguration of a new heaven and a new earth. Until that day Christians must live virtuously and do all they can to mitigate social evils, but they should never entertain illusions of success.

But there the similarities end. The essential core of Pentecostal faith is experience, in particular a vivid encounter with the Holy Spirit, often in the form of ecstatic speaking in unknown tongues. Fundamentalism, in contrast, is a religion based on texts, a Bible free from error that provides every believer with clear, self-evident rules for obtaining salvation. While Pentecostals revere the Bible, know it thoroughly, and quote it often, they also hear God speaking through supernatural signs and wonders. Though the Bible's authority is absolute in every way, experience is yet another source of authority, writes Grant Wacker, "more flexible and more workable than the otherworldly dictates of Scripture, doctrine, or Holy Spirit inspiration."[11]

Classic fundamentalism also cares little for spiritual pyrotechnics, especially for claims of healing or prophecy outside the bounds of biblical orthodoxy. It is at heart a rationalist faith, insisting that the Bible can withstand even the harshest scientific inquiry without faltering. A charismatic believer might applaud these efforts but not find them necessary for belief. "The difference," writes Harvey Cox, "is that while the beliefs of the fundamentalists . . . are enshrined in formal theological systems, those of Pentecostalism are imbedded in testimonies, ecstatic speech, and bodily movement." They have often "felt more at home singing their theology, or putting it in pamphlets for distribution on street corners," not writing it down.[12]

Outside the Western world, the Pentecostal/charismatic revival is different from fundamentalism in another important historic way. Christianity came to the Southern Hemisphere first as a missionary movement, exported from nineteenth-century Europe and the United States. Though missionaries themselves had an uneasy, sometimes even antagonistic relationship to colonialism, their message often carried with it assumptions of Western superiority and the "white man's burden." But the recent growth of Christianity, from the mid-twentieth century until the present, has come from a different source and under different circumstances. It is not, most scholars agree, an indigenized form of Western Christianity, the direct fruit of European and American missionary labors, but something new: a network of independent churches that have grown up largely outside the "old Christendom."

Christianity began to flourish, in other words, when Western nations were forced to loosen their grip on their colonial empires, as they became absorbed in the great twentieth-century upheavals of war and economic disruption. In part the change was the fruit of a new internationalism, of emerging enthusiasm for a "world Christianity" in the years after World War I. It also grew from a rethinking of missionary strategy, emphasizing the presence of God across diverse cultural boundaries. Colonial structures also became harder and less profitable to maintain:

after World War II nineteenth-century empires were in full retreat, and by the 1960s more and more nations in Africa and Asia demanded and won independence. During the Cold War era Western missionaries also began to take on a lower profile. Rather than invite political reprisals on local communities, they concentrated on handing over schools and churches to local control.[13]

All this proved a formula for success. "While old structures sagged from the top down," writes missionary scholar Dana Robert, "new growth was occurring from the bottom up."[14] The great growth of African Christianity, for example, has been among thousands of independent, predominantly Pentecostal/charismatic churches, whose numbers skyrocketed from some 60,000 in 1970 to 213,500 in 1995. Chinese houses churches grew silently under many years of Communist domination, outside of Western purview, and are now flourishing in numbers that are nearly impossible to estimate. Worldwide, these "postdenominational" churches are estimated to have grown from 95 to 386 million believers just from 1970 to 2000, while those in denominational settings increased from about one million to one and one-half million.[15]

This means that the current wave is not simply a culturally refracted version of Western Christianity but a unique new form of an old faith, with its own categories of belief and behavior. Prominent missionary scholar Andrew Walls in fact argues for two different narratives for early medieval Europe and modern Africa. When the first missionaries arrived in northern Europe, their Christian message reflected the power of Hebrew monotheism and the political realities of life in the shadow of the Roman Empire. Those early missionaries declared that the Christian God was the true and only god, and that he demanded sole allegiance. "When the faith came north," says Walls, it "found no shadow of itself in the faiths it displaced. Odin was not God, nor was Thor, nor Frey." Converts faced a choice between the old gods or citizenship in an emerging Christendom, centered in Rome and bound together by the Latin liturgy. In contrast, the nineteenth-century encounter between missionaries and the Southern Hemisphere took place under a politically and intellectually fracturing Christendom and within a missionary theology emphasizing the immanence of God within all human societies. "Christian preachers," says Walls, "found God already there, known by a vernacular name." Instead of demanding that native people set aside their own theological language, biblical translators began to use indigenous titles for the deity, not so much "bringing God to the people, so much as bringing him near." In other words, Walls suggests, the theological narrative at the core of African Christianity is not one of crisis and choice but of more gradual spiritual cultivation.[16]

The exact contours of the "next Christendom," as it has been dubbed by the historian Philip Jenkins, are impossible to judge, but one thing seems certain: the growing edge of modern Christianity owes far less to the European Enlightenment and the battles between faith and rationality that have followed in its wake.

The burden of Western Christians, to somehow prove that religion is not intrinsically opposed to ordered scientific thought, is not necessarily a universal one.[17]

This does not mean that the Enlightenment is unimportant outside of Europe and the United States; but it does mean that we need to be careful in applying that historical narrative where it does not belong. The rapid growth of evangelical churches in Latin America, for example, has relatively little to do with fears of secular modernity or, some critics argue, opposition to change. "There is little militant defense of tradition," writes Daniel H. Levine, "and scant appeal to the reconstruction of some past golden age." In fact, the success of evangelicalism in Latin American fundamentalism owes more to the rejection of Roman Catholic hegemony and a desire for freedom from the kinds of traditionalism it has long represented.[18]

Fundamentalism, in contrast, is a creature of Western-style modernity. In the United States it grew out of a Protestant tradition already deeply rooted in Enlightenment ideals, particularly the assumption that religious truth is accessible to anyone equipped with normal human "common sense." The Bible was not an esoteric document requiring special knowledge but the plain story of God's will, meant to be read and understood by everyone.[19] If anything, the American fundamentalist movement intensified the claim that the Bible's truth was evident to anyone with a rational mind; it stood on an inerrant Bible, one entirely free of any error of fact and whose perfection would always be upheld by clear, unbiased scholarship. In fundamentalist eyes the liberal New Testament scholars at secular universities were the ones unwilling to give the Bible a fair shake, all too quickly retreating into myth and metaphor when the going got rough. In many ways the present-day battles over scientific creationism and the "new atheism" reflect this deep-seated faith in the basic rationality of religion. They are not epic battles between believers and nonbelievers but, at heart, family squabbles between two groups both passionately committed to the pursuit of scientifically verifiable truth.[20]

This is not to say, however, that Pentecostals and charismatics are too unsophisticated or too spiritually minded to take a political or intellectual stand; they simply approach such problems from a different angle than a fundamentalist would. In the United States, for example, charismatics have adapted fairly easily to some aspects of modernity, a fact not lost on their more world-denying fundamentalist critics. In the 1990s the most telling rift was between Jerry Falwell, a church pastor and biblical moralist through and through, and the genial Pat Robertson, founder of the Christian Broadcasting Network and host of a long-running talk show, *The 700 Club*. Both have been politically active and have shared a similar Republican-leaning agenda but in profoundly different ways. Falwell's Moral Majority sought to mobilize true Christian believers into a single movement against secular humanism; Robertson, who ran for president in 1988, founded the Christian Coalition, an organization dedicated to building a broad grassroots effort and turning existing party structures toward moral and spiritual purposes.[21]

It is also an enormous leap to assume that Pentecostal and charismatic churches have no social message; they are predominantly the churches of the poor, and their social disenfranchisement is not just a matter of abstract cultural symbolism but tied to life-and-death issues of social justice. In fact, it may well be that Western scholars are some of the least well situated to understand the possible future of this newly emerging Christendom. They are separated from its growing edges not just by geography but also by their own intellectual framework, by understandings of religion and secularity handed down from the eighteenth-century Enlightenment. It is almost as if a community in a desert monastery, arguing over fine points of Greek translation, tried to imagine the consequences of Martin Luther's protest at the door of the Wittenberg cathedral—or, perhaps more properly, to chart the rise and fall of Aztec empires or the Ming dynasty in China.

Dualisms?

The other problem with applying the fundamentalist label has to do with the history of religion in the United States. American church life has always resisted simple categories, especially the dualisms implied in a concept like fundamentalism. Lacking any significant religious establishment, outside of New England at least, denominational diversity flourished mostly unchecked and by the early nineteenth century defied most attempts at classification. The sheer variety of American religious groups and their unparalleled ability to track the winds of popular opinion also meant that malcontents would have great difficulty in identifying a single focus of complaint, much less in making their charges stick. Most would-be critics found it easier to burrow into another spiritual niche, throwing the occasional brickbat to make sure that they would be left alone, but not ignored.[22]

This was certainly the case with American fundamentalists. Though they enjoyed some success in building a presence within northern Baptist and Presbyterian churches, they were quickly marginalized by denominational politics. What looked like major victories in the early 1920s had largely faded a few years later; by the late 1920s most observers assumed that the battles were over and that the fundamentalists had lost. In the decades ahead, however, the movement prospered as never before, as the next generation settled into building a separate infrastructure of colleges, seminaries, missionary agencies, and denominations. As fundamentalists recovered new zeal for evangelism—the goal of "winning America back for Christ"—they also began to lose some of the hard edges that held them together during the combative 1920s. Over the course of just a few decades, American fundamentalism showed itself to be thoroughly adaptable to changing circumstances and remarkably adept in taking advantage of denominational pluralism.[23]

If anything, decentralization has grown more acute in recent years. Under the centripetal forces of globalization American evangelicalism today is less and less a native tradition and one increasingly fed by immigrants and evangelists from Africa, Latin America, and Asia. It seems likely that in years ahead American Christianity will look more and more like the new forms emerging in the rest of the world and less and less like the traditional faith inherited from early modern Europe.[24] And so we might say that American fundamentalism is itself an unstable category, and the twentieth-century United States an unlikely place for getting a conceptual handle on it.

What the American setting does offer is access to a very long and thoughtful discussion about the nature of militant religion, carried on by people struggling to understand what they were seeing. In fact, the earliest scholarship on fundamentalism, by H. Richard Niebuhr and Stewart Cole, appeared just a few years after the major controversies of the 1920s had died down. The writings of both men were essentially attempts to bring some order to bear on a confused situation, using the best tools that recent scholarship had to offer. In his classic text *The Social Sources of Denominationalism* (1929), and later in an influential essay written for the *Encyclopedia of the Social Sciences* in 1937, Niebuhr explained the fundamentalist controversy as a conflict between a modernizing bourgeoisie and rural communities still clinging to small-town agrarian values.[25] This made sense: just four years earlier the Scopes Trial had pitted scientists against anti-evolutionists in a Tennessee courtroom, dramatizing Niebuhr's argument that fundamentalism represented an epic clash between two ways of life, one thriving and the other on a path toward irrelevance and extinction. It also cemented the popular image of fundamentalism as something rural, southern, and uneducated, deeply out of step with the progressive flow of American life.

Niebuhr also used secularization theory to chart fundamentalism's trajectory. Led by Max Weber and later by Ernst Troeltsch, early-twentieth-century scholarship had sought to explain what was perceived as the demise of religion and the emerging contours of modernity—two developments assumed to be intrinsically incompatible. They envisioned the triumph of scientific rationality as part of a great inexorable wave of change, leaving only odd bits of religion floating in its wake. In classic secularization theory, therefore, fundamentalism was little more than the last gasp of a reactionary faith unsuited for the rigors of the twentieth century.[26]

Stewart Cole's *History of Fundamentalism*, published in 1931, took Niebuhr and Weber a step further, applying the theories of clinical psychology to explain the presence of reactionary faith in a progressive age. In an era fascinated with mental health and the boundaries of "normality," Cole depicted fundamentalism as a psychic "maladjustment" to the modern world, the backward-looking faith of conservative people "opposed to social change" who simply lagged behind the changing times. They were, in other words, the polar opposite of the extroverted democratic faith of mainline Protestant churches that Cole and his colleagues believed would serve American society best.[27]

The assumption that fundamentalism was out of sync with the modern world grew stronger even as American fundamentalism itself showed signs of accommodation. By the 1950s, when a "neo-evangelical" movement brought increasingly mainstream conservative Protestant figures such as Billy Graham to the fore, old-style separatism was a thing of the past. Yet secularization theory was still the "reigning dogma in the field" of sociology during the 1970s, and American religious historians were still primarily interested in white mainline Protestants.[28] Except for Richard Hofstadter's *Anti-Intellectualism in American Life* (1962), which devoted a chapter to religion, scholarly interest in fundamentalism rarely extended beyond small groups of specialists.[29]

But the outside world would soon change all that. In the 1980s Niebuhr's and Cole's analyses of "fundamentalism" resurfaced in scholarly studies and later in popular phraseology as the "culture wars," taken from the sociologist James Davison Hunter's influential book published in 1991. Nothing less seemed adequate to describe the acrimony of those years, as liberals and conservatives clashed regularly over abortion and evolution, family values and freedom of choice. Hunter described a deep polarization over "fundamentally different conceptions of moral authority, over different ideas and beliefs about truth, the good, obligation to one another, the nature of community, and so on." Religion was, therefore, the source of cultural conflict at its deepest level.[30]

By that time, however, many evangelicals themselves objected to the fundamentalist label for a host of different reasons. Among evangelical scholars, for example, a deep fault line separated those identified with Wesleyan and holiness traditions from those in Reformed and Calvinist churches. At issue was George M. Marsden's seminal work *Fundamentalism and American Culture,* which provided for the first time a rich intellectual account of the movement's rise in the late-nineteenth and early-twentieth centuries, emphasizing the central role of churches in the Reformed (Calvinistic) tradition. Marsden's work also credited fundamentalism as the source for the progressive "neo-evangelical" revival of the 1940s and 1950s and the making of modern-day evangelicalism.[31]

Marsden's Wesleyan critics countered quickly, emphatically rejecting his suggestion that contemporary evangelicalism and fundamentalism were basically two versions of the same thing. A volume of essays edited by the holiness scholars Donald Dayton and Robert K. Johnston, *The Variety of American Evangelicalism,* listed an almost bewildering array of denominations and religious movements under that rubric: Holiness churches, Baptists, Adventists, Missouri Synod Lutherans, Mennonites, charismatics, and Pentecostals. Somewhere toward the back was fundamentalism, receiving only partial, somewhat grudging credit for playing a formative role.[32]

All parties, however, agreed on one central point: that it was inaccurate to call any contemporary evangelical of any type a fundamentalist. The word was simply too controversial, especially as it took on increasingly negative connotations in the politically charged 1980s and 1990s: not surprisingly, white middle-class American evangelicals objected vehemently to any and all comparisons with Middle Eastern terrorists.

The scholarly picture was changing as well, verifying the shift away from an all-out culture war. Extensive survey data compiled by the sociologist Christian Smith, for example, found rank-and-file evangelicals remarkably similar to their secular neighbors and friends. In basic practical ways—income, education, the prevalence of two-career couples, and even rates of political participation—they were first and foremost white middle-class Americans. Evangelicals were "embattled," Smith argued, mostly in rhetorical and symbolic ways, not in political or economic matters, or in any sense that an old-school fundamentalist would recognize.[33]

The other change in thinking after the 1980s concerned secularization theory. The eye-popping growth of Christianity in Africa and Asia—and its continued vitality in the United States—visibly contradicted the notion that religion was somehow declining or that it would eventually succumb to the power of scientific rationality. The new Christendom evinced a vividly supernatural faith that seemed to be adapting extraordinarily well to the modern world. Indeed, many Pentecostal and independent churches thrived best in the cities experiencing the fastest population growth; increasingly they were not just the churches of the poor but of the aspiring and the upwardly mobile as well. The new challenge for scholars, therefore, was accounting for the persistence of faith, not its disappearance.

As the narrative of decline began to weaken, researchers began to find religion turning up everywhere. The sociologist Callum Brown, for example, found traditional faith deeply embedded in twentieth-century Britain, a society long assumed to be "post-Christian." Closely analyzing the dress, speech, and behavioral habits of ordinary people, Brown concluded that the "death of Christian Britain" had not really occurred until the early 1960s. Before that time it was largely a figment of the scholarly imagination, rooted more in secular prejudice than in fact. Religious decline was, in Brown's view, "a moral judgement, whether brandished by Christians, atheists, social scientists or philosophers."[34]

With classic secularization theory went the old dualism between religious and secular, as well as the old fundamentalist narrative of eternal warfare between faith and unbelief. The fundamental transition into modernity, as the theorist Charles Taylor has written, was not the loss of religion but the addition of many new secular alternatives. The Western world, said Taylor, had gone "from a society in which it was virtually impossible not to believe in God, to one in which faith, even for the staunchest believer, is one human possibility among others."[35] The real problem for religious believers, therefore, is not some external enemy, whether in the form of radical atheism or Western-style modernity, but pluralism, the open and negotiated character of modern belief—in other words, the absence of any single enemy at all.

This does not mean, however, that religious absolutism does not exist. We could say that it is both everywhere and nowhere in the world today. Modern social media, for example, have given militants unprecedented access to broad audiences, as well as the ability to hone and target their message to the most likely converts, rendering it all but invisible to the public at large. But for all its specificity, an electronic message is impossible to control. Once an e-mail leaves the screen it is no longer the property of the sender—it can be forwarded and edited at will; an entry on an accessible site such as *Wikipedia* can be created by knowledgeable experts but also changed by a random visitor. The word of absolute divine truth goes out today in an inherently unstable form. Indeed, the diffuse nature of electronic media mirrors Charles Taylor's pluralistic secular age, in which religious certainties coexist with a thousand variations on the truth. This is not a world in which fundamentalists—or secularists—can do battle easily. There are too many places for heretics and fanatics to hide, too many "others" for the true believer ever to quiet or convince.

Conclusion

Even though *fundamentalism* is a problematic term with a complicated relationship to religious realities on the ground, it is still has its uses. There is no denying that militant antimodern religion exists and that it continues to play a role in world affairs today. But especially in these complicated times, it is important to understand its origins and to gauge its importance carefully. The deepest misconceptions about confrontational religion take root when it is either taken too seriously or not seriously enough—as, on the one hand, archaic and strange or, on the other, a paramount threat to peace and security. Both are ways of denying its validity, of defining and quarantining an other.

Moreover, religion with sharp angles may well be a necessary part of modern life. As Lionel Caplan wrote in 1987, "We are all of us, to some degree and in some senses, fundamentalists."[36] In other words, many different people, not just the militant few, have reason to be uncomfortable with modernity and its progressive disenchantment of the world. Increasing personal liberation and technological progress have, after all, emerged alongside unprecedented political and ecological destruction; we carry a complicated, dangerous burden. Perhaps for that reason alone we might well pay attention to a warning or perhaps even join in a lament about our modern age, even if the words are not our own.

Notes

1. This often-quoted phrase is from George M. Marsden, *Fundamentalism and American Culture: The Shaping of Twentieth-Century Evangelicalism, 1870–1925* (New York: Oxford University Press, 1980), 4.

2. See Gabriel A. Almond, Emmanuel Sivan, and R. Scott Appleby, "Fundamentalism: Genus and Species," in *Fundamentalisms Comprehended*, ed. Martin E. Marty and R. Scott Appleby (Chicago: University of Chicago Press, 1995), 399–424.

3. Almond, Sivan, and Appleby, "Fundamentalism: Genus and Species," 402.

4. Bruce Lawrence, *Defenders of God: The Fundamentalist Revolt against the Modern Age* (San Francisco: Harper & Row, 1989), 2. See also Bronislaw Misztal and Anson Shupe, "Making Sense of the Global Revival of Fundamentalism," in *Religion and Politics in Comparative Perspective: Revival of Religious Fundamentalism in East and West*, ed. Misztal and Shupe (Westport, Conn.: Praeger, 1992), 3–10.

5. See for example, Gananath Obeyesekere, "Buddhism, Nationhood, and Cultural Identity: A Question of Fundamentals," in *Fundamentalisms Comprehended*, 231–56; William E. Shepard, "Fundamentalism Christian and Islamic," *Religion* 17 (October 1987): 355–78, and the discussion and response by Bruce Lawrence, Azim Nanji, and William E. Shepard, *Religion* 19 (July 1989): 275–92; H. Paul Chalfant, Ted Jelen, and William H. Swatos Jr., "Book Review Symposium on *Fundamentalisms Observed*," *Review of Religious Research* 35 (September 1993): 63–75.

6. Michael Hamilton points out that "for every dollar evangelicals spend on political organizations, they spend almost $12 on foreign missions and international relief and development," "$13 in evangelical book and music stores," and "almost $31 on private elementary and secondary schools." See "More Money, More Ministry: The Financing of American Evangelicalism since 1945," in *More Money, More Ministry: Money and Evangelicals in Recent Norman American History*, ed. Larry Eskridge and Mark Noll (Grand Rapids: Eerdmans, 2000), 129–31. This more irenic portrait of evangelicals is found in Christian Smith, *American Evangelicalism: Embattled and Thriving* (Chicago: University of Chicago Press 1998), and Christian Smith, *Christian America: What Evangelicals Really Want* (Berkeley: University of California Press, 2000). See also Clyde Wilcox, *Onward Christian Soldiers? The Religious Right in American Politics* (New York: Westview / Harper Collins, 1996). The classic text on political second thoughts is Ed Dobson and Cal Thomas, *Blinded by Might: Can the Religious Right Save America?* (Grand Rapids: Zondervan, 1999).

7. Tony Dokoupil, "Faith beyond His Father's," *Newsweek*, January 17, 2009. Other sources abound: for example, D. Michael Lindsay, *Faith in the Halls of Power: How Evangelicals Joined the American Elite* (New York: Oxford 2007, 34).

8. Dana Robert, *Christian Mission: How Christianity Became a World Religion* (Malden, Mass.: Wiley-Blackwell, 2009), 70.

9. See Grant Wacker, *Heaven Below: Early Pentecostals and American Culture* (Cambridge: Harvard University Press, 2001); David Edwin Harrell, *All Things Are Possible: The Healing and Charismatic Revivals in Modern America* (Bloomington: Indiana University Press, 1975).

10. David Barrett, George T. Kurian, and Todd M. Johnson, *World Christian Encyclopedia*, vol. 1 (New York: Oxford University Press, 2001), 19.

11. Wacker, *Heaven Below*, 84.

12. Harvey Cox, *Fire from Heaven: The Rise of Pentecostal Spirituality and the Reshaping of Religion in the Twenty-First Century* (Reading, Mass.: Addison-Wesley, 1995), 15.

13. Dana Robert, "The First Globalization: The Internationalization of the Protestant Missionary Movement between the World Wars," *International Bulletin of Missionary Research* 26

(April 2002): 50–66; Grant Wacker, "Second Thoughts on the Great Commission: Liberal Protestants and Foreign Missions," in *Earthen Vessels: American Evangelicals and Foreign Missions, 1880–1980*, ed. Joel A. Carpenter and Wilbert R. Shenk (Grand Rapids: Eerdmans, 1990), 281–300; Richard Pierard, "*Pax Americana* and the Evangelical Missionary Advance," in *Earthen Vessels*, 155–79.

14. Robert, *Christian Mission*, 69.

15. David Barrett, George T. Kurian, and Todd M. Johnson, *World Christian Encyclopedia*, vol. 1 (New York: Oxford University Press, 2001), 10, 12.

16. See Andrew Walls, "The Evangelical Revival, the Missionary Movement, and Africa," in *The Missionary Movement in Christian History: Studies in the Transmission of Faith* (Marynoll, N.Y.: Orbis Books, 1996), 79–101, and Walls, "Origins of Old and New Southern Christianity," in *The Missionary Movement in Christian History*, 70, 71.

17. Philip Jenkins, *The Next Christendom: The Coming of Global Christianity*, 2nd ed. (New York & Oxford: Oxford University Press, 2007).

18. Daniel H. Levine, "Protestants and Catholics in Latin America: A Family Portrait," in *Fundamentalisms Comprehended*, ed. Martin E. Marty and R. Scott Appleby (Chicago: University of Chicago Press, 1995), 163f.

19. Mark Noll, "Common Sense Traditions and American Evangelical Thought," *American Quarterly* 37 (Summer 1985): 220–57.

20. On fundamentalism and the Bible, see Marsden, *Fundamentalism and American Culture*, 109–123. See also Ronald Numbers, *The Creationists: The Evolution of Scientific Creationism* (Berkeley: University of California Press, 1993).

21. See, for example, Francis Fitzgerald, "A Disciplined Charging Army," *New Yorker*, May 18, 1981, and David Edwin Harrell, *Pat Robertson: A Life and Legacy* (Grand Rapids: Eerdmans, 2010).

22. The best single overview is Nathan Hatch, *The Democratization of American Christianity* (New Haven: Yale University Press, 1990).

23. Joel A. Carpenter, *Revive Us Again: The Reawakening of American Fundamentalism* (New York: Oxford University Press, 1997).

24. Paul Numrich *The Faith Next Door: American Christians and Their New Religious Neighbors* (New York: Oxford University Press, 2009); Diana Eck, *A New Religious America: How "Christian America" Has Become the World's Most Religiously Diverse Nation* (San Francisco: Harper Collins, 2002).

25. H. Richard Niebuhr, *The Social Sources of Denominationalism* (New York: Holt, 1929), 184, 185; H. Richard Niebuhr, "Fundamentalism," in *Encyclopedia of the Social Sciences*, vol. 6 (New York: Macmillan, 1937), 525–27l.

26. William H. Swatos and Kevin Christiano, "Secularization Theory: The Course of a Concept," *Sociology of Religion* 60 (Fall 1999): 1069–4044.

27. Stewart Cole, *History of Fundamentalism* (New York: Richard R. Smith, 1931), 53.

28. Swatos and Christiano, "Secularization Theory," 209–28.

29. Richard Hofstadter, *Anti-Intellectualism in American Life* (New York: Knopf, 1962).

30. James Davison Hunter, *Culture Wars: The Struggle to Define America* (New York: Basic Books, 1991), 49.

31. The connection is spelled out most clearly in Marsden's *Reforming Fundamentalism: Fuller Seminary and the New Evangelicalism* (Grand Rapids: Eerdmans, 1987).

32. Donald Dayton and Robert Johnston, eds., *The Variety of American Evangelicalism* (Downers Grove, Ill.: InterVarsity Press, 1991).

33. Smith, *American Evangelicalism.*

34. Callum Brown, *The Death of Christian Britain: Understanding Secularisation, 1800–2000*, 2nd ed. (New York: Routledge, 2009), 12, 13, 33.

35. Charles Taylor, *A Secular Age* (Cambridge Harvard University Press 2007), 3, 22.

36. Lionel Caplan, introduction to *Studies of Religious Fundamentalism* (Albany: State University of New York Press, 1987), 22.

"America Is No Different," "America Is Different"—Is There an American Jewish Fundamentalism?

Part I. American Habad

Shaul Magid

Fundamentalism is arguably one of the most widely used and least understood terms in the popular discourse about religion. We find it applied to all kinds of groups, religions, communities, even societies. The formal term applies to a defined group of American Protestants at the beginning of the twentieth century who viewed themselves as part of a particular spiritual trajectory that extended back at least to the 1740s in America and likely to the seventeenth century in England. [1] In its modern context it usually refers to Protestant communities who strictly adhere to five basic principles: 1) biblical inerrancy or scripturalism; 2) virgin birth; 3) substitutionary atonement; 4) bodily resurrection; and (5) Christ's divinity.[2]

Fundamentalism has more specifically been applied to various branches of Judaism both in Israel and in the Diaspora. It largely applies to three distinct communities: 1) Hasidism, 2) non-Hasidic ultra-Orthodoxy, and 3) religious ultra-nationalism (i.e., the settler movement in Israel).[3] The first and second have coalesced into an umbrella group that has become known as *haredi* Judaism.[4] A portion of the ultra-nationalist camp has also taken on a *haredi* persona under the term *hardal* (*haredi leumi*, or haredi national religious). These fundamentalist Jewish communities do not view themselves as partners. In fact, many are vehemently oppose one another. For example, the Satmar branch of Hasidism (the focus of a subsequent essay) is at war with the ultra-nationalist Zionist "fundamentalists" in Israel.[5] And the Habad branch of Hasidism has been in an ideological war with

Satmar for decades. While there is more sympathy between Habad and the ultra-nationalists, Habad does not view itself as Zionist, which is the backbone of the ultra-nationalist ideology in Israel. And even within these subcultures there is dissent. Some are more tolerant toward Zionism, others are vehemently opposed to it. Some are accommodating to secularism and even study in universities, others shun secular knowledge except as they apply it to vocational needs.[6] Jay Harris is surely correct that *fundamentalism* is a subjective term, used as a pejorative, the definition of which depends on where the accuser stands in the trajectory of tradition. Yet it seems too dismissive to simply abandon the term as describing certain contemporary Jewish movements, especially in America.[7]

Almost all the studies on Jewish fundamentalism focus on postwar communities, suggesting by implication that ultra-Orthodoxy in prewar Europe, while similar in tenor and even in substance to its postwar progeny, cannot properly be called fundamentalist. This is curious for a numbers of reasons. First, it raises the question of whether Jewish fundamentalism is a post-Holocaust phenomenon. Second, given that postwar Jewry has two main centers, Israel and North America (smaller haredi communities do exist in other parts of the Jewish Diaspora), it raises the question of whether Jewish fundamentalism can exist only in 1) a society where Jews comprise the dominant culture (Israel) or 2) a society where religious freedom and disestablishment are the societal norms (America).[8] That is, does the activism necessary to constitute contemporary Jewish fundamentalism require a level of freedom of expression that exists only for Jews in Israel and other democratic countries where freedom of religion is assured?[9] Moreover, while Israel and the United States both offer conditions conducive to Jewish fundamentalism, each has distinctive qualities. Thus it would be necessary to view American and Israeli ultra-Orthodoxy as different not only in context but also in substance. One of the deficiencies of the many excellent studies on Jewish fundamentalism is that they generally do not distinguish between Jewish fundamentalism in Israel and in the United States. While it is true that many of the ultra-Orthodox communities in Israel have companion communities in the United States and vice versa, those communities are situated in very different social and political contexts that produce different programmatic agendas, if not in principle then certainly in practice.

In this essay and the one that follows I focus on two Jewish fundamentalist groups in the United States: Habad and Satmar. I argue that their fundamentalism agendas, while originating in prewar Europe, are products of the United States and thus particular to the American context. Here I respectfully disagree with those who argue that *fundamentalism* is not applicable to Judaism.[10] In part my position stems from my assumption that the "American" nature of Jewish fundamentalism is as much sociological as it is theological. That is, I believe it is a mistake to look only at the theological premises of Christian fundamentalism and then determine whether they cohere with a Jewish case. Under such criteria Judaism would certainly not reach the fundamentalist bar. But the theological premises of Judaism—

excluding perhaps biblical inerrancy—differ enough from those of Christianity that any comparison purely on theological grounds is unhelpful. Religious communities are not simply products of their theological convictions as much as they would like us to believe they are. They are also responding and adapting to societal conditions and are in a constant state of absorbing and reframing the ethos of the world in which they live, sometimes consciously, sometimes not. Thus, while ostensibly remaining true to their theological principles inherited from a very different societal context, religious communities can be quite innovative, even radical, in the name of continuity and tradition. In a religious tradition with the interpretive history and skills of Judaism, external values and perspectives are easily absorbed, almost seamlessly, making the novel appear ancient and the new appear authentic. The question is thus not whether insiders in these communities think they are absorbing American fundamentalist positions. Surely they do not. It is, rather, whether we on the outside can ascertain if the community's "lived religiosity" reflects an ethos in concert with external forms of belief.

Jewish fundamentalism in America is a postwar phenomenon generated by at last three issues: 1) the destruction of European Jewry in the Holocaust; 2) the coalescence of Zionism around a Jewish state; and 3) the corruption of tradition via the predominance of Reform and other progressive Judaisms on American soil. Each one of these issues resonates in particular ways in the United States which served as the tolerant new home for most of world Jewry who chose not to immigrate to Mandate Palestine / Israel.

While the term *fundamentalism* can apply to Judaism, particularly in America, its particular context within a minority community in a free society gives it distinctive qualities. While the issues confronting Christian and Jewish fundamentalisms in America may seem similar, these fundamentalisms are also confronting very different challenges. The Jewish challenges focus on being a minority group ostensibly threatened by at least two things: 1) the erasure of Jewish identity as the final phase of assimilation; and 2) the irreparable distortion of Judaism as it was previously known and practiced through the teachings and influence of progressive Jewish movements (Conservative, Reform, Reconstructionist). The major nemesis of Jewish fundamentalisms in the United States is therefore not secular America but progressive American Judaism. Making full use of the secular American landscape, the rise of Jewish fundamentalism in America has become an internal battle for the soul of American Judaism. While assimilation and the transformation of tradition are not unique to the United States, the battle lines were different in prewar Europe and contemporary Israel where traditional Judaism had, and has, a stronger foothold in society's civil religion.

Jewish fundamentalism in Israel is different from that in America for at least four reasons. First, these battles are not being waged under the gaze of a Gentile society, and therefore Israelis are less concerned with how Jewish divisiveness in their society will be viewed by non-Jews. Second, most of the fundamentalist communities in Israel are politically empowered through representation in the Israeli Parliament and thus have at their disposal all the tools of the democratic process to achieve their goals. Third, there is no sharp division of church and state in Israel which enables fundamentalist Judaism there to affect secular Israelis more profoundly than it affects their counterparts in America. Because Israel is a society comprising mostly Jews, the pressure to view the "other" in a positive light is less pressing. This may seem counterintuitive given Israel's precarious political reality. However, regarding internal affairs the alienation of the secular Jew from the fundamentalist Jew is sharper in Israel than in the United States where Jews, even those with opposing views, see themselves as part of a minority that needs to present a united front against the pressures and seductions of the society in which it lives. In Israel, fundamentalist groups can be both activist *and* separatist and receive government funding to support their agendas. Finally, the messianic or redemptive component of some but not all Jewish fundamentalisms is much more acute in Israel than in America. Notions of redemption, in both religious and secular garb, permeate Israeli religion and culture in ways quite different from the ways they do in similar communities in America.

Therefore, while the fundamentalist groups examined here and in the next essay are not exclusive to America, their existence in America is an integral part of their project. The adjective *American* is a description of substance and not merely of geography. America presents a religious, cultural, and legal context that enables them to express themselves in particular ways. These expressions, while certainly a manifestation of their own religious tradition, are also a specific articulation of American religion, in this case, American fundamentalism.

Millennialism and Messianism: "Premillennialist" and "Postmillennialist" Judaism

Scholars of non-Protestant fundamentalisms often list the basic principles of Protestant fundamentalism to show how their tradition can or cannot cohere with many of those principles. Hence, some argue, there can be *no* Jewish fundamentalism. Others suggest that while Jews cannot abide by some of the specifics of Protestant fundamentalism there are some broader paradigms indicative of fundamentalist movements that accurately describe some maximalist Jewish perspectives. Here Gabriel A. Almond, R. Scott Appleby, and Emanuel Sivan's broad definition of fundamentalism might suffice. "Fundamentalism, in this usage, refers to a discernible pattern of religious militance by which self-styled 'true believers' attempt to arrest the erosion of religious identity, fortify the borders of the religious community, and create viable alternatives to secular institutions and behaviors."[11] Many of those who write about fundamentalism stress that it is not only situated in modernity but is also, in fact, a product of modernity.[12] In this sense fundamentalism is a particular construction of "tradition" that is uniquely equipped to confront modernity and offer an alternative template for human civilization. Almost all fundamentalisms in contemporary America are committed to some form of activism to oppose either secularism or liberal religion or both.[13]

Millennialism is one of Protestant fundamentalism's founding principles.[14] Millennialism is a belief in society's close proximity to the end-time and invites either political activism to create conditions for the imminent redemption or cultivates a separatist mentality that builds walls against the impure influence of decadent society. Both of these options exhibit a highly charged sense of urgency. Dispensationalist millennialism has been influential in millennial communities. Many contemporary Protestant fundamentalists and evangelicals (a similar but not identical group) view themselves as either living immediately before the new, and final, dispensation or already part of a new dispensation.[15] George M. Marsden offers a succinct definition of dispensational premillennialism.

According to the dispensationalist's scheme of world history, the current dispensation, or "church age," was marked by the regressive corruption of so-called Christian civilization and the apostasy of its large churches. Only a remnant of its true believers would remain pure. The kingdom of Christ would not be brought in by united Christian effort, as the social gospel had promised, but only by the dramatic return of Jesus to set up his millennial kingdom in Jerusalem. Dispensationalism thus suggests that Christian political efforts were largely futile. Believers should give up on the illusion of "Christian civilization."[16]

While there are substantive differences between dispensational millennialists and nondispensational millennialists, for our limited purposes these distinctions are not relevant.[17] The relevant point here is whether these terms can be adapted to Jewish fundamentalism in America. For most Jewish fundamentalists messianism is an operative and often a central tenet of their religious worldview. The messianist stances of the two American fundamentalisms under examination, Habad and Satmar, loosely cohere with the pre- and postmillennialist perspectives of Christian fundamentalism, albeit each refracts its view through its respective theological lenses.[18] While dispensationalism is a category specific to Christian theological teaching, Rabbinic Judaism posited a similar framework in its description of history as constituting three distinct periods, each consisting of two thousand years: two thousand years of confusion (from Adam to Sinai), two thousand years of Torah (from Sinai to the advent of the Messiah), and two thousand years of redemption (from the Messiah until the world-to-come).[19] While the rabbinic sages were noncommittal with regard to how historical events correspond with these three "dispensations," post-rabbinic rabbis in the medieval and modern period, including Habad and Satmar, often interpreted historical events in light of this framework. Similarly, while the anti-Christ is a Christian category, Jews have correlate terms (e.g., Satan, the demonic "other side," the *yezer hara* or evil inclination) that appear disguised as positive forces but are from the side of destruction. Satmar, in particular, views Zionism in this way.

Many premillennialists claim to live "outside" history, viewing society's state of irreligion as irredeemable and even a necessary part of the divine plan to bring the end-time. Based loosely on the Augustinian principle of the incurable evil nature of the world and the human soul, premillennialists remain wed to the notion that the "return of Christ" is literal and that his empirical return must precede any discussion of true redemption. Postmillennialists, in contrast, adapt a spiritual return to Christ, leaving open the possibility of viewing history in a progressive state toward the final end-time.[20] The premillennialist belief in redemption solely by divine fiat, including the advent and ultimate destruction of the anti-Christ, promotes a religious perspective that no human agency *in the world* is possible to bring about the end-time. Hence in many cases there is no systematic commitment to social change as the prelude to the end-time.[21] In Christianity the purer form of premillennialism is no longer common. There is a lively debate among scholars of Christian fundamentalism as to the state of pre- and postmillennialism today. George M. Marsden argues that most premillennialists today have adopted an activist posture more common in postmillennialism, suggesting that the two categories are less distinct than they may have been earlier in American history.[22] David Harrington Watt has a different take on the transition of postwar American fundamentalism. He argues that the template remains premillenial although he acknowledges that the dispensational focus of prewar premillennialism has dissipated. In any case premillennialism does remain and is quite influential in postwar evangelical Christianity, especially regarding its attitude toward the State of Israel.[23] We shall see how this is also true of our Jewish cases.

Postmillennialists have a more optimistic view of history, including in some cases even relegating the secular/political spheres to a redemptive role, believing the contemporary moment represents the first stages of the end-time.[24] Most believe that the redemptive era has begun and that the coming of Christ will mark its conclusion. The active transformation of society in postmillennialism has strong Calvinist inclinations and has its roots in America in the Great Awakening, especially in the sermons of Jonathan Edwards, and later grew in progressive communities such as those that embraced the Social Gospel movement and other forms of liberal Protestantism.[25] More traditional postmillennialism is expressed in various evangelical movements today, in the "family values" movement in the early 1990s and even arguably among some Tea Party activists who have entered the halls of Congress to stem the tide of post-Christian secularism in favor of an American society more deeply rooted in Christianity and its values.

Jewish fundamentalists whom I consider postmillennialist messianists, such as contemporary Habad, have very specific and complex views about tradition in juxtaposition to—and in symbiosis with—the secular, and exhibit moderate separatist tendencies even as they engage in evangelism and political action. While Habad views itself as antithetical to, and to some extent at war with, American

Reform Judaism, both share a concerted effort to transform society through Jewish values. Reform has adapted many secular principles as part of its religious ideology. Habad rejects secularism in principle yet readily engages with and utilizes the fruits of secularism (such as technology, free speech, and the freedom of religious expression, language, and nomenclature) to further its postmillenial agenda.[26] What separates them is what each views as the essential character of Judaism and the vision of what a transformed society would look like.

Another important component of American Jewish fundamentalist identity is how these individuals view the United States. Many Jewish premillennialists (Satmar is the example in the next essay) view America as not significantly different from other diasporic venues, except for the fact that American freedom is more spiritually dangerous than circumstances in previous host cultures where Jews may have been physically threatened but spiritually safe. That is, America requires Jewish premillennialists to be more steadfast in protecting the values they hold dear. As we shall see with Satmar, in the United States separatism becomes sacrosanct and legal stringencies become more operative. Many Jewish postmillennialists (for example, Habad) explicitly hold America to be different, the place God has chosen to complete his mission. Habad often refers to America (and Canada) as a "country of kindness" (*medinah shel hesed*), pointing to a substantive difference in setting from all other Jewish diasporas. This difference becomes a central tenet of Habad's postmillennialism.

In order to analyze Jewish fundamentalism in the United States, these movements must be situated within the larger culture in which they exist and not only within the traditions from which they draw. Jewish movements take part in the general millennial spirit even though some specifics of Christian millennialism are foreign to them. For example, the notion of dispensations is largely based on an interpretation of a series of opaque verses in the ninth chapter of the book of Daniel that has attracted the attention of many Jewish scholars throughout the ages. The Babylonian Talmud provides us with its own rendering of the ninth chapter of the book of Daniel.[27] The notion that the Messiah will rule for one thousand years before the world will be fully transformed is a talmudic teaching and has been interpreted creatively by post-rabbinic Jews.[28] In short, there are many Jewish ideas of redemption that underlie Jewish fundamentalisms, some of which are cosmological, astrological, and some which view historical events, such as the Lisbon earthquake in 1755, the exile of the Jews from Spain in 1492, World War I, or the First Gulf War, as signs of the redemption.[29] It is also important to distinguish between messianism and ideas of redemption in Judaism, categories that surely overlap but are not identical.[30] While the coming of the Messiah is surely a dominant part of Jewish redemptive thinking, it is not the sole criterion for Jewish redemptive ideologies. As will become clear regarding American Habad, and as is true with other modern ultra-Orthodox Jews such as the first chef rabbi of Mandate Palestine Abraham Isaac Kook (d. 1935) and his followers, in postmillennial fashion Jews can tolerate the notion that redemption can begin before the arrival of the Messiah.

I do not argue that either of these groups is overtly influenced by American Christian fundamentalists, although Habad is certainly aware of tactics used by other fundamentalists and freely borrows from them.[31] Grand Rabbi Menahem Mendel Schneerson of Habad was actively involved with the public-school prayer issue and openly supported the position of Jerry Falwell in favor of a moment of silence in public schools.[32] He also challenged church-state law in the Supreme Court in 1989 with his construction of menorahs in a public square in Philadelphia, in San Francisco, and in other American cities and towns. It was a highly symbolic and, to my mind, intentional, choice to erect the first public menorah at the foot of the Liberty Bell in Philadelphia in 1974.[33]

I situate these groups around the question, "Is America different?" That is, does America provide a diasporic context unique in Jewish history that would enable, or require, traditional Jews to respond to the challenges of Jewish survival in new ways? If America is not different for the Jews than, say, Germany, Poland, or Hungary, how does this impact the way the group lives "in" America? Alternatively, for the premillennial Satmar Hasidim, it seems America is *not* different, but, while proclaiming America as not different, the group acts differently in America, and its position even vis-à-vis Israel and Zionism is partially an outgrowth of its American context.[34] Thus in America even this extreme branch of Hasidism, with its ideological separatism and premillenial tendencies, does not fully disengage from its external environment.

American Habad as a Jewish Postmillenial Fundamentalism

The Hasidic sect known as Habad or Lubavitch (from the Belarus town where it was founded) had very humble beginnings.[35] Its founder, R. Shneur Zalman of Liady (d. 1812), was a disciple of Dov Baer, the Preacher of Mezritch (d. 1772), a disciple of the founder of Hasidism, R. Israel Baal Shem Tov (d. 1760).[36] After Dov Baer's death his disciples slowly dispersed to various parts of Eastern Europe and began to establish Hasidic courts. While many courts were established in Poland, Galicia, and Hungary, R. Shneur Zalman and later his son Dov Baer (no relation to the Preacher of Mezritch) established a court in Belarus, an area largely cut off from Hasidic activity.[37]

During its early years Habad developed an ideology of outreach to Jews living in more isolated parts of Russia. This program was not only practical but also part of a larger messianic agenda, an ideology much less developed than it would become in America. In line with kabbalistic sources, this ideology held that the power of Jewish observance had the potential to bring about redemption. Maximizing that power by encouraging otherwise "fallen" Jews to engage in certain acts and behaviors was fostered through various means. While active in certain parts of Eastern Europe, as a movement Habad remained small yet grew exponentially in America after World War II. This growth was largely the result of the innovative and courageous leadership of its seventh grand rabbi, Menahem Mendel Schneerson (1902–1994) who became the movement's leader in 1951 after the death of his father-in-law, the sixth grand rabbi R. Joseph Isaac Schneersohn (the younger Schneerson dropped the second *h* in his last name after immigrating to America).

While Habad historiographers like to emphasize the continuity between Habad's European roots and R. Menahem Mendel's agenda in America, the picture is more complex. While it is true that the campaign mission that became the signature of Habad in America had roots in Europe, the difference between the European model and its American counterpart is more than situational.[38] The fifth Lubavitcher Rebbe, R. Shalom Dov Baer Schneersohn (1860–1920), assumed the role of rebbe in 1893 and reigned during the heyday of the Jewish Enlightenment in Eastern Europe, including the advent of Zionism. He was the last Habad rebbe to live and die in Europe and witnessed firsthand the secularization of European Jewry and the struggles of traditional societies to stem the tide of modernity.

Like many Christian millenialists and Jewish messianists, R. Shalom Dov Baer viewed the degradation of society as the "birth pangs of the Messiah," the beginning of the end of civilization as we know it.[39] He understood his times according to the (premillennial) Talmudic teaching that the world would descend (perhaps *needed* to descend) into chaos immediately before the advent of the Messiah.[40] He referred to his students as "pure ones" (*temimim*) in the military language common among later fundamentalists, nomenclature that would be deployed somewhat differently by R. Menahem Mendel Schneerson in America. R. Shalom Dov Baer charged his disciples to "wage war" against the Enlightenment, including Zionism. His was a classical premillenial charge, not a call to transform the world through kindness but to wage war against those creating darkness. His weapon of choice was the proliferation of Torah, mitzvot, and *frumkeit* (a Yiddish term referring to religious practice and behavior). R. Shalom Dov Baer's approach was not dissimilar from the one adopted by Hungarian Hasidism in the late nineteenth century that became the signature of Satmar in America.

R. Shalom Dov Baer's war was not expressed as quietist piety or absolutist separation. He initiated "missions" to the far-flung parts of Russia and Siberia to provide Jews there with basic resources and religious materials. The sixth rebbe of Habad, R. Joseph Isaac Schneersohn (1880–1950), continued these activities in Russia, secretly thwarting authorities and organizing clandestine missions that landed him in a Russian prison. With the intervention of world leaders, including American statesmen, R. Joseph Isaac was released from prison in 1927; he migrated for a time to Warsaw and then to America in 1940.

These Habad "missions" would continue in an attempt to counter Jewish assimilation in America and reached new heights with the seventh rebbe Menahem Mendel Schneerson who transformed the Habad mission program from a premillenial Manichean battle of light against darkness to a postmillenial attempt to transform the world, including outreach to Gentiles, something unprecedented in Hasidism in general and Lubavitch in particular.

Habad in America was the brainchild of R. Joseph Isaac, the father-in-law of R. Menahem Mendel. Their visions, however, were not identical. Upon his arrival in the United States R. Joseph Isaac proclaimed "America is no different," a call that remained operative for Habad until his death in 1950. This proclamation insinuated that the Habad program in Europe, including the battle against secularism and Zionism, would continue on American soil.[41] The very proclamation "America is no different" suggests an anxiety about the new challenges America posed to ultra-Orthodoxy. The dominance of non-Orthodox Judaism, the religious freedom, the absence of systemic anti-Semitism, and the economic and educational opportunities in the United States all suggested that America was indeed different. Yet R. Joseph Isaac, even though he had strong messianic inclinations, viewed America as the next phase of exile and did not believe that America required a new Hasidic agenda. The insular premillennial inclinations that drove his prewar agenda largely remained intact even as R. Joseph Isaac instructed certain Hasidism to reach out to the assimilated Jews on college campuses in the winter of 1948.[42]

R. Menahem Mendel Schneerson did not lead the cloistered life of his father-in-law or his predecessors.[43] Growing up in the court of Habad in Russia, he later lived in Berlin and Paris, studied in universities in both cities, and worked as an engineer in the U.S. Navy Yard upon his arrival in the United States, all things unusual for someone being cultivated to become the leader of a Hasidic dynasty. While there is considerable debate between those inside Habad and scholars who study them as to the extent and nature of his engagement with liberalism and secularism, there is little doubt that, in contrast to his father-in-law, for R. Menahem Mendel America was, in fact, different although the specific nature of that difference is never explicitly developed.[44] He was fond of referring to North American as a "nation of kindness" (*medinah shel hesed*) and followed and participated in political matters that were both directly and indirectly relevant to his constituency.

In this way R. Menahem Mendel's attitude reflected a common postmillennial sentiment that argued "America has a special place in God's plans and will be the center of a great spiritual and moral reform that will lead to a golden age or 'millennium' of Christian civilization."[45] On this reading, R. Menahem Mendel gestures to a position taken by Jonathan Edwards who preached that salvation "would begin in America."[46] Of course for R. Menahem Mendel this meant the coming of the Jewish Messiah and the return of all Jews to the land of Israel. Yet America was an important conduit for this unfolding. He often invoked the national American slogan *E pluribus unum* (from many, one) as both a justification for his engagement with American society and a metaphysical principle in concert with Habad's acosmic worldview.[47] Unlike previous Habad rebbes whose interests were solely with their constituents and other Jews in need, R. Menahem Mendel entered the political arena on such issues as public-school prayer (even though few of his disciples' children attended public school) and was responsible for a Supreme Court case on the issue of church-state matters when he directed his disciples to erect large Hanukkah menorahs in town squares to foster Jewish pride. He had influence in the halls of Congress, appointing his close disciple Lev Shemtov as a permanent emissary to the Hill, and R. Menahem Mendel Schneerson was awarded the Congressional Gold Medal, one of the highest honors for an American citizen, in 1994. In short, American Habad's attitude toward its host culture was decidedly different from that of other Hasidic communities who engaged in government matters only as they related to those communities. American Habad is an example of a Jewish fundamentalism that navigates between a firm commitment to "fundamental" doctrinal beliefs and proactive engagement in the larger to world in order to transform it and thus achieve its goals. On this point Aviezer Ravitzsky sums up Habad position succinctly. "On the one hand, Habad Hasidism adheres to a consistent, radically conservative posture regarding matters of faith and religious norms: it clearly rejects such concepts as liberalism, pluralism, and universal human equality. . . . On the other hand, more than any other trend in contemporary *haredi* Jewry, Habad Hasidism displays a dynamic and activist attitude, approaching reality as a field of movement and change, consciously expanding the boundaries of its religious involvement."[48]

R. Menahem Mendel's "Army of God" (*Tzivos Ha-Shem*), Habad's youth movement, was not constructed as an army of warriors of light against darkness, as the youth movements of his predecessors had been, but rather as a body of representatives of Judaism to an assimilated Jewish as well as to a Gentile public who had little exposure to traditional Judaism.[49] For example, in 1988 Tzivos Ha-Shem sponsored a musical and cultural arts fair in New York City and in 2004 opened a Jewish Children's Museum in Brooklyn's "Museum Row," a very different tack from the polemics against Zionism and the Jewish Enlightenment (*Haskalah*) in prewar Habad and in other postwar Hasidic groups.[50] While R. Menahem Mendel advocated strict adherence to Jewish law and practice, he instructed his disciples to be tolerant of nonpracticing Jews and to offer them a taste of Judaism (or Yiddishkeit) that might, or might not, take root later. He advocated using traditional religion as a source of identity and pride even for those who did not practice. In some ways this is a novel attempt to use tradition as a tool of Jewish secularism. Moreover, in addition to his advocacy of Jewish ritual as central to Jewish survival, he stressed matters of Jewish doctrinal belief (focusing on Maimonides's Thirteen Principles of Faith), a campaign that touched many who would not adopt the rigorous life of ultra-Orthodoxy.[51] While surely not pluralistic in any formal sense, the American Habad program was one of tolerance and flexibility. The Manichean premillenial tenor of Habad's previous agenda seems to have disappeared.

Three examples serve to illustrate the ways in which American Habad moved from the Jewish premillennial posture of R. Shalom Dov Baer and R. Joseph Isaac to the Jewish postmillennialism of R. Menahem Mendel. The first is the Habad Noahide Law campaign. The second is Habad's anti-Zionist engagement with the Jewish state, and the third is the peculiar nature of Habad's rejection of Jewish secularism as an operative category.

Throughout his career R. Menahem Mendel broadened the missions of his predecessors with what became known as *mivtzoyim*, expansive missionary activities to bring Torah and mitzvot to unaffiliated Jews around the world.[52] In 1992, when the messianic fervor of Habad was sharply on the rise, largely due to R. Menahem Mendel's failing health, he instituted what was an unprecedented program in the annals of ultra-Orthodox, or even Orthodox, Judaism. As a way of preparing the non-Jewish population of the United States for the impending redemption, R. Menahem Mendel initiated a massive educational campaign about the Noahide Laws, the seven laws instituted by the rabbinic sages that Gentiles are required to fulfill to be considered "righteous Gentiles" in the messianic era.[53] While the initial impetus for this move was with his immediate predecessor R. Joseph Isaac upon his release from prison in 1927, R. Menahem Mendel's audacious and sustained campaign was the first time traditional Jewish outreach devoted considerable resources toward influencing the non-Jewish world regarding Jewish ideas of messianism and the role of the Gentile in that end-time vision.[54] Pamphlets were printed and distributed widely, R. Menahem Mendel spoke publicly about the importance of the Noahide Laws, and Habad emissaries across the country (and beyond) began exposing their Gentile neighbors to this idea.[55] In some way this was the culmination of the turn toward a Jewish postmillennialism focused on transforming the world while maintaining allegiance to its own strict doctrinal principles. Instead of hunkering down and "waging war" against the forces of darkness, R. Menahem Mendel positively engaged the larger world in an attempt to prepare individuals for the redemptive era that he believed had already begun.

The second example is contemporary Habad's engagement with Zionism and the Jewish state. From R. Shalom Dov Baer onward, Habad Hasidism was anti-Zionist. R. Joseph Isaac actively opposed the establishment of a Jewish state and sided with some of the most vehement anti-Zionists of his era, even though he did initiate Kefar Habad, the first Hasidic agricultural community in Israel. Both R. Shalom Dov Baer and R. Joseph Isaac exhibited what could be viewed as premillennial attitudes that the state was apostasy, a corruption of true Jewish messianic ideals, and, in fact, antimessianic.

Unlike his Habad predecessors and many of his ultra-Orthodox rabbinic contemporaries R. Menahem Mendel actively engaged with secular Israeli prime ministers and parliamentarians, evincing a hawkish and uncompromising stance of territorial compromise founded on his understanding of Jewish law with regard to preparation for the coming of the Messiah. He openly supported political parties in the Israel Parliament and urged his constituents to vote in Israeli elections. In an Israeli election in 1988 a picture of R. Menahem Mendel Schneerson appeared on Israeli voting cards encouraging voters to vote for Agudat Israel, his party of choice.[56] Here anti-Zionism (which often refuses to engage in the politics of a *treife medina,* i.e., a non-kosher state) is combined with messianic activism. R. Menahem Mendel's rejection of any land-for-peace initiative is not founded on the argument of security or Zionism more generally but rather on his messianic vision that the era of redemption had begun and Jewish sovereignty in the entire land of Israel is a requirement for its continued unfolding, an idea that has parallels among many Christian Zionist fundamentalists in America.[57]

Whereas most *haredi* anti-Zionists reflect premillennial tendencies arguing that we can do nothing other than perform mitzvot and wait for the Messiah, R. Menahem Mendel's postmillennial turn offers a different approach. His argument against Zionism was not so much that we must wait patiently in the Diaspora for the Messiah to come but that we must contest the Zionist's secular narrative of redemption. As Maya Katz argues regarding Habad's revision of the Hanukkah menorah, R. Menahem Mendel wanted to embrace the rich cultural life of Diaspora Judaism as a messianism in and of itself.[58] His problem with Zionism was less political (the existence of a Jewish state) and more cultural (rejecting the secular narrative of Zionism's cultural revolution). He offered what he deemed was a religious and authentic cultural paradigm as the foundation of his messianic vision. In this sense Habad's anti-Zionism was a postmillennial response to Zionism as a secular form of, or substitution for, traditional Judaism.

The final example requires us to touch briefly on Habad's metaphysical worldview. In accordance with kabbalistic teaching Habad believes that the Jewish soul contains a dimension of divinity that is absent in the non-Jewish soul. *Tanya,* a book written by R. Shnuer Zalman of Liady, is Habad's major source for its metaphysical system. This book makes a categorical distinction between the divinity of the Jewish soul (*neshama elohit*) and the pure corporeality (*neshama behamit*) of the Gentile soul. (The Jewish soul has *both* a divine and corporeal component, while the Gentile soul has *only* a corporeal component.) While Habad has often been accused of having a doctrine that constitutes a form of spiritual racism, Elliot Wolfson has shown that this doctrine is not exclusive to Habad Hasidism or Hasidism more generally but permeates much of kabbalistic literature upon which *Tanya* is based.[59] In any case Habad in America has done something quite ingenious with this doctrine. As we have seen, the war against secularism in general and Jewish secularism in particular was paramount in the Habad teachings of R. Shalom Dov Baer and R. Joseph Isaac. In the postwar period, especially in the United States, there appears to have been a shift in emphasis that may point to a change in orientation. Habad's belief that all Jews, secular or religious, contain the divine spark of a Jewish soul (in Yiddish it is called the *pintele Yid,* or the Jewish spark) leads them to the conclusion that "secularism," expressed as a deep rejection of religious belief and practice, is simply impossible for the Jew.[60] Espousing an acosmic worldview that all but erases the distinction between the sacred and the profane, Habad in general and American Habad in particular denudes secularism for the Jew by claiming it does not exist.[61] On this Aviezer Ravitzky notes, for Habad "Jewish religious identity is a matter of essence and substance; it is a given objective fact. It is not based on ethnic, cultural, mental or historical factors, or even on the actual relationship of the individual to the Torah and to halakha (Jewish law), but rather the divine nature of the Jewish soul." [62]

On this reading, "secular" Jews should not be rejected or marginalized. Rather they should be given access to their "inner-souls," to their "Jewish spark," after which they will, of their own accord, come to see the truth of traditional Judaism. The divisiveness and rancor of prewar Habad against the "secularists" and Zionists have been transformed into a campaign to get American Jews to "know themselves."[63] While spiritual self- knowledge has its roots in prewar Jewish pietism and is expressed in similar ways in earlier Hasidism, this idea has arguably undergone a transformation in American Habad, not only in rhetoric but also in substance.[64] Cultural, ideological, and historical factors melt away when the Jewish soul is able to breathe. The way back to tradition for the Jew is not to be convinced of Judaism's truth but to be reintroduced to one's own self.[65] The Gentile may have to be convinced that the Noahide Laws are true. The Jew, however, has only to know who he or she is. In Habad the Gentile must be convinced via rational means; the Jew must be woken up emotionally and spiritually.

As much as all of this is founded on metaphysical grounds, some of which are quite jarring to the modern ear, I suggest that this is a novel way to confront secularity. This old idea is applied in a new way that results in tolerance, patience, and the erasure of the siege mentality that dominated Habad before its arrival in America. It is another example that illustrates an "America is different" sensibility and in which R. Menahem Mendel's revision of his predecessor's thinking embodies an American form of postmillennial fundamentalism committed to the transformation of a society already in the early stages of redemption. Jewish secularism need not be the object of consternation and confrontation; it must be massaged until it disappears since it is, for the Jew, only an illusion.

"Come to my Garden": "Holy Folly" as Jewish Postmillenialism

These attitudes can be drawn from one seminal essay in R. Menahem Mendel's writings. His writings, both in Hebrew and Yiddish, are voluminous. For example, his public discourses are collected in *Likkutei Sihot,* consisting of thirty-nine volumes. His longer essays are collected in *Torah Menahem,* in forty-five volumes. His letters, *Igrot ha-Kodesh,* are collected in twenty-six volumes. One of his most celebrated essays is the inaugural lecture he delivered when he became rebbe of

Habad in the winter of 1951.[66] Entitled "*Bati le-Gani*" ("Come to my Garden" [Song of Songs 5:1]), it is a kind of blueprint for his entire institutional and spiritual career and one that captures American Habad's postmillenial agenda.

This lecture is a metaphysical reflection on the kabbalistic idea of the divine presence descending into the material world. Much has been made of his reference to the *shekhina* (divine presence) as the seventh realm of divine emanation at the time that he is becoming the seventh rebbe of Habad.[67] It is often viewed as an early, albeit esoteric, proclamation of his messianic status. Most of the lecture is based on the kabbalistic idea of "turning inside out" (*itkafya ve-itkafya*), in R. Menahem Mendel's language, transforming darkness into light. Darkness is depicted as the concealment of divine light from the upper worlds, and the job of the Jew is to disclose that light in material realms. This activity is accomplished not solely by means of personal worship (for example, mitzvot and prayer) but also by an active engagement with the world and, in particular, with other Jews.

The orientation is made clear but never explicit in the second part of the lecture. After the first metaphysical section, R. Menahem Mendel turns to the notions of "profane folly" and "holy folly."[68] Although he never says so explicitly, it is plausible that "profane folly" is a thin veil for "secularism" practiced by the Jew. He argues that profane folly conceals divinity. Thus, when Jews who are engaged in profane folly (which could just as easily be intellectual as materialistic) commit a sin, they don't feel that they are separating themselves from godliness, because their folly has already concealed it. Secularism thus makes religious experience inoperable. The way out of sin, or to transcend secularism, is to recognize what it does that requires someone else to disclose the divine nature of the individual's Jewish soul. There is, of course, a circular logic at play. If the Jew sees the sin for what it is, it is a sign he is experiencing things from his divine spark. If he does not, it is a sign that his divine spark remains concealed.

R. Menahem Mendel proceeds in the final section of the lecture to talk about "holy folly," tying it to an earlier discussion of how animal sacrifices brought divine light into the world. This holy folly is described as part of the prophetic vocation. Harkening back to the beginning of the lecture, he states, "And this is what it means, *make me a sanctuary and I will dwell among you*" (Exodus 25:8), "among each one of you."[69] By means of divine worship one activates the reversal of darkness to light, that is, one turns (*lehafokh*) that which is below consciousness (*da'at*) in this world to a state of consciousness. Here he interjects the Yiddish *fun velt,* in addition to the Hebrew '*olam* (world), to suggest, I think, that he is now talking practically about *this very world* and not a kabbalistic hypostasis of it. In other words the vocation of the Hasid is to engage in the world and disclose its divinity, including engaging with nonreligious Jews (enactors of profane folly) and showing them the divinity of their own souls. This can be done only by interactive worship, or holy folly, with the belief that darkness can be dispelled through engagement rather than confrontation. And so officially began postmillenial Habad fundamentalism.

This charge was accompanied by a growing belief over time that R. Menahem Mendel was himself the Messiah and that his directives were a secret message to the "pure ones" (*temimim*) of what needed to be accomplished before he could reveal himself as such. This belief reached a crescendo in the 1990s and then came crashing down after his death in the summer of 1994. Habad is still reeling from this tragedy, some believing he did not die, others continuing his work and remaining agnostic about his messianic status.

Habad did not change its daily routine of religious life (*halakha*) after R. Menahem Mendel's proclamation in 1991 that the Gulf War was the beginning of Armageddon. And his death in the summer of 1994 did not result in sweeping practical changes to coincide with the claim of his postmortem messianic status. In my view, the transformation from Habad's prewar premillennialism to an American postmillennialism is the trademark of American Habad and is an integral part of their messianic program.[70] Martin Katchen argues just the opposite when he writes that "Lubavitch has remained faithful to its premillennial belief system. It will not be stampeded by events into declaring a premature entry into the Messianic Age in the absence of a messianic faith to accomplish it. In this, Lubavitch remains faithful to the best traditions of Judaism."[71] My disagreement with this assessment is based on two points. First, the extent to which "American is different" (as a postmillennial position) runs through R. Menahem Mendel's entire American career, and Habad's continued adherence to *halakha* is no proof that substantive, even radical, changes have not taken place. Second, in the postwar period in the United States, Christian premillennialism more generally adopted postmillennial positions or activism or at least made gestures toward postmillennial positions. On my reading, American Habad, under the tutelage of its leader and for both similar and different reasons, followed suit.

Notes

1. See George M. Marsden, *Fundamentalism and American Culture: The Shaping of Twentieth-Century Evangelicalism, 1870–1925*, 2nd ed. (New York: Oxford University Press, 2006), 221–28. There he argues that "in many respects fundamentalist Christianity was not unique to America" (221). Yet he acknowledges that the term *fundamentalist* was coined in the United States around 1920 and thus has a certain American resonance (250).

2. For a brief discussion, see A. Hastings, A. Mason, and H. Pyper, eds., *The Oxford Companion to Christian Thought* (Oxford: Oxford University Press, 2000), 255–57. On the complex nature of the principle of scriptural inerrancy, see Richard T. Antoun, "The Complexity of Scripturalism," in *Understanding Fundamentalism: Christian, Islamic, and Jewish Movements*, 2nd ed. (Lanham, Md.: Rowman & Littlefield, 2008), 37–54. Jay Michael Harris has a slightly different set of characteristics. See Harris, "'Fundamentalism': Objections from a Modern Jewish Historian," in *Fundamentalism and Gender*, ed. John Stratton Hawley (New York: Oxford University Press, 1994), 137.

3. These are the Jewish communities examined in the multivolume Fundamentalism Project, 1992–1995, published by the University of Chicago Press, as well as in *Jewish Fundamentalism in Comparative Perspective: Religion, Ideology and the Crisis of Modernity*, ed. Laurence Silberstein (New York: New York University Press, 1993).

4. It is important to note that Hasidic and non-Hasidic ultra-Orthodoxy now include a large contingent of Mizrahi Jews who come from the Maghreb, Levant, and Yemen.

5. For a thorough description of ultra-Orthodoxy as it developed in Eastern Europe, see Michael Silber, "The Emergence of Ultra-Orthodoxy: The Invention of a Tradition," in *The Uses of Tradition: Jewish Continuity since Emancipation*, ed. Jack Wertheimer (New York & Jerusalem: Jewish Theological Seminary Press, 1992), 23–84. For the history of Gush Emunim and the settler movement, see Ehud Sprinzak, *The Ascendance of the Israeli Right* (New York: Oxford University Press, 1991).

6. For a discussion of these oppositions, see Alan Mittleman, "Fundamentalism and Political Development: The Case of Agudat Yisrael," in *Jewish Fundamentalism in Comparative Perspective*, ed. Laurence Silberstein (New York: New York Unversity Press, 1993), 216–22.

7. See Harris, "Fundamentalism," 142, 143.

8. Here I respectfully disagree with Jay Michael Harris when he writes about "the modernity that prevailed among the Orthodox of the nineteenth century and prevails today among the 'fundamentalists' of our time" (Harris, "Fundamentalism," 150). I would argue that in many ways our "modernity" is quite different, especially with regard to the Jews' place in society, opportunities, and religious freedoms, all of which affect how these ultra-traditional communities fashion themselves today.

9. I would include here other democratic countries that respect religious freedom such as Canada, Australia, countries in Western and Central Europe, Argentina, and so on. Jay Michael Harris bases his criticism of the use of the term *fundamentalism* for Jewish groups largely on the fact that they are based on older European precedents. While acknowledging those precedents, I argue here that, in fact, the American instantiation of these communities differs enough from their European forbearers (largely due to the new context in which they live) that their differences may efface their similarities, at least when it comes to defining them under the term *fundamentalist*.

10. See, for example, Harris "Fundamentalism," 137–73; Leon Wieseltier, "The Jewish Face of Fundamentalism," in *The Fundamentalist Phenomenon: A View from Within, A Response from Without*, ed. Norman Cohen (Grand Rapids: Eerdmans, 1990), 194; and Charles Liebman, *Deceptive Images: Toward a Redefinition of American Judaism* (New Brunswick: Transaction Books, 1988), 43–60. Wieseltier mistakenly collapses the term *fundamentalism* to refer to a few precepts: 1) the inerrancy of scripture and 2) the rejection of historical progress. He notes that "Judaism is based on the authority of commentary," which is surely true, but he does not address the position of the *inerrancy* of commentary, which is not prevalent but surely exists in some of the circles we are discussing. Moreover, he simplifies the notions of the inerrancy of scripture and scriptualism, which is a much more nuanced view of the matter. See, for example, "The Complexity of Scripturalism," in Richard T. Antoun, *Understanding Fundamentalism: Christian, Islamic, and Jewish Movements*, 2nd ed. (Lanham, Md.: Rowman & Littlefield, 2008), 37–54. Or, in the case of Habad, the inerrancy of the Rebbe himself! In terms of historical progress Wieseltier ignores many ultra-Orthodox texts, Hasidic and non-Hasidic, that make such claims about history. R. Teitelbaum of Satmar surely did not believe in historical progress, and one could argue that R. Menahem Mendel's assertions against evolution and against the scientific idea of the earth revolving around the sun (because it ostensibly contradicts Talmudic teaching) come close to a rejection of historical progress if such progressive ideas contradict traditional teaching. In the end Wieseltier defines for himself "normative

Judaism" (based on his reading of Maimonides), and then asserts that fundamentalism is not part of it. But is not normativity, at least to some degree, itself a subjective category? And today, given the prevalence of ultra-Orthodox Judaism, can we really say that Maimonides the rational theologian is the template of normative Judaism?

11. Gabriel A. Almond, R. Scott Appleby, and Emanuel Sivan, eds., introduction to *Strong Religion: The Rise of Fundamentalisms around the World* (Chicago: University of Chicago Press, 2003), 17.

12. Peter Berger, *Homeless Mind: Modernization and Consciousness* (New York: Vintage Books, 1974). Jacob Katz makes similar comments about the "modernity" of ultra-Orthodox Judaism. See his discussion in "Orthodoxy in Historical Perspective," *Studies in Contemporary Jewry*, vol. 2 (1986): 3–17. Cf. Katz, *A House Divided: Orthodoxy and Schism in Nineteenth-Century Central European Jewry* (Hanover, N.H.: Brandeis University Press, 2007).

13. Marsden, *Fundamentalism* 2005 postscript.

14. Marsden, *Fundamentalism and American Culture*, 5, 232.

15. Ibid., 233–35. Cf. Glenn W. Shuck, *Marks of the Beast: The Left behind Novels and the Struggle for Evangelical Identity* (New York and London: NYU Press, 2005), 29–52.

16. George M. Marsden, *Understanding Fundamentalism and Evangelicalism* (Grand Rapids: Eerdmans, 1991), 101.

17. For some of differences between dispensational and nondispensational premillennialists, see Marsden, *Fundamentalism and American Culture*, 51, 52. Cf. David Harrington Watt, "The Private Hopes of American Fundamentalist and Evangelicals, 1925–1975," *Religion and American Culture* 1 (Summer 1991): 155–75.

18. On messianism in R. Menahem Mendel Schneerson, see Max Kohanzad, "The Messianic Doctrine of the Lubavitcher Rebbe, Rabbi Menahem Mendel Schneerson (1902–1994) (Ph. D. thesis, University of Manchester, 2006), and Elliot Wolfson, *Open Secret* (New York: Columbia University Press, 2009).

19. Babylonian Talmud, Sanhedrin 97a. The Christian dispensationalist breakdown is somewhat different. Its most popular formulation in the United States may be from the Scofield Bible commentary adopted by John Nelson Darby that offers a sevenfold scheme. See C. I. Scofield, *The Scofield Reference Bible* (New York: Oxford University Press, 1909).

20. See the discussion in Ernest Lee Tuveson, *Redeemer Nation: The Idea of America's Millennial Role* (Chicago and London: University of Chicago Press, 1968), 26–39. Marsden argues that this attitude became common after the Civil War partly as a response to the bloody war and partly influenced by Darwin's challenge to religious doctrine, the growing emergence of urban life in United States, and the rise of biblical criticism. Timothy Weber offers the opposite assessment when he writes that "postmillennialism lost credibility after the Civil War because in the eyes of most people things were getting worse, not better." See Weber, *On the Road to Armageddon: How Evangelicals Became Israel's Best Friend* (Grand Rapids: Baker, 2004), 42.

21. See Sivan, "The Enclave Culture," in *Strong Religion*, ed. Almond, Appleby, and Sivan, 44.

22. See Watt, "Private Hopes," 160–62. "Many evangelicals remained within the general premillenial framework but explicitly rejected some of the distinctive tenets of dispensationalism in which the fundamentalists had found so much spiritual sustenance" (162).

23. See Weber, *On the Road to Armageddon*, esp. 95–128, 213–48.

24. In Judaism the great Jewish postmillennialist might be Rabbi Abraham Isaac Kook (d. 1935), the first chief rabbi of Palestine.

25. See Ruth Bloch, *Visionary Republic: Millennial Themes in American Thought 1756–1800* (Cambridge: Cambridge University Press, 1985), 22–50.

26. See, for example, Jan Feldman, *Lubavitchers as Citizens* (Ithaca and London: Cornell University Press, 2006). This is also to some extent true with Jewish premillennialists such as Satmar, especially regarding Kiryas Joel and church-state matters, but Habad is much more open to the secular world as a tool to foster redemption than Satmar.

27. Babylonian Talmud, Sanhedrin 97a.

28. See, for example, Gershom Scholem, *Origins of the Kabbalah* (New York: JPS, 1987), 460–75; Haviva Pedaya, *Nahmanides, Cyclical Time and Holy Text* [Hebrew] (Tel Aviv: Am Oved, 2003); and Moshe Idel, "The Jubilee in Jewish Mysticism," in *Fin de Siecle—End of Ages* [Hebrew], ed. J. Kaplan (Jerusalem, 2005), 67–98. On the astrological aspects of Jewish messianism, see Idel, "Saturn and Sabbatai Tsevi: A New Approach to the Study of Sabbateanism," in *Toward the Millennium: Messianic Expectations from the Bible to Waco*, ed. P. Schafer and M. Cohen (Leiden: Brill, 1998), 173–202.

29. For example, see the long essay by the thirteenth-century rabbinic leader Moses Nahmanides, "The Book of Redemption" [Hebrew], in *Kitvei Ramban*, vol. 1 (Jerusalem: Mosad ha-Rav Kook, 1963), 261–95, available in English as *Ramban: The Book of Redemption*, trans. Charles Chavel (New York: Shilo, 1978). Cf. "Essay on Redemption" by the eighteenth-century Italian kabbalist Moses Hayyim Luzatto, in *Sifrei Ramhal: Hoker ha-Mekubal be Milkhamot Moshe* (Jerusalem, n.d.). These are two of many such essays in post-rabbinic Judaism. Menahem Mendel Schneerson claimed the First Gulf War was part of the apocalyptic wars of Gog and Magog and the anti-Zionist R. Hayyim Elazar Shapira of Munkacz (the Satmar Rebbe's teacher), among many others perhaps including the Zionist R. Abraham Isaac Kook, thought the World War I was the beginning of the messianic wars of redemption.

30. See Moshe Idel, "Multiple Forms of Redemption in Kabbalah and Hasidism," *Jewish Quarterly Review* 101, no. 1 (2011): 27–70.

31. See, for example, Maya Katz, *The Visual Culture of Chabad* (Cambridge: Cambridge University Press, 2010), 144–73.

32. Jerry Falwell's Moral Majority was considered perhaps the most popular fundamentalist group in postwar America. When *Time* magazine devoted its September 1985 issue to fundamentalism in the United States, they chose to put Falwell on the cover.

33. See Katz, *The Visual Culture of Chabad*, 204–24. It is also significant that many of the groups that contested the legality of the public menorah lighting were Jewish, such as the American Jewish Congress.

34. On the social life of Satmar more generally, see Israel Rubin, *Satmar: Two Generations of an Urban Island*, 2nd ed. (New York: Peter Lang, 1997); and Jerome Mintz, *Hasidic People: A Place in the New World* (Cambridge: Harvard University Press, 1992), 309–27.

35. *Habad* is an acronym for wisdom (*hokhma*), understanding (*bina*), and knowledge (*da'at*) in kabbalistic nomenclature.

36. On the Baal Shem Tov as the founder of Hasidism, see Moshe Rosman, *Founder of Hasidism: A Quest for the Historical Ba'al Shem Tov* (Los Angeles and Berkeley: University of California Press, 1996); and Immanuel Etkes, *The Besht: Magician, Mystic, and Leader* (Waltham, Mass.: Brandeis University Press, 2005).

37. The ascendance of Dov Baer to become the second rebbe of Lubavitch was a hotly contested episode in the history of Hasidism. R. Shnuer Zalman's eldest son Moshe was passed over and eventually converted to Christianity. See David Assaf, *Untold Tales of the Hasidim* (Waltham, Mass.: Brandeis University Press, 2010), 29–96.

38. See, for example, Yitzchak Krauss, *The Seventh: Messianism in the Last Generation of Chabad* [Hebrew] (Tel Aviv: Yediot Ahronot and Chemed Books, 2007).

39. See, Babylonian Talmud, Ketubot 111a. On R. Menahem Mendel Schneerson's rendering of this idea in English, see *From Exile to Redemption*, vol. 1 (Brooklyn: Kehot, 1992), 53–66.

40. See Babylonian Talmud Sanhedrin 97a.

41. See Menahem Friedman, "Habad as Messianic Fundamentalism: From Local Particularism to Universal Jewish Mission," in *Accounting for Fundamentalisms: The Dynamic Character of Movements*, ed. Martin E. Marty and R. Scott Appleby (Chicago: University of Chicago Press, 1994), 340.

42. See Mintz, *Hasidic People: A Place in the New World*, 29: "The shared mission of Hasidic Jewry in New York City was to recreate the world that had existed in prewar Europe. In part this was a debt that they owed to a generation that had been destroyed. It was a way too of affirming victory over those who had tried to annihilate them."

43. Most recently, see Samuel Heilman and Menahem Friedman, *The Rebbe* (Princeton: Princeton University Press, 2010), 65–89.

44. See, for example, in Jan Feldman, *Lubavitchers as Citizens* (Ithaca: Cornell University Press, 2003), 38–59; 111–134. Cf. Friedman, "Habad as Messianic Fundamentalism," 340–45.

45. Marsden, *Understanding Fundamentalism and Evangelicalism*, 112.

46. Jonathan Edwards, "Some Thoughts Concerning the Present Revival of Religion in America (1742)," in C.C. Goen, ed., *The Works of Jonathan Edwards*, vol. 4 (New Haven: Yale University Press, 1972), 353.

47. See his use of that term as a justification for his public menorah campaign in *Chabad Magazine* (November 1994): 49, cited in Katz, *The Visual Culture of Chabad*, 211. On the acosmism and its political ramifications, see Wolfson, *Open Secret*, 27–65.

48. Ravitzky, "The Contemporary Lubavitch Hasidic Movement," in *Accounting for Fundamentalisms*, ed. Marty and Appleby, 305.

49. See Susan Fishkoff, *The Rebbe's Army* (New York: Schocken Books, 2003), 46–65; 339–60.

50. Katz, *The Visual Culture of Chabad*, 197, 198.

51. On the thirteen principles of faith, see Marc B. Shapiro, *The Limits of Orthodox Theology: Maimonides' Thirteen Principles Reappraised* (Oxford: Littman Library of Jewish Civilization, 2004).

52. The *mivtzoyim* campaigns started after 1967 when R. Menahem Mendel announced his *tefillin* campaign following the Six Day War. See Katz, *The Visual Culture of Chabad*, 174, 180n12.

53. See, Aviezer Ravitzky, "The Contemporary Lubavitch Hasidic Movement," 309–13, and Elliot Wolfson, *Open Secret*, 229, 230. On the Noahide Laws more generally, see David Novak, *The Image of the Non-Jew in Judaism* (New York: Edwin Mellen Press, 1983); and Novak, "Noahide Law: A Foundation for Jewish Philosophy," in *Tradition in the Public Square: A David Novak Reader*, ed. R. Rashkover and M. Kavka (Grand Rapids: Eerdmans, 2008), 113–44. Cf. Michael Broyde, "The Obligation of Jews to Seek Observance of Noahide Laws by Gentiles: A Theoretical Review," *Tikkun Olam: Social Responsibility in Jewish Thought and Law*, ed. David Shatz, Chaim I. Waxman and Nathan J. Diament (Northvale, N.J.: Jason Aronson, 1997), 103–43. See Martin Katchen, "Who Wants Moshiah Now?," *Australian Journal of Jewish Studies* 5, no. 1 (1991): 70–72.

54. Wolfson, *Open Secret*, 229. The only comparable campaign to my knowledge was the reform rabbi Isaac Mayer Wise's attempt in the mid-nineteenth century to make American Christians "denationalized" Jews. See Isaac Mayer Wise, *American Israelite*, May 14, 1875, cited in Dena Wilansky, *Sinai to Cincinnati* (New York: Literary Licensing, 2012, 1937), and Benny Kraut, "Judaism Triumphant : Isaac Mayer Wise on Unitarianism and Liberal Christianity," *AJS Review* 7 (April 1982): 194n46.

55. Books began to appear written by Jews about the concept of the righteous Gentile. See, for example, Michael Shelomo Bar Ron, *Guide for the Noahide: A Complete Manual for*

Living by the Noahide Laws (Lightcatcher Books, 2010), and Michael Ellias Dallen, *The Rainbow Covenant: Torah and the Seven Universal Laws* (Lightcatcher Books, 2003). This is an instance of two works written by traditional Jews published by a Christian press to encourage Gentiles to live by the Noahide Laws. Moreover, the U.S. Congress passed a resolution in 1991 designating "Education Day" in honor of R. Menahem Mendel. Part of this resolution proclaimed the Noahide Laws as the basis of human civilization. See H. J. Res. 104, Public Law 102–14 passed on March 26, 1991.

56. See Ari Goldman "Israelis Vote, and the Lubavitchers Rejoice," *New York Times*, November 14, 1988.

57. See, for example, Timothy Weber's *On the Road to Armageddon*. It should be noted that most of the Christians who shared the Habad rebbe's view were dispensationalist premillennialists. On Christian Zionism most recently, see Shalom Goldman's *Zeal for Zion: Christians, Jews and the Idea of the Promised Land* (Chapel Hill: University of North Carolina Press, 2009).

58. Katz, *The Visual Culture of Chabad*, 202.

59. This doctrine has crept into more mainstream Jewish life in the depiction of the fictious Ladover Hasidic sect (obviously taken from Habad) in Chaim Potok's national best-seller *My Name Is Asher Lev* (New York: Random House, 1972); see 187–89. On the more widespread history of this doctrine, see Elliot Wolfson, *Venturing Beyond: Law and Morality in Kabbalistic Ethics* (New York: Oxford University Press, 2006), 17–128. Cf. Wolfson, *Open Secret*, 239–40.

60. Jonathan Sarna succinctly describes a *pintele yid* as "a dormant Jewish homunculus waiting to burst forth." See Sarna, "Ethnicity and Beyond," in *Ethnicity and Beyond*, ed. Eli Lederhendler (New York: Oxford University Press, 2011), 108. This idea is quite common in Hasidic literature, including Habad. See, for example, the celebrated "*Bati le-Gani*" essay, R. Menahem Mendel's inaugural sermon as rebbe of Habad in 1951. See *Torat Menahem: Sefer Ma'amarim Bati le-Gani*, vol. 1 (Brooklyn: Lahak Hanochos, 2008), 9.

61. The idea that the "Jewish spark" is "asleep" in "exile" appears in the first master of Habad, R. Shneur Zalman of Liady. See, for example, in his *Torah 'Or* (Brooklyn: Kehot, 1991), 28 c/d. Cf. Elliot Wolfson, *A Dream Interpreted in a Dream* (New York: Zone Books, 2011), 202–8. Thus secularism, like exile, is a kind of dream state where the dreamer does not even know she is dreaming.

62. Ravitzky, "The Contemporary Lubavitch Hasidic Movement," 311. This idea is rooted in earlier kabbalistic literature that argues that Jews really cannot sin. See, for example, Zohar 3.16a. More precisely, the belief is that only the lower dimension of the Jewish soul can sin (*nefesh*), but the higher divine element (*neshama*) cannot. This becomes a central theme in Habad as expressed in R. Menahem Mendel's essay "*Bati le-Gani*" cited above.

63. The whole notion of "knowing oneself" as a religious precept is very much a part of the contemporary American spirituality that matured with New Age religion in the 1980s. While American Habad draws from Hasidic literature that similarly emphasizes self-knowledge as a spiritual precept (drawing from earlier sources), Habad's utilization of this idea is in concert with contemporary spiritual trends in America.

64. See, for example, Simon Jacobson's *Toward a Meaningful Life: The Wisdom of the Rebbe Menahem Mendel Schneerson* (New York: William Morrow, 1995).

65. The idea of sin as a severance of the individual Jew from his or her true divine self is a common theme in later spiritual Jewish theologies. See, for example, a similar locution defining repentance in R. Abraham Isaac Kook's *'Orot Ha-Teshuva* 15:10 (Jerusalem: Gar Or Press, 1977), 143, 144. Another example can be found in the little-known early-twentieth-century Hasidic writer R. Menahem Mendel Eckstein. See his *Ta'anei Ha-Nefesh le-Hasagat Ha-Hasidut*, 46, cited in Daniel Reiser, "To Fly Like Angels: Imagery or Waking Dream in Hasidic Mysticism in the First Half of the Twentieth Century" [Hebrew] (Ph.D. thesis, Hebrew University, Jerusalem, 2011), 233, 234.

66. It should be noted that every year R. Menahem Mendel would give additional "*Bati le-Gani*" lectures to commemorate the yahrzeit of his father-in-law, the sixth rebbe of Habad. These are collected in *Torat Menahem: Sefer Ma'amarim Bati le-Gani*, 2 vols. (Brooklyn: Lahak Hanochos, 2008).

67. See, for example, Wolfson, *Open Secret*, 11, 18, 41.

68. On the rabbinic distinction upon which this is based, see Babylonian Talmud, Ketubot 17a.

69. This is a common midrashic reading of the verse. An early Hasidic rendering can be found in *Keter Shem Tov*, collected teachings of the Baal Shem Tov (Brooklyn: Kehot, 1987), section 319, pp. 186–89.

70. On the changes that took place in the movement following his death in 1994, see Yori Yanover and Nadav Ish-Shalom, *Dancing and Crying: The Truth about the Habad Movement* [Hebrew] (New York: Meshy Publishing, 1994).

71. Katchen, "Who Wants Moshiah Now?," 74, 75.

"America Is No Different," "America Is Different"—Is There an American Jewish Fundamentalism?

Part II. American Satmar

Shaul Magid

When Hillary Clinton was campaigning for a New York State Senate seat in 2000 she met with a group of Hasidic women from the town of New Square in Rockland County, north of New York City. New Square is an incorporated village made up almost exclusively of Hasidic Jews, mostly descendants from the Hasidic town of Skver and it environs in present-day Ukraine. She began her talk by noting what a pleasure it was to address a group of *American* Jewish women. I wonder how these Hasidic women who live in a separatist religious enclave, primarily speak Yiddish, and are mostly unaware of the basic elements of American culture, music, and fashion, felt about being referred to as American Jews.

Satmar Hasidism and American Jewish Premillennialism

Formally, of course, they are American Jews; most hold American passports, pay taxes, and vote in American elections. Their Americanness, and more specifically, their being part of American Jewry, is a much more complicated story. The Hasidic Jews of New Square, and their "cousins" in the Satmar communities in Williamsburg, Brooklyn, and Kiryas Joel, a short distance from New Square, have little interaction with American Jews or American Judaism. And yet they are a part of American Judaism even against their will. This identification is more than circumstantial. Satmar Hasidism in the United States is what it is because of and in response to the American landscape in which it lives, and its distinctive brand of separatist fundamentalism shares some substantive components with Christian premillenial fundamentalism in America.

Satmar Hasidism is probably the second most recognizable Hasidic community in the postwar United States, largely as a consequence of its radical separatist and vehemently anti-Zionist ideology. The name *Satmar* comes from the Romanian town Satu Mare (also spelled Szatmar) in present-day Romania, thirteen kilometers from the Hungarian border where the young scion of a rabbinic and Hasidic family, R. Yoel (Joel) Teitelbaum (1887–1979), first attracted a following in the interwar period. R. Teitelbaum was a child prodigy from a family of rabbis and Hasidic masters that extends back to R. Moshe Teitelbaum of Satorakja-Ujhel (1759–1841)—better known by the title of his book *Yismakh Moshe*—one of the great masters in the first generations of Hasidism.[1]

Given his Hasidic lineage, it is somewhat surprising that the young R. Teitelbaum functioned not as a Hasidic rebbe in Satmar but as a rabbinic authority and spiritual leader of a relatively small community in a town whose Jewish community consisted of a mix of Hasidic, non-Hasidic, Zionist, and nonreligious Jews. R. Teitelbaum's radical separatist and anti-Zionist ideology, for which he later became famous, was not new—nor was it limited to Hasidic Judaism—but it was an extension of Hungarian ultra-traditionalism from the middle decades of the nineteenth century.[2]

Hungarian Jews were exposed to the Jewish Enlightenment earlier than most of Eastern European Jewry. The reformist community in Hungary, known as the Neologs, was influential and challenged the hegemony of traditional Judaism before similar communities arose in Poland and Galicia. This in part sparked a vehement rejection of religious innovation known as the *Austrittsgemeinde*, led by, among others, R. Moshe Schreiber, better known as Hatam Sofer (1762–1839), perhaps the most influential leader of Hungarian Jewry in the modern period.[3] Sofer's motto "innovation (*hadash*) is prohibited in the Torah"—a clever wordplay on Leviticus 23:14 prohibiting the consumption of new grain before Passover—served as the banner of the traditionalist camp. The spiritual progeny of R. Sofer developed a separatist mentality and waged war against modernity that by the late nineteenth century included Zionism.[4] R. Teitelbaum was very much a part of this non-Hasidic Hungarian traditionalist tradition, and the Satmar dynasty he built in postwar America remained committed to the principles he learned in prewar Hungary. In fact, R. Teitelbaum arguably became the best-known carrier of this Jewish separatist mentality in the twentieth century, making separatism into a devotional doctrine.[5]

In contrast to R. Menahem Mendel Schneerson of Habad discussed in the previous essay, R. Teitelbaum did not represent a long Hasidic tradition, even as he was part of a long line of Hasidic leaders. Satmar Hasidism is solely the product of R. Teitelbaum's learning, leadership, and charisma. Satmar may be one of the only Hasidic dynasties that has no distinctive *Hasidic* ideology and even harbors a disdain for mysticism more generally. In fact, R. Teitelbaum was alleged to have said that the tradition of the Baal Shem Tov, the founder of Hasidism, is no longer operative. In this sense Satmar Hasidism is a kind of anti-Hasidic Hasidism, anomalous among other Hasidic sects, especially Habad, which claims to have a direct line to the mystical ideology of Hasidism's founder.

Many of R. Teitelbaum's followers in Satmar were among more than one million Hungarian and Romanian Jews exterminated in the last years of World War II. The dynasty R. Teitelbaum built in America consisted largely of Hungarian and Romanian Holocaust survivors who were members of other Hasidic sects or traditional communities that were destroyed.[6] Escaping almost certain death in the Bergen-Belsen concentration camp via the famous Katzner transports (ironically, it was a Zionist transport that saved his life), R. Teitelbaum immigrated to Brooklyn, New York, in 1946 after a brief stay in Jerusalem. He retained strong connections to his Jerusalem community and became the honorary head of its rabbinical court called the Edah Haredit.[7] In America many survivors who had lost their communal affiliation coalesced around him, as he was arguably the most charismatic ultra-Orthodox Hungarian figure to survive the war.

In this sense Satmar Hasidism as we know it today is a postwar American phenomenon, even as it embodies an ideology that stretches back to prewar Hungarian ultra-Orthodoxy. As we shall see, the Americanism of Satmar is more than situational. Satmar's unrelenting war against Zionism is a battle that only increased after the Six-Day War in 1967. It was at that time that many ultra-Orthodox Jews reconciled with the existence of the Jewish state, its increased focus on punctilious observance and extreme modesty, and its separatist ideology that resulted in the emergence of Kiryas Yoel, a rural Satmar enclave in Rockland County, New York— all products of a Jewish premillennialist sentiment that has roots in prewar Europe but is made possible by living in the United States.

While much has been written on the sociopolitical and spiritual dimensions of Satmar Hasidism, mostly concerning the unrelenting anti-Zionism, my interest in this essay is quite narrow, with a focus on three issues: 1) Satmar's relationship to Jews who do not agree with their separatist and anti-Zionist principles, Orthodox or non-Orthodox; 2) R. Teitelbaum's desire to create an "American *shtetle*" or enclave community in rural Upstate New York; and 3) R. Teitelbaum's unwavering critique of Zionism that became more vociferous as Israel became more accepted by ultra-Orthodox communities, American Jews, and the West after 1967. Rather than soften his position on Zionism, the "triumph" of the Six-Day War made him more resolute that Zionism was the most egregious error committed by the Jewish people in their long history.

As we have seen in the previous essay on Habad, premillennialism, specifically post–Civil War dispensationalist premillennialism, was founded on the Augustinian principle that "Christ's kingdom, far from being realized in this age or in the natural development of humanity, lay wholly in the future, was totally supernatural in origin, and discontinuous with the history of this era. . . . For the [premillenial] dispensationalists the prophecies concerning the kingdom referred wholly to the future. This present era, the 'church age,' therefore could not be dignified as a time of the advance of God's kingdom."[8] It is not only that this age *cannot* be a part of the unfolding redemption; it is that this age represents the *necessary* decline of civilization that will be radically reversed when the Messiah arrives (or, in Christianity, returns). R. Teitlebaum was quoted as saying that "the Rambam [Moses Maimonides, the twelfth-century legalist and philosopher] says that we do not know how the Messiah will come until he comes, so let us wait patiently *without taking any action* toward the redemption, and let us have faith that God will fulfill the promises of the prophets at the time he sees fit."[9] It is significant to note that Maimonides does not explicitly say we should not take any action, only that we should "wait each day for him to arrive." Elsewhere R. Teitelbaum writes that "the future redemption will come solely on the merit of the Great Avenger, [we must] wait until the coming of the messiah and should not turn [or be seduced by] any other redemption, heaven forbid, before the coming of the messiah."[10] This premillenial passivity does not yield pacifism. As a premillennialist, R. Teitelbaum was at war with the world, particularly the Jewish world, because his ideology is founded on the biblical idea in the book of Daniel of the false prophet or, in Christianity, the anti-Christ who appears in the book of Revelation.[11] This satanic figure impersonates and even acts like a messenger from God but is an evil force intended to draw society to its doom. As we will see, for R. Teitelbaum, the Jewish "anti-Christ" is secularism and, more important, Zionism. This idea is very much in concert with many premillenial Protestants in America who have deemed the pope and the Roman Catholic Church more broadly as the anti-Christ. The circularity of this premillenial logic is that success in this world is a sign of its having roots in the demonic realm that must be resisted. The messianic ideology, with roots in Rabbinic literature, that the world must come to the very precipice of destruction before it will be redeemed, lies at the center of Satmar's separatism.

Satmar: Separatism as Devotion

This spiritual separatism, largely adopted from his great-grandfather R. Moshe Teitelbaum and from R. Moshe Sofer, is not only a practical way to avoid foreign influence. It becomes as well a spiritual value in and of itself. It is a devotional posture that enables one to be in constant awareness of the illusory nature of social progress. And it is not by any means limited to separating from the Gentile world. Jewish unity is not a premessianic goal for Satmar but a consequence of "false prophecy" that precedes redemption. The satanic force can appear inside Judaism as easily as outside of it, perhaps even more easily. According to this demonological view of history, hatred is the only proper response to the forces of evil that pervade the world.[12] "The Rebbe [R. Teitelbaum] often repeated the words of R. Yehoshuah of Belz: Separatism was of such importance that if a city had no wicked Jews, it would be worthwhile to pay some wicked Jews to come and live there so that the good Jews would have something to separate from. The very act of declaring separateness from the wicked strengthens the commitment of the righteous."[13] Citing the Talmudic passage (Babylonian Talmud Sotah 49b) "just before the messiah comes truth will be divided into flocks (*ne'ederet*)," R. Teitelbaum wrote that "in these years as falsehood spreads those who practice the truth will grow fewer and fewer. The flock of truth must separate again and again from those who go astray. Every time a part of the small group of the faithful takes a step in the wrong direction, those who remain faithful must once again separate from them."[14] This suggests an infinite regress of separation until evil is destroyed by divine fiat. The postmillenial spirit of Habad resulted in spreading its message of *Yiddishkeit* (Jewishness) to Jews and the Noahide Laws to non-Jews as a prelude and even prerequisite for the final redemption. This is countered by Satmar's premillennial ideology of separation as a spiritual discipline. The world is dominated by the forces of evil. God does not want us to erase them by engaging them. He wants us to separate ourselves to prevent contamination. Only separation, and not engagement or transformation, can save the dwindling remnant. Concerning extreme separatists in various religions, Emmanuel Sivan writes that "there is no concern for the klal or umma of the so-called believers, for one is faced with an 'infidel society', and 'evil kingdom'. Doomed to damnation it can be saved, if at all, either by messianic intervention or by imposing the divine law upon one and all once the elect take power by force."[15]

R. Teitelbaum spoke and wrote with great passion about worldly matters and engaged with the New York State and U.S. governments to assure the rights and safety of his community. He did not advocate living "off the grid" in a desolate area independent of governmental influence, as did David Koresh's Branch Davidians in Waco, Texas. Quite the opposite, as we will see with regard to Kiryas Joel, his separatism was activist. He was engaged with government agencies. American liberal democracy was very much a tool of Satmar's Hasidic separatism. Absolute separatism was relegated only to the Zionist entity, because he felt that Zionism was the great sin of modern Jewry, the very root of modernity's false prophecy. For example, it was said that when he visited Israel to bring much-needed financial resources to his community there, he refused to handle Israeli money or to make use of Israel's buses or other public services. While R. Teitelbaum viewed American democracy in purely utilitarian terms, he viewed Zionism in absolutist terms.

It is significant to note that while Satmar is not overtly messianic like Habad, and in some ways can even be construed as antimessianic, in other ways it is no less messianic than Habad. The difference between their messianisms is very much a product of their respective postmillennial and premillenial dispositions. R. Menahem Mendel believed that we are living on the cusp, or even inside of, the messianic era and that we (Jews *and* Gentiles) must do the final work to complete the process. This position argues that the beginning of the age of redemption precedes the coming of the Messiah. Many of R. Menahem Mendel's disciples considered him the Messiah (many even after his death), and at times he appeared to be in agreement with that assessment. R. Teitelbaum held that any belief that humans can do anything to erase evil and bring Messiah is blasphemy, even idolatry. The Messiah will usher in redemption by destroying the illusion of historical progress.[16] Only the Messiah can finally erase the stain of satanic temptation. Thus, religious Jews, even ultra-Orthodox ones, who capitulate to Zionism (for R. Teitelbaum the satanic "other"), whether ideologically or practically, are implicated in this idolatrous act. He eschewed all rebbe worship and would have thought it absurd for anyone to consider him Messiah. Rejecting the miraculous nature of the Six-Day War, R. Teitelbaum spoke out against being impressed with miracles, whether they come from holy men or men of unknown reputation.[17]

For R. Teitelbaum evil will reign and even increase until it will be eradicated in the end-time. Jews must separate themselves from all manner of evil, mourn the destruction, and await the redemption.[18] In many ways what separates Habad and Satmar on this point is that Habad is committed to the kabbalistic idea of eradicating evil by transforming it, and Satmar is committed to a Manichean, perhaps Gnostic, worldview that humans cannot eradicate evil. In this sense Satmar is perhaps the least mystical sect of Hasidism. It is worth noting that this antimystical worldview is also common among certain branches of Christian fundamentalism in America. While kabbalah plays a role in R. Teielbaum's teachings, it does not do so as a template of his worldview but simply as part of the canon of classical Jewish literature. The Hatam Sofer, whose influence is pervasive in Satmar's ideology, was not a mystic, and R. Teitlebaum's sermons collected in the multivolume *Divrei Yoel* do not exhibit strong mystical tendencies. At odds with these views, R. Menahem Mendel's teachings are saturated with Habad's distinctive acomsic mystical worldview, and one cannot adequately understand Habad's social program without understanding its kabbalistic foundation.[19] American Habad is perhaps the most overt case of applied mysticism in Judaism since the Sabbatean heresy in the seventeenth century.

One of the most overt expressions of Satmar's separatism in America was R. Teitelbaum's dream of establishing a Satmar enclave in a rural community in close proximity to Brooklyn. This would enable his Hasidim and their families to escape the secular temptations of the city while remaining close enough to New York's commercial center where many had businesses. Kiryas Yoel in Monroe Township is about fifty-five miles north of New York City. It was established in 1974.[20] In one sense R. Teitelbaum wanted to establish an "American *shtetl*."

However, as Nomi Stolzenberg astutely notes, this *shtetl* is perhaps more a product of his imagination than it is a reflection of any real prewar *shtetl* in Europe. "Kiryas Yoel is, in many respects, more insular, more homogenous, more exclusive than the European *shtetl.* It is stricter in its observance and, symptomatically, the rates of yeshiva learning and life-long Torah study are far higher in Kiryas Yoel than they were in Europe." It is precisely the American context of this *shtetl* that makes it possible. The ability for this American fundamentalist community to realize this vision of separation is "in part because the American welfare system alleviates the pressure to find *parnasa* [a livelihood] that weighed on most European Jews. All of these features that distinguish the 'American *shtetl'* from the European one are clearly signs of the community's success in resisting assimilation and Americanization (even as the community avails itself of the American system's largess)."[21]

While R. Teitelbaum fanatically advocated against reaping any benefit from the Zionist state, he was fully open to participating in the commercial life of America's liberal democracy. This attitude was not hypocritical because he was in full agreement with the divine decree of exile and Jeremiah's call for the Jewish exiles to make homes in the Diaspora until the coming of the Messiah (Jeremiah 29:4–7). Alternatively, his attitude toward the State of Israel was purely ideological and uncompromising. For him, the Zionist state was an act of heresy that not only "forced the end" (the blasphemous rabbinic category against premature messianism) but also was an embodiment of the demonic force that was testing the Jewish people's resolve to resist the temptation of premature redemption.[22] To reap benefit from Israel was to participate in an egregious act and, from his perspective, the most serious antimessianic endeavor imaginable. In this sense his protest against any redemptive quality of the Jewish state is an expression of his premillenial messianism.

Kiryas Joel was a party in a Supreme Court case in 1994 (Kiryas Joel v. Grumer) regarding the establishment of a public-school district for this American town made up solely of Satmar Hasidim.[23] Among other things, winning this case would give the Kiryas Joel school district access to state funds for certain school programs, such as assistance for special-needs children. (The particulars of this case are beyond the scope of this essay.) Stolzenberg notes that Kiryas Joel was able to establish itself as a "public" community which enabled it to be more separatist than its European predecessors. By internalizing "American liberal and cultural norms" Kiryas Joel established a self-segregated community that is as "deeply rooted in fundamental principles of liberalism and individual rights and the free market as it is opposed to them." [24] While the ideal of Satmar separatism is rooted in Hungarian ultra-Orthodoxy, its success in America is in part due to America's commitment to religious freedom and the ways in which closed communities such as Satmar can use that to their advantage. Thus, as was the case with the Habad missionary program, the *American* in Satmar's "American *shetl*" is more than a geographical adjective.

Satmar's Anti-Zionism and Its American Articulation: 'Al Ha-Geulah ve 'al Ha-Temurah

Satmar is perhaps best known for its vehement position against Zionism. Much has been written about Satmar's anti-Zionism and its roots in prewar European Orthodoxy, and I will not rehearse those observations here.[25] While Orthodox anti-Zionism was popular before the Holocaust and even after the establishment of Israel in 1948, the Six-Day War in 1967 softened many of the remaining anti-Zionist Jews, both Orthodox and Reform. While many remained less than enthusiastic about the Jewish state, the anti-Zionist rhetoric diminished precipitously by the early 1970s. The exception to this rule was R. Teitelbaum.

After the Six-Day War in 1967, Jews worldwide celebrated Israel's victory over its Arab neighbors, including gaining sovereignty over East Jerusalem and many "biblical" lands in what became known as the West Bank. The victory resulted in an increased sense of security many Jews felt about the fledging Jewish state. In light of, and in spite of, this new triumphalist spirit R. Teitelbaum, by then quite frail, set out to write an anti-Zionist manifesto that sought to prove that the Zionist victory was yet another illustration of Zionism as the "anti-Christ." This work, "On Redemption and on Exchange" (*'Al ha-Geulah ve 'al ha Temurah*), is based on a midrashic reading the book of Ruth 4:7. The book of Ruth has often been given messianic import since it ends with a genealogy leading to King David, the messianic symbol in classical Judaism. The midrash links the illusion of "redemption" (*geulah*) to "exchange" (*temurah,* its opposite) in the midrashic case, the sin of the golden calf in Exodus 32. R. Teitelbaum makes his case that Zionism is a contemporary golden calf, and all who participate in it, even if they outwardly do not support it, are guilty of the gravest sin in Jewish history.

The initial reviews of this book were predictably negative, although some praise came from the ultra-Orthodox circles in Jerusalem and other pockets in the Diaspora.[26] Most Jews were understandably at a loss as to how to understand R. Teitelbaum's sustained anti-Zionism in the wake of what many viewed as a miraculous victory for Israel and the Jews. While many ultra-Orthodox Jews understood and sympathized with R. Teitelbaum's misgivings about the establishment of a secular state, the Six-Day War resulted in free access to the Wailing Wall and other holy sites, including Rachel's tomb in Bethlehem, Joseph's tomb in Nablus, the Tomb of the Patriarchs in Hebron, and the Temple Mount in Jerusalem (even though many ultra-Orthodox Jews do not visit the Temple Mount because of a prohibition against setting foot on its sacred ground). Thus, while many in the ultra-Orthodox camp still refused to celebrate Israel Independence Day, many recognized Jerusalem Day (commemorating the "unification" of Jerusalem in 1967) as a day of thanksgiving. For many, this was not about the secular state but about divine intervention. In this regard it is useful to consider the introduction to *'Al ha-Geulah ve 'Al ha-Temurah* in order to make some suggestions as to what is really at stake in this book. It is in this late work that his most pungent version of anti-Zionism, and its American context, emerge.[27]

In his introduction to *'Al ha-Geulah ve 'Al ha-Temurah* R. Teitelbaum makes a series of audacious claims that, given the charged rhetoric, makes one wonder what is really at stake. He claims that Zionism is not only a contemporary embodiment of the golden calf; it is also "thousands of times worse than the golden calf" (19), worse than the Sabbatean heresy that racked world Jewry in the seventeenth century (22), an instance of Jewish idolatry that requires martyrdom (10), and the work of Satan himself (7, 17).[28] He believed that this was the final test that the messianic generation had to overcome (6, 10). Like a lone wolf in the wilderness after 1967, he watched as Zionism engulfed the entire Western world. For him, the fundamental premillennial framework of waiting patiently for redemption was shattered by the "satanic miracle" (7, 17) that he claimed was founded on a Talmudic teaching suggesting that Satan is given dominion in order to test humanity. Zionism and its acceptance resulted in the fate of the Jews delivered to satanic powers (18). "It is known from writers and books that any time there is an arousal of redemption from above . . . , Satan cleverly intervenes to transform it into a false redemption" (20). This satanic dominion, R. Teitelbaum argues, is strengthened by Torah-observing Jews who support the Zionist project. "Religious Jews with their leaders who are drawn after them [the Zionists] give strength and power to the heretics [*apikorsim*] in a powerful way" (19). While many of these themes exist earlier in *Vayoel Moshe,* written in the late 1950s, the language here is much sharper and the stakes are much higher. R. Teitelbaum knew that the events of 1967 made it more difficult for sympathizers to maintain their resolve in the face of what so many viewed as a miraculous moment in Jewish history.

While we cannot know for certain what precipitated this escalation of rhetoric, we might consider three possibilities. First, R. Teitelbaum witnessed how the "religious" consequences of the Six-Day War (i.e., the "unification of Jerusalem," access to holy places, and so forth) softened the attitudes of many who were sympathetic to his absolutist ideology before 1967. Viewing the events of 1967 as another manifestation of "false redemption" facilitated by the dominion of evil, he needed to reiterate his position to an ultra-Orthodox community vulnerable to succumbing to the illusion of historical progress.[29] In classic premillenial fashion R. Teitelbaum held that the illusion of historical progress is the most useful tool Satan has to do his work.

Second, his call to dismantle the Jewish state may have in part been a consequence of the reality of Jewish life in America. That is, when Jews were in danger in prewar Europe he spoke out against the establishment of a Jewish state as an act of heresy. And even though he finally wrote *Vayoel Moshe* in the late 1950s, the trauma of the Holocaust and instability of world Jewry were still quite palpable. But by the late 1960s ultra-Orthodox Jewish life (which was his focus) had reestablished itself in the safe haven of America. Whatever negative things he may have said about America, like R. Menahem Mendel, R. Teitelbaum knew that America was a place where Jews could practice their religion in relative safety. Hence, the dismantling of the Jewish state would not by definition put the Jewish people in grave danger. This conclusion of course assumes many things that could not be taken for granted (for example, open immigration to democratic countries such as the United States), but it may have enabled him, coupled with his belief in the impending redemption, to invoke the absolutist rhetoric prominent in *'Al Ha-Geulah*. For R. Teitelbaum, the only safe haven for Jews was the life of mitzvot and separation from the forces that seek to undermine the religious life. The notion that Jews could be safe by having an army was anathema from his premillennialist perspective.

Unlike R. Menahem Mendel, whose anti-Zionism was really about the cultural project of secular nationalism, R. Teitelbaum exhibited an anti-Zionism that was primarily political. Secularism was not the issue. For him, secularism was anathema by definition, and he did not have to convince his readers of that. The issue was the heretical use of political power as an insurance of Jewish survival that undermined his premillenial ideology. As a postmillennialist, R. Menahem Mendel held that the political could be used as a tool to procure redemption's unfolding as a long as it adhered to traditional theological principles. Hence he strongly advocated against the relinquishing of even "one inch" of territory as a theological precept and not a matter of security, and he supported the secular government of Israel as a means to achieve that theological end.

Finally, it seems that *'Al- Ha-Geulah* is a new and increasingly desperate articulation of R. Teitelbaum's theology of separatism adopted from his prewar Hungarian predecessors. It is not distinct from his activity in creating Kiryas Joel and, like the founding of Kiryas Joel, is made possible by his American context.[30] As Nomi Stolzenberg notes in her analysis of Kiryas Joel, liberal America made Kiryas Joel as an "American *shetl*" more relevant—and more possible—than anything that could have been created in Europe. Before 1967, Zionism did not have the same cachet among secular American Jews or among Americans generally. For many American Jews, Israel was not on their radar before 1967. While President Truman supported the establishment of Israel (after much heated discussion in his cabinet), subsequent American administrations before 1967 were more tepid in their support.

The Six-Day War changed that for American Jews and most of the Western world.[31] As we have noted, for R. Teitelbaum, separatism was more than pragmatic;

it was devotional. Each new moment in history introduced another opportunity to separate from evil. After 1967, Zionism was not only an ideology of "some" Jews; it became the default ideology of most Jews, and many ultra-Orthodox Jews in America who were not Zionists could not retain their ideological commitment to wage war against it. For R. Teitelbaum, the disease that infected modern Judaism now became a pandemic infecting most of the world. *'Al ha Geulah* was thus his final act of separatism, a message not only to Jews but to the world as well. It is thus not surprising that in subsequent years Satmar has become more vocal and more activist in its message, translating some material into English and presenting its case on the Internet. While R. Teitelbaum remained primarily concerned with his community and supporters, after 1967 he viewed the world as increasingly hypnotized by the successes of the Zionist state. Hence he widened his lens to include not only the ultra-Orthodox community but the larger world as well, with its shift in political policy toward what he deemed was the antithesis of his vision of redemption. Not enough attention has been paid to the extent to which *'Al Ha-Geulah,* written in the dense style of rabbinic prose, is actually a book that has as much to say to the Gentile world as it does to the world that can read and understand it. I would argue that this is not the case with his earlier *Vayoel Moshe,* which is more limited in scope and in many ways offers a view that is more in line with a prewar European mindset.

If our assessment is correct, R. Teitelbaum's ideology, especially as expressed in *'Al Ha-Geulah,* is very much an American Jewish fundamentalism. The reality of non-Orthodox Judaism as the template of American Judaism that supported his theology of separatism, his use of American goods and resources in the establishment of Kiryas Joel, and his belief that Zionism's universal acceptance after 1967 required a more radical act of separatism than before—all speak to an individual who, consciously or not, viewed his new home in America as a platform to develop and even radicalize an ideology born in prewar Europe.

Satmar and Habad: Fundamentalists or Religious Maximialists?

Some theorists deploy terms such as *strong religion* or *religious maximalism* to describe a series of religious extremist movements that have risen in contemporary society.[32] Given the limitations of the term *fundamentalism* discussed in the other essays in this book, it is worth considering whether, in fact, a term such as *religious maximialism* might better capture the nature of the Habad and Satmar communities. While I am not in principle wed to the term *fundamentalism* as a description for American Habad and Satmar, I do feel that previous attempts to invalidate such a description are largely based on a resistance to viewing ultra-Orthodoxy in America as sharing some fundamental similarities with its fundamentalist Christian counterparts. Thus, the differences between Christian fundamentalism and ultra-Orthodox Judaism are highlighted in order to distance the latter from the former.[33]

There is no doubt that Christian fundamentalisms have their own distinct history and are, in large part, a product of American religious history. And there is no doubt that Habad and Satmar emerge in prewar Europe under very different cultural and political circumstances, and their American instantiations largely continue the ideological program initiated in Europe. Having said that, in this and the preceding essay we have seen that the term *fundamentalism* may do some important work in helping us to understand the ways in which these movements have absorbed, both consciously and unconsciously, the liberal democracy of America such that their positions cannot be adequately understood outside of their American context.[34] The fact that until recently most studies on the ideology of Habad and Satmar do not distinguish between Israel and America, two very different cultural and political climates, underscores what is in need of correction.[35] The problem I have with terms such as *religious maximalism* is that they are largely culturally neutral. They capture different forms of extremism across diverse cultural and political divides but often do not focus on the ways in which these movements constitute interesting amalgams of Old-World traditions and ideologies and contemporary concerns and how many of them adapt forms of maximalism from outside their own systems.

My choice of the term *fundamentalism* to describe Habad and Satmar in America is precisely to underscore the specificity of these American versions of Jewish ultra-Orthodoxy in two ways. First, to suggest that it is the legal and cultural ethos of religious freedom in America (nonexistent in prewar Europe) that shapes these ultra-Orthodox responses to modernity. Second, to show that while Judaism and Christianity are quite different in their understandings of messianism and redemption, both emerge from the same biblical tradition and thus draw from similar, if not identical, texts to articulate their respective visions. Highlighting the differences between them is useful and important. But that should not efface the very real similarities, in temperament if not also in substance, that exists between them.

In fact, it may be precisely in ultra-Orthodoxy that these similarities can be seen. This is because much of modern progressive Judaism was formed in response to Christianity, highlighting the distinctiveness of Judaism in light of Christianity.[36] Ultra-Orthodox Judaism, however, was not threatened by Christianity in the same way as other forms of modern Judaism. Its constituents were not converting in large numbers, and it had limited social interaction with Christian society. Hence there is an absence of an apologetic tenor in ultra-Orthodox Judaism that enables some of those similarities to emerge. It is precisely ultra-Orthodoxy's distance from Christianity that allows its theological proximity to it to become apparent. Using categories such as *postmillennial* and *premillenial* to describe

Habad and Satmar is one way of examining these distinctive Jewish maximalisms in their American context.

How Habad and Satmar Have Contributed to Jewish Americanization

When we think of Americanization as the American Jewish project, we often think of progressive Judaism's acculturation and assimilation. This often takes the form of amelioration and accommodation to the ethos of liberal (Protestant) religion and secular culture that is perhaps most prominent in classical Reform Judaism. This and the preceding essay have set forth the position that the turn to multiculturalism and the celebration of diversity beginning in earnest in the late 1970s have created space for a new form of Americanization: the return to tradition. American Jewish fundamentalism is part of that story.

This return to tradition grew out of the counterculture of the 1960s, resulting in the Baal Teshuva movement in the 1970s and 1980s, the return to religious practice in Reform Judaism, and the growth of religious nostalgia in the rise of Habad. A renewed sense of Jewish "difference" was promulgated by radical movements, such as Meir Kahane's Jewish Defense League in the late 1960s, and very different kinds of inclusive programs, such as Birthright Israel in the early 2000s.[37] The fundamentalism of Habad and Satmar is part of this phenomenon. This is most apparent, and arguably successful, in American Habad, whose program of offering secular Jews a taste of authentic Yiddishkeit (Jewishness) has changed the sense of identity for many American Jews. While many who are touched by Habad do not become a part of its community or adopt its fundamentalist ideology, many are given a new sense of Jewish identity through its unapologetic approach to Jewishness that serves as a counter to Reform's accomadationalist approach. Most American Jews who are convinced that the State of Israel is a positive development are not receptive to Satmar's absolutist anti-Zionist ideology. Yet Satmar's uncompromising practice, devotion to Old-World traditionalism, and willingness to confront America's democratic process to achieve its goal of separation has gained moderate respect among some American Jews who have a nostalgic sense of the Old-World Judaism they have abandoned.

This new phase of multicultural Americanization arguably puts groups such as Habad and Satmar in proximity to Christian fundamentalists, surely not in basic beliefs and practices but more subtly in orientation and commitment to use the secular government and the benefits of religious freedom for the purpose of promulgating their religious agendas. Habad's mitzvah campaign, R. Menahem Mendel's advocacy of public-school prayer (in support of Jerry Falwell), and Habad's claim of the legality of erecting Hanukkah menorahs in public squares and Satmar's claim to the right of state funding in Kiryas Joel are some examples of how each in its own way both functions within the parameters of the disestablishment clause and challenges its legitimacy with regard to free public worship and support. Their respective views and visions of redemption inform their larger programs not unlike the views and visions of the various kinds of Christian fundamentalism. And both Habad and Satmar, whether they openly acknowledge it or not, seem to work under the assumption that America is, indeed, different. And for each, the nature of that difference informs the core of their fundamentalist approaches.

Notes

1. For more on his background, see Allan Nadler, "Politics and Piety: The Satmar Rebbe," *Judaism* 31 (Spring 1982): 135–52. More recently, see the hagiography culled from the eight-volume Hebrew *Moshian shel Yisrael:* Dovid Meisels, *The Rebbe: The Extraordinary Life and Worldview of Rabbeinu Yoel Teitelbaum*, trans. Y. Green (Published privately by Dovid Meisels, 2010).

2. See Michael Silber, "The Emergence of Ultra-Orthodoxy: The Invention of a Tradition," in *The Uses of Tradition: Jewish Continuity since Emancipation*, ed. Jack Wertheimer (New York & Jerusalem: Jewish Theological Seminary Press, 1992), 23–84.

3. See Jacob Katz, "Toward a Biography of the Hatam Sofer," in *Profiles in Diversity*, ed. Frances Malino and David Sorkin (Detroit: Wayne State University Press, 1998), 223–66.

4. On Sofer and his thought in relation to Jewish fundamentalism, see Jay Michael Harris, "'Fundamentalism': Objections from a Modern Jewish Historian," in *Fundamentalism and Gender*, ed. John Stratton Hawley (New York: Oxford University Press, 1994), 151–55.

5. This separatist mentality was forged in Mandate Palestine/Israel by R. Asher Zelig Margoliot whose community still exists today as the "Edah Haredit" in Jerusalem and other pockets in Israel. Yehudah Liebes analyzed the separatist nature of this group, comparing them to the Dead Sea Scroll sect of late antiquity. See Liebes, "The Ultra-Orthodox Community and the Dead Sea Scroll Sect" [Hebrew], *Jerusalem Studies in Jewish Thought* 3 (1982): 137–52.

6. See Jerome Mintz, *Hasidic People: A Place in the New World* (Cambridge: Harvard University Press, 1992), 7–43.

7. On the Katzner affair, which alleged Zionist collaboration with the Nazis to save Hungarian Jews, see Ben Hecht, *Perfidy* (New York: Milah Press, 1997).

8. George M. Marsden, *Fundamentalism and American Culture: The Shaping of Twentieth-Century Evangelicalism, 1870–1925*, 2nd ed. (New York: Oxford University Press, 2006), 51.

9. Shlomo Yaakov Gelbman, *Moshian shel Yisrael*, Kiryas Yoel, volume 7, 141–42.

10. R. Yoel Teitelbaum, *'Al ha-Geulah ve 'al ha- Temurah*, new ed. (Brooklyn, 2001), 20.

11. On the "great tribulation" so prominent in Revelation, see also Matthew 24:2: "Nothing will escape destruction. No stone upon a stone will not be thrown down."

12. Satmar's worldview as "demonological" is discussed as Norman Lamm's "The Ideology of Neturei Karta: According to the Satmarer Version," *Tradition* 13 (Fall 1971): 38–53. In his Hasidic teachings R. Moshe Teitelbaum describes how hatred between the righteous and the sinners is natural and a good thing because it keeps them apart. See R. Moshe Teitelbaum, *Yismakh Moshe*, vol. 2 (Jerusalem: Gross Brothers, 1989), 72c.

13. Shlomo Yaakov Gelbman, *Moshian shel Yisrael*, vol. 3, 247. This reflects the attitude initially proposed by R. Moshe Sofer (Hatam Sofer) regarding separating from religious innovators (reformers). See Sofer, *Kan Sofer* #39, 38, cited in Allan Nadler, "The War on Modernity of T. Hayyim Elazar Shapira of Munkacz," *Modern Judaism* 14 (October 1994): 234. "The general principle is to distance oneself from the innovators; we must form a strong fortress to assure that the community is divided into two camps, so that the separation between the Jews and the innovators will be as great as the distance between heaven and earth. Only in this way shall we succeed."

14. R. Moshe Teitelbaum, *Kuntres Hiddushei Torah,* 5 vols. (Brooklyn, 1962–1969), parshat Eikev 5717, cited in Meisels, *The Rebbe*, 159.

15. Emmanuel Sivan, "The Enclave Culture," in *Strong Religion: The Rise of Fundamentalisms around the World,* ed. Gabriel A. Almond, R. Scott Appleby, and Emmanuel Sivan (Chicago: University of Chicago Press, 2003), 44.

16. Richard Hofstadter notes in reference to certain forms of premillennialist fundamentalists in America that for them "history is a conspiracy, set in motion by demonic forces of almost transcendent power." See Hofstadter, *The Paranoid Style in American Politics, and Other Essays* (1952; repr. Cambridge: Harvard University Press, 1996), 29.

17. See *'Al Ha-Geulah ve 'al ha-Temurah,* 13. He often cited a teaching by R. Kalonymous Kalman Epstein of Cracow (1754–1823) on Deuteronomy13:2 about the signs of a false prophet. R. Epstein warned of the weakness of those who pursue a man simply because he ostensibly performed miraculous deeds. See R. Epstein, *Meor ve Shemesh* (Jerusalem, 1986), 2: 162d.

18. The belief that we are living through the "birth pangs of Messiah" was very much in line with R. Teitelbaum's teacher R. Hayyim Elazar Shapira of Munkacz. See Nadler, "The War on Modernity," 237 and 260 n26. See Teitelbaum, *'Al ha-Geula ve al ha-Temurah,* 3.

19. This is argued quite convincingly in Elliot R. Wolfson's *Open Secret* (New York: Columbia University Press, 2009) and, I think, points to a weakness in Samuel Heilman and Menahem Friedman's biography of R. Menahem Mendel entitled *The Rebbe* (Princeton: Princeton University Press, 2010).

20. See Mintz, *Hasidic People*, 198–215.

21. "What does Kiryas Joel Tell us about Liberalism in America?" (with Nomi M. Stolzenberg). *The Fritz Bamberger Memorial Lecture.* Hebrew Union College, November 21, 2006, 52, 53.

22. See Teitelbaum, *Vayoel Moshe* (Brooklyn: Joseph Dov Ashkenazi Books, 1961), "Essay on the Three Oaths." Cf. Aviezer Ravitzky, "Forcing the End: Radical Anti-Zionism," in *Messianism, Zionism, and Religious Radicalism*, trans. Jonathan Chipman (Chicago: University of Chicago Press, 1996), 40–78.

23. See Mintz, *Hasidic People*, 309–27.

24. David Myers and Nomi Stolzenberg, "What Does Kiryas Joel Tell Us about Liberalism in America?," 53. On R. Teitelbaum's relationship to America, see Allan Nadler: "At all his political rallies, a huge American flag covered the wall behind Teitelbaum's podium. He constantly urged his Hasidim to be upright citizens faithful to the statutes of American law." Nadler, "Politics and Piety," 147.

25. For some examples in English, see Aviezer Ravitzky, "Forcing the End: Radical Anti-Zionism"; Allan Nadler, "Politics and Piety"; Lamm, "The Ideology of Neturei Karta: According to the Satmarer Version"; and Zvi Jonathan Kaplan, "Rabbi Joel Teitelbaum, Zionism, and Hungarian Ultra-Orthodoxy," *Modern Judaism* 24 (May 2004): 165–78. Cf. David Sorotzkin, "Building the Earthy and Destroying the Heavenly: The Satmar Rebbe and the Radical Orthodox School of Thought" [Hebrew], in *The Land of Israel in Twentieth-Century Jewish Thought,* ed. Aviezer Ravitzky (Jerusalem: Yad Ben-Zvi, 2004): 133–67.

26. After a careful study of the work, the chief judge in the ultra-Orthodox rabbinical court, P. Pinhas Epstein, said, "*Vayoel Moshe* is something that I think I could have written. But *'Al ha-Geulah* where the Rebbe exposes the falsifications of the religious Zionists, is a feat that no one could duplicate." Cited in Meisels, *The Rebbe*, 516.

27. I choose to limit myself to the twenty-six page introduction because this is the only part of the book he wrote himself. The remainder of the book contains collected oral teachings that were edited by his students.

28. See Nadler, "Politics and Piety," 138. Nadler notes that Teitelbaum took this so seriously that he said that "a Jew ought to give his children up to Christian missionaries rather than

entrust them to the Zionist authorities." Satmar was also accused of stealing Yeminite children from Israel and bringing them to be raised in the Satmar community in America. Stories of Yeminite children being taken from their religious parents upon arrival in Israel in 1948 and raised in youth villages is a tragic part of early Zionist history and has lately received new attention as some of the children, now aging, have been telling their stories.

29. See Nadler, "Politics and Piety," 136 and 137, where he makes a similar, albeit not indentical, suggestion. On the analogy with Sabbateanism, see Nadler, 142.

30. It is certainly true that this theology of separatism remained operative in his community in Israel. But '*Al Ha-Geulah* was written in America and was part of a much larger ideological project undertaken by Satmar there. I am not aware of any analysis of the American context of this work or of any attempt to view it in light of R. Teitelbaum's American program.

31. France's loaning its fighter jets to the Israeli army in 1967 greatly helped the war effort. Ironically, it was the occupation, the consequence of the Six-Day War, that turned many of those same countries against Israel.

32. See, for example, *Strong Religion: The Rise of Fundamentalisms around the World*, ed. Gabriel A. Almond, R. Scott Appleby, and Emmanuel Sivan (Chicago: University of Chicago Press, 2003), and Bruce Lincoln, *Holy Terrors: Thinking about Religion after September 11* (Chicago: University of Chicago Press, 2003).

33. See, for example, Leon Wiesltier, "The Jewish Face of Fundamentalism," in the *The Fundamentalist Phenomenon: A View from Within, A Response from Without,* ed. Norman Cohen (Grand Rapids: Eerdmans: 1990), 192–98, and Jay Michael Harris, "'Fundamentalism': Objections from a Modern Jewish Historian," in *Fundamentalism and Gender*, ed. Hawley, 137–73.

34. The term has also recently been used to describe ultra-Orthodoxy in Israel. See Nurit Stadler, *Yeshiva Fundamentalism* (New York & London: New York University Press, 2009). Stadler, whose study focuses primarily on gender in Jewish ultra-Orthodoxy, acknowledges the contextual origin of the term but uses it, suggesting that it has already been deployed to describe various religious traditions. See pp. 6–10.

35. Recent studies of Habad, such as M. Avrum Ehrlich's *The Messiah of Brooklyn,* Sue Fishkoff's *The Rebbe's Army,* Jan Feldman's *Lubavitcher's as Citizens,* and Maya Katz's *The Visual Culture of Habad,* and Israel Rubin's *Satmar: Two Generations of an Urban Island* and the forthcoming book by David Myers and Naomi Stolzenberg, *American Shtetl: Politics and Piety in Kiryas Joel, New York,* are noteworthy exceptions to this rule. In fact I think the scholarship on these movements is in a crucial state of transition, with the American context becoming more of an integral part of the analysis.

36. See, for example, *Judaism despite Christianity: The 1916 Wartime Correspondence between Eugen Rosenstock-Hussey and Franz Rosenzweig,* new ed., ed. Eugen Rosenstock-Hussey (Chicago: University of Chicago Press, 2011); Leo Baeck, *The Essence of Judaism* (New York: Schocken Books, 1948); Baeck, "Romantic Religion," in *Jewish Perspectives on Christianity,* ed. F. Rothschild (New York: Crossroads, 1990), 56–91; Baeck, "Two World Views Compared," in *The Pharisees and Other Essays* (New York: Schocken Books, 1947), 125–48; and Martin Buber, *Two Types of Faith* (New York Macmillan, 1951).

37. For an insider's view of the Jewish Defense League, see Meir Kahane, *The Story of the Jewish Defense League* (New York: Chilton Books, 1975). On Birthright Israel, see Shaul Kelner, *Tours That Bind: Diaspora, Pilgrimage, and Israeli Birthright Tourism* (New York: New York University Press, 2010).

The Jewish Settler Movement and the Concept of Fundamentalism

Jean Axelrad Cahan

It is not clear when the term *fundamentalism* was introduced into the scholarly literature with regard to Judaism. It may have been in the wake of the 1979 Iranian Revolution, but it is also possible that the development of Khomeinism was itself in part a reaction to the Six-Day War of 1967.[1] Be that as it may, in this essay I argue that the term *fundamentalism,* when applied to the Israeli–Jewish context, and to the settler movement in particular, is of ambiguous explanatory value. A problem arises immediately in that the term is applied to groups that are diametrically opposed in important respects. Second, the term is both quite general, including features that belong to many groups, and quite specific in its inclusion of features that are peculiar to Christianity. This universal/particular character may be the result of different approaches to the topic of religious radicalism: social-scientific ones, which seek generalizations, versus explorations in the humanities, for example, in the history of religion, which tend to have a more phenomenological approach and are more sensitive to distinctiveness. In this regard the term *fundamentalism* may resemble the term *genocide*: while we may wish to include a certain case of mass death in the general category of genocide for public-policy or political purposes, what is most interesting and meaningful about that case may be precisely what we learn from disaggregating it from others. In my view the term *fundamentalism* is too disconnected from Jewish thought and history to provide an explication of the distinctive beliefs and motivations that seem to be at issue. But the term does point, in a hand-waving, shorthand sort of manner, to one salient characteristic shared by many religious activists, including Jewish ones: the belief that they have the capacity and the opportunity to be historical agents in a unique way, by undertaking actions that will hasten the movement of history toward a redeemed end-state. This leads them to question and sometimes outright deny the legitimacy and authority of the existing State of Israel and of international legal bodies. Ultimately, however, the term is too burdened by ideational and political biases to be a sound scholarly tool.

In this essay I concentrate on settlers in the West Bank, especially in the town of Hebron, which has a foundational role in Jewish religious history. Hebron is often seen as "the most militant Jewish ghetto" in the West Bank.[2] According to Ian Lustick, the Hebron settlers represent "a fundamentalist belief system so radically different from the liberal-humanitarian ethos shared by most Israelis and Americans that it can transform even the slaughter of defenseless people into a virtuous act."[3] It is a belief system, says Lustick, which is equivalent to Muslim fundamentalism in its power "to impel masses of believers to employ war, revolution and terrorism to meet their religious and political obligations."[4] Although the ultra-Orthodox sector of Israeli society is also often viewed as fundamentalist, especially by non-Israeli commentators, its political aims and methods are quite different from those of the settler movement. The ultra-Orthodox generally oppose territorial expansion into the West Bank (called "Judea and Samaria" by religious Jews) on religious grounds, namely, that this is a process that should be initiated and brought to fruition through divine power. Many of them opposed the foundation of the State of Israel for the same reason. Nonetheless, they view it as a religious obligation to maximize the level of religious observance in the land of Israel. The settlers, though often pious (but not all settlers are religious, as we shall see), are focused less on living up to an idealized, maximal level of observance or imposing religious observance on others than on the problem of redemption in a more cosmic, messianic sense, and their role in it. Thus while both groups challenge the authority of the state, and especially that of the Supreme Court of Israel, the problem each group poses for the Israeli political and legal systems is somewhat different. The ultra-Orthodox seek to narrow the space between religious and political institutions; they seek to alter the conditions and structures on which modern democratic states have been more or less based since the seventeenth century. The settlers, by contrast, are oriented toward Israel's future in what others regard only as a literal geographic sense but which to them is a "sacred space" sense and a fulfillment of divine promises. The settlers are more likely to use active resistance, and sometimes violence, in order to achieve their aims.

Before entering into a detailed discussion of the settler movement, it is useful to consider some of the features of the "standard model" of fundamentalism. Numerous scholars of Jewish fundamentalism have used the term freely without much concern for stating a precise definition. Thus although Lustick claims that "the Jewish fundamentalist movement, and the settlers in the territories who have been its spearhead, have 'emerged as the greatest obstacle to meaningful negotiations toward a comprehensive Arab-Israeli peace settlement,'"[5] fundamentalism is broadly equated with simple extremism of some vague type. Nor does his lengthy description of three key figures behind the religious ideology of Gush Emunim (the "vanguard" of part of the settler movement) advance the conceptual issue. Ehud Sprinzak lays out a conception of the "radical right" in Israel, giving a more nuanced account of historical developments in Israel. Sprinzak argues that the radical right includes about a half dozen political parties, in addition to Gush Emunim, which formed after the 1978 Camp David accords between Israel and Egypt. These parties have both secular and religious members and come out of both historical labor Zionism and religious Zionism. In Sprinzak's view, the radical right is ultra-nationalist and antidemocratic, but not fundamentalist and not fascist: "The characterization of the entire new camp as fundamentalist is untenable. Although Gush Emunim and Kach [probably the most extreme right-wing religious party of Meir Kahane] are very influential, they are only a small part of the new phenomenon. Most of the leaders of the radical right and the vast majority of its followers are not religious fundamentalists, and their support of the politics of the new extremists does not depend on their commitment to the literal texts of the Torah."[6] Like Lustick, Sprinzak does not explicitly explore definitions of fundamentalism, but it is evident from the text as a whole that he equates fundamentalism with scriptural literalism.

The Settlers and the Standard Model

Various overlapping lists of features have been presented, by which a group may be identified as fundamentalist and comparable to American Protestant fundamentalists in the early twentieth century, with whom the term originated. The list that follows is a compilation from those put forward by other scholars. Characteristic number 6 appears on everyone's list.[7]

1. Hostility to many aspects of modernity, especially reason and science as sources of authority.
2. Desire to recapture a way of life and set of religious traditions believed to have prevailed in pre-Enlightenment times.
3. Constituting an "enclave" culture, with tight religious and personal boundaries, and a sense of "besetment," from within which everyone on the outside is regarded with suspicion.
4. "Sacralization" of the enclave—the view that there is a special religious virtue pertaining to this religious minority, in choosing to belong to it and enduring its hardships.
5. Insistence on adherence to an essential or fundamental core of religious ideas and principles which have been selected from a much richer and more ambiguous context. Ignoring tradition of religious commentary and interpretation which developed over centuries. Thus, formation of a very crude theology with simplistic ideas of reward and punishment, among other things.

6. Literal readings of religious texts, and especially those containing the essential or core ideas and principles.
7. Belief in the inerrancy of sacred texts and their current "true" interpreters.
8. Treatment of women as second-class citizens, or outright oppression of them.
9. Having the view that the current historical conjuncture provides a unique opportunity for carrying out some or all of the essential ideas and principles, especially in the form of political action.
10. Willingness to use and justify violence in pursuit of certain sacralized aims.
11. Rejection of the existing nation-state and political system, whether democratic or not.

In my opinion, only two of the commonly mentioned features—numbers 6 and 9—apply substantially to religious settlers in the West Bank. Number 10—willingness to use violence—applies to some degree, but I do not think that it is clearly an integral part of the settler movement. Although number 3—constituting an enclave culture—seems a likely candidate, the sense of besetment among settlers may not be much greater than that of Israelis or Jews in general, including the Left, which favors giving up all settlements. Moreover, perhaps the most notorious settlement, Hebron/Kiryat Arba, is actually one of the most open in terms of accepting new residents, so the characteristic of having tight religious and social boundaries does not quite fit here. Number 4—sacralization of the enclave—also seems prima facie a plausible candidate, but I have not found evidence for it either in the scholarship or in person. The other criteria either apply only in a weak, partial sense or not at all. Therefore the concept of fundamentalism, or even the notion of "family resemblances" which has been widely mentioned in the literature on fundamentalism, seems unpromising in this context. A further problem is that, contrary to popular belief, the majority of settlers are not in fact religious: probably only 20 percent of all settlers are religious.[8] This has led certain scholars to the formulation of concepts of fundamentalism which are at bottom political, not religious; the concept has been stretched to the point of absurdity, for if fundamentalism is no longer a religious phenomenon, then their definitions have become completely detached from the project of comparison with the original Protestant version. Again, I shall have more to say about this below.

With regard to other criteria of fundamentalism, Jay Harris has argued persuasively that hostility to modernity, desire for return to a pre-modern way of life and oppression of women (1,2,8) will not withstand scrutiny. Briefly stated, Harris argues that the term "modernity" itself is too undifferentiated to be illuminating. Modernity has brought about an inextricable bundle of trends, both desirable and undesirable, but defining which is which is a highly subjective matter. We tend to apply the term "fundamentalist" as well as the terms "conservative" and "liberal" in non-neutral ways, depending on whether we approve or disapprove of the trend, idea or practice under consideration. Moreover, it is not at all obvious that women are suffering from the restrictions they accept.[9] Based on my own informal interviews with women settlers in the West Bank, it would seem that many have arrived at a combination of traditional religiosity with economic and political activism that is much closer to a feminist understanding of equality than it is to oppression.

Regarding characteristic 5—insistence on a fundamental core of ideas—we shall see the religious settlers are not radicals or innovators in the way that American Protestant fundamentalists might have been in the early twentieth century. They have not introduced a simplified, modified, or selective creed. It is true that they emphasize certain ideas, in particular the historical right of Jews to the land of Israel as it was defined in biblical times, and hastening the arrival of messianic times and final redemption. They do select biblical texts to justify claims to the land, and they do read these passages literally, but they are otherwise quite traditional, religiously speaking. Menachem Friedman has argued that on the ground of Gush Emunim's (the main religious settler organization) emphasis on redemption and the uniqueness and urgency of the historical conjuncture provided by the Six-Day War (1967), the settlers should be regarded as innovative religious radicals as opposed to conservative religious radicals, fundamentalists, or zealots.[10] But viewing oneself as the agent of divinely approved or transcendent historical and political forces is not distinctive of the settlers and should not be regarded as an innovation. Moreover, of those who are religious (many but not all from the Gush Emunim movement), their religious inspiration comes largely from the religious Zionist or Modern Orthodox tradition of textual interpretation and system of education. That is, they have been educated in a tradition which, while innovative to some extent in the early twentieth century in its acknowledgement of the value of secular learning, did not share Protestant fundamentalism's penchant for reductionism and literalist readings. On the contrary, religious Zionism, and especially the writing of the controversial Rav Avraham Yitzchak Kook, is permeated by the very complex interpretive habits of Talmudic study; in Kook's case there is the further influence of kabbalah, which gives much scope to metaphor and symbolism even as it enjoins concrete actions and practices in everyday life.

A brief history of the settlers in Hebron, commonly viewed as the most fanatical, is useful in order to substantiate the claim that the term *fundamentalism* does not provide much, if any, analytic insight. Since in my view the settlers are not religious radicals in either a conservative or an innovative sense, the question remains of what is motivating them to persist in their activities.

Brief History of Hebron

Although the settlement movement obviously extends beyond the town of Hebron, this may be a particularly useful case to examine because of the intense religious associations for Jews as well as Muslims and Christians. The town, more specifically the Cave of Machpelah, is viewed in each of these religious traditions as the burial place of the biblical patriarchs and matriarchs: Abraham, Isaac and Jacob, and their wives Sarah, Rebekah, and Leah. In addition, on the basis of the Hebrew Bible it is believed that Abraham resided there for some time and that King David was anointed and governed there for seven years. Religious Jews more oriented toward the mystical ideas of kabbalah hold that the cave is over or near the entrance to the Garden of Eden and that in the age of final redemption the divine presence may be encountered there. The book of Genesis gives an account of Abraham's purchase of the cave and the surrounding field in Hebron for Sarah's burial (Genesis 23:17–20). Jews lived there intermittently from biblical times onward, under both Christian and Muslim ruling authorities.

Beginning about 1260, with the restoration of Muslim rule by Saladin and his Mameluk soldiers, a small Jewish community, comprising perhaps twenty families, may have reestablished itself in Hebron. But in 1267 an edict prohibited non-Muslims from entering the Machpelah enclosure. Jews were forbidden to ascend any higher than the seventh step outside the southeastern wall, where they were permitted to squeeze messages through a space between stones. That prohibition would remain in place exactly seven hundred years.[11]

While a detailed exploration of the intervening centuries is beyond the scope of this essay, traveler reports dating from the nineteenth century suggest that during the first half of the century about 750 Jews, both Ashkenazic and Sephardic, lived there, alongside numerous Muslim families. The town specialized in glass manufacture as well as fruit production, especially production of grape sugar.[12] At that time Arab–Jewish relations in the town appear to have been fairly stable. The town and the whole Jerusalem district belonged to the Ottoman Empire; they were governed indirectly from Istanbul through notable local Arab families, who also served as tax collectors. In 1917 British forces occupied Hebron as part of the British Mandate of Palestine. During the following decade additional Jewish families arrived from Lithuania, seeking both to avoid the draft into the Lithuanian army and to contribute to the life of the religious community in Hebron. In August 1929 an attack carried out by some Arabs in Hebron—part of the ongoing struggle over immigration to Palestine by Jews since the latter part of the nineteenth century and of a more widespread series of attacks in other cities—caused the death and mutilation of sixty-seven Jews and severe injuries to many others. Women were raped, synagogues and Torah scrolls, some dating to the expulsion from Spain at the end of the fifteenth century, were desecrated or destroyed. On the third day of the attack, British soldiers, having failed to intervene effectively, transferred the remaining 484 Jews to Jerusalem. The immediate aftermath of this episode brought an ambivalent response from various Jewish organizations, and this perhaps carried over into the mixed signals of more recent Israeli governments. On the one hand there was concern over the fate of fellow Jews. On the other hand there was disdain for what was perceived to be the outdated, even medieval religiosity of the Hebron Jews. Today there is, in addition, a determination to maintain the reach of Israeli state law. At the time of the massacre, secular Zionist groups condemned the Hebron Jews for conducting themselves as the Jews of Kishinev did during the infamous 1903 pogrom—they had not resisted but had gone like sheep to the slaughter.[13] Subsequently, in the early 1930s, attempts were made by Jewish families to return to Hebron, but hostilities between Arabs and Jews made this practically impossible. From 1929 to the 1970s, the site of the centuries-old Avraham Avinu synagogue, a few hundred yards from the cave, became a combination of garbage dump and goat- and pigpen.[14]

In 1967 circumstances came together that both allowed and required Jews and Israelis to rethink their relationship to Judea and Samaria, that is, the lands to the north and southeast of Jerusalem, part of the West Bank, which were the heartland of biblical Israel. In May of that year Rabbi Zvi Yehuda Kook, son of Avraham Yitzchak Kook, former chief rabbi of Mandate Palestine and a leader of modern Orthodoxy, gave an impassioned speech calling for a reunification of the boundaries of the State of Israel with the boundaries of the biblical land: "They [the secular Zionists and the British] have divided my land. Where is our Hebron? Have we forgotten it? And where is our Schechem? And our Jericho?—Will we forget them?"[15] By the middle of June of the same year, after the Six-Day War, Israel was unexpectedly in military control over these areas as well as the Old City of Jerusalem and the Western Wall. With the surrender of the mainly Arab town of Hebron and the setting up of provisional Israeli military headquarters, Rabbi Shlomo Goren hurried to the Cave of Machpelah with a Torah scroll, *shofar* (ram's horn), and Israeli flag. It is possible that he was the first Jew in seven humdred years to go beyond the seventh step and enter the cave. Thus for religious Jews the Six-Day War, which resulted in an improbable military victory and recovery of so many holy sites, came to be seen not only as a sign of divine intervention, but a sign that a final redemptive process had begun as well. The war seemed to some to have created a unique opportunity—one that had not existed for thousands of years—to return to the spiritual and physical home of biblical ancestors. Although Hebron in particular had become in most respects a backwater, it had continued to have a religious significance for Jews that can hardly be overstated. Its reduced appearance could not detract from its religious meaning: "Hebron, isolated for nearly twenty years at the western edge of the Kingdom of Jordan . . . , had fallen on hard times. During the 1948 war, many Hebron Arabs—

educated and prosperous residents conspicuous among them—had fled to Jerusalem, to northern West Bank cities, or to Jordan. With the city cut off from Beersheva, its traditional marketing center to the south (but within the borders of Israel after 1948) those who remained behind, joined by war refugees, suffered severe economic deprivation."[16] But because of the religious and historical significance of Hebron, in April 1968 at Passover, Rabbi Moshe Levinger sought and obtained permission from the military authorities to bring a group of Jews to an Arab-owned hotel, later called the Park Hotel, to spend the first night of the holiday. When the first night and day were over, they refused to leave and indeed have remained in Hebron and the nearby town of Kiryat Arba ever since.

From 1968 to the present the number of Jewish settlers in the Hebron district has grown, and numerous violent clashes have taken place between the settlers and the surrounding Arab population. After a series of killings of Jewish yeshiva students in March 1994, the settler Baruch Goldstein went to the Muslim side of the Cave of Machpelah during prayer services and opened fire, killing twenty-nine worshippers and wounding many others. Today there are about five hundred Jews in the former Jewish quarter near the cave. The quarter consists essentially of one curtailed street and a very few side lanes, with a handful of low, small apartment buildings clustered around the reconstructed Avraham Avinu Synagogue. Approximately five thousand Jews live in Kiryat Arba a couple of miles away. The greater part of the city of Hebron is home to about one hundred sixty thousand Arabs. Wire fencing and police barricades separate the Jewish quarter from the rest of the city. Security arrangements in the rest of the city are divided between Palestinian and Israeli authorities according to the Hebron Protocol of 1997. Access to the Cave of Machpelah, which is on the main street of the old Jewish quarter, is governed by the protocol and provides for separate Muslim and Jewish entrances, a fixed schedule for when services may take place, and times when either Muslim or Jewish groups are to have exclusive use of the main halls of the structure.

The Jewish Underground

Although Levinger's group became an inspiration to other settlers, the impact of the conspiracies of the Jewish Underground movement (*machteret*) may ultimately have been greater, because it concentrated attention on threats to the authority of the Israeli state in a more drastic way. While government-authorized settlements throughout the West Bank receive considerable economic support, Israeli governments have from time to time shown willingness to dismantle settlements, even when under politically conservative leadership: Yamit in the Sinai in 1982, and Gush Katif and other settlements in Gaza in 2005. To this extent the settlement issue remains "manageable." The Jewish Underground, which included inhabitants of Hebron as well as settlers from other parts of the West

Bank, threatened to ignite a conflagration, literally and politically, involving the entire region. Members of the underground spent months planning and executing several violent actions, carrying out attacks on five Arab West Bank mayors and on the Hebron Islamic College. They saw themselves as retaliating against murders of Jews and incitement to violence against Jews by members of the college. The most dangerous component of the underground conspiracy, however, was a plan to blow up the Dome of the Rock and the Al-Aqsa Mosque on the Temple Mount in Jerusalem. The plot was discovered before it could be carried out; the conspirators were tried and given prison sentences ranging from life terms to terms of a few years.

The sheer existence of the underground has been interpreted by some as encapsulating the conflict between Israel's social democratic tradition on the one hand and the fundamentalist minority, the "redemptionist extravaganza of the settlers," on the other.[17] Lustick maintains that the underground had widespread support, as is evident from a petition launched to seek amnesty for members. He fails to note, however, that ultimately the petition did not succeed and that in fact there was not widespread support for it: "[An] attempt in the Knesset to pass an amnesty law to release those members of the 'Jewish Underground' still in jail failed by a substantial margin, even though Prime Minister Shamir voted in its favor."[18] Moreover, reading the memoir of one of the participants in the underground, Haggai Segal, with the expectation of finding some religious "redemptionist extravanganza," one may be surprised to find a considerable degree of political self-consciousness. Segal's account suggests that the conspirators were aware that their actions might be no different from ordinary murder and criminality and that the religious justification for their planned actions—national redemption—would only be discernible retrospectively. They also realized that since "no *halakhic* [religious law] authority can be found to lead our operation, there is no further need to consult with rabbis or *halakhic* scholars on anything to do with its execution." [19] But whatever their level of political consciousness, it is undeniable that many of the religious settlers explicitly or implicitly declare a willingness to jettison democratic methods and use all available means to further the goal of reclaiming all of the land of Israel (*eretz Yisrael*). Numerous statements by settler leaders, especially in Hebron, attest to this attitude:

> An Israeli state which limits or inhibits the settlement of Israel by its people loses . . . its moral and legal authority altogether.[20]
>
> The evacuation of a Jewish settlement constitutes an illegal order and soldiers must refuse to carry it out.[21]
>
> Our idea is very simple. The difference between one part of Eretz Yisroel and the other is an odd idea. The Jewish spirit, throughout all generations, was

> that there was a place called Eretz Yisroel. Not two parts, Eretz Yisroel and the other, Palestinian Autonomy.[22]
>
> Jewish immigration to Israel and settlement are beyond law. The settlers' movement comes out of the Zionist constitution and no law can stop it. . . . For those to whom the Bible and the religious prescripts are beyond the law there is no need to say anything further.[23]

There is also evidence to show, however, that other important religious leaders did not feel that the people were ready to be redeemed; they were not in a spiritual condition to re-ascend the Temple Mount, the resting place of the divine presence. Thus Rabbi Tau, a prominent figure in Mercaz HaRav (the religious Zionist center that educated several Gush Emunim leaders), viewed the situation this way: "[Since] Begin returned from Egypt [in the preparations toward the Camp David accords] and one hundred forty thousand people assembled in a public square in Tel Aviv and danced because peace was at hand, Rav Zvi Yehuda determined that 'the people are not with us' and therefore we must cease our efforts. The men of action of Gush Emunim didn't agree and our paths parted. There is no mandate for five thousand people [in the Sinai settlement of Yamit] to coerce the Jewish people to revolt against the spirit of the nation, and to erase that which was done publicly—this is a revolt against the kingship of God."[24]

Ian Lustick, Anita Shapira, and others have noted that there is a certain logic to the view expressed by Moshe Levinger in the quotation above. Many of the late-nineteenth-century Jewish immigrants to Palestine (not the long-standing inhabitants, such as those living in cities like Hebron) were also thought of, by themselves and others, as "settlers." They lived in small self-supporting communities in the swamps of the coastal plain and sometimes in the northern region closer to Lebanon. Shapira, whose general approach is one of seeking to understand the ideological superstructure, the "defensive ethos" of founding myths of the early Zionists, has analyzed the varying attitudes of those settlers to self-defense, abandonment of a settlement, and refusal to vacate a settlement in the face of Arab violence that can be seen as early as 1908. It becomes evident in the course of her nuanced work that there were profound conceptual and therefore political failings on the part of the Jews, under both Ottoman and British rule. But it is equally clear from her work that under no circumstances would the Arabs relinquish their central claim to exclusive possession of the entire land and the "prerogative of preventing Jewish immigration."[25] What this means for our problem is that while the post-1967 settlers pose an enormous problem for Israeli law and democracy, Israel itself came into existence partly through earlier legal, but nonetheless contested, settlement movements that had nothing to do with religious fundamentalism. The existence of a contested settlement in the Palestinian region is not a novel phenomenon, and it is primarily a political, not a religious, problem.

Are the Settlers Fundamentalists? And Is Fundamentalism Religious, Political, or Both?

Having cursorily reviewed the history of Hebron, what can we conclude about the settler movement there and its characterization as fundamentalist? From a secular point of view, bluntly stated by Prime Minister Yitzchak Rabin, the town of Hebron is of no significance, and it does not matter if a Jew has to enter Hebron with a Jordanian visa, that is, if Hebron is under Jordanian or Palestinian military and governmental control. But for religious Jews, Hebron is second only to the Western Wall in holiness; and it is vital to have ready access to it for religious services and simply to be in a sacred place where the divine presence is held to exist or may be anticipated. As we saw, access to the Cave of Machpelah by Jews was virtually nonexistent for seven hundred years. After the events of 1929, the remaining structures of the Jewish quarter were simply trashed. The fact is that under Muslim, Ottoman, British, and Jordanian (after 1948) sovereignty, access to a major holy site for Jews, and even the presence of Jews in the town where they had had a community historically, was either severely restricted or not tolerated at all. So at a minimum one issue that must enter into both the calculations of the settlers and of the Israeli government is whether, under any future agreement in which land is traded for peace, religious Jews could reasonably expect even the limited access and living conditions in Hebron that they now have under Israeli rule. There is the further question, though, of whether Jews' wish to return to Hebron in the sense of maintaining a small presence in the centuries-old Jewish Quarter near the cave, and a larger one in Kiryat Arba (which also has Biblical associations), is a problem about fundamentalism. While the insistence on maintaining a presence is problematic in several respects, it does not seem to be a problem about fundamentalism. The issues are legal, political, and perhaps military. The underlying question for the State of Israel and for the international community is about the legal and political merits of a claim of a right to worship at a holy site and the claim of a right to return to a place historically populated by both Jews and Arabs. It does not seem to me that as historical and religious claims there is anything distinctively "fundamentalist" about them. But I would be inclined to agree that the claims just mentioned might be fundamentalist in the language in which they are sometimes justified and through the methods by which they may be pressed. I therefore agree that is fair to say the following: "[Jewish] fundamentalists believe they can circumvent hermeneutic processes and gain direct access to the meaning of Scripture. They subordinate democratic values to the authority of their own leaders."[26] And: "A key element in Jewish fundamentalism, as in any fundamentalist movement, is the belief that its adherents possess special and direct access to transcendental truth, to a true vision of the future course of events, and to an understanding of what the future requires."[27]

"For Jewish fundamentalists, history is God's means of communicating with his people. Political trends and events contain messages to Jews that provide instructions, reprimands, and rewards. Political and historical analysis, properly undertaken, is equivalent to the interpretation of God's will.[28]"

Settlers' claims to ownership, not mere presence, based on a literal reading of the Bible, do not recognize the legal and political complexities of a situation in which biblical law, in the eyes of most other people, has at the very least been superseded by human international law; and their expressed willingness to trade democratic political processes for a "higher" religious goal, such as redemption of holy land, threatens to vitiate the distancing between religion and state that Westerners regard as essential and that took centuries to achieve. But for the purposes of this volume the problem is that this is not unique to religious groups, or to the West Bank settlers in particular. It could be argued that the idea of history being God's way of communicating with his people, or of some other transcendent force being at work in history and politics, is true of almost any movement with huge political ambitions, whether it has a religious dimension or not. For Lustick and others whom I shall mention shortly, this is ultimately the point: fundamentalism is at bottom a political phenomenon, a "political style" and not a religious phenomenon. Referring to the uncompromising nature of the settlers' stance, Lustick argues that "every movement or cause is potentially fundamentalist"[29] and adds that "it is absolutely necessary to separate it [the term *fundamentalism*] from its etymological origins relating to American Protestantism."[30] The settlers, ultra-Orthodox Jews, and whatever other religious maximalists there may be, are simply "the religious wing of the fundamentalist movement."[31] Lustick is accordingly led to label as fundamentalist two Jewish revolts of the Second Temple period. But as Shaye Cohen, an authority in the field, has shown, the motivations of all the participants were much more varied and complex than Lustick allows.[32] The primary terms of analysis have thus shifted from politicized messianic redemptionism to religiously framed nationalism or imperialism. If that is the case, there is no point to retaining the term *fundamentalism*; we can just use already existing notions in political science and history. Many historical and political actors, from Alexander the Great down to Hitler and Stalin, have had a sense that divine providence, historical forces, fate, or some other "higher" authority, inaudible to everyone else, is calling to them and justifying their actions. *Fundamentalism* does not seem to me to add anything by way of explanation of either religious worldview or political method. Why not just say that the religious Jewish settlers, who give literalist readings of certain texts but not others, are fundamentalist in this sense, and use certain fairly familiar political methods to further their religious aims: civil disobedience[33]; aggressive rhetoric; intermittent assaults and violence toward Arabs; legal and political challenges to the authority of the Israeli state? Nonetheless, the Jewish settlers are deemed by scholars such as Lustick both to be fundamentalists and to play a key role in the larger Arab-Israeli conflict, a situation worthy of further comment regarding the political interpretation of fundamentalism.

As indicated above, Ian Lustick, Ehud Sprinzak, Malise Ruthven, S. Eisenstadt, and other scholars have arrived at a view in which fundamentalism is primarily a political phenomenon utilizing religious language and resources to further essentially political ends. According to this view, religion is at most a useful set of myths that serves to mobilize "the masses" in certain extreme directions. "The heart of the fundamentalist project . . . lies not in religion but in the essentially modern agenda of extending or consolidating the power of the national state," writes Ruthven.[34] Indeed religion has become "secularized," by which he seems to mean infused with nationalism. "By deliberately exploiting eschatological expectations of the religious right, secular right-wing Zionists acknowledge that religion is a more effective ideological basis for expansionist aims than secular nationalism."[35] But it is difficult to find evidence for the claim that the secular right-wing nationalists in Israel seek to exploit the religious right. Rather, in the Knesset and in other forums, both groups form coalitions for various purposes, and not necessarily or only for a territorial expansionist agenda.[36] Sprinzak at one point uses the term *secular neo-fundamentalism* to refer to "older Israelis who are charmed by Gush Emunim's energy but are not Orthodox." As mentioned earlier, however, he eventually concludes that "most of the leaders of the radical right and the vast majority of its followers are not religious fundamentalists and their support of the politics of the new extremists does not depend on their commitment to the literal texts of the Torah" (20).

The notion that all settlers are fundamentalists, where fundamentalism is merely a religiously extreme ideology used to disguise expansionist nationalism/imperialism/fascism, that is, a political phenomenon, has led to an overemphasis on the religious settlers as an obstacle to a peace agreement in the larger Arab-Israeli conflict. But that conflict obviously long predates the actions of the Hebron settlers in 1968 or the formation of Gush Emunim in 1974; it involves questions about the armistice line from the war of 1947–1948; the right of return for both Arab and Jewish refugees and expellees; recovery of lost property; access to religious sites; security; water; and many other issues. It is simply not plausible to reduce the larger conflict to the topic of the West Bank settlers after 1967. Nonetheless Ruthven, Lustick, and others insist on the settlers' central role. Ruthven writes:

> It is the religious factor, not the conflict of interests, that threatens to prevent a settlement. On the Jewish side, orthodox settlers from Gush Emunim, the Bloc of the Faithful, absolutely refuse to abandon the West Bank settlements that

> are obstructing the peace process because, they insist, the land was originally given to the Children of Israel by God. They are duty bound to hold it in trust until the coming of the Messiah, whose return is imminent. On the Arab side, religious Palestinian Muslims refuse (unlike their more secular counterparts) to recognize the State of Israel, having declared the whole of Palestine (including the West Bank and the land occupied by Israel since its foundation in 1948) to be a *waqf*, or religious trust, which cannot be governed by non-believers.[37]
>
> People will respond positively to political messages couched in language associated with religion, because religion is thought of as "good." But the use of such language also tends to transcendentalize disputes, elevating them, as it were, from the mundane to the cosmic level. The result is that conflicts are absolutized, rendering them more intractable.[38]

While Ruthven is correct that the settlers see themselves as "God's agents" in hastening the redemption of the world, the idea of return to Eretz Yisrael, the emergence of a messianic era, and final redemption have always been part of Jewish religious thought. But at various times and places the messianic idea has been "privileged" by certain groups, to the great consternation of mainstream authorities. It was the achievement of the renowned scholar Gershom Scholem to bring this more to light. It seems to me that the religious settlers are just such a group: a minority of religious believers, otherwise quite traditional, who seize on the redemptive idea in Judaism and seek to actualize it in the present, challenging prevailing political authorities in the process. For thousands of years religious Jews did not have and could not have political, let alone expansionist-national, aspirations. The Six-Day War created what Marxist-Leninists would call a revolutionary moment, a historical opening for the normally quiescent redemptive idea, and some of the religious Zionists seized it. Moreover, it is not difficult to see in the history of the early stages of Zionism both an affinity with socialist revolutionary aims and style and a tendency to view the situation in Palestine as offering revolutionary potential. [39] In a sense the settlers could be as readily viewed as similar to a left-wing revolutionary vanguard as to a right-wing fascistic movement. Therefore I would say this about the religious settler movement: Extreme? In a political sense, yes, in that they insist upon the decisive character of the current historical conjuncture and are willing to engage in active, sometimes violent, resistance to Israeli and to international law. Out of the religious mainstream? Yes and no, because apart from the literal readings of biblical texts about land, and focus on final redemption, they are otherwise quite traditional and not maximalists as concerns religious observance. Religiously or politically innovative? No.

Before 1967 no one had any expectation that the West Bank could be reclaimed by Jews. Religious Zionists, including those trained at the Mercaz Ha Rav Yeshiva who later became leaders of the settler movement, such as Moshe Levinger in Hebron, were engaged in traditional text study, which is replete with metaphorical and symbolic interpretations, that is, not bent on literalist readings and not reducible to a relatively small number of religious ideas or principles in the way of early-twentieth-century American Protestant fundamentalism. Nor were the religious Zionists of the 1960s antimodern; they are not antiglobalization today. Rabbi Avraham Yitzhak Kook, head of the Mercaz Ha Rav Yeshiva, himself underwent considerable harassment within the Jerusalem community during the 1920s for the excessive modernism and liberalism of his ideas—for example, recommending physical exercise and acquaintance with secular learning. One of his principal works, *Orot* (Lights), reveals considerable influence of Western philosophy. Another figure who may be considered an early religious Zionist, Haim Hirschensohn (1857–1935), aimed to reconcile democracy and *halachah* (Jewish religious law). Among other things, Hirschensohn repeatedly stated the necessity of adhering to international laws and conventions in the process of settlement of Palestine.

In my opinion, then, the relationship between traditional Jewish religion, which includes a normally quiescent faith in the coming of a messianic era, and nationalist-expansionist aims is far from being a necessary one. To the extent that it exists in the form of aggressive religious Zionism, as in the person of Moshe Levinger, it is the result of a vast number of historical contingencies. The picture painted by Lustick, Ruthven, and others of large numbers of Jewish "fundamentalists" cynically using religious ideas and language to further their nationalist or imperialist aims and to block regional peace is simply not accurate. While the religious settlers constitute a vociferous and especially committed minority within the settler movement as a whole, there is nothing to be gained in understanding their claims, their motives, or their behavior by labeling them fundamentalist. On the contrary, insofar as it has become a term applied broadly and rather indiscriminately to the political right or used to refer to groups deemed to be the principal threat to peace in the Middle East, the word *fundamentalist* has lost much of its potential explanatory power in the study of religion and serves mainly to obscure the complexities of both political and religious realities.

Notes

I would like to thank Rabbi Jonathan Gross and Mrs. Esti Herscowitz, for guiding me through various settlements in the West Bank.

1. The topic of the spreading of the term *fundamentalism* to religions other than Christianity is raised by William O. Beeman, "Fighting the Good Fight: Fundamentalism and Religious Revival," in *Anthropology for the Real World,* ed. Jeremy MacClancy (Chicago: University of Chicago Press, 2001).

2. Jeffrey Goldberg, "Among the Settlers: Will They Destroy Israel?" *New Yorker,* May 31, 2004, 5.

3. Ian S. Lustick, *For the Land and the Lord: Jewish Fundamentalism in Israel.* NewYork: Council on Foreign Relations, 1988. Transcribed for Columbia International Affairs Online edition, May 1998. Reissued by the Council on Foreign Relations in 1994. Preface to the 1994,

edition, p.1. Main text retrieved from www.sas.upenn.edu/penncip/lustick; preface retrieved from http://www.sas.penn.edu/penncip/lustick/preface.html, 1 October 2012.

4. Ibid.

5. Ibid, preface, 3.

6. Ehud Sprinzak, *The Ascendance of Israel's Radical Right* (Oxford: Oxford University Press, 1991), 20.

7. Malise Ruthven, *Fundamentalism: The Search for Meaning* (Oxford: Oxford University Press, 2001); John S. Hawley and Wayne Proudfoot, introduction to *Fundamentalism and Gender*, ed. John Stratton Hawley (New York: Oxford University Press, 1994), especially pp. 17–23; Gabriel A. Almond, R. Scott Appleby, and Emanuel Sivan, *Strong Religion: The Rise of Fundamentalisms around the World* (Chicago: University of Chicago Press, 2003); Laurence J. Silberstein, "Religion, Ideology, Modernity," in *Jewish Fundamentalism in Comparative Perspective: Religion, Ideology and the Crisis of Modernity*, ed. Silberstein (New York: New York University Press, 1993); Hava Lazarus-Yafeh, "Contemporary Fundamentalism in Judaism, Christianity, Islam," *Jerusalem Quarterly* 47 (Summer 1988); Raphael Israeli, *Muslim Fundamentalism in Israel* (London: Brassey's UK, 1993), 11.

8. Cf. Ehud Sprinzak, "The Politics, Institutions and Culture of Gush Emunim," in *Jewish Fundamentalism in Comparative Perspective*, ed. Silberstein, 136; Goldberg, "Among the Settlers," 5; David Weisburd, *Jewish Settler Violence: Deviance as Social Reaction* (University Park: Pennsylvania State University Press, 1989), chapter 3; Charles S. Liebman, "Jewish Fundamentalism and the Israeli Polity," in *Fundamentalisms and the State: Reclaiming the Sciences, the Family, and Education*, ed. Martin E. Marty and R. Scott Appleby (Chicago: University of Chicago Press, 1993), 73.

9. Jay M. Harris, "'Fundamentalism': Objections from a Modern Jewish Historian," in *Fundamentalism and Gender*, ed. Hawley, chapter 6. See also Deborah Bernstein, *The Struggle for Equality: Urban Women Workers in Pre-State Israeli Society* (New York: Praeger, 1987), and David Harrington Watt, "Jews, Fundamentalism, and Supersessionism," *Fides et Historia* 40 (Winter–Spring 2008): 1–23.

10. Menachem Friedman, "Jewish Zealots: Conservative vs. Innovative," in *Jewish Fundamentalism in Comparative Perspective*, ed. Silberstein, 161.

11. Jerold S. Auerbach, *Hebron Jews: Memory and Conflict in the Land of Israel* (Lanham, Md.: Rowman & Littlefield, 2009), 36.

12. Information on Hebron in the nineteenth century falls within the contested field of the history of Palestinian national self-consciousness. The basic facts mentioned here can be found in Baruch Kimmerling and Joel S. Migdal, *The Palestinian People: A History* (Cambridge: Harvard University Press, 2003); James Parkes, *Whose Land? A History of the Peoples of Palestine* (Harmondsworth, U.K.: Penguin Books, 1970), 227.

13. Auerbach, *Hebron Jews*, 74.

14. Ben Zion Tavger, *My Hebron*, translated Pnina Tadmor (Hebron, 2009). According to this autobiographical account, Ben Zion Tavger was a physicist and dissident from the Soviet Union who immigrated to Israel in the 1970s and spent much of the remainder of his life clearing out the site of the Avraham Avinu Synagogue with the help of a small number of Arabs and Jews.

15. Quoted in Auerbach, *Hebron Jews*, 80.

16. Ibid., 83.

17. Lustick, *For the Land and the Lord*, introduction.

18. Erik Cohen, "The Changing Legitimations of the State of Israel," in *Israel: State and Society, 1948–1988*, ed. Peter Y. Medding (Oxford: Oxford University Press, 1989), 164, n. 34.

19. Haggai Segal, *Dear Brothers: The West Bank Jewish Underground* (Woodmere, N.Y.: Beit Shamai Publications, 1988), 137.

20. Rabbi Jacob Ariel, writing in the settler newspaper *Nekuda*, cited in Auerbach, *Hebron Jews*, 173.

21. Rabbi Shlomo Goren, cited in Auerbach, *Hebron Jews*, 173.

22. Rabbi Moshe Levinger, quoted in Ellen Cantarow, "Gush Emunim: The Twilight of Zionism?" *Media Monitors Network*, February 27, 2001.

23. Rabbi Ben Nun, quoted in Ruthven, *Fundamentalism*, 161.

24. Cited in Eliezer Don-Yehiya, "The Book and the Sword: The Nationalist Yeshivot and Political Radicalism in Israel," in *Accounting for Fundamentalisms: The Dynamic Character of Movements*, ed. Martin E. Marty and R. Scott Appleby (Chicago: University of Chicago Press, 1994), 277.

25. Anita Shapira, *Land and Power: The Zionist Resort to Force, 1881–1948* (Oxford: Oxford University Press, 1992), 115.

26. Hava Lazarus-Yafeh, cited in Silberstein, "Religion, Ideology, Modernity," in *Jewish Fundamentalism in Comparative Perspective*, ed. Silberstein, 7.

27. Ian Lustick, "Jewish Fundamentalism and the Israeli-Palestinian Impasse," in *Jewish Fundamentalism in Comparative Perspective*, ed. Silberstein, 112.

28. Ibid., 113.

29. Lustick, *For the Land and the Lord*, chapters 1, 3.

30. Lustick, "Jewish Fundamentalism," in *Jewish Fundamentalism in Comparative Perspective*, ed. Silberstein, 105.

31. Lustick, *For the Land and the Lord*, chapters 2, 3.

32. Ibid. Shaye J. D. Cohen, *From the Maccabees to the Mishnah* (Philadelphia: Westminster, 1989), chapter 2.

33. A leader of the far-right movement Zo Artzeinu, Moshe Feiglin, aligns himself strongly with Martin Luther King's movement and tactics of civil disobedience in his memoir *Where There Are No Men: Zo Artzeinu's Struggle against the Post-Zionism Collapse* (Jerusalem: Published by Jewish Leadership, 1999).

34. Ruthven, *Fundamentalism*, 187.

35. Ibid., 159

36. Cf. Liebman, "Jewish Fundamentalism and the Israeli Polity."

37. Ruthven, *Fundamentalism*, 3–4.

38. Ibid., 166–67.

39. Cf. Shapira, *Land and Power*, 70 and passim.

The Concept of Global Fundamentalism

A Short Critique

Simon A. Wood

The concept of fundamentalism as a global rather than merely a Protestant phenomenon has been a controversial topic for at least three decades, particularly since the publication of the Fundamentalism Project (edited by Martin E. Marty and R. Scott Appleby) in the 1990s. Yet one point acknowledged by most scholars who write about fundamentalism is that the concept is—or has been—somewhat vague. Scholars have disagreed, however, on whether it is necessarily or inherently so. Very broadly speaking, fundamentalism is defined in terms of resistance to modern "threats" or opposition to modern secularism. Beyond that, it is difficult to pin down precisely what the words *fundamentalism* and *fundamentalist* mean, and this difficulty is the object of this book. Several scholars have observed that the general designation of fundamentalists as religiously committed people who uphold "fundamentals" is not, in itself, particularly useful, or that it is premised upon what may appear to be a rather circular argument: fundamentals are the doctrines or practices that fundamentalists uphold; fundamentalists are people who uphold fundamentals. This differs from the more limited and specific designation of fundamentalism as a subset of Protestantism. In the early twentieth century fundamentalists can be identified as a group of North American Protestants who upheld certain fundamentals that, in their view, modernists were forsaking. These include biblical inerrancy and adherence to what was taken as the literal meaning of certain critical passages, such as those referring to the resurrection. Fundamentalists certainly did not read *all* of the Bible literally. In this context what is signified by *fundamentalism* is reasonably clear: a trend within American Protestantism embodied by those who held to such principles as set out in a series of pamphlets entitled *The Fundamentals.* Several decades later, in the 1970s, *fundamentalism* identified the movement led by Jerry Falwell and like-minded Protestants. At that time Falwell described himself as a fundamentalist.[1]

The considerably more ambitious concept of fundamentalism as a global phenomenon can be traced to the late 1970s or early 1980s. At a 2009 conference marking the thirty-year anniversary of the Iranian Revolution, historian Evrand Abrahamian observed that early Western reports on Khomeini's rise referred to him as other than a fundamentalist.[2] The notion that a Muslim could be fundamentalist had yet to gain much currency. Fairly quickly, however, Western observers began to suggest that *fundamentalist* was an appropriate term with which to label Khomeini and other leaders of what became known as the Islamic revival. There are two important corollaries to this development. First, whereas Khomeini's unforeseen success had rather dramatically caught Western observers off guard, fundamentalism was seen as a concept that might help people to understand it. Reviewing the Fundamentalism Project, Earle H. Waugh noted that Khomeini "forced the hand of the academic establishment."[3] In view of the Imam's achievement many came to feel that prevailing theories on religion's role in modern society—the general outlines of secularization theory—were in need of some revision. Three decades on, Khomeini's catalyzing influence endures.[4] The concept of fundamentalism, then, has significant implications for wider issues concerning religion's station in the modern world. Second, the description of Khomeini as a fundamentalist implied that there was some manner of familial relationship between the Imam and Protestant fundamentalists such as Falwell. That is, differences notwithstanding, if the same word labeled the two, there must be substantive similarities between their agendas. If Khomeini was an Islamic fundamentalist, then he stands in relation to Islam as does Falwell in relation to Protestantism. This notion of similarity has been elaborated in the Fundamentalism Project, and more recently in books by Gabriel A. Almond, R. Scott Appleby, Emmanuel Sivan, Malise Ruthven, Karen Armstrong, and others.

These authors argue for similarity through the rubric of "family resemblances." The case they advance is straightforward: however different Protestant and Islamic fundamentalists may be, they can be shown to belong to the same "extended family," one that also includes Jews, Hindus, Buddhists, Confucianists, and others.[5] A helpful summary of this case is provided in *Strong Religion: The Rise of Fundamentalisms around the World* by Almond, Appleby, and Sivan. This book outlines the genealogy and properties of fundamentalism, updating the Fundamentalism Project and condensing its five heavy volumes into less than three hundred pages. It posits such fundamentalist family resemblances as a dualistic black-and-white "enclave culture," reification, selective retrieval and fortification of tradition, the upholding or idealizing of a "sacred past," and belief in scriptural inerrancy (other works on fundamentalism refer not merely to inerrancy but to fundamentalist literalism).[6] Appendices tabulate degrees of subscription—high, medium, low—to various of these notions, providing a measurement for membership in fundamentalism's extended family. The notion of family resemblances undergirds the very significant claim that *fundamentalism* has become or is becoming an important and extremely useful umbrella term. As such, it stands alongside other useful umbrella terms such as *capitalism, socialism,* and *nationalism.*[7]

With an umbrella term one may identify and label important structural similarities, such as that between African and Latin American socialism. In the same manner the term *fundamentalism* enables identification and labeling of similarity with regard to global trends within various religions. This greatly facilitates the task of comparing recent developments within Christianity, Islam, and Judaism, if not world religions generally. Again, if we describe Khomeini as a fundamentalist, we are claiming that he has something important in common with certain Protestants, Jews, and others. The extent to which this notion has taken hold is reflected in a great variety of scholarly and journalistic writing, and in the adoption of dictionary and encyclopedia definitions of fundamentalism. For example, in the Oxford University Press Very Short Introductions series one finds Ruthven's thoughtful *Fundamentalism: A Very Short Introduction* alongside similar introductions to capitalism, socialism, nationalism, terrorism, and many other important historical phenomena. Ruthven deems the case for family resemblances compelling.[8] In the view of this leading publisher, then, fundamentalism is an identifiable and discrete phenomenon of unquestionable importance.

At the same time, and notwithstanding the currency it has gained, the concept has had its critics. Those who deem it unhelpful have advanced at least three general types of criticism. First, it is suggested that it is simply too vague to be useful, that the term labels a phantom or is a dead metaphor.[9] In other words the signifier lacks a concrete signified; the term does not label a discrete reality. In this vein Jay Michael Harris finds that because the term has been applied to so many diverse forms of Judaism (for example, ultra-Orthodox, Zionist, anti-Zionist), it creates more confusion than clarity.[10] Second, the term has been criticized as offensive. That is, some find that *fundamentalism* has effectively become a term used to label people with unreasonable, extreme, or disagreeable views. This in turn creates problems of definition as there is no consensus, scholarly or otherwise, on what constitutes an unreasonable view. The strong association of fundamentalism with unreasonableness or extremism is likely reflected in how few people today describe themselves as fundamentalists. This is the case even among American Protestants, the community where one might expect the term to be most applicable and least problematical. For instance, Bob Jones University does not presently identify itself as a fundamentalist institution. Third, critics have found that the concept is too shot through with specifically Christian tropes to be meaningfully applied to other religions. It is suggested that while all religiously motivated people act upon some set of fundamental principles while discarding others, the specific "fundamentals" of Protestant fundamentalism are quite different to the principles underlying, for instance, what has been called Islamic, Hindu, or Buddhist fundamentalism.

In light of these issues some critics have suggested discarding the term, while others have suggested replacing it with another. For Islamic cases many have found the term *Islamism* (or *political Islam*) preferable.[11] One of the more promising broad alternatives is Bruce Lincoln's "maximalism," which he counterpoints with the "minimalism" of the post-Enlightenment West. Lincoln argues that terms *maximalism* and *fundamentalism* are not at all synonymous. His proposal is not one of merely replacing a vague and contestable term with another that is equally vague and contestable.[12]

Fundamentalism: The Case for Careful and Flexible Use

Advocates of the concept have acknowledged and grappled seriously with such dissenting views and determined that it is substantive and rigorous enough to withstand them. Some argue that nothing is gained by replacing the term with alternatives such as *Islamism* or *political Islam*, or that alternatives may be misleading.[13] Most notably, where critics have deemed the concept vague, advocates, while acknowledging certain difficulties in its application, have deemed it flexible. They have stressed that it is a broad rubric and that individuals and movements need not fully exhibit every fundamentalist characteristic to be described as such. In other words advocates find critics understanding the concept in overly rigid terms. In the case of Asian religions, however, critique has led to or coincided with a partial retreat from the thesis that the concept applies globally. In particular, the critique that the concept is too deeply embedded in one tradition (Protestantism) or set of traditions (Abrahamic) to be transferable to others is not easily rebutted. For instance, Asian religions lack clear analogs, if any, to Protestant eschatology. Perhaps more significant, Protestant fundamentalism is specifically concerned with scripture: the very term derives from the "fundamental doctrines" set down in God's revelation. Yet, broadly speaking, Hinduism and Buddhism lack an equivalent or similar conception of revelation: truth is not revealed at a given point in time but exists to be discovered. The Buddha did not receive revelation but discovered truth, as had innumerable Buddhas before him. More generally, Hindus and Buddhists do not regard scripture or the notions of inerrancy or literalism in Protestantlike terms. This is seen in what is may be the primary candidate for a Buddhist fundamentalism, Sinhala Buddhism. The Sinhala stance toward scripture is different from that of Protestants in general and Protestant fundamentalists in particular. The primary Sinhala text, the Mahavamsa, is neither canonical nor, by a strict definition, scriptural.[14] Applying the concept here, then, might necessitate something considerably more complicated and complicating than flexible use. Such lack of fit has led some to downplay, if not discard, the idea that fundamentalism takes Asian forms. In this vein Almond, Appleby, and Sivan distinguish "pure"

Abrahamic fundamentalisms from "mixed," "synthetic," or "ethnonationalist" Hindu and Buddhist fundamentalisms. Appleby further comments: "Hinduism and Buddhism do not readily lend themselves to the political dynamics of fundamentalism."[15] In sum, at least some advocates acknowledge that, at a minimum, the concept works less well for Asian religions than for Abrahamic religions.

For advocates, this refining might be seen as one instance of a more general process whereby difficulties surrounding the term are resolved over time. This takes us to the heart of the issue: "As Martin E. Marty has noted, some who attack the word fundamentalism will use words like 'capitalism,' 'socialist,' 'nationalist,' 'revolutionary,' 'liberal,' 'conservative,' all of which were born in specific circumstances before they were translated into such general 'umbrella' terms. Careful scholars and publics will take care to see exactly how the various fundamentalisms invest their antisecular and antimodernist movements with meanings."[16] Marty's suggestion, here endorsed by Almond, Appleby, and Sivan, and elsewhere by Ruthven, is that when fundamentalism recently appeared on the scene it was a new phenomenon. As such, it needed "a new name." Thus, to deny the term because of its recent coinage or its lack of analogs in other languages would be "silly."[17] The implication here is that umbrella terms such as *fundamentalism, capitalism,* and *socialism* all undergo a comparable evolution. Initially obscure or applying to a specific set of circumstances, they gradually acquire a broad sphere of application and become powerful "comparative constructs," constructs that enable identification or differentiation of patterns of behavior: family resemblances.[18] There is, according to this view, only one substantive difference between fundamentalism and less controversial umbrella terms. Where all such terms follow a path from linguistic obscurity to general acceptance, *fundamentalism* is simply at an earlier stage of the process than the likes of *capitalism, socialism,* or *nationalism.* After all, the idea of global fundamentalism is, historically speaking, very recent indeed. Hence, to reject it because of its original embeddedness in one set of (American Protestant) circumstances, or because it remains to date somewhat vague, would be shortsighted. Carefully used, the term can facilitate illuminating and valuable research. The argument here is that the term's present-day currency, such as it is, provides a sufficient basis for its continued usage and suffices for faith in its potential. Provided scholars are careful, it can be expected that, in time, *fundamentalism* will become as uncontroversial as *capitalism, socialism,* or *nationalism.* As the juncture at which difficulties raised by critics are fully resolved lies at an unspecified future point, this argument requires patience together with care. In the immediate timeframe it may prove effectively untestable, if not immunized from critique.

The Case against the Concept of Global Fundamentalism

I find that the arguments of Marty et al., while stimulating, are not fully satisfactory. The case for care, flexibility and, by implication, patience is insufficient.

I take as my starting point an observation by Daniel Martin Varisco. Where Marty finds that we can better understand *fundamentalism* by setting the term alongside *capitalism, socialism* and *nationalism,* Varisco suggests that we can better understand it by setting it alongside *Mohammedanism.* This points us toward a very different kind of precedent.[19] As a signifier or broad label, *Mohammedanism* has largely fallen into disuse due to problematics similar to those presently found with *fundamentalism.* It is now generally considered misleading if not simply offensive (the *American Heritage Dictionary* labels it "n. offensive"). The signifier does not align well with what it would signify. As a term applied to one religion only, *Mohammedanism* is not analogous to *fundamentalism* in every respect. Yet its history nevertheless demonstrates that a term's currency at a given juncture does not, in itself, foreshadow its ongoing usage or definitive establishment. A similar observation can be made regarding *primitive religion,* another once popular rubric that has largely fallen into disuse. Thus, *fundamentalism* might presently lie on a trajectory previously traced by *Mohammedanism* or *primitive religion,* rather than one previously traced by *capitalism, socialism,* and *nationalism.* Efforts to disestablish the term are likely to be an uphill struggle, and far more works presently argue in favor of it than against it. But the precedents of *Mohammedanism* and *primitive religion* suggest that they may nevertheless be worthwhile.

Following a brief discussion of the case for disestablishment, Almond, Appleby, and Sivan defend the concept thus: "When they are carefully defined, comparative constructs help us differentiate patterns of activism. They reflect and systematize the findings of case studies in order to build a cross-cultural vocabulary useful for making structured comparisons of movements and groups. *'Fundamentalism,' in this usage, refers to a discernible pattern of religious militance by which self-styled 'true believers' attempt to arrest the erosion of religious identity, fortify the borders of the religious community, and create viable alternatives to secular institutions and behaviors.*"[20] I take the italicized sentence as a representative definition of global fundamentalism. The key phrase is *discernible pattern.* That is, as the concept is applied beyond its origins one must be able to see how Islamic and Jewish (if not Hindu and Buddhist) religious militancy follow the same general pattern as Protestant fundamentalism: all must be shown to belong to the same family. Several other features of fundamentalism supplement this basic definition. Fundamentalists are related to each other through their common rejection of modern secularism. Further, their struggle against it eclectically incorporates past and present, tradition and modernity. Specifically, fundamentalists selectively retrieve and fortify religious fundamentals while also embracing opportunities provided by new technologies and at least some aspects of modern ideology. In other words, as advocates take pains to emphasize, fundamentalism is oversimplified and misrepresented when it is described as a simple rejection of modernity. Rather, it is both a reaction to *and* a child of modernity: it is not restorationism, primitivism, or an ultraconservative isolationism. "Sacred past" notwithstanding, fundamentalists do not seek a turning back of the clock.

The general hypothesis here, I find, is reasonably clear, although the category of those who practice selective retrieval and fortification can scarcely be limited to those who are identified as fundamentalists.[21] For instance, it is very difficult to conceive of how Islamic modernism (for example, as represented by Muhammad Abduh and Rashid Rida) is not to a considerable extent an exercise in selective retrieval and fortification. Beyond this concern, I would like to investigate whether what is called Islamic fundamentalism conforms to what the concept of global fundamentalism would lead us to expect. I find that it fails to conform. In other words, I find that what is called Islamic fundamentalism is neither shown nor seen to belong to the same "pattern of activism" as Protestant fundamentalism. It does not share a "family resemblance" with it. The two phenomena, rather than representing analogous or familial manifestations of a global trend, are quite different. I illustrate my case by reference to the discourses of Mawlana Mawdudi and Khomeini.[22] The concept's advocates frequently, if not invariably, reference or describe the two as Islamic fundamentalists. We have already noted the ayatollah's specific pertinence. Mawdudi, while lacking Sayyid Qutb's profile in the West, is arguably the most influential Sunni Muslim intellectual to be labeled a fundamentalist.[23]

What is at stake here is not only the concept of an Islamic fundamentalism, but the global concept per se. The retreat from world religions (fundamentalism is a feature of all religions) to Abrahamic religions (fundamentalism is a feature of Abrahamic religions) heightens Islam's relevance, already of historic significance. One might be able to relinquish Asian cases partially yet retain a global concept. After all, Christians and Muslims alone account for a significant proportion of humanity. But if Islam is removed from the picture the global thesis is void. While, to be sure, Mawdudi, Khomeini, and their movements in no way circumscribe what is viewed as Islamic fundamentalism, they may certainly be taken as seminal representatives of it. My argument thus develops as follows: if the two cannot be shown to fit a paradigm indicative of family resemblance with other fundamentalists, the concept of an Islamic fundamentalism is called into question. This, in turn, undermines the concept of global fundamentalism as a broad signifier or umbrella term. The effort to employ such terms is highly worthwhile, but they are helpful only up to a point. They are unhelpful in cases wherein preoccupation with similarity and pattern effectively becomes inadvertence to difference. Where the discrepancy between signifier and signified entails stretching the former far beyond what "flexible use" would allow, if not simply deforming it, the exercise becomes dubious.

My investigation, then, concerns the ways in which the discourses of Mawdudi and Khomeini fail to conform to the concept. First, there is scant evidence for literalism, reification of tradition, or selective retrieval and fortification of tradition in a fundamentalist vein. Mawdudi and Khomeini decisively rejected literalism. Take for instance Mawdudi's Quran commentary and explication of the Quranic reference to its *mutashabihat,* or allegorical content.[24] Likewise, Khomeini's embrace of mystical unveiling and Imami gnosis or esoteric (*marifah, irfan*) as complementing exoteric (*ilm*) hardly lend to characterizations of literalism (on this point, see also the essays by Lynda Clarke in this volume). As regards the two's upholding of Quranic inerrancy (frequently conflated and confused with scripturalist or Quranic literalism), this is an unexceptional and normative Islamic doctrine. As such, any individual's embrace of it in no way suffices for identification of that person as a fundamentalist or differentiation from the wider community. I am certainly not alone in suggesting that by that measurement all (or very nearly all) Muslims would be fundamentalists, in which case the term lacks meaningful specificity.

As regards reification of tradition, the evidence is also clear, and here careful investigation produces results opposite to conformity with the concept. Take for instance Khomeini's seminal doctrine, guardianship of the jurist. This is premised upon Imamic or juristic authority to supersede tradition. The divinely revealed law or shariah, far from being reified or frozen, may be overruled by authority intrinsic to an individual. Further, this doctrine represents novelty established far more than tradition selectively retrieved and fortified. It is based to a considerable extent on Khomieni's idiosyncratic reading of tradition, one not easily explicated in terms of global trends or analogs. By my reading, his conception simply does not stand in relation to Shiite tradition as do the "fundamentals" emphasized by American Protestants in relation to Christian tradition. Khomeini was criticized by his co-religionists for advocating an idea deemed novel, unsupported by tradition, or strange. While those who disagreed with American fundamentalists' reading of tradition found much to criticize therein, it is unlikely that they would have been perplexed by ideas such as Trinity, biblical inerrancy, virgin birth, substitutionary atonement, physical resurrection, and the millennium. Further, it is also unclear that Sunni analogs to Khomeini's claim that the ruler-jurist may override the shariah on the basis of his intrinsic personal authority would be easily identifiable. Such lacks of alignment call the notion of a discernible pattern or family resemblance into question.

These significant concerns noted, I focus on the claim that the engine driving fundamentalism is resistance to modern secularism, resistance again following a discernible and global pattern. I suggest that the agendas of Mawdudi and Khomeini were substantively formed and framed by endemic conditions. They do not embody Sunni and Shiite manifestations of global fundamentalism. The distinctive features of their movements, I find, originate more in the distinctive environments of the subcontinent and Iran than in the rejection of ideas originating in Europe's enlightened cafes. I am not suggesting that the effort to identify or posit familial relationships or global analogs through umbrella terms is not worthwhile. Rather, I suggest that no relationships or analogs are found that are captured at all well by the term *fundamentalism.* Alternatives are, at minimum, less problematical. To be sure, Mawdudi and Khomeini veneered their programs with rhetoric that, at least initially, sounds very fundamentalist. Yet this packaged discourses that diverge from the concept far more than conform to it. To be sure, both combined what they saw as the best of tradition with the best of modernity. Yet this feature, as such, is insufficient to differentiate them from other religious reformers or to distinguish them as fundamentalists.

Mawdudi coined many of the tropes that subsequently came to characterize what has been identified as fundamentalist discourse. In Vali Nasr's wording, Islamic fundamentalism is Mawdudi's "brainchild."[25] Almond, Appleby, and Sivan note Mawdudi's establishment of fundamentalism's "religiopolitical idiom."[26] This might be encapsulated by his revision of the notion of pagan ignorance, later adopted by Qutb. Where normatively *al-jahiliyyah* ("the era of ignorance") had referred to the pagan ignorance of pre-Islamic Arabia, Mawdudi characterized the Muslim society of his day as pagan or ignorant of true Islam. He determined that most of his Muslim contemporaries, and certainly their leaders, were not true Muslims at all. Subcontinental Islam was lax with regard to the religion's exoteric dimension, outward observance, and incorporated much that for Mawdudi was simply not Islamic. Hence he distinguished the nominal Muslim majority from a minority of "true" Muslims, to be led by his party Jamaat-e Islami, a bedrock of orthodoxy. Such a conception may appear to align with a key family resemblance, a dualistic or enclave culture characterized by a black-and-white mentality brooking no compromise or shades of gray. This sense of alignment might also be reinforced by Mawdudi's uncompromising rhetoric in favor of an exclusively Islamic state as the only acceptable arrangement for postcolonial Muslim life. Mawdudi rejected secularist propositions as "un-Islamic," "heathen," and "anthropocentric." He argued that Muslims must live according to shariah and under the leadership of pious men committed to Islamic orthodoxy. This entailed the purging of syncretism and un-Islamic economic, social, or political conceptions and arrangements.

The fundamentalism of Mawdudi's program might appear evident. The crux of the matter, however, is that while the engine driving his project was the perception of threat, this was something very different to what the concept would lead us to expect. Fundamentalism, whatever else it may embody, represents a reaction to the enlightened or modernist critique of tradition and the marginalization of religion through the establishment of secular institutions and behaviors. The origins of American fundamentalism are traceable to the refusal to alter traditions and dogmas threatened by modern dictates. By contrast, Mawdudi was driven to action by the perception of a specifically and in fact uniquely Hindu threat. His object was not a felt need to reject enlightened thought. His work rather originates in the distinctive context of prepartition India and intra-Muslim debates about security. More than anything, Mawdudi's discourse was framed by his reading of subcontinental demography and its implications for independent Muslims. His primary concerns, then, were demographic. He felt that wherever the two are insufficiently separated a much larger (Hindu) majority will inevitably marginalize a (Muslim) minority.[27]

Given the stark demographic imbalance, Mawdudi rejected the vision of a unified India favored by India's traditionalist ulama. At least in the view of their critics, most ulama were satisfied by Hindu reassurances that Muslim and other minority rights would be guaranteed by India's "secular" character. Critically, Mawdudi viewed the movement for a unified India as an essentially Hindu struggle and, as such, one that Muslims could not rely upon. On this point, as is frequently the case in discussions concerning the developing world, the concept of fundamentalism becomes intertwined with the history of colonialism and its aftermath: fundamentalist rejection of Western thought links with fundamentalist rejection of Western rule. Hence it is notable that Mawdudi did not conceive of his struggle at all in this way. He did not deem his effort substantively an exercise in resisting colonial rule and criticized Muslims who subscribed to what he labeled blind anti-imperialism. In his view replacement of the British Raj with a Hindu Raj would be scant improvement.[28] Here again we see Mawdudi's object, quite out of keeping with the concept, as specifically Hindu. Further, where Islamic fundamentalism has a reputation for critiquing the political quiescence of traditionalist ulama, Mawdudi's critiques were informed by the ulama's specific stance on Hindu–Muslim relations. To be sure, Mawdudi's criticisms of the ulama's "establishment Islam" were not limited to this issue—consider his views on traditionalist indifference to modern learning.[29] Yet his opposition to the political positions favored by most Indian ulama was to a notable extent driven by distinctively Indian circumstances.

Mawdudi also rejected Muslim secularism, deeming the proposal of Muhammad Ali Jinnah (d. 1948) for a separate Muslim state untenable. Whereas fundamentalism is defined in terms of a global opposition to secularism, Mawdudi's views on this matter were again framed by local conditions. He argued that while any step separating Muslims from Hindus was a step in the right direction, Muslim secularism did not go far enough. Given the proximity of India, a secular Muslim state incorporating a Hindu minority with political rights would effectively be one with a built-in fifth column, giving India a ready means to encroach upon the Muslim position. As Nasr has persuasively argued, it was this contingency that underlay Mawdudi's call for Islamic exclusivism, political marginalization of non-Muslims, and his antisecularist rhetoric. Mawdudi's positions on Sufism and Islamic economics, positions commonly associated with fundamentalism, were similarly based. Fundamentalism is known for hostility toward mysticism (on this point, see the essay by Khalid Yahya Blankinship in this volume), a stance sometimes associated with the so-called proto-fundamentalism of Muhammad Ibn Abd al-Wahhab (d. 1792). Yet, notwithstanding his own lineage, Mawdudi was leery of Sufism due to the bridge it forms between Hindu and Muslim practice. His rejection of usury derived from the desire to distance Muslims from a Hindu-dominated sector of the economy. Along similar lines, Mawdudi's insistence on shariah for Muslims might be taken together with his advocacy of the Laws of Manu for India, something that would disadvantage Muslims living under them.[30] Mawdudi's views might, per the concept, seem indicative of a fundamentalist effort to "fortify the borders of the religious community," but he was not here addressing an erosion of religious identity caused by the rise of modern secularism.

On these matters the West and its political domination were secondary concerns for Mawdudi, especially prepartition. Elaborating this point, Nasr describes Mawdudi's fundamentalism as a case of "radical communalism." I suggest taking this insightful reworking a step further. Nasr finds that, contrary to the prevailing understanding of the concept, Mawdudi's case is one of fundamentalism rooted in communalism.[31] I suggest characterizing it as a case of communalism rather than fundamentalism. The detonations of the terms *communalism* and *fundamentalism* are sufficiently different that it is questionable whether it remains useful to apply the latter. The primary intention was securing communal rights rather than imagining and advocating a certain form of Islam, or one that aligns with the concept, and is therefore helpfully labeled fundamentalist. In other words, understanding Mawdudi in terms of the rhetoric with which he packaged his case is insufficient.

This is also seen in Mawdudi's postpartition shift from the rhetoric of rejecting Western political conceptions and arrangements to the pragmatics of accommodation. Pakistan created, he came to find his fears of a Hindu fifth column largely unrealized. This precipitated a reworking of his stance on electoral process and national statehood. He acknowledged the parliament's legitimacy and participated in the national discussion on the nature of Pakistan's constitution, while his party participated in every election up to his death in 1979.[32] In this he was unconstrained by some of his earlier rhetoric dismissing secular politics which, it might be said with a little irony, he came to read less than "literally." The same might not be said for at least some of his interpreters. While advocates of the concept note that fundamentalists have accommodated themselves to modern politics, it is not easy to square this with the definition quoted above: fundamentalists *"attempt to . . . create viable alternatives to secular institutions and behaviors."*[33] This raises the question of how far someone who is labeled a fundamentalist can go in negotiating the same politics of modernity as anyone else who is politically engaged before that term's use becomes dubious. Either it continues in spite of its representatives behaving, so to speak, quite uncooperatively, or it is reworked in an attempt to address the discrepancy. But this reworking involves going far beyond what flexible use would allow.

As for Mawdudi's political engagement, this incorporated an eclectic mix of Western and Islamic vocabulary. He idealized a "theodemocracy" and a "democratic caliphate" with constitutional checks and balances, a parliament, and an elected presidency.[34] This could, per the concept, be taken as illustrative of fundamentalism as both rejection of modernity ("theo-," "caliphate") and child of modernity ("democratic"). Yet it is more helpful to consider it as substantively and categorically an assimilation of modernity that, through political need, is couched in Islamic vocabulary. Mawdudi addressed a Muslim audience disempowered by the related legacies of colonialism and loss of position relative to Hindus. At the same time he did so as one who was unquestionably drawn not only to Western technology but also to significant aspects of Western thought. What integrates these elements is the appeal of and desire for power. On this point it might be suggested that there is nothing specifically or distinctively fundamentalist in that. Where classical Islam had empowered Muslims, what had drawn Mawdudi to the modern West was its contemporary demonstration of power.[35] Thus he found that borrowings from the West facilitating Muslim empowerment should be encouraged: radio waves could disseminate Islamic messages as much as any other; modern thought could animate Muslim minds as much as any other. He also commented: "On the one hand we have to imbibe exactly the Qur'anic spirit and identify our outlook with the Islamic tenets while, on the other, we have to assess thoroughly the developments in the field of knowledge and changes in conditions of life that have been brought during the last eight hundred years; and . . . we have to arrange these ideas and laws of life on genuine Islamic lines so that Islam should once again become a dynamic force; the leader of the world rather than its follower."[36] Where, again, fundamentalists are considered "modern creatures," in Mawdudi's case such description does not go far enough. He was not merely a modern but a modernizer, socially, politically, and culturally. The demands of local audience, the need to win popular Muslim subscription to this agenda, led him to frame it with Islamic referents.

This is not to suggest that Mawdudi should necessarily be labeled an Islamic modernist—Mawdudi was critical of Indian Muslims he identified as such. That said, it is unavoidable that much of his program recalls the paradigms of Islamic modernism more than those of fundamentalism. Yet excluding *modernist* still leaves us with several alternatives that are preferable to *fundamentalist.* While labeling such a complex individual will always be an exercise in falling short, *communalist* is clearly more applicable to Mawdudi than *fundamentalist.* Applying *maximalist* and *Islamist* to Mawdudi is also likely to be fruitful. Whatever the benefits, limitations, and vagueness of these terms in what they positively connote (and these have not been investigated in detail here), neither has been shown to connote what is patently inapposite. At least by this criterion, they are preferable to *fundamentalism.*

Turning to Khomeini, his pertinence lies more than anything in his political success, something Mawdudi lacked. Where Mawdudi's influence over Muslims globally has been pervasive, Khomeini's has been limited by his Shiism. But his "fundamentalist state" is seen as the preeminent example of an Islamic form of fundamentalism. Khomeini engaged different conditions to those Mawdudi faced, and the resulting vision was also different. Yet with regard to rhetoric a similar dynamic applies: seemingly fundamentalist language veneers something very different from fundamentalism. In *The Revealing of Secrets* (1944) Khomeini rejects constitutionalism, legislation, and representation as corrupt notions implicated with Western ills. In *Islamic Government* (1970) he avers that rulers should not legislate but rather implement divine legislation, shariah, which is fully comprehensive.[37] In various 1970s pamphlets he advocates an all-pervasive Islamic system and ideology (*maktab-i tawhid*).[38] The language of Iran's eclectic constitution follows Khomeini's lead. The state's raison d'is specified as establishment of shariah, while authority is religiously based. On these points we again find what might seem indicative of a family resemblance, dualism, or enclave culture. Almond, Appleby, and Sivan rate Khomeini "high" with regard to dualism.[39]

Khomeini's dualistic language, however, supplemented quite different elements, while packaging a worldview that departs from the concept much more than conforms to it. Far from calling for a theoretical or actual enclave, Khomeini was aware of the limitations of a hermetically sealed Islam. His ideology was eclectic yet flexible with regard to culture. For instance, while delineated in the vocabulary of Shiism, Khomeini's ruler-jurist also recalls Sunni and Western notions, al-Farabi's virtuous ruler and Plato's philosopher-king. In addition, Khomeini called for the integration of Islam not only with technology but also with modern civilization (*tamaddon-i jadid*). Here, *novel* appears a more apposite description than *fundamentalist.* One also notes his relentless critique of traditionalist Islam. His comments about *akhunds* or "pseudo-saints" recall modernist critiques of traditionalist ulama, such as Rida's descriptions of those he labeled *muqallidun* ("imitators").[40] To be sure, advocates of the concept note and even emphasize fundamentalist denunciations of traditionalist Muslims' political quiescence and ideological inertia. But Khomeini's specific critiques are quite insufficient to differentiate him as a fundamentalist from other Muslims critical of establishment Islam. On this point the concept does not enable us to separate clearly what is called fundamentalism from what is called modernism. Accommodating this difficulty again entails going far beyond what flexible use would allow: stretching or deforming the concept in ways that lack consistency as it is applied to some cases but not others. If Khomeini's rejection of traditionalism renders him a fundamentalist, the same would apply to Abduh and Rida, who are generally considered seminal modernists.[41]

The limitations of comprehending Khomeini in terms of fundamentalism are also seen with regard to nationalism which, by definition, is not a variety of fundamentalism. Fundamentalists are said to reject nationalism's "polytheistic" violation of Muslim unity, and counterpoint divided nation-states with the vision of a unified global ummah.[42] While Khomeini rejects nationalism in such works as

Islamic Government, labeling post-Ottoman states artificial creations,[43] taken as a whole his career was scarcely that of an antinationalist. Indeed, while his program was distinctly Shiite, it was also that of an Iranian national and, for many of his followers, that of a patriot. Khomeini did not unambiguously favor ummah over nation. While the relationship between the two notions inevitably involves tension, Khomeini's nationalism is palpable. He upheld nation and patriot, asserting that Iranians must uphold their distinct culture. Importantly, while perceiving that culture as Islamic and Shiite, he also considered it a national culture, differing from those of non-Iranian Muslims who were involved in their own national struggles. His conceived state, then, was Islamic *and* national. Scarcely in a fundamentalist vein, he called for strong state centralization funded through taxation and for clear borders secured by a modern army. Nationalist sentiment had facilitated cooperation with secularist and leftist opponents of the shah. Granted, this may have been somewhat cynical or achieved through concealing "true colors." Islamic agendas were not highlighted in the early stages of the revolution. Yet, tellingly, strong nationalist sentiment persisted well after the purging of former allies and establishment of a highly repressive clergy-dominated Islamic state and was ongoing after Khomeini's death. One might also consider here the continuing marginalization of Iran's Kurds. Further, notwithstanding efforts to export it, Khomeini's revolution remained generally confined within Iran's borders. This perhaps reflects its character as more Iranian and Shiite than global.

Khomeini unquestionably buttressed his vision for Iran by drawing on past memories, another key family resemblance. It should be noted, however, that strictly speaking the notion of a sacred or golden past is at odds with the Shiite worldview, wherein the sacred age lies in the future (on this point see the essays by Lynda Clarke in this volume). Where Muslim secularists drew on Phoenician, Mesopotamian, Egyptian, and other legacies to buttress various nationalisms, Khomeini drew on another ancient heritage, Shiism. He appealed to popular shared memories of its leading figures, especially the First, Third, and Sixth Imams.[44] Khomeini certainly opposed secularist nationalisms, and his combining of Shiite past and Iranian present may appear somewhat contradictory, paradoxical, or in need of interpretation (for example, to integrate Iran's history with that of the Imams, none of whom were Persian). On this point I note the thesis of Vanessa Martin, an authority on Khomeini. Martin finds Khomeini's combining of tradition and modernity, as such, insufficient to differentiate him from the like of his Baathist contemporaries, whom one would scarcely describe as fundamentalists.[45] One might compare Saddam Hussein's appeal to Nebuchadrezzar's legacy with Khomeini's appeal to that of Imam Husayn. It is not easy to see how one is intrinsically more anachronistic or antimodern than the other. Where, again, the concept allows for combinations of past and present, of tradition and modernity, it does not provide us with tools to readily differentiate specifically fundamentalist combinations from others. On this point the concept appears applicable not only to what is called fundamentalism but also to what is unquestionably not fundamentalism. Here the term again fails a key test for a successful umbrella term, facilitating differentiation and separation.

There is another telling sense in which Khomeini does not fit the profile of a fundamentalist. Two decades ago Ervand Abrahamian argued that Khomeini was more populist than fundamentalist.[46] To be sure, the concept has been refined, expanded, and expounded since then. Yet I find that those who continue to describe Khomeini as a fundamentalist have not sufficiently addressed this issue. That is, comprehending Khomeini entails consideration of both religious sensibility and the politics of modernity. The concept, I find, insufficiently reckons with the latter. On the one hand Khomeini's movement was distinctively Shiite, one outworking of the Imamic legacy. Highly symbolically and without precedent, Khomeini's followers identified him as "Agent of the Imam" (*naib-i imam*). Even more dramatically, Khomeini shunned a public opportunity to deny being the awaited Hidden Imam, silence taken by some as a tacit affirmation. As Imam, Khomeini was seen as embodying Imamic virtue, frugality, piety, purity, justice, gnosis, and divine light, while he described the shah as an embodiment of the Imam's enemy, *taghut,* illegitimate despotism. This symbolism may appear to lend well to the concept. Conflict was certainly depicted dualistically, the choice offered darkness (shah) or light (Imam).

On the other hand apparent conformity belies the integration of Shiism with an unambiguously populist movement. In short, significantly, much of Khomeini's success derived from factors other than religion, factors not illuminated by the concept of fundamentalism. Most notable, his support did not rest primarily on a religious foundation. He was far from universally recognized as a religious leader and was by no means the only or preeminent "model for emulation" (*marja-i taqlid*).[47] We have noted fundamentalism's reputation for wresting authority from a quiescent religious establishment, yet far more was at play in the case at hand. Disputation about Khomeini's status involved a complex and ongoing intra-Shiite discourse about the nature of authority. It is difficult to see how the concept might be illuminating here. For instance, it hardly seems helpful to imagine Khomeini as a fundamentalist and clerics who opposed him as traditionalists or antifundamentalists. In addition, it is difficult to find in this any immediate familial resemblance to developments within Sunnism or Protestantism. This might be a case where a global view can take us only so far.

While religious authority was controversial, popular appeal was less so. Khomeini successfully identified and harnessed resentment with the shah, projecting himself as embodying the mass interest. That is, he had a popular touch, speaking for those he labeled "disinherited" (*mustazafin*). Here we meet another critical juncture in our investigation. Where Mawdudi addressed a disempowered audience (i.e., relative to precolonial Indian Muslims), Khomeini's audience was unempowered. He spoke to and for Iranians alienated from modernization's benefits, chastising his opponent for failing to provide for his people's basic needs. In so doing, he presented a modern challenge, highlighting the regime's profligacy, pro-Western partiality, and social, economic, and political failings. Here, global analogs are found more in developing-world populisms than in religious fundamentalisms. To be sure, in rallying his movement Khomeini integrated populist critique with religious trope. He identified the mass experience with Imamic suffering and righteousness, and averred, "Islam is for the poor." But rather than understanding this in terms of fundamentalism, it is more helpful to view it as an embodiment of populism, populism couched in what we might call "indigenous rhetoric," the rhetoric of Shiism.

This feature, I find, is unremarkable and unexceptional. Khomeini addressed a traditionally minded audience for whom religious symbolism had potent appeal. Given the preoccupation with the regime's (scarcely unique) pro-Western partiality, Western vocabulary would be a hard sell. Other constituencies might be responsive to leftist calls for class revolution and proletarian dictatorship, or other slogans taken from Western ideology. But un-Westernized rural Iranians and the urban poor would surely be more responsive to the themes of Shiite social justice and such slogans as "Islam is taking from the rich and giving to the poor." Whatever else he may have embodied, Khomieni's populism is unavoidable. His religious symbolism rallied a significant portion of the populace in a modern political movement that shares significant similarities with others in a populist vein. The resulting constitution follows Khomeini's lead, integrating notions of popular sovereignty and populist economics with religious language. This combination might be better understood in terms of the integration of Iranian populism with Iranian Shiism than in terms of global fundamentalism.

In sum, like Mawdudi, Khomeini is not helpfully described as a fundamentalist. Alternative descriptions are more promising. Whatever the shortfalls of such terms as *Islamist* (or *political Islamist*), *maximalist, populist,* and *communalist*, none bring difficulties equivalent to those discussed above. The lack of alignment between Khomeinism and fundamentalism might be reflected by his followers' inability to find an indigenous or Islamic equivalent to the term with which Western observers were describing their leader: *bonyadgara* represents a Persian appropriation or approximation of the English *fundamentalist.*[48] If what is called Islamic fundamentalism differs substantively from Protestant fundamentalism, it is perhaps unsurprising that, appropriations aside, languages such as Persian and Arabic lack any terms that are genuinely equivalent to *fundamentalist.*

Conclusion

Efforts to construct and deploy broad umbrella terms that capture structurally similar developments within different global settings are integral to the study of culture. The argument outlined above is framed by the suggestion that some umbrella terms work better than others. Of the criteria that must be satisfied for such terms to be useful, the most important is their capacity to identify and differentiate. I have suggested that in the case of fundamentalism this criterion has not been fulfilled. In critical cases what is identified as fundamentalism does not align with the definition of fundamentalism. Conversely, key features defined as fundamentalist—selective retrieval and fortification of tradition; challenging a quiescent traditionalist establishment; forming eclectic combinations of tradition and modernity—are also found in phenomena that are clearly not fundamentalism. Thus, regarding both identification and differentiation the term falls short. The concept has a specific dependence on Islam. Thus, its inapplicability to Mawdudi and Khomeini—whose careers are integral to any discussion of Islamic fundamentalism—creates a problem that is unresolved, and perhaps unresolvable. While advocates of the concept have noted differences between Christian, Jewish, and Muslim engagements with modernity, they have insufficiently theorized the ways in which these differences bear on and undermine the concept of a genuinely global phenomenon.

Notes

1. David Harrington Watt, "Meaning and End of Fundamentalism," *Religious Studies Review* 30 (October 2004): 271–74.

2. Ervand Abrahamian, "The Islamic Republic after Thirty Years" (keynote address for conference, "The Iranian Revolution: Thirty Years," held at Rutgers University, February 7–8, 2009).

3. Earle H. Waugh, "Fundamentalism: Harbinger of Academic Revisionism," *Journal of the American Academy of Religion* 65 (Spring 1997): 162.

4. See the reference to Khomeini on the back cover of Gabriele Marranci's *Understanding Muslim Identity: Rethinking Fundamentalism* (New York: Palgrave Macmillan, 2009).

5. Karen Armstrong, *The Battle for God: A History of Fundamentalism* (New York: Ballantine Books, 2001); Gabriel A. Almond, R. Scott Appleby, and Emmanuel Sivan, *Strong Religion: The Rise of Fundamentalisms around the World* (Chicago: University of Chicago Press, 2003); Richard T. Antoun, *Understanding Fundamentalism: Christian, Islamic and Jewish Movements*, 2nd ed. (Lanham, Md.: Rowman & Littlefield, 2008); Malise Ruthven, *Fundamentalism: A Very Short Introduction* (New York: Oxford University Press, 2007).

6. On this point see, for example, Muhammad Ayoob, *The Many Faces of Political Islam* (Ann Arbor: University of Michigan Press, 2008), 7–8; Lawrence Davidson, *Islamic Fundamentalism* (Westport, Conn.: Greenwood, 1998), 17; Gustaaf Houtman, "Benazir Bhutto (1953–2007): A Conversation with Akbar Ahmed," *Anthropology Today* 24, no. 1 (2008): 5; Mehran Kamrava, "Reformist Islam in Comparative Perspective," in *The New Voices of Islam*, ed. Kamrava (London: I. B. Tauris, 2006), 10; Martin E. Marty and R. Scott Appleby, *The Glory and the Power: The Fundamentalist Challenge to the Modern World* (Boston: Beacon, 1992), 149; David Zeidan, *The Resurgence of Religion: A Comparative Study of Selected Themes in Christian and Islamic Fundamentalist Discourses* (Leiden: Brill, 2003), 81.

7. Almond, Appleby, and Sivan, *Strong Religion*, 16–17.

8. Ruthven, *Fundamentalism: A Very Short Introduction*, ix.

9. Watt, "Meaning and End of Fundamentalism."

10. Jay Michael Harris, "Fundamentalism: Objections from a Modern Jewish Historian," in *Fundamentalism and Gender*, ed. John Stratton Hawley (New York: Oxford University Press, 1994), 142.

11. On Islamism, see Richard C. Martin and Abbas Barzegar, eds. *Islamism: Contested Perspectives on Political Islam* (Stanford: Stanford University Press, 2010).

12. Bruce Lincoln, *Holy Terrors: Thinking about Religion after September 11* (Chicago: University of Chicago Press, 2003), 5. See also Mark Juergensmeyer, "Thinking about Religion after September 11," *Journal of the American Academy of Religion* 72 (March 2004): 221–34.

13. Mansoor Moaddel and Karam Talattof, eds., *Modernist and Fundamentalist Debates in Islam: A Reader* (New York: Palgrave Macmillian, 2000), 2–3; Almond, Appleby, and Sivan, *Strong Religion,* 16.

14. On Sinhala Buddhism and fundamentalism, see Tessa J. Bartholomeusz and Chandra R. De Silva, eds., *Buddhist Fundamentalism and Minority Identities in Sri Lanka* (Albany: State University of New York Press, 1998).

15. R. Scott Appleby, "Fundamentalism," in *Encyclopedia of Politics and Religion,* 2nd ed., ed. Robert Wuthnow (Washington, D.C.: CQ Press, 2007), 320.

16. Almond, Appleby, and Sivan, *Strong Religion,* 16–17.

17. Ibid., 17.

18. This is also the view of Ruthven. Ruthven, *Fundamentalism: A Very Short Introduction,* 5.

19. Daniel Martin Varisco, "The Tragedy of a Comic: Fundamentalists Crusading against Fundamentalists," *Contemporary Islam* 1 (October 2007): 212n11. Varisco also compares the term *fundamentalism* to the word *Negro.*

20. Almond, Appleby, and Sivan, *Strong Religion,* 17. Italics in original.

21. On this point, see also Watt's "Meaning and End of Fundamentalism."

22. Many of the points developed here are discussed in greater length in my article "Rethinking Fundamentalism: Ruhollah Khomeini, Mawlana Mawdudi, and the Fundamentalist Model," *JCRT* 11 (Spring 2011): 171–98. I have also argued that it is unhelpful to label Rashid Rida (d. 1935) a fundamentalist. See Wood, *Christian Criticisms, Islamic Proofs: Rashid Rida's Modernist Defence of Islam* (Oxford: Oneworld, 2008), 48–64.

23. According to the *Encyclopedia of Politics and Religion,* Khomeini represents "the most prominent and politically consequential example of Islamic fundamentalism," while Mawdudi's influence on contemporary Islamic fundamentalism is deemed pervasive. Appleby, "Fundamentalism," 325.

24. Mawlana Abul-Ala Mawdudi, *Towards Undersanding the Qur'an,* vol. 1 (Leicester: Islamic Foundation, 1988), 238. The Quranic verse commented on here is 3:7.

25. Sayyid Vali Reza Nasr, "Communalism and Fundamentalism: A Reexamination of the Origins of Islamic Fundamentalism," *Contention* 4 (Winter 1995): 122–23.

26. Almond, Appleby, and Sivan, *Strong Religion,* 24–25, 107.

27. Nasr, "Communalism and Fundamentalism." Nasr elucidates the ways in which Mawdudi's agenda was framed and informed by specifically subcontinental contingencies.

28. Ibid., 126.

29. See Charles J. Adams, "Abu-'l A'la Mawdudi's Tafhim al-Qur'an," in *Approaches to the History of the Interpretation of the Quran,* ed. Andrew Rippin (New York: Oxford University Press, 1988), 321–22.

30. Nasr, "Communalism and Fundamentalism," 130–33.

31. Ibid., 136.

32. Hamid Enayat, *Modern Islamic Political Thought* (London: I. B. Tauris, 2005), 102. Nasr, "Communalism and Fundamentalism," 135.

33. Almond, Appleby, and Sivan, *Strong Religion,* 17. Italics in original.

34. Sayyid Vali Reza Nasr, *Mawdudi and the Making of Islamic Revivalism* (New York: Oxford University Press, 1996), 88.

35. Nasr, *Mawdudi and the Making of Islamic Revivalism,* 51.

36. Quoted in Nasr, *Mawdudi and the Making of Islamic Revivalism,* 51.

37. Ruhollah Khomeini, *Islamic Government: Governance of the Jurist* (*Velayat-e Faqeeh*) (Tehran: Institute for Compilation and Publication of Imam Khomeini's Works, 2002), 16, 20, 29–30, 46.

38. For a detailed discussion tracing the development of Khomeini's thought in these works, see Vanessa Martin, *Creating an Islamic State: Khomeini and the Making of a New Iran* (London: I. B. Tauris, 2000), chapter 5.

39. Almond, Appleby, and Sivan, *Strong Religion,* 247.

40. Khomeini, *Islamic Government,* 16, 42–43, 47, 71–72.

41. On this point, see Wood, *Christian Criticisms, Islamic Proofs,* 48–64. For an alternative view, namely, that Abduh and Rida are fundamentalists rather than modernists, see Johannes J. G. Jansen, *The Dual Nature of Islamic Fundamentalism* (Ithaca: Cornell University Press, 1997), 29–40.

42. Almond, Appleby, and Sivan, *Strong Religion,* 41.

43. Khomeini, *Islamic Government,* 24.

44. Ibid., 11, 14, 44, 73–75, 66.

45. Martin, *Creating an Islamic State,* xii. Martin is only marginally concerned with fundamentalism yet finds the concept inapplicable to Khomeini (although not to Islam per se).

46. Ervand Abrahamian, *Khomeinism: Essays on the Islamic Republic* (Berkeley: University of California Press, 1993), 13–38.

47. Martin, *Creating an Islamic State,* 165–66.

48. On this point, see Abrahamian, *Khomeinism,* 13. Also releveant is the Persian *osulgara,* which might be taken as an equivalent term. Also relevant is the Arabic *usuli.* But to the extent that *usuli* connotes "fundamentalist" (and not something completely different) it represents an appropriation of the English term.

Muslim "Fundamentalism," Salafism, Sufism, and Other Trends

Khalid Yahya Blankinship

When the term *fundamentalism* began to be applied to various trends among Muslims in the 1970s, it soon came into wide and somewhat indiscriminate use. But what exactly its users meant by the term and why especially they began to use it at that time have remained rather unclear. While at its origin in 1920, the term referred to a specific Christian movement and tendency in the United States, even being taken up by some as a self-identity, it also tended from the outset to be used to classify others rather than the self. After it began to be applied to non-Christians, especially Muslims, its coherence dwindled, as different commentators used it rather indiscriminately to refer to various tendencies and trends among Muslims. The result today has been a confusion of different definitions, often mutually exclusive or contradictory. Thus, for example, the well-known historian Ira M. Lapidus has observed: "Since the 1970s latent Muslim identifications have begun to assert themselves in a worldwide Islamic revival. This revival is commonly characterized as 'Islamic fundamentalism.' This term has some validity, in that many movements so labeled do indeed seek to return to the Quran and the teachings of the Prophet, but otherwise it is at best only an umbrella designation for a very wide variety of movements, some intolerant and exclusivist, some pluralistic; some favorable to science, some anti-scientific; some primarily devotional and some primarily political; some democratic, some authoritarian; some pacific, some violent."[1] Lapidus then goes on to avoid using the term.

Use of *Fundamentalism* in Academic Works

Nevertheless, the term *fundamentalism* applied to Muslims remains alive and well, as exemplified by the book of essays titled *The Fundamentalist Mindset*, published as recently as 2010, with a foreword by the prestigious Martin E. Marty, who has devoted his career to promoting the broad use of the term and is as unapologetic as ever for using it.[2] Although trying to show that it is not primarily aimed at the Muslims by describing and analyzing those the authors deem to be Christian, Jewish, and Hindu fundamentalists as well, the work well underlines its purpose both by trying to base its analyses on psychology and by focusing especially on the connection of the claimed fundamentalists with violence, a theme popular with the security establishments in the dominant countries and those countries' media and publics as well.[3] Typically, as in the massive Fundamentalism Project series of books presided over by Marty, those using the term *fundamentalism* in *The Fundamentalist Mindset* have remained hesistant or reluctant to define it. Thus, the writers given the task of proposing a definition first reprise the idea of vague "family resemblances" among fundamentalisms across religions first. Then they go on to say of those who use the term, who include themselves, that "their approach is comparative and phenomenological; they believe there is something important happening in the world that sharply differentiates such movements from traditionalism, conservatism, and orthodoxy. But it is dangerous to be more concrete. Given its protean and elusive nature, a simple definition of fundamentalism risks being simple-minded. The movement of those we call fundamentalist is too new historically for there to be a clear and agreed-upon definition. In fact we argue in this book for the benefits of ambiguity, which makes for a larger conceptual umbrella."[4] Thus the authors relieve themselves of having to offer a clear definition of what they broadly claim applies to huge masses of people, while at the same time giving themselves authority to call others by this designation based on their own subjective assessments of the others' "mindsets," as in the book's title.[5]

However, despite its lack of a specific definition, *The Fundamentalist Mindset* offers the following characteristics or perhaps modalities of fundamentalism: "dualistic thinking; paranoia and rage in a group context; an apocalyptic orientation that incorporates distinct perspectives on time, death, and violence; a relationship to a charismatic leadership; and a totalized conversion experience."[6] By this kind of negative and unfavorable description, users of the term *fundamentalism* usually mean by it followers of religion who are both authoritarian and so bound to dogmatic teachings that they are incapable of discussing or debating anything and thus must be excluded from the framework of acceptable discourse. Even with this type of characterization, those designated as "fundamentalists" are actually quite diverse, so that the single, clear unifying characteristic described by the term, particularly in the Muslim context, is that it is exclusively used to designate others, never the self. This othering naturally has raised questions about the validity of the term's use, as well as about the purposes of those using it. Criticism of the use of the term has led to the alternative designations *Islamist* and *Islamism,* but these share the same problems of being as overgeneralizing and nondistinguishing as *fundamentalist* and *fundamentalism,* because, being built on the word *Islam,* they can only refer to Islam and Muslims in general, yet they are taken to designate only certain Muslims and not others.[7] All of these terms, because never applied to the self, tend at least to distance and delegitimate the other, whether that is the intention of the speaker or writer using them or not.

Another broad set of definitions focused on Muslim fundamentalism is offered by Youssef M. Choueiri in his book *Islamic Fundamentalism: The Story of Islamist Movements*, which links *fundamentalism* and *Islamism* even in its title. Indeed, in his preface, dated 2009, to the third edition, Choueiri manages to mention the terms *fundamentalism, Islamist, jihad, Jihadism, Taliban,* and *Islamic radicalism* all in the confines of less than a page.[8] In his introduction to the second edition, dated 1997, Choueiri strongly defends the use of the term *fundamentalism* against critics. His excuse is that since the Middle Ages the Muslims have used the term *usuli,* meaning a religious scholar who studies the bases or fundamentals of either the law (*usul al-fiqh*) or the creed (*usul al-din*).[9] Yet this original usage, indicating only the particular specialization of a kind of religious scholar, actually has a positive meaning for Muslims[10] and does not at all match the broad sweep of definitions of modern fundamentalism, which rather generally point to mass movements largely of laypeople, not religious specialists. One would understand from Choueiri's linkage of the modern meaning of usuli to the classical one that fundamentalists are simply dogmatic theologians, and thus he even retrojects the term into the distant past by calling medieval theologians fundamentalists.[11] However, echoing the statement of Strozier et al. given above, Choueiri states that he has redefined the term, "for lack of a better word, to convey a less rigorous connotation." This new meaning is adopted "to refer to Islamic systems of thought and political movements that emerged from the eighteenth century onward in countries as far apart as Saudi Arabia, Indonesia, Nigeria and India," a stunningly far-flung array of both times and places which seem to form an undifferentiated unity in his thought that is nearly coterminous with the modern Muslim world.

Additionally, Choueiri states of Islamic fundamentalism that "its direct meaning is assumed to indicate a certain intellectual stance that claims to derive political principles from a timeless, divine text."[12] While such a feature may seem clearly to distinguish religious believers from nonbelievers and thus offer a criterion for giving the religious specific designations, it is doubtful whether *fundamentalism* is up to playing that role. That is because of its utter lack of specificity, despite Choueiri's defense of it. Actually, all human beings must have "fundamentals" by which they live, whether they are derived from scriptural sources or from personal experience. The only exceptions would be those who are confused. Therefore, human beings who believe they are not confused could all be classified as "fundamentalists."

As for the notion that fundamentalists must be more rigid in their thinking because they rely on "a timeless, divine text," Choueiri himself observes about fundamentalism, that "intellectually and politically, it espouses a creative interpretation of its revealed text," and "this paradoxical approach, straddling simultaneously creativity and adherence to fundamentals, leads to a constant updating of the text in order to keep abreast of new developments and discoveries."[13] How then are the so-called fundamentalists more text-bound in their thinking than others, if they too are constantly changing and reinterpreting in the light of new developments? In this case it is difficult to see how fundamentalists are to be diffentiated from other humans, some of whom are more rigid than others, just like the alleged fundamentalists. And certainly most humans through experience have learned to be somewhat sure of themselves in their core beliefs about life, whether or not those beliefs include what are conventionally construed as religious tenets. Furthermore, if one were to seek a true text-based fundamentalism that goes back to an invariable, physically manifested text that allows no deviation from its conclusions at all, surely modern science itself, or rather the discourse of scientism that is based on it, which revives or continues the ancient reductionist, materialist, and usually atheist tradition of Leucippus, Democritus, Epicurus, and Lucretius, should be considered a leading candidate for the title of fundamentalism. Also, if the problem is really one of sticking to a hallowed text as closely as possible, surely some other, better terminology could be considered, even if itself not without problems, such as *textualism*, or *scripturalism*, or even *literalism*. But then these do not have the pejorative charge that *fundamentalism* has.

Furthermore, Choueiri indeed does not conceal that he views what he describes as Islamic fundamentalism unfavorably. Thus he cites "irreconcilable differences between modernity and an obsolete system that was basically medieval in its outlook and institutions," which renders any program or proposals of those he deems Islamists "untenable."[14] He further claims that utopian ideals are secular and rationalist, and, since "Islamist" ideals are neither of these, they must be characterized as "more akin to dystopia with all its attendant negative aspects."[15] However, it is doubtful whether Choueiri's sweeping generalizations themselves are tenable, and, because sweeping, they appear to exclude the totality of what he deems to be Islamic fundamentalist discourse from the realm of acceptable or even entertainable views. How broad his categorization is becomes further apparent when one considers the groups he includes under Islamic fundamentalism, which he has subdivided into three trends that also occupy three historical periods: revivalists (1744–1885), reformists (1839–1954), and radicals (1945–present).[16] This tripartite division is also utilized by Bruce Lawrence, except that he replaces the radicals category with fundamentalists, thus reducing the scope of fundamentalism for him only to this third category.[17] By presenting modern Muslim history in this way, Choueiri is able to label all significant modern Muslim movements, whether militant or quietist, as fundamentalist and then to assert that all have ended by now in the radical category, while Lawrence places them simply in the fundamentalist category.

Choueiri is not alone in viewing and using fundamentalism as an unfavorable and pejorative attribute of others than himself. In *Strong Religion: The Rise of Fundamentalisms around the World,* Gabriel A. Almond, R. Scott Appleby, and Emmanuel Sivan even state that "our use of the largely pejorative term 'fundamentalism' only for religious movements with which we disagree therefore reflects our liberal religious or secular biases and distorts our findings." To be sure, they are here only stating their opponents' objections to their use of the term *fundamentalism*; however, they are aware and accept that the term is largely pejorative and show that it is not to be applied to themselves in their rebuttal, in which they consider that the objectors are asking to include under "fundamentalism" only such secularist groups as Marxists, state socialists, "virulent strains of nationalism evident in the modern world," or other extremist revolutionary movements, without once considering whether their own hegemonistic and intolerant neoliberalism should be included as well. They say, "One hesitates to call such secular movements 'fundamentalist,' however, because they are pseudo-religious rather than authentically religious. They may call upon their followers to make the ultimate sacrifice, but, unlike the monotheistic religions, especially Christianity and Islam, they do not reassure their followers that God or an eternal reward awaits them. The absence of a truly 'ultimate' concern is decisive in the dynamics of such groups, just as a belief in a heaven or paradise serves as a framework for and legitimation of self-martyrdom in the monotheistic religions."[18]

So in their book, written in the aftermath of September 11, 2001, Almond, Appleby, and Sivan eventually thus reduce fundamentalist religion to repulsive terrorist violence and political agendas. They attribute the concept of martyrdom to religion, yet they ignore the fact that suicide bombers and other self-sacrificing individuals are not necessarily motivated by religion, as has been established by Robert Pape in his book *Dying to Win: The Strategic Logic of Suicide Terrorism,* in which he points out that the large proportion of suicide bombing by the Tamil Tigers organization in Sri Lanka came from an organization adamantly opposed to religion, and that "suicide terrorism is mainly a response to foreign occupation."[19] One might add that the self-sacrifice of Nathan Hale (1755–1776), the American martyr executed by the British during the Revolutionary War, was capped by Hale's statement, "I regret that I have but one life to lose for my country."[20] What of the whole concept of dying gloriously in war, celebrated by the Roman poet Horace (65–8 B.C.E.) in his famous line, "Dulce et decorum est pro patria mori," meaning "It is sweet and glorious to die for one's country"?[21] And lest one object that Hale and Horace are not referring to suicide, let us remember that war is often suicidal, as eloquently demonstrated by human-wave charges leading literally to millions of deaths in World War I. Nor can Western people, after World War II, claim either to have avoided the mass killing of civilians or the doctrine of collateral damage, claiming that such killings are just too bad. Based on these facts, why should the nationalists, patriots, Hale, Horace, and those who appreciate them not also be labeled fundamentalists?

In fact, such broad designations as *Islamic fundamentalism* seem to arise as arbitrary markers to differentiate "good Islam" from "bad Islam," as in Mahmood Mamdani's work *Good Muslim, Bad Muslim: American, the Cold War, and the Roots of Terror.*[22] The need for "good Islam" is that, with rare exceptions, those opposed to Muslims exercising political influence do not think it wise to attack all Muslims at once because Islam is so large in the world demographically, estimated as of 2010 to amount to 23.2 percent.[23] Thus *Islamic fundamentalism* becomes a catchall term simply to refer to groups that one does not like. From the non-Muslim viewpoint, this could designate any Muslims who are seen as inimical or resistant to progress, democracy, Western control, modernization, or secularization, or simply those who exhibit too much interest in or devotion to religion in any form, and Choueiri's broad brush, for example, or that of Strozier and his coauthors, seems to cover all of these in whole or in part. Such labeling represents a long colonialist tradition of trying to find a suitable catchall term by which to designate and thereby impugn disfavored Muslims. During the British Empire, the pejorative label *Wahhabi,* which, like *fundamentalist,* has generally not been used by any Muslims as a term of self-description, was frequently used for this purpose; it has also undergone a certain revival of usage to attack those whom one does not like.[24] The use of *Islamic fundamentalism* since the end of the 1970s represents a continuation of the hunt for a suitable term of denigration.

One must note that these terms have been used to designate both Muslims with activist political agendas and others who are conservative practicioners of Islam as a religion. Naturally it is the politically active who worry many non-Muslim writers, especially those concerned with security and connected with Western governments. However, as we have seen, the definitions offered above for Islamic fundamentalism and cognate concepts include both the politically active and inactive. This inability to distinguish one from the other in detail may be attributable to the fact that different specific Muslim ideologies do not separate the two. Rather, political activism can come from members of any Muslim tendency and most commonly instead depends on local political conditions, ever the main motivators of action. Probably only a minority of Muslims are actually politically active in any significant sense, but those are embedded in the same general and multifaceted Muslim identity as the inactive Muslims are, whence the difficulty of differentiating. But those promoting such concepts as Islamic fundamentalism need some specific ideological underpinning for their discourses. Hence the hunt for some more specific identification for the "bad" Muslims.

The extent to which this highly constructed discourse of "good" versus "bad" Muslims has been accepted as normative is shown by Natana J. DeLong-Bas in her book *Wahhabi Islam: From Revival and Reform to Global Jihad,* whose subtitle shows the same tripartite division as that of Choueiri and Lawrence discussed above, except that DeLong-Bas has replaced the radicalism or fundamentalism of the others here with "global jihad." This she conflates with "Islamic fundamentalism," stating, for example, that "fundamentalists stress . . . fighting . . . until a universal Islamic order ruled by God's law is established," a position which it is doubtful that very many persons actually uphold, so contrary is it to the actual political situation in the contemporary world.[25] In her work, in order to show the innocence of the Wahhabi founder Muhammad ibn Abd al-Wahhab (1703–1792) from the charge of violence, she attempts to transfer the blame to the medieval Hanbali scholar Ibn Taymiyyah (1263–1328),[26] a move that is oversimplifying, decontextualizing, and of dubious validity.[27]

Fundamentalism and Salafism

Some seeking to identify a coherent Muslim opponent have settled on the Salafi trend in contemporary Sunni Islam, often conflating it with or designating it "Islamic fundamentalism"[28] or Wahhabism.[29] Unlike fundamentalism and Wahhabism, Salafism is often or even usually a self-designation,[30] and as such it possesses, to some extent, despite numerous tensions within it, a coherent doctrine and program that can be described and characterized. Adding to the confusion of descriptions, the Salafis are characterized both as modern reformists and as religious conservatives, and indeed Salafism has been influenced by modernism while trying to preserve some of the main characteristics of classical Islam. The Salafi movement has drawn such attention to itself because, construed broadly, it constitutes the main modern revival and reform trend of Sunni Islam, has exhibited great vitality, and involves the largest portion of the religiously minded among the intelligentsia and the modern educated, not to mention the recent showings of strength by a Salafi-oriented political party in Egypt's elections. The Salafi movement also presents a convenient target because it promotes a conservative and broad application of Muslim practice, which is seen as noticeable, alien, and alienating by many non-Muslims. But the Salafi movement in general includes diverse positions on many matters, including both activism and political quietism, and the quietist trend remains much the larger, making it difficult coherently to include such quietists under the same category as political activists, let alone combative revolutionaries, in what is called Islamic fundamentalism. Nevertheless, this lumping together of Salafis with other Muslim "fundamentalists" continues in scholarly literature as well as in popular journalism.

As a descriptive term for a particular tendency in Islam, the name Salafism (*al-salafiyyah*), referring to the pious predecessors (*al-salaf al-salih*) of the first three or so generations of Muslims, first arose in the late nineteenth century in the context of a modernizing reform movement responding to the arrival of modernity in the Muslim world. It seems first to be adopted as the name of a movement by Jamal al-Din al-Afghani (Asadabadi) (1838–1897) and Muhammad Abduh (1849–1905) in Cairo in 1879, at a time of great ferment owing to the incipient British colonization of Egypt. However, al-Afghani and Abduh were only part of an already existing reform movement with older roots, as has been extensively studied by David Dean Commins.[31] Somewhat influenced by the teachings of the eighteenth-century Arabian scholar Muhammad ibn Abd al-Wahhab and the Hanbali tradition going back to Ibn Taymiyyah in the fourteenth century, the reformers, who gradually became identified as Salafis, sought to simplify the religious teachings of Islam and to return to the original, prescriptive texts of the Quran and hadith as sources of authority. This return to the Quran and hadith repeated a long-term trend in Islam often identified with Ahl al-Hadith or Hanbalism but sometimes also carried out by others, as in the case of the earlier Hanafi revival of the hadith in India.[32]

While such revivalism seems to match the idea of a "return to the fundamentals," as noted by Lapidus above, it actually was more complicated than that. For example, neither al-Afghani nor Abduh, the one a philosophically minded revolutionary of Iranian Shii origin, the other a rather liberal Egyptian Azhari, present the picture of a Salafi that one now would expect, and indeed both have been disowned by many later Salafis. Also, some early Salafi positions, such as that of support for Kemalist secularist changes in Turkey in the early 1920s, were repudiated by later Salafis. The pivotal figure here was Abduh's student and helper, the more conservative Lebanese scholar Muhammad Rashid Rida (1865–1935), who joined Abduh in Cairo in 1897.[33] In the period 1924–1926 Rida helped to bring the Salafiyyah into a closer alignment with the Saudi religious establishment,[34] an alliance that was further reinforced in the 1960s by the Saudi King Faysal with his policy of "Islamic solidarity,"[35] which brought many reform-minded Egyptians and others to Saudi Arabia to live and work, developments studied in detail by Reinhard Schulze. Thus the Salafi movement became one of the main protagonists in Muslim cultural and political struggles. Although many now use the terms *Salafism* and *Wahhabism* interchangeably, and although they did become closely related and influence each other, they retain some important distinctions, especially concerning the authoritative status of the Saudi religious establishment,[36] which illustrates how dangerous it is to generalize about religious groupings, as they maintain many differences and are in a continuous state of flux. It is significant that Commins and Schulze, historians who have studied the Salafi reform movement in great detail, do not refer to it as fundamentalist nor make use of such terminology.

To examine one of a variety of current basic Salafi teachings, one might consider the book *Ma la yasau al-Muslim jahluhu* (What a Muslim Cannot Afford to Be Ignorant about), by two Salafi shaykhs, Abd Allah al-Muslih and Salah al-Sawi.[37] Although the book, seeking a general audience, does not identify itself as Salafi, in fact Dr. Salah al-Sawi is a well-known and self-identifying Egyptian Salafi, and the contents display the basic Salafi beliefs. The book consists of three major sections: 1) Pillars of Belief (*arkan al-iman*, pp. 13–128); 2) Pillars of Practice (*arkan al-islam*, pp. 129–209); and 3) The Building of the Family in Islam (*bana al-usrah fi al-islam,* pp. 211–257), the last of these also including some additional material. The greater length of the first section is typical of the Salafi concern for correct doctrine, but most of the content is normal in a general presentation of Islam. However, one must attend to the peculiarities of the Salafi mission included within the book, because these constitute salient and effective points of difference. Thus, the doctrine of *al-wala wa-al-bara* ("following and shunning"), which is basically a doctrine of separatism and is a hallmark of much modern Salafi teaching, is stated briefly (pp. 39–41),[38] although it must be observed that the writers do not require a total shunning of a backsliding Muslim. Relating this to "fundamentalism," one might inquire whether separatism is a sufficient ground on whch to regard a group as fundamentalist. That is, are all separatists to be considered fundamentalists, and if so, what is the particular use of the term *fundamentalist* with regard to them, when *separatist* would seem more to the point and accurate?

A further significant point made by al-Muslih and al-Sawi that might be used to accuse Salafis of fundamentalism is the doctrine of the superior or highest Imamate (*al-imamah al-uzma*), meaning the necessity of establishing a paramount Muslim political leadership under one particular Imam (pp. 107–8).[39] This accusation is possible because such a doctrine expresses a political concern. Likewise, the authors state that obedience to the rulers is required unless they command something sinful or unlawful (pp. 109–10). These points might seem to amount to or at least to imply a political program, but they are laid out without any detail, and in fact they are also standard doctrines from the medieval law, where they are likewise laid out, though rarely elaborated.[40] Indeed the well-known historical theorist Ibn Khaldun (1332–1406), who has never been accounted a "fundamentalist," has a long explanation in his famous *al-Muqaddimah* on the necessity of the superior Imamate.[41] Therefore it seems doubtful that having such a doctrine on the necessity of orderly government can be taken as a defining indication of something called fundamentalism. While one group might hold certain rules of government to be "fundamental," another group might hold some other, opposite doctrine to be the same, and it is not clear which, if any, could be termed real fundamentalists. Thus, for example, some uphold the existing royal government of Saudi Arabia, and some support the concept of a more ideal Muslim government, while many eschew politics altogether. The doctrines as stated by al-Muslih and al-Sawi are minimal because they constitute a broad umbrella on which all Muslims should be able, in their view, to agree. Also, even though the bare political doctrine exists, there is no plan to implement it and no real emphasis on it. Indeed most Salafis appear either to support the existing governments or to be apolitical, like the famous Salafi hadith expert Muhammad Nasir al-Din al-Albani (1914–1999), whose pronouncements on the hadith have come to be taken almost as canonical by many, if not most, Salafis.[42] Although numerous Salafi and other conservative Muslim groups have various positions about government, the one group that stands out in emphasizing the need to have a single Muslim government under a single Imam over the Muslim world and in having a detailed description of such a regime is the non-Salafi Hizb al-Tahrir al-Islami (The Islamic Liberation Party) founded in 1953 by the Palestinian shaykh Taqi al-Din al-Nabhani (1909–1977). Yet that group, while greatly hallowing the history of the early caliphates, also provides no practical program to achieve the implementation of their plan.[43]

Al-Muslih and al-Sawi go on to mention the two ways of implementing the teachings of Islam: faith (iman) and struggle (jihad) (pp. 111–13). Yet their description of struggle, although mentioning the armed struggle and noting that most of the classical texts on struggle refer to the armed one, includes as well, under the title of jihad, teaching and learning in the mosque, while placing the most emphasis on preaching, as well as on struggling to overcome the self. Of course, the entire subject of armed struggle, which also may be termed just-war doctrine, is dealt with in some detail in most medieval legal compendia and thus does not stand out as a particular characteristic of Salafi doctrine. It is doubtful that the unelaborated presence of Muslim just-war doctrine in a text can be taken as a sign of "fundamentalism," for, were that the case, the generality of Muslims would have to be considered fundamentalists. Even Sufis, who are sometimes viewed as pacifists, in fact have endorsed the existence of just wars and historically have fought in what they have deemed to be just wars.[44] Indeed since most human beings believe in, or at least acquiesce in, the idea of just war under certain circumstances, even if war seems to be less favored now than at any previous time in human history, then most of humanity likewise would have to be considered fundamentalists. And al-Muslih's and al-Sawi's position is quite irenic, given that they emphasize that study, knowledge, preaching, and overcoming the self are also forms of jihad. Further on, this position of theirs is confirmed by the section on relations with peaceable non-Muslims (p. 122), which definitely offers a picture of peaceful coexistence, and that on the necessity of consultation (*shura*) (pp. 123–24), an emphasis which reflects democratizing tendencies of contemporary society. Both of these suggest modernist influence.

Finally, on the issue of women, where Salafis and other Muslims called fundamentalists are routinely excoriated by Western commentators both in the press and in academia, al-Muslih and al-Sawi adopt a moderate position as well, noting that the *qawamah,* or charge given to the man in the house in marriage, is to be a charge of care, protection, and responsibility and not of force and control, and that the marriage tie is to be built on the basis of mercy, affection, and mutual rights (p. 217). In this as in other areas, while al-Muslih and al-Sawi do not perhaps match the expectations of contemporary Western societies' demands for complete individual freedom and equality, they undoubtedly present a modernizing paradigm overall. It is not clear, then, why especially they or the Salafis or other Muslim groups should have to be lumped together under so obviously hostile label as *fundamentalist* when there is such a spectrum of opinion and when they seem to be in their own fashion in conversation with their modern environment, even in a book that is almost a kind of catechism meant didactically to inculcate a particular point of view.

In fact, if one examines other works among the well-known, most widely distributed, and essential texts of the Salafis, one sees that these also are primarily concerned with matters that would not strike the academic purveyors of the concept of fundamentalism as essential or relevant, nor those fearing Muslim political influence or power as very important. For example, the Salafi publishing house Dar-us-Salam of Riyadh, Saudi Arabia, one of the most important Salafi publishing houses in the world, offers a set of seven essential texts in English called the Islamic Library that is quite popular: a translation of the Quran, two secondary medieval hadith collections, a recent Salafi biography of the Prophet Muhammad, two books on correct belief dating from the eighteenth and nineteenth centuries, and a recent Salafi book on the pillars of faith and practice.[45] The last of these, *Arkan al-islam wa-al-iman wa-ma yajibu an yarifuhu kull muslim an dinihi*, by Muhammad ibn Jamil Zaynu (1925–2010), offers an interesting and fairly close parallel with the book of al-Muslih and al-Sawi already cited. Even the titles are similar: What a Muslim Cannot Afford to Be Ignorant about and What Every Muslim Must Know about His Religion. Like the book of al-Muslih and al-Sawi, it covers belief and practice, devoting much more space to the latter, including instructions on how to perform the required rituals. Like the other book, Zaynu's work contains only a little material that does not concern the norm of general Sunni Muslim beliefs and practices. It even parallels al-Muslih and al-Sawi in placing the family immediately after the basic practices in the order of things.[46] Zaynu also presents a considerable section on things that cause one to exit from the religion, with the usual Salafi complaints against veneration of saints, calling on them for intercession, and visiting graves being mentioned as vitiating one's faith.[47] An additional section near the end warns that various kinds of financial instruments involving interest are forbidden, including home mortgages.[48] Thus while Zaynu places a little more emphasis on regarding certain categories of backsliders as unbelievers, the works are remarkably similar, and neither of them contains anything that could be considered a plausible or certain indication of "fundamentalism."

The two works on belief or creed in the Islamic Library, *Kitab al-tawhid*, by Ibn Abd al-Wahhab, and *Taqwiyat al-iman*, by Shah Ismail al-Dihlawi (1779–1831), are older and hence a bit more archaic-seeming in their concerns. They mostly contain quotations from the Quran and the hadith, with some commentary, denouncing polytheism, amulets, sacred trees and stones, sacrifices made to other than God, worshiping at graves, honoring the tombs of dead saints, seeking intercession from other than God and his Prophet, sorcery, soothsaying, magic, omens, astrology, showing off, exaggerated respect for religious leaders, specific phrases not to say, denying God's names and attributes, denying the divine decree, making pictures, and wrong kinds of oaths.[49] It is difficult to see why any of these points would elicit a charge of fundamentalism. The only aspect of the books' contents that would allow suggesting that term would be that all of these sins are associated with unbelief, so that their practicioners are considered by the writers to have exited from the religion and placed their eternal souls in danger. This undoubtedly amounts to an exclusivism, but it is questionable that exclusivism can be defined as fundamentalism, because others, both Muslim and non-Muslim, religious and nonreligious, are exclusivist in various ways and to sundry degress and yet are not so identified, and also because it would seem more appropriate to call practicioners of exclusivism exclusivists, if they truly exclude others from the group.

Fundamentalism, Sufism, and Salafism

Nevertheless, such labeling also has received reinforcement when Muslims have taken it up to describe other Muslims whom they dislike for one reason or another. First of all, political rulers find such labels convenient for labeling and distancing the opposition, as well as asserting that the opposition, being "fundamentalist," must be excluded from all consideration of its views. This situation also applies to competing visions of Islam by different Muslims, who are sometimes anxious to dump the "fundamentalist" charge on their rivals, a phenomenon that is in particular visible among some Sufis who would like themselves to be seen as the "good Muslims" versus the Salafi "bad Muslims." Such labeling actually continues the long-standing polemic of Sufis against Wahhabis dating to the eighteenth century, a discourse which now comes back to help reinforce the new labeling, whether by using the term *fundamentalism,* one of its translations in another language such as *al-usuliyyah* in Arabic, or one of the other unfavorable identifying terms that have been created in the press or academia, to mark the anti-Sufis. This process has led to a generally abiding hostility between Salafis and Sufis, even though the early Salafi movement concentrating on reform initially drew considerable inspiration and support from Sufi orders.[50]

An example of particularly strident and focused polemic against the Salafis, Wahhabis, and Muslim fundamentalists is that of the Lebanese scholar Muhammad Hisham Kabbani (al-Qabbani in Arabic) (b. 1945). Kabbani follows the Hanafi school of law and is a shaykh of a branch of the Naqshbandi Sufi order. Because of this background, his polemic parallels that of the non-Muslim critics of Salafism, Wahhabism, and fundamentalism in some respects but differs in others. First, he regards Salafism and Wahhabism as one and the same thing, stating baldly, "In essence, Salafism and Wahhabism are the same, but the latter is identified by its founder while the former takes the name of the Salaf and makes it its own."[51] Further, he clearly identifies both Salafism and Wahhabism with fundamentalism as well as Islamic radicalism.[52] That this polemic has a clear political agenda is illustrated plainly by an article by Paul A. Goble (b. 1949), the political analyst and Central Asia expert, "Uzbekistan: Analysis from Washington—Fighting

Fundamentalism with Sufism," published on the Radio Free Europe–Radio Liberty website.[53] Significantly, Goble states,

> In many respects, this attempt to use Sufism to combat fundamentalism is fighting fire with fire. While followers of the two trends dislike one another and disagree on many theological and practical points, they share in common a distaste for many of the actions and corruption of the successor regimes in Tashkent and elsewhere in Central Asia.
>
> Moreover, the two groups have in common an underground kind of organization, fundamentalism because of its radical rejection of all civil authorities and the Naqshbandi Sufi order because its propagation has always been based on groups of the followers of a particular saintly leader. By their very nature, such organizations are often beyond the control of the state.

He thus suggests that the outcome may be similar and that there are organizational similarities between the fundamentalists and the Sufis. Kabbani also became closely connected with Uzbekistan's Karimov regime at least for a time starting in August 2000, the month before Goble's article was published, and cooperated in, or possibly even inspired, its attempts to promote the Naqshbandi Sufi order to counter non-Sufi fundamentalists, who are also identified as Salafis and Wahhabis.[54] This is possibly one of the most overt cases of trying to exploit the term *fundamentalism* as an accusation for political purposes.

While this political use of *fundamentalism* parallels that of several of the other writers cited in this article, Kabbani's detailed writings on Salafism and Wahhabism are concerned with other matters entirely, rather different from the concerns of academics. Mostly, Kabbani's writings are concerned with matters of belief where the Salafis and Wahhabis clash with his own esoteric Sufi tradition. Most of this debate, from both the side of the Salafis and that of equally argumentative Sufis such as Kabbani, surely would seem remote, imaginary, and irrelevant to most non-Muslim observers and even to some Muslims. The main issues are issues of creed or belief (*aqidah*), and many of them have been argued over furiously since the Middle Ages. Indeed, regarding the two important medieval icons of the Salafis Ibn Taymiyyah and Ibn Qayyim al-Jawziyyah (1292–1350), Kabbani states: "There is no doubt that these two scholars had the ability to exercise ijtihad [personal reasoning] in the areas of mu'amalat [laws governing society]. In fact, they gave many good fatwas in this area. Moreover, they did not attempt to bring about major changes in 'ibadat [forms of worship], although they diverged substantially from the Ahl al-Sunna in their ijtihad. However, they did pursue change in the area most crucial to Muslim unity and soundness of religion: they went astray in the area of 'aqida [belief system] and completely left the pure teachings of the original scholars of the Salaf [early generations of pious predecessors]."[55] Thus focusing on deviations in creed, Kabbani mentions the intolerance of the anthropomorphizing Hanbali beliefs in contrast to his own Ashari theology,[56] the charges of anthropomorphism leveled against Ibn Taymiyyah, Ibn Qayyim al-Jawziyyah, and others,[57] the charge that Ibn Taymiyyah authorized Muslims to fight other Muslims,[58] the rebellion of the Wahhabis against the legitimate Muslim state and their destructiveness,[59] the contentiousness of Muhammad Nasir al-Din al-Albani,[60] the dispute over whether or not God has a direction, which is up, according to the Salafis,[61] the impropriety of likening God to created things,[62] the Salafi attack on Sufism,[63] the validity of using weak hadiths,[64] and the acceptance of the Sufi Abd al-Qadir al-Jilani and others by Ibn Taymiyyah.[65] Another volume by the Iraqi scholar al-Zahawi and translated by Kabbani also criticizes the early violence of the Wahhabis,[66] and especially their pronouncing scholars and others of the past and present who disagreed with them to be unbelievers outside of the pale of Islam,[67] but at the same time reproves their deviance from traditional eschatological and otherworldly beliefs. Thus al-Zahawi and Kabbani disapprove of Salafi or Wahhabi reforms, such as their prohibiting seeking the intercession of dead shaykhs[68] or visiting their tombs.[69] Curiously, apart from the charges of violence and exclusivism, hardly any of these Salafi tenets that Kabbani is criticizing are claimed to be aspects of fundamentalism, yet they have actually been central to this internal Muslim debate.

One may admit that indeed the Salafi mission (*dawah*) is quite narrow and strict in its teaching. It not only requires conformity and assent to a particular creed that is quite detailed and occasionally excludes those who do not agree to this creed from the pale of Islam, but it also insists on the scrupulous application of a particular practice that is quite specific in many of the details it imposes. But even many Sufis, who are not often, if ever, called fundamentalists, uphold a parallel narrow insistence on a detailed set of beliefs and practices that also extends to excluding others from Islam. Thus the teaching of Ahmad Rida Khan Barelwi (1856–1921), the Qadiri Sufi founder of the Ahl-i Sunnah movement in India, issued fatwas denouncing the Deobandis and the liberal reformers of the Aligarh movement both as non-Muslims.[70] Similarly, the rather exclusivist Habashi movement founder and Rifai Sufi Abd Allah al-Harari (1920–2008) denounced the Wahhabis as unbelievers and non-Muslims.[71]

Conclusion

It is quite obvious that different religious groups try to establish and maintain their distinctiveness by the creation of religious boundaries, sometimes identified as religious particularism.[72] Actually all people are selective in their lives, at least to some extent, whether they are religious or not, which means they set up some boundaries. And for a group to preserve an extensive set of special teachings and way of life, as all organized religions do, the members will need to set more extensive structures as part of their framework for teaching, which inevitably means more boundaries to include some things and exclude others. Because this is a universal trait of religions, religious groups cannot be taken to task for "fundamentalism" merely for trying to keep up such boundaries. However, it is also clear that such boundaries can be more or less sharply drawn, and the sharpness of such boundaries is indeed one of the criteria of fundamentalism cited by Almond, Appleby, and Sivan.[73] And it would seem reasonable to consider some Salafis and Wahhabis, with their sometime denunciations of other Muslims as unbelievers who should be shunned, as intentionally drawing such sharp and distinguishing boundaries. But this is still not sufficient to justify the application of *fundamentalism* or any of its substitutes or cognates to them. As John L. Esposito has said, "I regard 'fundamentalism' as too laden with Christian presuppositions and Western stereotypes, as well as implying a monolithic threat that does not exist; more fitting general terms are 'Islamic revivalism' or 'Islamic activism,' which are less value-laden and have roots within the Islamic tradition. In recent years, the terms 'political Islam' and 'Islamism' have become more common usage. Islam possesses a long tradition of revival (tajdid) and reform (islah) which includes notions of political and social activism dating from the early Islamic centuries to the present day. Thus I prefer to speak of Islamic revivalism and Islamic activism rather than of Islamic fundamentalism."[74] While *Muslim* rather than *Islamic* may also be preferable as an adjective here, the principle of adhering to more clearly specifying and less pejorative terms finds justification. One does not have to like or approve of the stricter or sharper boundaries and criteria set up for group approval of one's actions by the Salafis to appreciate the need for a less loaded and more accurate set of descriptive terms. Salafi exclusiveness can be described simply as exclusivism.

Thus it would be desirable for the field of Muslim studies to distance itself from broad claims about the unified identity of very diverse groups, each of which deserves consideration separately and on its own. At the same time it would be desirable to abandon the term *fundamentalism* altogether, since it is being used primarily as a term of abuse.[75]

Notes

1. Ira M. Lapidus, *A History of Islamic Societies*, 2nd ed. (Cambridge: Cambridge University Press, 2002), 823.

2. Charles B. Strozier, David M. Terman, and James W. Jones, with Katherine A. Boyd, *The Fundamentalist Mindset: Psychological Perspectives on Religion, Violence, and History* (Oxford: Oxford University Press, 2010), xvii–xxi.

3. Indeed Marty's foreword portrays this threat in the most menacing terms. Strozier et al., *The Fundamentalist Mindset*, xvii–xviii; also, the book's cover design bears lurid red spots clearly representing bloodshed.

4. Ibid., 11.

5. The recourse to authorization based on psychology is reminiscent of the egregious stereotyping of Raphael Patai in *The Arab Mind* (New York: Scribners, 1973).

6. Strozier et al., *The Fundamentalist Mindset*, 11. Note that identifying the motivation of the other as irrational rage is a trick of propaganda as old as politics, as it is found even in

the ancient Roman motif of "the wrath of Hamilcar" as the cause of the Second Punic War of 218–201 B.C.E. On this, see especially Polybius (c. 200–c. 118 B.C.E.), *Histories*, III.10–12.

7. Notwithstanding the recent book, Richard C. Martin and Abbas Barzegar, eds., *Islamism: Contested Perspectives on Political Islam* (Stanford: Stanford University Press, 2010), in which some of the authors advocate the use of *Islamism* while others oppose it. Sidahmed and Ehteshami use *Islamic fundamentalism* in their collection's title but then repudiate it, while, along with their contributors, preferring *Islamism* throughout. Abdel Salam Sidahmed and Anoushirvan Ehteshami, *Islamic Fundamentalism* (Boulder, Colo.: Westview Press, 1996), 2–5.

8. Youssef M. Choueiri, *Islamic Fundamentalism: The Story of Islamist Movements*, 3rd ed., (London: Continuum, 2010), vii.

9. Ibid., 1–4.

10. Ejaz Akram, "The Muslim World and Globalization: Modernity and the Roots of Conflict," in *Islam, Fundamentalism, and the Betrayal of Tradition: Essays by Western Muslim Scholars*, rev. ed., ed. Joseph E. B. Lumbard (Bloomington, Ind.: World Wisdom, 2009), 291 n. 10.

11. Choueiri, *Islamic Fundamentalism*, 3.

12. Ibid., 7.

13. Ibid., 10.

14. Ibid., 5.

15. Ibid., 6.

16. Ibid., 4, 7–8, 237.

17. Bruce B. Lawrence, *Shattering the Myth: Islam beyond Violence* (Princeton: Princeton University Press, 1998), 40–105.

18. Gabriel A. Almond, R. Scott Appleby, and Emmanuel Sivan, *Strong Religion: The Rise of Fundamentalisms around the World* (Chicago: University of Chicago Press, 2003), 15.

19. Robert A. Pape, *Dying to Win: The Strategic Logic of Suicide Terrorism*, New York: Random House Trade Paperbacks, 2006, 16–17, 21–23. See also Talal Asad, *On Suicide Bombing* (New York: Columbia University Press, 2007), 54, 109 n. 25, citing a Pape article of 2003.

20. Hale's story is indeed featured on the CIA website at https://www.cia.gov/news-information/featured-story-archive/2007-featured-story-archive/nathan-hale.html (accessed October 1, 2012).

21. Horace, *Odes*, III.2.13; quoted sarcastically by the World War I antiwar poet Wilfred Owen (1893–1918) in his poem "Dulce et Decorum Est Pro Patria Mori," available at http://www.oucs.ox.ac.uk/ww1lit/collections/item/3303?CISOBOX=1&REC=1 (accessed October 1, 2012).

22. Mahmood Mamdani, *Good Muslim, Bad Muslim: America, the Cold War, and the Roots of Terror* (New York: Pantheon Books, 2004), 15 and passim.

23. "The Global Religious Landscape: A Report on the Size and Distribution of the World's Major Religious Groups as of 2010," Pew Forum on Religion & Public Life, Pew Research Center, December 2012, at http://www.pewforum.org/files/2012/12/globalReligion-full.pdf, 9, 22, 50 (accessed September 1, 2013).

24. Charles Allen, *God's Terrorists: The Wahhabi Cult and Hidden Roots of Modern Jihad* (Cambridge, Mass.: Da Capo Press, 2007). "Wahhabis" are called fundamentalist by Malise Ruthven, *Fundamentalism: A Very Short Introduction* (Oxford: Oxford University Press, 2007), 87–88; Rebecca Joyce Frey, *Fundamentalism* (New York: Facts on File, 2007), 94; Timothy R. Furnish, "Islamic Fundamentalism," in *Encyclopedia of Fundamentalism*, ed. Brenda E. Brasher (New York: Routledge, 2001), 238; for its application to contemporary Central Asian Muslim movements, see Alexander Knysh, "A Clear and Present Danger: 'Wahhabism' as a Rhetorical Foil," *Die Welt des Islams*, new series 44, no. 1 (2004): 3–26; Hamid Algar, *Wahhabism: A Critical Essay* (Oneonta, N.Y.: Islamic Publications International, 2002), 45; for its use as a pejorative term and sometimes, rarely, a self-identification, see 'Abd Allâh Sâlih

al-'Uthaymîn, *Muhammad ibn 'Abd al-Wahhâb: The Man and His Works* (London: I. B. Tauris, 2009), 110–111.

25. Natana J. DeLong-Bas, *Wahhabi Islam: From Revival and Reform to Global Jihad* (Oxford: Oxford University Press, 2004), 243.

26. Ibid., 240–43, especially 242.

27. This move is challenged by Yahya Michot, *Muslims under Non-Muslim Rule: Ibn Taymiyya on Fleeing from Sin; Kinds of Emigration; the Status of Mardin; Domain of Peace/War, Domain Composite; the Conditions for Challenging Power,* trans. Jamil Qureshi (Oxford: Interface Publications, 1427/2006), 123–24.

28. Roel Meijer, ed., *Global Salafism: Islam's New Religious Movement* (New York: Columbia University Press, 2009), 1–2, 37; Hamid Enayat, *Modern Islamic Political Thought* (London: I. B. Tauris, 2005), 69, 81; As'ad AbuKhalil, *The Battle for Saudi Arabia: Royalty, Fundamentalism, and Global Power* (New York: Seven Stories Press, 2004), 68.

29. Vincenzo Olivetti, *Terror's Source: The Ideology of Wahhabi-Salafism and Its Consequences* (Birmingham, U.K.: Amadeus Books, 2002), 20.

30. Thomas Hegghammer, "Jihadi-Salafis or Revolutionaries: On Religion and Politics in the Study of Militant Islam," in *Global Salafism: Islam's New Religious Movement,* ed. Roel Meijer (New York: Columbia University Press, 2009), 248–49.

31. David Dean Commins, *Islamic Reform: Politics and Social Change in Late Ottoman Syria* (Oxford: Oxford University Press, 1990), and Commins, *The Wahhabi Mission and Saudi Arabia* (London: I. B. Tauris, 2006), both of which deal extensively with how Najdi reformism both paralleled and successively influenced developments in Iraq and Syria, a trend that later took place in Egypt as well.

32. This revival was led by Abd al-Haqq ibn Sayf al-Din al-Dihlawi (958–1052/1551–1642), a Hanafi Sufi. Abd al-Hayy ibn Fakhr al-Din al-Hasani (d. 1341/1923), *al-Ilam bi-man fi tarikh al-Hind min al-alam, al-musamma bi-Nuzhat al-khawatir wa-bahjat al-masami wa-al-nawazir* (Beirut: Dar Ibn Hazm, 1420/1999), vol. 2, pt. 5, pp. 553–57.

33. Commins, *Wahhabi Mission,* 137.

34. Reinhard Schulze, *A Modern History of the Islamic World,* trans. Azizeh Azodi (New York: New York University Press, 2002), 67–68, 71–72.

35. Reinhard Schulze, *Islamischer Internationalismus im 20. Jahrhundert: Untersuchungen zur Geschichte der Islamischen Weltliga* (Leiden: Brill, 1990); Schulze, *Modern History,* 18–19; Stéphanie Lacroix, "Between Revolution and Apoliticism: Nasir al-Din al-Albani and His Impact on the Shaping of Contemporary Salafism," in *Global Salafism: Islam's New Religious Movement,* ed. Roel Meijer (New York: Columbia University Press, 2009), 62–63; Algar, *Wahhabism,* 47–50.

36. Lacroix, "Between Revolution and Apoliticism," 61, 66–68, 72–73; more baldly stated by her in her "Al-Albani's Revolutionary Approach to Hadith," *ISIM Review* 21 (Spring 2008): 6–7.

37. Abd Allah al-Muslih and Salah al-Sawi, *Ma la yasau al-Muslim jahluhu* (Cairo: Islamic Foundation of America, 1416/1995).

38. This doctrine is strongly promoted by a widely circulated recent book by Muhammad ibn Said al-Qahtani, *al-Wala wa-al-bara fi al-Islam* (Cairo: al-Fath li-al-Ilam al-Arabi, 1402[/1982]). For a useful and nuanced study of the concept, see Joas Wagemakers, "The Transformation of a Radical Concept: *al-wala' wa-l-bara'* in the Ideology of Abu Muhammad al-Maqdisi," in *Global Salafism: Islam's New Religious Movement,* ed. Roel Meijer (New York: Columbia University Press, 2009), 81–102.

39. For a study of the superior Imamate, affirming it, see Abd Allah b. Umar b. Sulayman al-Dumayji, *al-Imamah al-uzma inda ahl al-sunnah wa-al-jamaah* (Riyadh: Dar Tibah li-al-Tibaah wa-al-Nashr, 1409[/1989]). It is possible that the authors have drawn the phrase *al-imamah al-uzma* from this book.

40. The best-known, if idealistic, medieval elaboration on government is Abu al-Hasan Ali b. Muhammad al-Mawardi (364–450/975–1058), *The Ordinances of Government: Al-Ahkam al-Sultaniyyah,* trans. Wafaa H. Wahba (Reading, U.K.: Garnet, 1996); also Abu'l Hasan al-Mawardi, *Al-Ahkam As-Sultaniyyah: The Laws of Islamic Governance,* trans. Asadullah Yate (London: Ta-Ha Publishers, 1416/1996).

41. Abd al-Rahman Ibn Khaldun al-Maghribi, *Tarikh Ibn Khaldun: Kitab al-ibar wa-diwan al-mubtadi wa-al-khabar fî ayyam al-arab wa-al-ajam wa-al-barbar wa-man asarahum min dhawi al-sultan al-akbar* (Beirut: Dar al-Kitab al-Lubnani, 1956–1961, Vol. 1 reprinted 1982), 7 vols, 1: 336–42. For the English translation, see Ibn Khaldun, *The Muqaddimah: An Introduction to History,* trans. Franz Rosenthal (London: Routledge & Kegan Paul, 1958), 3 vols., 1: 385–94.

42. Lacroix, "Between Revolution and Apoliticism," 68–71.

43. Suha Taji-Farouki, "Islamic State Theories and Contemporary Realities," in Abdel Salam Sidahmed and Anoushirvan Ehteshami, eds. *Islamic Fundamentalism* (Boulder, Colo.: Westview Press, 1996), 38–47.

44. Muhammad Hisham Kabbani, *Islamic Beliefs & Doctrine According to Ahl al-Sunna: A Repudiation of "Salafi" Innovations,* 2nd ed. (Mountain View, Calif.: As-Sunna Foundation of America, 1993), 1: 231–32. His list is not exhaustive, however.

45. http://store.dar-us-salam.com/Eng_Pkgs/009.html (accessed October 1, 2012).

46. Muhammad bin Jamil Zeno, *The Pillars of Islam & Iman & What Every Muslim Must Know about His Religion* (Riyadh: Dar-us-Salam Publications, 1997), 224–27. The Arabic version: Muhammad ibn Jamil Zaynu, *Arkan al-islam wa-al-iman wa-ma yajibu an yarifuhu kull muslim an dinihi* (N. p.: Jamiyyat Ihya al-Turath al-Islami, Idarat Bana al-Masajid wa-al-Mashari al-Islamiyyah, 1408[/1988]), 177–79.

47. Zeno, *Pillars of Islam,* 38–55; Arabic: Zaynu, *Arkan al-islam,* 23–36.

48. Zeno, *Pillars of Islam,* 238–41; Arabic: Zaynu, *Arkan al-islam,* 187–88.

49. Muhammad bin Abdul-Wahhab, *Kitab at-Tauhid* (Riyadh: Dar-us-Salam Publications, 1416/1996); Shah Ismail Shaheed, *Taqwiyat-ul-Iman (Strengthening of the Faith)* (Riyadh: Dar-us-Salam Publications, 1416/1995).

50. Schulze, *Modern History,* 24, especially 307n34.

51. Jamal Effendi al-Iraqi al-Sidqi al-Zahawi, *The Doctrine of Ahl al-Sunna Versus the "Salafi" Movement: A Complete Refutation,* trans. Muhammad Hisham Kabbani (Mountain View, Calif.: As-Sunna Foundation of America, 1996), 3.

52. See, for example, the article "Islamic Radicalism: Its Wahhabi Roots and Current Representation," by an organization that he founded and continues to govern as its chairman, The Islamic Supreme Council of America (ISCA) See
http://www.islamicsupremecouncil.org/home/about-us.html and
http://www.islamicsupremecouncil.org/understanding-islam/anti-extremism.html.

53. Paul Goble, "Uzbekistan: Analysis from Washington—Fighting Fundamentalism with Sufism," published September 9, 2000, at http://www.rferl.org/content/article/1094729.html (accessed October 1, 2012).

54. As shown in Kabbani's own bio on his organization's website at http://naqshbandi.org/about/Sh_Kabbani_bio.htm (accessed October 1, 2012).

55. Kabbani, Islamic Beliefs & Doctrine, 1: 44.

56. Ibid., 8–10, 48–78.

57. Ibid., 44–47, 84–97, 101–143, 183–189, 193–210, 213–214; Zahawi, *The Doctrine of Ahl al-Sunna,* 35–41, 43–44.

58. Kabbani, *Islamic Beliefs & Doctrine,* 1: 42–43.

59. Ibid., 219.

60. Ibid., 79–83.

61. Ibid., 144–82, 200–203.

62. Ibid., 98–99, 190–92.

63. Ibid., 326–30.

64. Ibid., 331–35.

65. Ibid., 337, 354–56. That Ibn Taymiyyah himself, despite being possibly the greatest of all shaykhs for the anti-Sufi Salafis, was himself a Sufi, was famously argued by George Makdisi, "Ibn Taymiya: A Sufi of the Qadiriya Order," *American Journal of Arabic Studies* 1 (1973): 118–29.

66. Zahawi, *The Doctrine of Ahl al-Sunna,* 25, 27, 29–31.

67. Ibid., 24–25, 27, 35, 37, 45, 58–70, 106.

68. Ibid., 29–30, 45, 65, 71–92.

69. Ibid., 27–29, 37, 45, 67–68, 93–105.

70. Usha Sanyal, *Ahmad Riza Khan Barelwi: In the Path of the Prophet* (Oxford: Oneworld, 2005), 108.

71. Patrick Desplat. "The Articulation of Religious Identities and Their Boundaries in Ethiopia," *Journal of Religion in Africa* 35 (November 2005), 498, 500–501; Abd Allah Muhammad al-Shami, *al-Radd ala Abd Allah al-Habashi* (N. p.: Dar al-Ittila, n. d. [1980s]), 160–64. To see how anti-Wahhabi preaching is a central theme in the Habashi mission, see Abd Allah al-Harari, *Sarih al-bayan fi al-radd ala man khalafa al-Quran* ([Beirut]: Dar al-Mashari, 1415/1995), passim, especially pp. 135–245, 370–71, 395–98.

72. Fiona Bowie, *The Anthropology of Religion,* 2nd ed. (Oxford: Blackwell, 2006), 62–79; R. Stephen Warner, "Religion, Boundaries, and Bridges," *Sociology of Religion* 58 (Autumn 1997): 217–38.

73. Almond, Appleby, and Sivan, *Strong Religion,* 97–98.

74. John L. Esposito, *The Islamic Threat: Myth or Reality?* 3rd ed. (Oxford: Oxford University Press, 1999), 6.

75. Ruthven, *Fundamentalism,* 5.

Fundamentalism and Shiism

Lynda Clarke

This essay points to features of Shiism that inhibit the growth of Islamic fundamentalism seen in the Sunni world.[1] Much has been written, including many essays in the works of the Fundamentalism Project, about fundamentalism in relation to the Iranian Islamic revolution and other Shiite movements, but there has been no attempt to relate it to Shiism as a religious tradition with its own characteristics and conditions. Although also part of Islam, Shiism is very different from Sunnism, and its peculiarities should always be kept in mind. The four distinctive features treated here are the minority status of Shiites, quietism, clerical authority, and lack of literalism or scripturalism. As a result of these, Shiism is an inefficient conductor of fundamentalism, or at least of the fundamentalism that has been characteristic of modern Islam.

The very significant exceptions of Ayatollah Khomeini and the Islamic Republic of Iran are dealt with in the companion essay in this book, "Fundamentalism, Khomeinism, and the Islamic Republic of Iran." In both essays I refer to first- , second- , and third-wave Islamic fundamentalism. By first wave, I mean mass-based organisations that operate at the state level through political action, the prototype being the Muslim Brotherhood (founded 1928). By second-wave fundamentalism, I mean the utopian schemes of the Indo-Pakistani Abu al-Ala Mawdudi (d. 1979) and Sayyid Qutb (d. 1966) from Egypt. The third wave consists of clandestine groups that turn to spectacular violence to overthrow local governments and eliminate Western influence with the aim of establishing a true Islam worldwide, for example, the violent Egyptian grouplets arising in the 1970s and al-Qaeda. The three waves are quite different, although they all bear what I take to be the common mark of Islamic fundamentalism, that is, desire to establish the absolute rule of Islam.

The relation of each wave to Shiism is also different. Shiism has produced versions of the first two, in the form of the Dawah party, founded as a clandestine organization in the 1950s or early 1960s in Iraq, and, as I will assert in the next essay, Khomeinism, which borrows from the second wave. Shiites have not participated in the third wave, for reasons that will become clear below. The thing to notice here is that fundamentalism in each case begins in the Sunni world and then exercises influence on Shiites. It is not original with Shiism, although Shiites have in special conditions seized upon it and made it their own.

The Minority Situation

The situation faced by Muslim-majority nations today is essentially political. It involves an experience of Western encroachment and domination, followed by the political failures of successor states and regimes. James Piscatori points to the importance of the latter element when he characterizes Islamic fundamentalism as a "second-order reaction," a response not as much to the failures of modernization as to those of "leaders, religious as well as political, to deal with these failures."[2] The political nature of the situation helps to explain why the definitions and responses of Muslim fundamentalists are also political; why, for instance, the problem is defined as lack of Islamic rule and the solution is thought to lie in militant action and why fundamentalism is blended with nationalism and pan-Islamism. We come to see why Islamic fundamentalism is sometimes called "political Islam"; it is because Muslim fundamentalists answer to a political situation in political terms.

Islamic fundamentalism also, of course, addresses cultural concerns, often in deep and complex ways. These are, however, in the final analysis subordinate to political goals. This is evident in the idea advanced by Sayyid Qutb and others that cultural renovation and creation of an Islamic society are required to build an Islamic state capable of restoring the power of Islam. We will also see in the next essay how Ayatollah Khomeini entirely subordinates religion to politics. The editors of the Fundamentalist Project see fundamentalism arising in situations in which believers feel "beleaguered" by a "syncretistic, areligious, or irreligious cultural milieu"; but this does not fit the Muslim case. Muslims in Muslim-majority countries are not in reality faced by any serious "irreligious cultural milieu." What they feel "beleaguered" by is rather foreign culture as a symbol of foreign dominance associated with "ethnoreligiously alien, imperialistic, and exploitative forces."[3] Islamic fundamentalism is not a direct reaction to Enlightenment values or so-called modernity but to the perception that these are part of a political assault; that the West is engaged in a plot to penetrate Muslim lands culturally in order to take them over is something emphasized by all fundamentalists and believed by many others.

Shiites share in the Muslim political situation described above; but since they make up only 10 to 15 percent of the Muslim population worldwide, they are also in the situation of a minority. If the situation of Muslims overall is essentially political, the essence of the situation in which Shiites find themselves is their minority status; or, one might say, they are in a double bind. The minority situation involves both on-the-ground and psychological aspects, which reinforce each other. The result may be summed up as preoccupation with the majority; any attempt to conceive of a political end or take political action, the basic activities of Muslim fundamentalism, has to contend with the majority's limiting presence.

Shiites are particularly preoccupied by the Sunnis who enclose them because of Sunnite hostility. Despite occasional feelings of solidarity stirred by common experience with Western encroachment, the attitude of the majority of Sunnis toward Shiites is decidedly negative, ranging from discomfort with their "strangeness" to belief that they are dangerous heretics. Consequently, Shiites contemplating religiously articulated political action have to take into account the limitations of their numbers and possible Sunni reaction.

Shiites are sometimes able partially to escape the minority situation by working to gain power at the state level in countries where there are larger Shiite populations and relatively favourable conditions. This has been the case in Lebanon, where a rising Shiite population (usually estimated at about one-third), along with the weakness of the Lebanese state, less preoccupation with the Sunni majority because Lebanon itself is a patchwork of minorities, and aid from Iran has created space for religiously coloured political action. The principal or ultimate aim in these instances, however, is not countrywide institution of Shiism, as would be the case for Sunni fundamentalists, but gaining a measure of power for the community. Shiite groups are usually ready to engage in negotiation and compromise and attenuate or discard religious goals in order to secure communal advantage. Democracy can be considered as an option if it seems to promise increased influence. Even the radical Iraqi cleric Muqtada al-Sadr, noted for his opposition to the American occupation and building of a Shiite militia, has quite readily entered into the political process. The tendency of Shiites toward defensive consolidation is due not only to the objective minority situation, but also to a psychological horizon imposed by ultimate awareness that the prospects of establishing Shiite rule in a hostile environment are not good. Even when Shiites gain population and power within states, they remain aware that, as a minority worldwide, they are potentially faced with some form of Sunni coalition.

The limitations imposed on Shiite fundamentalism by the minority situation and differences with Sunni fundamentalism come into sharp focus on the transnational scene. The vision of Sunni fundamentalists is pan-Islamic and triumphalist. Sunni theorists such Sayyid Qutb and Mawdudi ultimately address not just Egypt, Arabs, or Indians, but all Muslims and the worldwide future of the One True Islam, an Islam that is assumed to be orthodox, that is to say, Sunni. The horizon of transnational action and imagination for Shiites is much more restricted. They are unable to see their way to Islamic triumphalism and utopianism, not only because of the hard reality of their small numbers, but also because of a certain mentality that comes from having historically settled with a minority status.

Even simple pan-Islamism is difficult for Shiites, since specifically Shiite ideas do not appeal to the majority and would increase hostility if they were openly propagated. One way Shiites have tried to overcome isolation is by promoting a movement of rapprochement (Arabic *taqrib*) through emphasizing common elements such as similar systems of law while downplaying problems such as the traditional Shiite dislike of the revered Companions of the Prophet. This strategy actually requires moving away from Shiite fundamentals such as the Imamate and strident conviction that is the mark of fundamentalism.[4]

There are also basic differences between Sunnism and Shiism in relation to sectarian strife. As the weaker party, Shiites usually try to avoid religiously based conflict. They are generally more interested in conciliation, since they have the most to gain; the rapprochement movement has always been stronger from the Shiite side. The attitude toward Shiites of the first and second waves of Sunni fundamentalism, in contrast, ranges from some openness (for example, the founder of the Egyptian Muslim Brotherhood Hasan al-Banna [d. 1949], who attended meetings of the Rapprochement Society in Cairo), to indifference (Sayyid Qutb, who does not address Shiism), to general hostility (the Iraqi branch of the Brotherhood).[5] With the rise of Islamic Iran and sharpening of sectarian conflict, animosity on the part of the Muslim Brotherhood and Sunni religious intellectuals has become much greater.

Third-wave movements such as al-Qaeda and the various al-Qaeda–like groups take the most vigorous approach, focussing on Shiism as a source of corruption that has to be removed in order for the true Islam to be restored and become strong. What seems to have happened is that the virus of local conflicts and enmities, for example anti-Shiite sentiment and fear of Iran in Saudi Arabia and the Gulf, has been transmitted through international networks and become a shared infection.[6] The emphasis in the third wave on militant action also exposes Shiites as a local, reachable target. Thus anti-Shiism, along with violence such as the bombing of shrines and religious processions in Iraq, has become "a constituent part of the ideology of Sunni militancy,"[7] and militants cooperate internationally to perpetuate such violence.

Shiites, in contrast, do not imagine overcoming the Sunni majority. They do at times engage in sectarian conflict, for instance in Iraq and rural Pakistan, but this violence is not part of an ambitious ideology and therefore local, that is, involving contiguous populations, usually reactive, and relatively small scale. Sunnis also do not present wide and provocative targets in the way Shiites do with their public, dramatic, apparently unorthodox rituals involving crowds of worshippers. It is unlikely that we will ever see spectacular, transnational, ideologically inspired action against Sunnites as we do against Shiites in Iraq and elsewhere.

Shiite action against the West has also been different from that of Sunnis. The most spectacular anti-Western actions in the last few decades have been produced by third-wave floating Sunni networks and individuals, the best known of which are al-Qaeda and its imitators. Why do we not see Shiites engaging in this kind of activity? One on-the-ground circumstance that may help to account for this striking fact is that it would be difficult for a Shiite network to establish a base in open territory such as a failed state, lawless frontier, or urban no-go area as Sunni groups have done, since Shiites in open territory are immediately exposed to the hostile majority. Another factor preventing the development of floaters is Shiite clerical authority, addressed below. The most basic reason, however, is the limited psychological horizon of an enclosed minority. Floater operations are more symbolic than strategic; they spring from the utopian aspiration to throw off Western influence and establish the power and dominion of Islam. It is difficult for Shiites to bring this kind of vision into focus, since they are preoccupied with their own problems as a minority and impeded in their ability to think utopia by the question of what that would be in Shiite terms. It would be difficult for a Shiite floater, including an immigrant or convert, to work out what and whom he is fighting for, especially when the lead in such actions has already been taken by virulently anti-Shiite Sunnis whose success is to be feared.

Shiites are also unlikely to mount third-wave type attacks against religious minorities, such as the bombings of synagogues in Tunisia and Istanbul in 2002 and 2003 and continuing attacks on churches in Iraq. The reasons for lack of interest in action of this kind against minorities seem evident enough. Shiites have too many problems of their own to think of attacking other minorities and are the primary target of local third-wave attacks themselves. As in the case of symbolic transnational action against the West, third-wave action against minorities is also made unlikely by fact that the Shiite psychological horizon does not extend to cleansing the Muslim world and setting up a new Islamwide order.[8]

These limitations do not prevent Shiites from engaging in anti-Western rhetoric. Shiites generally share in the political situation of other Muslims and are in close contact with them, so that their perspectives on the West tend to be similar and expressed in similar language. Because that situation involves the whole Muslim community and not Shiites alone, and also because anti-Western rhetoric acts as a kind of a warrant of solidarity with other Muslims, Shiites even routinely speak of relations with the West in all-Islamic rather than specifically Shiite terms, with Shiite symbolism (for example, the bravery of Ali, the martyrdom of Husayn[9]) reserved chiefly for internal consumption.[10] These habits carry over to movements that might be classified as fundamentalist. Iranian revolutionaries have described America as the "Great Satan" and attributed "arrogance" (*istikbar*, a sin of Satan; see Quran 2:34) to Western powers, and Hizbollah in Lebanon also has a quite elaborate anti-Western worldview;[11] but the language is not overtly Shiite.

Shiite anti-Western rhetoric would seem to be evidence of the dichotomous, "Manichean" worldview said to be characteristic of fundamentalism.[12] There, is, however, some difference between Sunni so-called Manichaeism and the Shiite worldviews just described. Sunni fundamentalism emphasizes the complete corruption of the West, including social and sexual mores; Western corruption is a prominent theme of both Mawdudi and Qutb and part of the justification of the third wave for killing Western civilians. Shiite statements, in contrast, tend to concentrate on politics and sometimes also deny a cultural dichotomy. Statements issuing from revolutionary Iran and Lebanese Hizbollah, for example, portray conflict with the West as essentially political and show some openness toward Western civilization and Christianity,[13] a perspective foreign to Sunni fundamentalism especially of the second and third waves. The populist movement led in Iraq by Muqtada al-Sadr following the 2001 American invasion has been described as leaning toward a "Shiite exclusivism" unusual in Iraq and "xenophobic";[14] but the anti-Westernism of the Sadrists developed face to face with Western forces, rather than purely as the outgrowth of an ideology.

The relative lack of anti-Western Manichaeism in Shiite movements is difficult to explain, especially in view of traditional Shiite views that are exclusivist (for example, legal rulings suggesting that unbelievers are unclean).[15] One possible reason for Shiites not joining wholeheartedly in the idea of a cultural dichotomy between Islam and the West is that they themselves are culturally suspect in the eyes of the Sunni majority. Openness in the high tradition cultivated by the clerics to rational discourse and philosophy may also be a factor. In the Islamic Republic of Iran, which wishes to project the image of a modern nation rather than the base of an inward-looking minority, that openness has been translated into an attempt to incorporate Western philosophic and social-scientific material into a new Islamic thought.[16]

Quietism and Discretion

Shiism began with a series of uprisings in the seventh and eighth centuries, and Shiites trace their school back to the struggle of Ali and Husayn against unjust rule. However, as Shiites became a minority movement under Sunni rule, a tradition developed that repudiated activism and forbade revolt. This religious attitude depended on the idea that victory and justice under the Imams would occur only in the future, at the hands of God and at a time unknowable to human beings. Classical Shiite texts present quietism as a central tenet especially of the revered fifth and sixth Imams, who are credited with establishing Shiism as an independent school. According to these figures, rising up against the established authorities is forbidden; the duty of Shiites is to endure oppression until the messianic return of the Twelfth Imam, the Mahdi. Shiites are also allowed and even, according to some sayings of the Imams, obliged to practise *taqiyah,* that is "discretion" in relation to their beliefs in the presence of the Sunni majority.

History and the course of events are not completely controlled by even very influential beliefs, and there have been instances in the past of open Shiite movements, most notably the fifteenth-century campaign that brought to power the Safavid dynasty which finally gave Iran the Shiite character it has today. Apart from these exceptional instances, quietism and discretion functioned well enough for Shiites, allowing them to coexist with the majority while maintaining a contrary worldview. Quietism also suited the Shiite clergy, who were left to build institutions and consolidate their authority without being expected to oppose non-Shiite authorities. Quietism and *taqiyah* finally bred a religious ethic which was inward-turning, otherworldly, and made a virtue of passivity. The incompatibility of this religious attitude with Muslim fundamentalism is obvious. It is antipolitical, denies the efficacy of revolutionary action, and places the utopia that fundamentalists want now or quite soon in a distant, indeterminate future.

The next essay demonstrates how Ayatollah Khomeini attempted to reverse the traditional Shiite attitude of otherworldly passivity by insisting that there is no separation between Islam and politics. Khomeini's political Islam was not, however, acceptable to all of the clergy, especially the higher-ranking figures. The tradition of quietism was represented at the time of the revolution at the most lofty level by Ayatollah Khoei, the chief grand ayatollah of the Shiite world resident in Iraq, as well as in Iran by Ayatollah Shariatmadari, successor apparent to Ayatollah Borujerdi who as chief grand ayatollah of the world from the mid-1940s to his death in 1961 had been the most quietist cleric of all. Ayatollah Khoei urged the clergy to withdraw from the political arena,[17] while Shariatmadari came out openly against theocracy and Khomeini's theory of rule of the jurist, preferring the constitutionalism he had advocated during the monarchy.[18] In the first years of the Republic, fundamentalist, statist Shiism was not endorsed by most leading clerics.[19]

Quietism, rejection of theocracy, and clerical constitutionalism remain well represented among the Shiite clergy. The common denominator of these tendencies is the distancing of Islam from politics, thus denial of the very basis of Islamic fundamentalism. Ayatollah Sistani of Iraq, heir to Ayatollah Khoei and probably the chief grand ayatollah of the world today, did bring his influence to bear on political affairs during the American occupation, most notably by issuing a fatwa in 2003 instructing his followers to reject the American plan to formulate a constitution before proceeding to popular elections.[20] This caused some foreign observers to worry that the ayatollah was not as quietist as had been thought, even that he might become Khomeini-like. Sistani's other interventions, however, were less overt and he did not openly condemn the occupation; his limited aim, quite typical for a cleric, was to gain more power for the community and some attention to Islamic law. The difference between Sistani and Khomeini can be seen in the religious instruction they give to the faithful, the chief function of a grand ayatollah. Sistani's "Treatise" (*Risalah*), the basic reference for an ayatollah's legal opinions, is concentrated, in traditional style, on the minute rules of prayer, fasting, pilgrimage, and alms, along with personal and commercial law. Khomeini's treatise is very similar, except that it also contains statements about the political nature of Islam and religio-political duties, for example, the inherently political nature of the Friday congregational prayer and pilgrimage and, in an unusual section on "defence," the duties of believers in resisting foreign domination. Political concerns penetrated to the heart of Khomeini's mission, while for Sistani and most other ayatollahs, law and guidance are aimed at forming a private world distant from the political sphere.

Nevertheless, some of my Shiite informants criticize even Sistani for being "too political." What I am calling quietism in fact embraces a range of attitudes, from an entire retreat into scholarly and pastoral concerns to willingness to deal, at a distance, with the powers that be. Since the title of ayatollah is acquired through clerical consensus and popular acclaim, the good number of high-ranking quietists reflects currency of these types of views among the clergy and worldwide Shiite population.

The impress of Shiite discretion, if not quietism, remained even with Khomeini. It is sometimes said that Khomeini forbade *taqiyah;* but this is not true. In *Islamic Government,* his manifesto composed some years before the Iranian Islamic revolution of 1979, he acknowledges that without it, Shiism "would have been destroyed," a view in line with his 1954 treatise on *taqiyah,* in which he discusses instances (admittedly limited) in which it may be applied. He does forbid *taqiyah* for clerics in particular in relation to the issue of Islamic government, especially "when the chief principles of Islam and its welfare are endangered."[21] This view is consistent with the classic Shiite position that allows *taqiyah* when harm is feared but forbids it when it would result in blood being spilled and religion violated.[22] For Ayatollah Khomeini, Western domination and corrupt rule, the triggers of Islamic fundamentalism, represent exactly those circumstances, and so *taqiyah* should be lifted. At the same time he continued to prescribe *taqiyah* for the sake of Shii–Sunni unity, recommending, for example, dropping Shiite features of prayer when there are opportunities to pray with Sunnis "so that Muslims do not [because of disunity] become debased among the nations and fall under the rule of infidels."[23]

The hard reality behind Khomeini's continuation of *taqiyah* is the minority situation. An exchange between two of my students, one Sunni and one Shiite, illustrates the effect of this reality on the outlook of Shiites living even in the West. The young Sunni man criticized *taqiyah* as being dishonest and cowardly; the Shiite, a young woman, angrily demanded: "What would you do if you came to a checkpoint and you were going to be killed because you were a Shia?" Preservationist thinking of this kind tends to restrain political activism. It was overcome for a time by enthusiasm for martyrdom during the revolution in Iran, but that is not very likely elsewhere where Shiites live as minorities.

Clerical Authority

This essay has concentrated so far exclusively on the Shiite clergy. Readers familiar with Sunni, Christian, and other fundamentalisms might wonder why. Where are the figures typical of fundamentalism emerging from outside the tradition to challenge traditional authority and remake religion? The answer lies in the extraordinary power of the Shiite clerics, which gives them a hold over religious discourse that is difficult to match. Strong clerical authority prevents fundamentalists from opposing the ayatollahs and creating space for their own ideas.

The Imamlike charisma of the leading Shiite clerics is one very important source of this power. Another lies in the Shiite structure of authority, which is quite different from that of Sunnism. Shiites must directly obey or "emulate" (*taqlid*) one of the grand ayatollahs, following him in all his religious rulings. Loyalty is owed personally to this living ayatollah rather than to the tradition in general as in Sunnism. The grand ayatollahs as well as other members of the upper ranks are required to reach a very high level of learning, which means a long initial course of study, generally more rigorous than that of Sunni institutions, followed by many additional years of study and teaching. Piety or "justice," involving not only rectitude but a kind of quiet dignity and retreat into learning, is also required. Grand ayatollahs are usually recognized only late in life and achieve their greatest prominence in old age. The figures of the grand and lesser ayatollahs provide a locus of charisma and authority that is missing in Sunnism, and their prestige and power elevate the religious class as a whole.

It seems then that for fundamentalism to take hold, it would have to be adopted by one of the clerics. This is exactly what happened with Ayatollah Khomeini. The result has been characterized as "clerical fundamentalism,"[24] an accurate description but one that needs explanation, since fundamentalists and traditional clerics are usually opposed. Sunni Muslim fundamentalists, for instance, deem the tradition upheld by the clerics to be corrupt and inauthentic, question their authority, and disparage them for their tolerance of the status quo. Mawdudi considers the clerics ignorant and their learning useless, and Qutb speaks of them as "professional men of religion" who misrepresent Islam with meaningless fatwas.[25] Ayatollah Khomeini was able to speak like a fundamentalist despite being a member of the religious class because he imagined the clergy to be divided between hidebound traditionalists sitting "in some corner in Najaf or Qom studying legal problems related to menstruation and parturition"[26] and clerical activists—the true clerics—who would act as a revolutionary vanguard. He was no doubt aided in this conception by the idea, also present in the Sunni tradition but much stronger in Shiism, that refusal by ulema to associate with rulers is a mark of piety.

Learned cleric and fundamentalist are different performances, and each is very strenuous. The extraordinary thing about Khomeini was that he was able to perform both as a learned ayatollah—a more exacting role, I would argue, than that of a Sunni shaykh or grand mufti—and fundamentalist. The difficulty in combining the two is confirmed by a widespread view of Khomeini as being more pious than learned. Learning is usually considered the more important qualification of a grand ayatollah, but it is sometimes said of Khomeini that his most outstanding quality was piety, understood in his case as political action and steadfastness. At the same time images of Khomeini never emphasized political power but rather the traditional, Imamlike characteristics of a grand ayatollah such as simplicity, otherworldliness, and "oppression" (Persian *mazlumiyat*), a kind of modest forbearance. It appears that a new type of clerical personality had to be created to accommodate fundamentalism. It seems, however, that the model of a thoroughly political grand ayatollah could be sustained by Khomeini alone. When the time came to consider succession to the position of "Supreme Leader" held by Khomeini after the revolution, no high-level cleric would accept the position, and the qualifications for the leader of very high learning and grand ayatollahship had to be struck from the constitution and more emphasis placed on "piety" along with mundane political attributes such as "administrative ability."[27] The present supreme leader, Ali Khamenei, did finally receive acclaim as a grand ayatollah and acquire a good number of followers. But his image is skewed toward politics, and his elevation rests mostly on what Max Weber calls "charisma of office" rather than personal qualities. Before Khamenei, Ayatollahs Muhammad Baqir al-Sadr of Iraq (killed by Saddam in 1979) and Muhammad Hussein Fadlallah of Lebanon (d. 2010) had recognized the difficulty of combining a reputation as a high-ranking cleric with political activity. They dealt with the issue by maintaining some distance from, respectively, the Iraqi Dawah Party and Lebanese Hizbollah. Although neither figure was actually a quietist, Sadr nevertheless faced problems in combining high clerical authority with leadership in a lay political party (which he finally exited), and Fadlallah found it necessary to transcend local entanglements in order to achieve the transnational following necessary for the rank of grand ayatollah.

Khomeini's vision of the Shiite clergy as the vanguard of fundamentalism has also been thwarted by the pluralism of the religious class. For the fundamentalist there is one evident truth and authority; but Shiite juristic theory gives each ayatollah his own authority which cannot be abridged by others. This theory has a reality; the ayatollahs are aware of their independence and do exercise it, usually within the restricted range of careful conservatism and the traditional concerns of the law but also sometimes in other affairs and in a more liberal way. Independence of thought certainly played a part in Khomeini's orientation toward politics and formulation of a Shiite fundamentalism; and it also contributed to opposing views, including those of Khomeini's initial heir apparent, Grand Ayatollah Montazeri, who was finally sent into internal exile for his objections to totalitarianism and then continued to move in ever more liberal directions up to his death in

2009. The Iranian regime has tried to solve the problem of clerical pluralism by proposing alternate models, for example, an arrangement in which other leading clerics confine themselves to nonpolitical matters or participate in some kind of council that cooperates with the Leader.[28] But these have not been accepted by the clerical hierarchy even inside Iran.

Nor has the bureaucratic participation of other clerics in the Islamic Republic affected the hold of the hierarchy. As the backbone of a regime that posits the rule of Islam and authority of a Supreme Leader, the government clerics may be considered fundamentalists by default, a kind of bureaucratized vanguard. They are, however, generally from the middle or lower ranks. Although some, for example, certain members of the Guardian Council, may be counted in the upper grades according to the traditional criterion of learning, the qualifications of others, for example, Ayatollah Hashemi Rafsanjani, who has served over the years as president and in many other capacities, are essentially political. There is actually a proliferation of ayatollahs as the title has come to be claimed much more widely in the Shiite world and particularly in Iran than before the revolution. It should not be thought that the presence of ayatollahs and other clerics in the republic indicates fundamentalisation of the Shiite clergy overall.

The few clerical figures outside Iran who lead political movements and seem at times to indulge in fundamentalism are also from the lower ranks, demonstrating once again the limited penetration of this kind of thought and action into the religious class despite the example of Khomeini. This is the situation of Muqtada al-Sadr of Iraq and Hasan Nasrollah, secretary general of the Lebanese Hizbollah. Neither of these has or indeed claims any rank in learning or religious following.[29] The function of their clerical robes is merely to identify them as legitimate leaders of Islamic movements, underlining once again the hold of the clergy over religious discourse and legitimacy. At the same time they are genuine members of the religious class and thus shadowed by the hierarchy; Sadr has had to deal with the weighty authority and quietism of the redoubtable Grand Ayatollah Sistani, and Iran-loyal Nasrollah with the success of Grand Ayatollah Fadlallah in building a Lebanese and international following. The peculiar feature of third-wave Sunni fundamentalism in which leaders from outside the religious class with little or no religious learning set themselves up as rivals to traditional authority by mimicking their language (as in the "fatwas" of Bin Laden), or even their dress and aspect (for example, Anwar al-Awlaki, the American-born commander of al-Qaeda in Yemen[30]), is not possible in Shiism. This is due not only to the weight of a hierarchy based on high standards of learning but also to the tight-knit nature of a relatively small Shiite religious class limited to a few centers of learning in Iran and Iraq.

The dominance of the Shiite religious hierarchy has resulted in a peculiar pattern in modern Shiite religious discourse. It leaves no room on the right for emergence of the lay anticlerical fundamentalism characteristic of Sunnism and even little for independent conservative movements. The space that remains open is on the left; here is where lay intellectuals and youth cluster to advocate "radical" ideas such as new hermeneutics, reduction of the role of Shariah, democracy, and so on. At the same time clerics with their autonomy and independence of thought are also active in antifundamentalism; two examples out of many are Shaykh Shams al-Din, the head of the Lebanese High Shiite Council who argued that, in the absence of the Hidden Imam, the people are to rule over themselves;[31] and Mohsen Kadivar, a mid-ranking figure from Iran who advocates a religiously conscious secularism. A number of grand ayatollahs, such as Fadlallah of Lebanon and Sanei of Iran, are also noted for progressive shariah opinions, for example in relation to gender. Religiously committed Shiites, including the idealistic youth who might in the Sunni world be drawn to fundamentalism, are thus either under the authority of learned clerics (some with attractively "radical," i.e., somewhat modern, ideas) or presented with a choice of other nonfundamentalist kinds of thought.

Lack of Scripturalism

Literalism or scripturalism has been identified as a key characteristic of fundamentalism, at least in the three Abrahamic faiths that focus on a sacred book. Scholars have been particularly struck by the similarity of Sunni fundamentalist attitudes toward the Quran to Protestant scripturalism. Ellis Goldberg sums up the parallels between the two: "Both early Protestantism and the [Sunni] Islamist movement seek to force believers to confront directly the authority of the basic texts of revelation and to read them directly, rather than through the intervening medium of received authority. Both believe that Scripture is a transparent medium for anyone who cares to confront it."[32] None of this is true of Shiism. For Shiites, the Quran is not "transparent." Rather it is thought to be intelligible only if properly interpreted, especially in light of the sayings of the Imams, who are its true exegetes. The text of the Quran is believed to have an esoteric dimension, principally hidden messages that point to the virtues of the Imams and their right to rule. A metaphorical reading or reading in accord with reason (*aql*) is also applied to passages that do not match tenets of Shiite theology, such as freedom of God from anthropomorphism and infallibility of the prophets. Even if everyday believers are not entirely conscious of these views, they do not encourage the idea that the Quran is a plain text that can be directly understood with the insight of faith. Shiism is not even very Quran-centric; a collection of moralistic sermons and wise sayings of the Imam Ali called "The Way of Eloquence" is also very popular, and hagiography, intercessory prayers, and rituals related to the Imams provide other foci.

Nor are the scriptures accessible "for anyone." Shiite doctrine holds that only the learned clerics with their arduously acquired knowledge can properly interpret the Quran and dicta of the Imams. The qualified cleric is the "learned one" (*alim*), while nonclerics with any other kind of education—certainly the scientific or technical training often possessed by Sunni fundamentalists—are "not-knowing" (*jahil*). The Sunni clerics, of course, also have specialized religious knowledge, but the division between knower and not-knower is not as firm as in Shiism, especially when compared to the traditionally scripturalist Hanbalism that feeds modern Sunni fundamentalism.[33] We expect the writings of fundamentalists to be directed at the masses they aim to move. It is for this reason that Mawdudi and Sayyid Qutb use a compelling literary style unburdened by traditional learning even in their multivolume Quranic exegeses. By contrast, even Khomeini's fundamentalist manifesto *Islamic Government* is addressed not to the masses but to seminarians who are charged with the mission of "disseminating religious knowledge," "teaching and convincing" the people and youth, and "helping them to mature."[34]

Scripturalism has serious consequences for authority, both of fundamentalist leaders and of individual believers. Leaders assert that the meaning they adduce is evident from the text itself; in this way they vault over the tradition and establish themselves on new ground free of traditional authority and the burden of producing learned arguments inconsistent with their education and aims. Scripturalism also grants authority to individuals by allowing them to verify their own understandings and feelings through attaching them to the text in some way. There is some tension here. Leaders are likely to be convinced that that their evident meaning is the only one, which believers are obliged to discover; but believers sometimes decide that they are hearing something different (usually more radical) that compels them to take their own path and tell that truth to others. This tension has contributed in Sunni fundamentalism to fractiousness and the emergence of grouplets. Finally, scripturalism authorizes action; leaders and individuals use the idea of a plain and direct text to make it into a program for action.

Once again Shiism is different in every way. Since evident meaning does not exist, there is little possibility of circumventing established authority and tradition by relying on supposedly clear texts. The one instance I know of a modern Shiite group attempting to present an independent reading of the Quran "in a simple language capable of being understood by all" is the series of booklets *How We Should Teach the Quran* issued by the People's Mujahidin.[35] The People's Mujahidin was a leftist organisation which proposed a "scientific-realist" approach to the Quran that would reveal its "essence" as a socioeconomic document and "guide for revolutionary action."[36] This seems like a fundamentalist approach, except that the Mujahidin, in characteristic Shiite fashion, treated exegesis as an exercise in using "elucidation and deduction"[37] to reach a nonapparent, in their case modernist or socialist, meaning. The words of the title, "how we should teach" (rather than "how to read"), refer to this special technique. The association of the Mujahidin with Ayatollah Mahmoud Taleqani, who also wrote on the socioeconomic dimensions of the Quran, suggests a continuing need for the validation of a cleric even though the group was anticlerical and claimed that the power of *ijtihad* (religious "independent reasoning)" belonged not to the religious class but to those able to perceive the Quran's social meaning.[38] The Iranian anticlerical grouplet calling itself Furqan, which is said to have based itself on the Quran and Sunnah (Furqan being an epithet of the Quran), might have been genuinely scripturalist and even fundamentalist; but it is hard to tell since it was always shadowy and seems to have disappeared after arrests for the 1979 assassination of Ayatollah Mutahhari, the revolution's philosopher and second most prominent figure after Khomeini.[39]

Lack of scripturalism and authority of the religious class (the two go together) along with quietism and the minority situation have not only inhibited but, with the exception of Khomeinism, virtually excluded Sunni-style fundamentalism. The fundamentalist groups, grouplets, and inspired individuals familiar from modern Sunni Islam are conspicuously absent among Shiites. This raises the question of a native Shiite fundamentalism. Western scholars have taken Sunni-style fundamentalism to represent Islamic fundamentalism overall; but does Shiism have the potential to produce a different model?

Such a potential might lie in Mahdism, a type of millennialism involving the near presence or imminent return of the Twelfth Imam. Expectation of the Twelfth Imam is part of the pietistic, Imam-centered, ritually lavish dimension of the tradition. Imamocentric Shiism is relatively free of clerical authority and a potential source of the emotion, certitude, and agency generated in Sunni fundamentalism by scripturalism; the final meaning of scripturalism, after all, is these qualities and not the fact of the text itself.[40]

There is, however, currently no sign of a Mahdism that could be sustained as a movement. One possibly full-blown millenarian Shiite group that has come to light in recent times—apparently around 2003, that is close to the Allied invasion of Iraq—involves a grouplet in the area of Basra, Iraq, said by one report to be following a guardian and prophet of the Mahdi, Ahmad al-Hasan. Al-Hasan asserted that there is no need for the *itjihad* of the clerics since he has direct insight into the Quran and is himself a sign of the imminent Return. Some sources also link a force calling itself the Army of Heaven (*Jund al-Sama*) involved in a battle in 2007 in Najaf (also in southern Iraq) to Ahmad al-Hasan or someone with a similar name.[41] The obscurity and confusion surrounding the group(s)[42] only underlines their marginality—or it might be said that revolutionary groups do often surface in these ways as they incubate, with some finally emerging as full-blown movements.

Mahdism has also been on the rise among some Shiites as a kind of amillennialism, a sense that the Mahdi is accessible and active in the present in various ways, for instance through receiving petitions at the pilgrimage site of Jamkaran near Qom, Iran, which has been built up since the 1990s into a large complex, appearing at crucial moments in battles, and otherwise watching over human life and events. Amillenniel Mahdism can be controlled by clerics and established institutions since it gives heightened but still routine meaning to contemporary events and conditions rather than reading them as signs of the Apocalypse and signals to engage in revolutionary action. An amillennial interpretation of Mahdism is aided by the fact that the Twelfth Imam is not a completely divine figure existing on some other plane whose appearance thus involves change in the natural order, but a very long-lived human being circulating unrecognized in the world. Mahdism has been reformulated in the Islamic Republic as a historical-progressive, scientific realization of the aspirations of all humankind.[43] In this very novel vision the bloody end-time battles of the classic texts in which the Mahdi and Shiites finally triumph over other Muslims are replaced with a scenario that transcends the limitations of Shiite minority status by moving up to the universal and makes Shiism and the Republic relevant to the modern world. It is this view and not, as reported in some Western media, fundamentalistlike apocalypticism that inspired former president Ahmadinejad. Although Mahdism was not encouraged by Khomeini in his time since he was a high-ranking cleric, the current vogue inside and outside Iran has its roots in the momentous events of the revolution and the ayatollah's own extraordinary charisma.[44] This undercurrent of Iranian fundamentalism is addressed in the next essay.

Notes

1. *Shiism* in this and the following essay refers to Twelver Usuli Shiism, the school of the vast majority of Shiites today, including virtually all in Iran.

2. James Piscatori, "Accounting for Islamic Fundamentalisms," in *Accounting for Fundamentalisms*, ed. Martin E. Marty and R. Scott Appleby (Chicago: University of Chicago Press, 1994), 361.

3. Gabriel A. Almond, Emmanuel Sivan, and R. Scott Appleby, "Fundamentalism: Genus and Species," in *Fundamentalisms Comprehended*, ed. Marty and Appleby (Chicago: University of Chicago Press, 1995), 404. If it is true, as Sayyed Vali Nasr believes (*Mawdudi and the Making of Islamic Revivalism* [New York: Oxford University Press, 1996], 49–50), that Mawdudi has somewhat more of a cultural focus, that may be because Muslims in the subcontinent are living in a non-Muslim cultural milieu and are thus also in a cultural situation.

4. The doctrine of the Imamate holds that only the charismatic descendants of Ali ibn Abi Talib, cousin of the Prophet and Shiite hero, were fit to rule, that these Imams or "leaders" were divinely elected, and that Sunni rulers usurped the Imams' rule, oppressed, and even murdered them.

5. For the Iraqi Brotherhood, see Werner Ende, "Success and Failure of a Shiite Modernist: Muhammad ibn Muhammad al-Khalisi (1890–1963)," in *The Other Shiites. From the Mediterranean to Central Asia*, ed. Alessandro Monsutti et al. (Berlin: Peter Lang, 2007), 237.

6. For example, feelings against Shiites and Sufis in Pakistan have local origins, but violent attacks arise within a network extending to Saudi Arabia, Kuwait, Jordan, and so on; see Thomas K. Gugler, "When Democracy Is Not the Only Game in Town," in *Trysts with Democracy: Political Practice in South Asia*, ed. Kenneth Bo Nielsen et al. (London & New York: Anthem Press, 2011), 281–95.

7. Sayyid Vali Reza Nasr, "Regional Implications of Shi'a Revival in Iraq," *Washington Quarterly* 27 (Summer 2004): 7–8. Nasr reviews violence against Shiites in Iraq, Pakistan, and Afghanistan.

8. Shiite-majority Iran takes action against Bahais and converts from Islam, although as part of a systematic national program rather than in the spectacular, transnational fashion of the third wave.

9. Husayn, a son of Ali, was martyred in 680 as he traveled to Iraq to answer calls of distress from the population. Shiites commemorate the incident annually with processions and lamentations.

10. For instance, the Charter of the Shiite Lebanese party and militia Amal downplayed Shiism, for example, by mentioning Ali only "in a cryptic manner" but referring to Jesus and some of the Companions respected by Sunnis; see Marius Deeb, "Shia Movements in Lebanon: Their Formation, Ideology, Social Basis, and Links with Iran and Syria," *Third World Quarterly* 10 (April 1988): 693.

11. Amal Saad-Ghorayeb, *Hizbu'llah: politics and religion* (London & Sterling, Va.: Pluto Press, 2002), 88–110.

12. Almond et al., "Fundamentalism: Genus and Species," 406–7.

13. For example, former president Ahmadinejad refers to the American "nation" as "God-fearing, truth-loving, and justice-seeking"; see his "Message to the American People" of November 29, 2006. Hizbollah claims that its conflict is not with Western or American peoples or even civilizations, which, it is said, are bound to have positive and negative elements like any other; see Saad-Ghorayeb, *Hizbu'llah*, 106–10. Shiite rhetoric against Zionism and Judaism is more likely to extend to religious and quasi-racial prejudice, although there is still some drawing back not found in Sunni fundamentalism; see Saad-Ghorayeb, *Hizbu'llah*, 134–86, and a speech ("not a fight between Judaism and other religions") entitled "The World without Zionism," delivered by Ahmadinejad on October 26, 2005 at a Tehran conference; the speech has been translated by Nazila Fathi as "Text of Mahmoud Ahmadinejad's Speech," *New York Times*, October 30, 2005.

14. Juan Cole, "The United States and Shi'ite Religious Factions in Post-Ba'thist Iraq," *Middle East Journal* 57 (Autumn 2003): 544.

15. See David M. Freidenreich "The Implications of Unbelief: Tracing the Emergence of Distinctively Shii Notions Regarding the Food and Impurity of Non-Muslims," *Islamic Law and Society* 18, no. 1 (2011): 53–84.

16. The English website of the Islamic Research Institute for Culture and Thought at http://en.iict.ac.ir/ provides vivid examples. Accessed September 2, 2013.

17. Shahrough Akhavi, "Elite Factionalism in the Islamic Republic of Iran," *Middle East Journal* 41 (Spring 1987): 191.

18. The fullest account of Shariatmadari in English is the admiring essay by Abbas Milani in *Eminent Persians: The Men and Women Who Made Modern Iran, 1941–1979*, 2 vols. (Syracuse: Syracuse University Press, 2008), 2: 367–76.

19. For a partial list of the quietists, see Akhavi, "Elite Factionalism," 191–92.

20. Andrew Arato, *Constitution Making under Occupation: The Politics of Imposed Revolution in Iraq* (New York: Columbia University Press, 2009), 91–93. The fatwa was reiterated some months later.

21. "Islamic Government," in *Islam and Revolution. Writings and Declarations of Imam Khomeini*, trans. Hamid Algar (Berkeley, Calif.: Mizan Press, 1981), 34, 144; *Risalah fi al-taqiyah*, in Khomeini, *al-Rasa'il*, ed. Mujtaba al-Tihrani (Qum: Mu'assasah-i Matbu'ati Isma'iliyan 1385/1965), 178.

22. See Lynda Clarke, "The Rise and Decline on Taqiyya in Twelver Shiism," in *Reason and Inspiration in Islam: Theology, Philosophy and Mysticism in Muslim Thought*, ed. Todd Lawson (London & New York: I. B. Tauris, 2005), 55–58.

23. *Risalah fi al-taqiyah*, 200. Khomeini calls this the *taqiyah* of "affable discretion" (*mudarah*).

24. Said Amir Arjomand, "Unity and Diversity in Islamic Fundamentalism," in *Fundamentalisms Comprehended*, ed. Marty and Appleby, 179–98.

25. See Abdullah Saeed, "Official Ulema and Religious Legitimacy," in *Islam and Political Legitimacy*, ed. Shahram Akbarzadeh and Abdullah Saeed (London & New York: Routledge Curzon, 2003), 26–27. Mawdudi moderated his attitude toward the clergy in the later part of his career as it became necessary to work with them in the context of Pakistani politics.

26. *Islamic Government*, 38.

27. See article 8 of the constitution, and, for further details of the episode, Daniel Brumberg, *Reinventing Khomeini: The Struggle for Reform in Iran* (Chicago: University of Chicago Press, 2001), 147–48.

28. Ayatollah Muhammad Ali Taskhiri, "Supreme Authority (Marji'íyah) in Shí'ism," in *Shiite Heritage: Essays on Classical and Modern Traditions*, ed. Lynda Clarke (Binghamton, N.Y.: Global Publications, 2001), 159–79; see also Said Amir Arjomand, *After Khomeini: Iran Under His Successors* (New York: Oxford University Press, 2009), 174–77.

29. It does seem that Sadr is currently trying to gain additional credentials.

30. Awlaki acquired a reputation among his young followers as an Islamic scholar by quoting past authorities whilst posing in a turban among volumes in Arabic; but he actually had no scholarly credentials at all. See Denis MacEoin, "Anwar al-Awlaki: 'I Pray that Allah Destroys America,'" *Middle East Quarterly* 17 (Spring 2010): 13–19.

31. See Chibli Mallat, *Shi'i Thought from the South of Lebanon* (Oxford: Centre for Lebanese Studies, 1988).

32. Ellis Goldberg, "Smashing Idols and the State: The Protestant Ethic and Egyptian Sunni Radicalism," *Comparative Studies in Society and History* 33 (January 1991): 4.

33. Hanbalism is one of the four Sunni schools of law, distinguished from the others by its high degree of fideism and scripturalism. Although it is the least widespread of the law schools today, its spirit is influential, partly because of the worldwide reach of the related Wahhabi sect established in Saudi Arabia.

34. *Islamic Government*, 126–29. These duties of the seminarians are the chief subject of the last chapter of *Islamic Government*.

35. *Chigunah Quran biyamuzim. Qismat-i duvvum: dinamism-i Quran* (Long Beach, Calif.: *Intisharat-i Sazman-i Mujahidin-i Khalq-i Iran*, 1358 [1979]), 5. References are to the second booklet, the only one I was able to obtain.

36. *Chigunah*, quoted in Ervand Abrahamian, *Radical Islam: The Iranian Mojahedin* (London: I. B. Tauris, 1989), 95–96.

37. *Chigunah*, 6 and passim. Deduction = *istinbat*, a term usually referring to deduction of legal norms performed by learned clerics.

38. Abrahamian, *Radical Islam*, 97 (from a passage translated from *Chigunah*).

39. See Shahrough Akhavi, *Religion and Politics in Contemporary Iran: Clergy-State Relations in the Pahlavī Period* (Albany: State University of New York Press, 1980), 177–78.

40. Anthropologist Richard T. Antoun points to "the emotional and inspirational qualities of scripture" and "their relation to the numinous" as elements of so-called literalism (*Understanding Fundamentalism: Christian, Islamic, and Jewish Movements* [Walnut Creek, Calif.: AltaMira Press, 2001], 37). Scholars of fundamentalism also emphasize that scripturalism

means focus on inerrancy rather than "mechanical literalism" (Malise Ruthven, *Fundamentalism: The Search for Meaning* [New York: Oxford University Press, 2004], 63); the Imams, who are considered to be inerrant (*ma'sum*), also provide such a focus.

41. See Reidar Visser, "Basra, the Reluctant Seat of 'Shiastan'," *Middle East Report,* no. 242 (Spring 2007), http://www.merip.org/mer/mer242/basra-reluctant-seat-shiastan (on the incident at Basra) (accessed September 30, 2011); David Cook, "Messianism in the Shiite Crescent," *Current Trends in Islamist Ideology,* 11 (April 8, 2011), http://currenttrends.org/research/detail/messianism-in-the-shiite-crescent (on the incident around Najaf) (accessed November 9, 2011).

42. Juan Cole, an experienced and careful observer of Iraqi Shiism, gives several widely differing accounts of the movement(s) at his blog *Informed Comment*: "Fighters for Shiite Messiah Clash with Najaf Security," posted January 29, 2007, at http://www.juancole.com/2007/01/fighters-for-shiite-messiah-clash-with.html (accessed September 2, 2013).

43. See Abbas Amanat's *Apocalyptic Islam and Iranian Shi'ism* (London: I. B. Tauris, 2009), 221–51. For amillennial Mahdism inside and outside Iran, see Jean-Pierre Filiu,"The Return of Political Mahdism," *Current Trends in Islamist Ideology* 8 (2009): 26–38, and David Cook, "Messianism in the Shiite Crescent," *Current Trends in Islamist Ideology* 11 (2011) at http://currenttrends.org/research/detail/messianism-in-the-shiite-crescent (accessed November 9, 2011).

44. See Said Amir Arjomand, "Millenial Beliefs, Hierocratic Authority, and Revolution in Shi'ite Islam," *The Political Dimensions of Religion*, ed. Arjomand (Albany: State University of New York Press, 1993), 219–39.

Fundamentalism, Khomeinism, and the Islamic Republic of Iran

Lynda Clarke

In the preceding essay I point out that the fundamentalism currently seen in Islam is not originally a Shiite phenomenon. Islamic fundamentalism began in Sunni circles and then found its way to the Shiite world. This influence was always limited by features of Shiism not consistent with Sunni-style fundamentalism such as quietism, nonliteralism, and extraordinarily strong clerical authority. Nevertheless, some Shiites did participate in Islamic fundamentalism since, as an essentially political movement, it provided a vehicle for addressing the great problems common to all Muslims of Western dominance and failure of local regimes. Thus the first wave of Sunni fundamentalism represented by the Muslim Brotherhood, a mass-based transnational movement originating in Egypt, was followed by the later Shiite Dawah, a transnational party originating in Iraq.[1] The second-wave utopian schemes of the Indo-Pakistani Abu al-Ala Mawdudi (d. 1979) and Sayyid Qutb (d. 1966) from Egypt are paralleled by Ayatollah Ruhollah Khomeini's widely known *Islamic Government* composed in 1970, which finally became the blueprint for the Islamic Republic. In the first part of this essay, I show how Khomeini absorbed the premises of Sunni fundamentalism and gave them a distinctive Shiite expression.

Sunni-style fundamentalism involves establishment of the rule of Islam in a state, and so participation of Shiites has been restricted above all by their minority status, what I call in the previous essay the minority situation. Because Shiites in most countries are small minorities enclosed by a generally unfriendly Sunni majority and amount to only 10 to 15 percent of Muslims worldwide, the space in which they can act politically as Shiites is limited.[2] The outstanding exception is Iran, where Shiites are an absolute and long-standing national majority making up 89 percent of the overwhelmingly Muslim population of the country.[3] In the three other countries where Shiites make up more than half the population—Azerbaijan (65–75 percent),[4] Bahrain (70 percent or less, excluding foreign nationals)[5], and Iraq (60–65 percent)[6]—they may be described as "functional minorities,"[7] since they have limited political power or, in the case of Azerbaijan, share in a culture in which religion is separated from politics and adherence to Islam is largely nominal or based on folk practice.[8] It is Iran with its majority Shiite population that has enabled a fundamentalist political Islam, by providing both a focus for Khomeini's imagined Islamic state[9] and the site on which to found the Islamic Republic. In fact, in Shiite-majority Iran, some aspects of Shiism such as strong clerical hierarchy functioned in ways that aided the establishment and survival of the Islamic state. Khomeinism finally produced the only stable Muslim fundamentalist polity in the world; the second part of the essay looks at the role of shiism in this accomplishment. The models of Khomeinism and the Islamic Republic, however, were finally too dependent on the special circumstances of Iran to work for other Shiite populations, as well as too Shiite to be acceptable to Sunnis; the third part of the essay examines the decline of the Republic's fundamentalist drive in the face of this reality.

Khomeini and Islamic Government

In his *Reinventing Khomeini* Daniel Brumberg discusses "Sunni realism," an orientation of classical Sunni political theory toward the idea that establishment of mundane rule is necessary for the preservation of religion. In the nineteenth and twentieth centuries, Sunni reformers faced with Western imperialism combined traditional realism with Western ideas of the nation-state to argue for powerful Muslim polities and a politically organized worldwide Muslim Community (*ummah*). Thus was the way paved for the Muslim Brotherhood, Mawdudi, and Qutb to reflect on the shape such an entity would take and how to arrive at it.[10] Shiism, in contrast, does not have a heritage of realism. Classical Shiite political theory is concerned instead with an ideal that cannot exist, that is, the rule of the Imam. Thus, apart from expectation that the Twelfth Imam will finally return at the end of time to establish justice,[11] Shiites are left with a gap between the ideal and reality.

Political thought, like politics, did not come to standstill because of this problem. The gap was dealt with in various ways. For example, soon after the disappearance of the Twelfth Imam in the mid–tenth century, it was allowed that participating in the government of a Shiite or even possibly non-Shiite ruler was legitimate if the holder of office could avoid doing evil and perhaps do some good.[12] Under the Iranian Shiite Safavid dynasty of the sixteenth to eighteenth centuries, the gap was bridged or partially so by an accommodation between the clergy and shahs that gave the latter a role as legitimate protectors of religion.[13] With the advent of the nation-state prominent clerics in Iran and Iraq, where there were enough Shiites to exercise some influence, pressured governments to give a greater role to religion and the shariah; Khomeini himself played this role in the mid-1940s by penning a treatise in which he objected to aspects of Pahlavi rule and suggested greater cooperation with the clergy.[14] A gap is also a space, and the absence of the ideal rule of the Imam has allowed many Shiite clerics and intellectuals to envision acceptable democratic or secular governments in the interim; a few of these figures will be met with below.

Khomeini finally dealt in his *Islamic Government* with the gap between ideal and reality by erasing it, an unprecedented move in Shiite thought. He did this by adopting the Sunni fundamentalist idea of a fully legitimate Islamic state realized in the present time; in effect, by making the state the ideal instead of the Imam. With this model and Shiite-majority Iran in mind, Khomeini was able to concentrate, in the fashion of Sunni fundamentalists, on a political response to Western dominance and failed local governments. By focusing on these common Muslim concerns he was also able to follow his Sunni model in speaking of liberation and Islamic rule for the whole of the Muslim world, a pan-Islamic voice little in evidence in pre–*Islamic Government* writings and declarations but common thereafter. Brumberg notes the similarity of Khomeini's ideas to Mawdudi's "theodemocracy" and the possibility of contact points with the Muslim Brotherhood.[15] *Islamic Government* also repeatedly uses the word *nizam* (system), a favorite term of the Brotherhood, Mawdudi, and Qutb.[16] The strongest evidence of Sunni influence on *Islamic Government,* however, is its conformance to the typology of Sunni fundamentalism, which can be followed point by point.

First, Khomeini's *Islamic Government* turns religion into politics; it is political to the extent that, as Bayat observes, it is "not concerned with intellectual and religious renewal [or] doctrinal reforms."[17] According to Khomeini, even the "forms of worship" in Islam are "usually linked to politics."[18] Second, Muslim fundamentalists believe firmly that Islam, understood principally as application of shariah, "cannot be implemented without the power of the state."[19] This is precisely the argument elaborated throughout *Islamic Government.* Third, fundamentalist thought typically proposes to "replace existing structures with a comprehensive system embracing law, polity, society, economy and culture";[20] just so, Khomeini believes Islam to be "a complete social system" containing regulations for "all the needs of man" from trade, marriage, and education to defence, economics, and so on.[21] Fourth, a "totalitarian impulse"[22] underlies the fundamentalist idea of a comprehensive system provided by religion; not only, according to Khomeini, are Islamic rule and law compulsory for Muslims, but it is also "the duty of all people to obey" the ruling jurist, whose "governmental power" is said to be, astonishingly, equal to that of the Prophet and Imams.[23] Khomeini also employs the "rhetoric of crisis,"[24] a fifth characteristic of fundamentalist manifestos; *Islamic Government* begins and ends with warnings about the plots of Jews and Western imperialists aimed at taking over and exploiting the Muslim world. Sixth, fundamentalist movements "deem political activism the necessary expression of socio-religious concerns,"[25] and *Islamic Government* is, above all, a call to action, with the first and last chapters devoted to exhortation punctuated with bitter condemnation of those who fail to act.

The most striking evidence of Khomeini's adoption of a Sunni fundamentalist model is his hearkening back to a golden age. Even allowing for the tendency of fundamentalist thought to be selective and reshape particular aspects of the tradition to its own ends,[26] this is difficult to fit to Shiism. The Shiite view of history is very different from that of Sunnism; for Shiites there is no ideal past and, very different from the motive spirit of Sunni fundamentalism, no past ideal community to imitate and recreate. Islamic history in the Shiite view is a record of injustice and oppression, with the ideal located in the future age of the Mahdi. Moreover, the reported sayings (*hadiths*) of the Imams actually forbid activism and command believers to await the return of the Mahdi at the end of time. Khomeini nevertheless does manage to follow his model by seizing on the time of the Prophet and Imam Ali, the only Imam to achieve somewhat tentative power, as a golden age in which there was a struggle to establish Islamic rule. He also suggests that the other Imams struggled in their own way for the sake of realizing an Islamic government in the future; this, according to Khomeini, was the meaning of the martyrdom of Husayn at Karbala, and the sixth Imam Jafar al-Sadiq also appointed judges and "laid down a pattern of government" despite having "no executive power" because he was "thinking of the future."[27] Thus in Khomeini's retelling, the ideal aspect of these times which is to be recreated and imitated is a forward-looking spirit of revolution.

Although Khomeini arrives at an Islamic state using a basically Sunni model, he does it in Shiite style. In the world of a traditional Shiite scholar, principles of fundamentalism such as Islamic government, absolutism, and total rule of the shariah irresistibly call to mind the Imam. The traditional Shiite theory of the ideal Islamic state is the theory of the Imamate. In this case it should not come as a surprise (although for some reason it has not been recognized) that *Islamic Government* or *Rule of the Jurist*—the alternate title of the work—follows the model of traditional treatises on the Imamate. *Islamic Government* resembles even the form of classical works on the Imamate, which routinely begin with chiefly rational arguments for the "necessity" (*wujub*) of a government and supremely qualified ruler (equivalent to chapter 2, "The Necessity/*Wujub* of Islamic Government") and continue with textual proof pointing to who that ruler actually is (roughly equivalent to chapter 3). If we follow Khomeini's rational proofs for the authority of the supreme jurist, we will see that they are, in fact, the traditional Shiite proofs for the necessity of Imamate. Khomeini repeats the statement of the classical treatises that "both reason (*aql*) and divine law" demonstrate that government is necessary to prevent "chaos,"[28] adding that, in the modern age "reason dictates that we establish a government" [also] for the purpose of "being able to ward off aggression and defend the honour of Muslims."[29] The classical theory holds that certain executive powers belonging to the Prophet must have been transferred to the Imams, since logically, these cannot fall into desuetude; similarly, Khomeini argues that the executive powers held by the Prophet and inherited by the Imams must have been transferred to the jurists, since logically, these cannot fall into desuetude.[30] This argument of continuity is the chief rational argument adduced by Khomeini in *Islamic Government,* as well as the chief rational argument advanced in traditional writings for the necessity of the Imam.

The classical treatises on the Imamate also assert that reason demonstrates that the Imams are the only ones fit to guide the community because they alone have perfect knowledge of the law and are protected from sin; similarly according to Khomeini, "reason dictates" that jurists who possess full knowledge of the law and are "just and untainted by major sin" are the only ones fit to guide.[31] The classical treatises state that the Imams, although they did not have prophethood, possessed the same knowledge and authority as the Prophet over the community in their times, and Khomeini argues that the jurists, although they do not have the same "spiritual virtues" as the Imams, have "the same [political] authority"[32] The one classical argument missing from *Islamic Government* is that there can be only a single true Imam in any time, and this was finally added when an article of the Iranian constitution allowing for a clerical leadership council in lieu of one ruling jurist was struck in the course of revisions shortly before Khomeini's death.[33]

Part of the conclusion of *Islamic Government* is that the jurist stands in place of the Imam. This is suggested in Shiite tradition by transfer of some of the Imams' charisma and legal functions to the jurists, and Khomeini duly cites relevant texts, from tenth-century hadiths to the reflexions of the nineteenth-century cleric Mulla Ahmad Naraqi.[34] But neither the private authority enjoyed by the Imams and jurists nor the advisory role favored (as is quite typical of clerics) by modern figures such as Naraqi fulfills the requirements of Khomeini's fundamentalism. Khomeini's goal is the absolute political rule of Islam—in Shiite terms, the rule of the Imamlike jurist—in a modern nation-state; this is the leap to Muslim fundamentalism. According to Khomeini, the jurist alone is to "conduct and administer the affairs of the Muslims," with the prerogative of the "same governance that was exercised" by the Prophet.[35] There has been a debate about the degree to which Khomeini's theory of rule of the jurist is congruent with earlier thought on juristic authority.[36] His theory is, in fact, quite original in that it makes the jurist's authority thoroughly political rather than religious or administrative. In order to set up this model Khomeini goes so far as to claim, very much against the tradition, that the chief function of the Imams was to "exercise government" rather than to expound the law.[37]

The Islamic Republic

In the previous section, it was argued that Khomeini's *Islamic Government* is a Shiite expression of the second-wave Sunni fundamentalism that seeks to outline the theory of an ideal state ruled by Islam. Khomeini brings the idea of the absolute rule of Islam into Shiism by radically reshaping native Shiite political theory, that is the theory of the Imamate. Can the "Islamic Republic" finally established on the basis of Khomeini's *Islamic Government* also be characterized as fundamentalist? This question has become a point of debate. The scholar to argue most adamantly that the revolution and republic are not fundamentalist is Ervand Abrahamian, who sees rather "social and economic populism."[38] Said Amir Arjomand objects, contra Abrahamian, that religion should be "taken seriously"[39] and believes that Iran presents a case of "clerical fundamentalism."[40]

The problem with the question seems to be focus on a pure type. One can characterize an idea, system of thought, group, or movement as fundamentalist, perhaps disagreeing on exact criteria; but as one moves up through these levels, fundamentalist ideas and aspirations, which are always utopian and thus aimed at the simple and pure, become ever more mixed with the real stuff of society and politics, that is to say, existing and developing culture, social structures, interests, institutions, and so on. It may be difficult to recognize fundamentalism in the Islamic Republic because it has reached the level of a relatively stable, functioning state, and fundamentalism that rises to this level will be faced with quantities of real material, at least a part of which has to be absorbed or accommodated in some way. Co-opting of populism and nationalism, something very evident in Khomeini's speeches and, according to Abrahamian, key to the survival of the Islamic Republic, is one way of accomplishing this.

At the same time Khomeini's fundamentalist vision does continue to color postrevolutionary Iran. The state imposes a version of Islamic law, the most cherished goal of Muslim fundamentalists; the idea of Islam as a complete way of life is carried through in Islamisation of education, culture, and the public space; and the totalitarian impulse embodied in the ruling jurist continues in the office of the guide (*Rahbar*) currently occupied by Ayatollah Khomeini's successor, Ayatollah Sayyid Ali Khamenei. Each of these elements is duly enshrined in the constitution: "sovereignty and legislative power" are reserved for God, with laws to be ultimately based on "revelation"; the state is charged with creating "an atmosphere conducive to moral virtue"; and "leadership (*imamat*) and ongoing guidance (*rahbari*)" are to play a "fundamental role" in securing the revolution.[41]

The more interesting question may be: How did a fundamentalist movement come into possession of a state, and how has the Iranian regime sustained itself and even flourished for more than thirty years? The question is important because the Islamic Republic is the only case in history in which fundamentalism has consolidated its hold over a stable state. Muslim fundamentalists have not been successful at all in founding Islamic states, despite the fact that they are essentially political movements with precisely that goal. If, as Martin Riesebrodt asserts, fundamentalism is "innovative and shrewdly adaptive,"[42] those qualities have not extended to state-building; the few other "Islamic states" in Sudan, Afghanistan and Somalia suggest that fundamentalism can only achieve tenuous power in situations of disorder.[43]

The first great difference in the Iranian case is that the movement personified by Khomeini managed to capture a coherent socially and economically developed state. The full circumstances of the capture are beyond the scope of this discussion; although it appears that even though the motifs of the revolution were religious, not all the participants wanted or expected the kind of Islamic state that finally emerged. For the purposes of this essay, we are interested in two features of the capture related to Shiism: the Shiite ideal of martyrdom and leadership of Ayatollah Khomeini.

Shiite ideals of martyrdom were crucial to the success of the Islamic revolution. The Shiite ethos of martyrdom centers on the slaughter of the third Shiite Imam Husayn at the hands of the Umayyads. Shiite martyrology also counts the other Imams and daughter of the Prophet as victims, and the deaths of all these figures are part of a sacred calendar. In the years leading up to the revolution, the traditionally Imamocentric and otherworldly view of martyrdom was challenged by activist interpretations both from within and without the religious establishment. The "People's Mujahidin," the largest of the militant groups opposing the shah's regime, cast its guerrillas in the role of martyrs, even citing the example of Che Guevara.[44] Ayatollah Khomeini, showing a fine political sense, extended the idea of martyrdom to the whole Iranian population and willingness to die simply by standing up to the bullets of the shah's army, thus not martyrdom encountered in the course of armed struggle but a fight *through* martyrdom, as the ayatollah said: "Fight through martyrdom, because the martyr is the essence of history."[45] The result was a series of encounters between the army and demonstrating crowds that produced large numbers of casualties whose deaths as martyrs were again commemorated, in accord with Shiite custom, forty days after each incident in fresh demonstrations. The morale of the army and legitimacy of the regime were finally worn away by the escalating cycle, and the bloodiest incidents are still marked today in the Islamic Republic in a kind of addition to the sacred calendar.

Ayatollah Khomeini himself acted as a charismatic focus of the revolution, the "charismatic and authoritarian male leader"[46] often found in fundamentalist movements. His charisma, however, was due not to his personal qualities alone but to an aura surrounding higher-ranking Shiite clerics. The highest members of the Shiite clergy, as noted above, have over the centuries taken on some of the charisma of the Imams. For example, they live modestly, and this, although not entirely explicit, is in imitation of the "oppressed" Imams. To give another example, the Imams were said to be possessed of a divinely conferred, inaccessible knowledge that obliged believers to follow them without question; just so, the elite ayatollahs hold office because of arduously acquired learning that ordinary persons must follow in order to gain salvation. This transferred charisma is not distributed evenly or universally among members of the Shiite religious class, and believers do understand that they are encountering men who are deputies of the Hidden Imam and not Imams themselves. But there is a sense of respect and awe for the chief ayatollahs, of whom there are a limited number and sometimes only one living at a time, which has no parallel in the Sunni world.

The charismatic cleric was thus already a familiar and compelling figure in Shiite and Iranian culture. To this familiar image Khomeini added the Imamlike quality of steadfastness in the face of oppression (not only had he been exiled by the shah, but his eldest son was believed to have been killed by the secret police). Finally, the ayatollah in his clerical robes combined defiance of the West with complete authenticity, answering to the nativism of elements of Iranian society who, although not religious in the traditional sense, were troubled by Westernization. It is fair to say that Iranians responded primarily to a model of Shiite charismatic authority elaborated by Khomeini rather than to his fundamentalist vision.

Iranians and Shiites worldwide also responded during the revolution to an undercurrent of messianism. The image of the Imamlike ayatollah sweeping away the unjust, overturning Western hegemony and establishing a radically new order recalled the final triumph of the Twelfth Imam, causing true believers, along with less traditional persons who shared in the culture of Shiism, to feel that they were witnessing events of cosmic significance. One again it was attachment to personality and expectation generated by latent messianism that provided the élan of the revolution rather than ideas about the rule of Islam or Islamic law. Sunni fundamentalists have no such resources.

The second great distinction of Khomeinist fundamentalism in Iran is that it managed to hold on to the captured state. Again, out of the factors that might help to explain this development, we single out two related specifically to Shiism: the idea that law can evolve and, most important, the religious hierarchy.

Shiite juristic theory requires that independent legal reasoning, known as *ijtihad,* be applied by high-ranking clerics in order to arrive at fresh shariah rulings for each new circumstance. In the past this theory did not much affect the conservatism and narrow focus of shariah rulings. Nevertheless, the constitution of the Islamic Republic takes up *ijtihad* and recasts it as a principle of legal and political dynamism by declaring that government and values are to be based on the "continuous *ijtihad* of fully qualified jurists."[47] The clause suggests that shariah may be changed or expanded to fit new circumstances; the following article, which speaks of employing the "most advanced sciences and arts" and "advancing them further," suggests some kind of progressivism.

Although the idea of a flexible shariah met with resistance from clerical conservatives, it was ultimately institutionalized at the behest of Khomeini himself in a "Council for Determination of the Interests of the Islamic *Nizam*" charged with certifying novel legislation as Islamic. The aim, however, was not to introduce a progressive shariah but rather to facilitate the functioning of the state. Khomeini made this clear in his famous dicta of 1987 and 1988 in which he declared that it was permissible to transform "Islamic systems" to better serve as "instrument[s] for the implementation of [state] policy." According to Khomeini, an Islamic government does not even have to "work within the framework of divine [shariah] injunctions," since it is "one of the foremost injunctions of Islam itself" with priority, when necessary, over "[certain injunctions related to] prayer, fasting, and the pilgrimage."[48] These ideas may seem surprising, but they are the logical end of the assertion already laid out in *Islamic Government* that Islam cannot be fully established or survive without an Islamic state—or it may be that they simply exhibit a development characteristic of totalizing ideologies in which loyalty to the apparatus that deals in the ideology ends up outweighing the ideology itself. Whatever the case, the tenet of Shiite jurisprudence that shariah is not fixed and timeless but an ongoing endeavor facilitated conduct of state in the name of Islamic law. Sunni legal theory and fundamentalist shariaism do not have this flexibility.

Sunni fundamentalist movements have also suffered from a lack of stable and politically qualified leadership. In Iran the backbone of a legitimate and stable ruling class was provided by the Shiite religious hierarchy. The revolution initially depended on a typically Shiite charisma magnified by Ayatollah Khomeini; but personal charisma is too fleeting and formless to provide a basis for governance. Numerous other members of the clergy, both high-ranking and low-, had participated in the revolution, and staff for the institutions of the state was subsequently drawn from the same group. Certain bodies, for instance the "Guardian Council" which interprets the constitution and supervises elections and "Council for Determination of the Interests of the Islamic Regime" mentioned above include clerical membership by law, and clerics also occupy many other official positions, in addition to acting as a collective éminence grise. The question of who can legitimately rule a theocracy is answered by the qualifications of the Shiite religious class, while the requirement of stability is met through the well-established and well-integrated clerical hierarchy. Nonclerical personalities also occupy high offices in the Islamic Republic, the previous president of the republic, Mahmoud Ahmadinejad, being one example. These cadres have qualifications as "Islamic intellectuals," but they do not have an independent discourse. They do not possess the natural legitimacy, epistemic authority, or cohesion of the Shiite clergy, and they could not have ruled an Islamic state or made the transition after Khomeini on their own.

The death of Khomeini in 1989 marked a critical juncture in the survival of the Islamic Republic. How would a solution be found to the always acute problem of succession after the disappearance of a charismatic leader? Again the clerical hierarchy supplied the answer. Although it was not possible to find a figure equal to Ayatollah Khomeini, his post could be occupied by a figure from the hierarchy with somewhat parallel attributes, that is another ayatollah. In the constitution devised by Khomeini and his associates, the clergy were charged with selecting that candidate. The new leader, effectively the ruling jurist described in *Islamic Government* and first personified by Khomeini himself, was to be designated by an "Assembly of Experts" composed of prominent clerics, with the workings of the assembly supervised in turn by the Guardian Council, also dominated by clerics. Sayyid Ali Khamenei, the successor *Rahbar* finally appointed in 1989, has managed to consolidate his power and perpetuate the Islamic Republic in concert with the same clerical establishment through a balancing of factions and interests characterized by Arjomand as "clerical conciliarism."[49]

The Islamic Republic and the Muslim World

Throughout its history Shiism has embraced aspects of Sunnism and made them its own. In the time of the Imams or shortly after, Shiite scholars took up the new science of scholastic theology (*kalam*) despite traditional objections to the use of reason and finally became the prime exponents of rational thought. Shiites adopted independent reasoning (*ijtihad*) as part of a model of jurisprudence taken from Sunnism and ended as the school of living, continuous *ijtihad.* In the twentieth century Shiism produced its own version of Sunni fundamentalism and established the only fundamentalist state in the world partly by drawing on the special resources of the Shiite tradition. Ironically, a utopia conceived by Sunnis found expression among Shiites. Fundamentalism, however, involves the precarious sphere of politics, and its mark on Shiism, let alone influence in the Sunni world, is not so sure.

The Islamic Republic has not been very successful in exporting its fundamentalist revolution, largely due to Iran's Shiite identity. Ayatollah Khomeini's ambition was to lead an all-Islamic movement. He often spoke as if he were at the head of a universal uprising, a role he is actually credited with in the constitution where he is given the title "great leader of the world-wide Islamic Revolution."[50] In order to sustain the idea of a worldwide movement, the ayatollah and his successors offer a revolutionary ideology washed of Shiism. De-Shiisation is already evident in *Islamic Government;* in addition to speaking in a pan-Islamic voice, Khomeini omits the early sectarian history, involving supposed usurpation of Ali's rightful rule by the first caliphs, that is the very raison d'être of Shiism but extremely offensive to Sunnis. He goes so far as to speak of the caliphs, including Umar, who is traditionally execrated by Shiites, in somewhat favorable or at least neutral terms.[51] Rapprochement (*taqrib*) and appeal to Muslim solidarity have remained the official tone and policy of the Iranian regime ever since. The Islamic Republic has vigorously promoted these causes by founding a very active and well-supported Rapprochement Institute and continually issuing calls for "Muslim unity";[52] readers may see for themselves the complete de-Shiitisation involved in these efforts by referring to the English-language site of the Institute at http://www.taqrib.info/english/index.php.

Shiite fundamentalism, then, or at least the kind of fundamentalism taken up by Khomeini and the Islamic Republic, does not conspicuously display the enclave culture[53] and strict maintenance of boundaries thought to be typical of such movements. Nevertheless, the editors of the Fundamentalism Project rate Shiites "high" on the "elect-chosen" and "boundaries" indicators of fundamentalist religion and assert that, for fundamentalist Shiites, "the sinful world" also includes Sunni Muslims.[54] Marvin Zonis and Brumberg go so far as to claim that Khomeini was hostile to Sunni governments because of a traditional Shiite belief that they are "intrinsically illegitimate." The evidence they give, however, shows clearly that governments such as that of Saudi Arabia were disdained not because of their Sunnism but for the purely political or political-religious reason that they refused to join in the worldwide Islamic revolution *despite being Muslim.*[55] What has happened with Khomeinism is that the typical Muslim fundamentalist emphasis on politics has translated into a preference for all-Islamic revolution over Shiite particularism. To put it a different way, Shiite particularism is not, due to the minority situation, efficient for politics, and Muslim fundamentalism tends to discard or remake the parts of religion that are politically inefficient. Khomeini and his successors could not entirely dispense with Shiite tradition, but they did as much as they could to give it a more acceptable public face.

Success with this strategy is difficult, however, because of deep suspicion of Shiism. Initially, the revolution did have widespread appeal. The example of a population throwing off the American "Great Satan" in the name of Islam stirred up pride and anticipation among many Muslims. The response, however, probably on the part of all Muslims but certainly of Sunnis, was simply to an Islamic movement and decidedly not to any of its Shiite features. Khomeini, for instance, was appreciated not as the grand jurist succeeding to the political prerogatives of the Imams, but as an Islamic leader, a Muslim success story so to speak. The chord struck in the Muslim world by the revolution was more political than religious; its political meaning as a Third World uprising resonated even in the West.[56] Once the euphoria of revolution lifted, the Shiite character of Iran became an ever-increasing liability. To give just one example, the influential Egyptian Sunni cleric Yusuf al-Qaradawi has in the past expressed support for Iran as a political entity and the Lebanese Hizbollah as a force fighting Israel; but in 2008 he cast suspicion on Iran by denouncing Shiites as heretics and raising the specter of Shiitisation of Sunni societies.[57]

Neither have the efforts of the Islamic Republic to gain influence among Shiite populations outside Iran gone smoothly. Appeals to fellow Shiites run up against the minority situation. Pakistan is a case in point. The Iranian Revolution inspired heightened religio-political consciousness among Pakistani Shiites, especially as clerics trained in Qom began to gain power over more traditional quietist leadership. Students stirred by events in Iran preached the Khomeinist creed of a political Islam and pan-Islamic, worldwide revolt against Western imperialism while openly displaying their Shiism, and in 1987 a Qom seminarian and agent (*wakil*)[58] of Ayatollah Khomeini, Allamah Husseini, founded a political party dedicated to Shiite rights and freeing of Pakistan from American influence. It was as if participants in the movement had, in the flush of the revolution, forgotten their precarious minority status (Pakistani Shiites are only 15 to 20 percent of the total population) while mixing the unmixable, that is, flagrant Shiism with nationalist plus pan-Islamic rhetoric. Renascent Sunnism, which had already been on the rise under President Zia-ul-Haqq, struck back with assassinations (including of Husseini) and bombings of Shiite sites and gatherings, which continue to this day.[59]

Khomeinist fundamentalism is also too tied up with Iran to go very far even with Shiites. Its real use has been not to inspire Islamic revolution but to raise the consciousness of Shiites and their ambitions for religious freedom and equality with their Sunni compatriots. Once the example of the revolution and republic fulfills this function, links with Iran become a liability as Shiite groups pursue their ultimate goal of integration into their home nations. Developments in Saudi Arabia illustrate this dynamic. The 1979 uprising of the Shiite minority (between 7 and 20 percent of the total population[60]) showed signs of inspiration from Iran, with some elements calling for an Iranian-backed revolution. A mere decade later, Hasan al-Saffar, the clerical leader of the radical Organization for Islamic Revolution in the Arabian Peninsula founded on the heels of the uprising, responded to overtures from the Saudi regime by renaming his party the Movement for Reform, negotiating with the king and advocating for Shiite religious and social rights as a part of a national development program.The earlier "anti-imperialism" of the movement, clearly styled after the Iranian worldview, was also dropped.[61]

Faced with limitations on ideological influence, the Islamic Republic has deemphasized export of the revolution and withdrawn to a strategic defensive position centered on national interest. The turn in foreign affairs to relative pragmatism dates to the end of the Iran–Iraq war in 1988, which revolutionary zeal had turned into a long and thoroughly disastrous attempt to "liberate" Iraq so that its people could establish Islamic rule as the next step in worldwide Muslim revolution.[62] Improvement of relations with the Gulf States and Saudi Arabia was vital to Iran's regional strategy and economic recovery after the war, and President (Ayatollah) Rafsanjani went to great lengths to convince Iran's neighbors that its focus had shifted from internationalist revolution to benign cooperation.[63] Politically unproductive relations with Shiite minorities, for example, in Pakistan, were also ended or reduced to religio-cultural ties, and relations emphasizing shared culture and economic interests rather than pan-Islamism were established with Central Asian states.[64] During this period Iranian leaders reconciled the founding myth of the Islamic Republic with their new tack by taking up the classic position of international revolutionists faced with the limitations of their creed: they asserted that "export" meant only export of ideas and a good example.[65]

Crucially for the question of fundamentalism, the ideological content of remaining Islamic alliances has been narrowed. First, steady and long-term alliances are with Shiites, presently in Iraq and Lebanon. The idea, so important to Muslim fundamentalism, of the march of all peoples toward Islamic government has been effectively replaced by Shiite solidarity; although the language of pan-Islamism, deeply embedded in Khomeinism and the constitution and certainly the more noble and enabling mandate, continues.[66] Second, the goal of even these Shiite alliances is not religious or ideological but strategic. Cultivation of Iraqi Shiites helps to keep the American occupiers of the country off balance and influence Iraqi governments toward a friendly attitude, while support of Lebanese Hizbollah is a card in the game with America and enhancer of prestige because of Hizbollah's success in fighting Israel. Third, there is increased emphasis on authority of the ruling jurist as an essentially political idea and *the* fundamental article of faith. Inside Iran, acceptance of Khomeini's theory of rule of the jurist demonstrates loyalty to the regime, so that those who publicly reject it may be charged with treason. Outside Iran, fealty to Khamenei and the jurist's rule indicates allegiance to the Iranian state rather than commitment to fundamentalism or any particular style of religion. Lebanese Hizbollah, for instance, does not care much if at all about the rule of Islamic law and has finally openly rejected the idea of an Islamic state, which it probably was never very serious about to begin with[67]; but a recent issue of the journal of the Rapprochement Institute mentioned above prominently features statements by Hizbollah's leader Sayyid Hasan Nasrollah declaring that Khamenei is a "Great Imam," with the most "clear and prominent" feature of his exceptional personality said to be the "political" one of "leadership."[68]

A separate essay has been devoted to Khomeinism because it has been by far the most prominent instance of Shiite fundamentalism, as well as the only Islamic fundamentalism to have captured and consolidated a state. It is in fact the only Shiite movement that fits the typology of Muslim fundamentalism by insisting that an authoritarian Islamic state is required to apply shariah as a compulsory system covering all areas of life.[69] Other Shiite groups that went in this direction did so under the influence of Khomeini's thought and the Iranian Revolution, adopting the concepts of Islamic government and rule of the jurist while maintaining associations with the Islamic Republic or elements within it. This was the situation of the Supreme Assembly for the Islamic Revolution in Iraq, founded in 1982 by Iraqi exiles with Tehran's sponsorship and espousing, as the name suggests, the establishment of an Islamic state in Iraq along with rule of the jurist.[70] Movements whose interests did not bring them as close to Iran may have found the example of the Islamic Republic empowering, but this did not lead them to conclude that they should adopt the Iranian model, which was ultimately not suited to local conditions and also involved loyalty to Iran because of the idea of the universal authority of the supreme leader. The Dawah Party is a classic example. Some Dawah members were attracted to the Iranian Revolution in the difficult days under Saddam. The Dawah, however, had been established as an independent, Iraq-centered organisation, and it rejected the theory of rule of the jurist during the 1980s even as it had to lean on Iran.[71] Although influenced by the Muslim Brotherhood, the Dawah never advocated the rule of Islam as consistently as its model and has ended in post-Saddam Iraq by advocating and participating in democracy.[72]

The editors of this volume report in their introduction that Western scholarly interest in Islamic fundamentalism began with the 1979 Islamic revolution in Iran. In this and the previous essay we have seen that the revolution and Islamic Republic that followed it are exceptional in the annals of Islamic fundamentalism and do not indicate its future. It must not be forgotten that the founding of the republic took place in a Shiite setting using Shiite ideas. Although Khomeini and the Islamic Republic strove to transcend sectarianism, the distinctively Shiite flavor of Khomeinism and Iranian fundamentalism along with Sunni hostility to Shiites excluded any chance of the Iranian example being followed in the Sunni world. Nor could the Islamic Republic serve as a precedent for Shiites outside Iran, since as beleaguered minorities they were incapable of realizing the political rule of Islam, the essence of Islamic fundamentalism. Certain features of Shiism such as devotion to martyrdom, charismatic leadership charged with latent messianism, an extraordinarily strong religious class, and relative openness to change in shariah came forward in Iran to aid the establishment and maintenance of an Islamic state in ways that might suggest that Shiism is an ideal vehicle for political Islam. None of these, however, is very relevant for Shiites in other countries, where the reasonable and possible is to gain some measure of power or security through entering into the political process while remaining discrete about Shiite identity. Political activity that is seen as religious and sectarian can be dangerous for such populations, as demonstrated by ongoing events in Bahrain.

Notes

1. For the influence of the Brotherhood and adoption of its program by the Dawah, see Faleh A. Jabar, *The Shiite Movement in Iraq* (London: Saqi, 2003), 80–81.

2. *Shiites* in this as in the previous essay refers to Twelver Usuli Shiites, who account for the vast majority of Shiites today, including virtually all Iranians. The other, much smaller Shiite minorities such as Ismailis and Nusayris (i.e., Alawis) do not engage in religio-political action. Intra-Shiite minorities express themselves in other ways, for instance, through nationalism.

3. CIA Factbook: https://www.cia.gov/library/publications/the-world-factbook/geos/ir.html. Accessed September 5, 2013

4. Anar Valiyev, "Azerbaijan: Islam in a Post-Soviet Republic," *Middle East Review of International Affairs* 9 (December 2005): 2.

5. Seventy is the highest percentage I see proposed. See, for example, Maximilian Terhalle, "Are the Shia Rising?," *Middle East Policy* 14 (Summer 2007): 70.

6. CIA Factbook: https://www.cia.gov/library/publications/the-world-factbook/geos/iz.html. Accessed September 5, 2013

7. *Functional minorities* is the useful phrase of Juan Cole, *Sacred Space and Holy War: The Politics, Culture and History of Shi'ite Islam* (London: I. B. Tauris, 2002), 7.

8. See Valiyev, "Azerbaijan."

9. *Islamic Government*, which was composed in the shrine-seminary city of Najaf, Iraq, while Khomeini was in exile, seems to present a universally applicable model of Islamic government; but with its many references to Iran and distinct Shiite features, such as the rule of an ayatollahlike grand jurist (which would require the assent of a Shiite population), the setting is certainly Iran. The pan-Islamic shading, clearly at odds with *Islamic Government*'s Iranian focus and Shiite flavor, is a result of the influence of Sunni fundamentalism.

10. Daniel Brumberg, *Reinventing Khomeini: The Struggle for Reform in Iran* (Chicago: University of Chicago Press, 2001), 55–61.

11. Shiites believe that the last or Twelfth Imam, also known as the Mahdi or Guided One, disappeared from view more than a millennium ago. The return of the Mahdi is awaited at the end of time when he will "fill the earth with Justice as it is now filled with oppression."

12. See Wilferd Madelung, "A Treatise of the Sharif al-Murtada on the Legality of Working for the Government," *Bulletin of the School of Oriental and African Studies* 43, no. 1 (1980): 18–31.

13. See Said Amir Arjomand, *The Shadow of God and the Hidden Imam* (Chicago: University of Chicago Press, 1984), along with the critical review of Arjomand by R. M. Savory in *American Historical Review* 91 (June 1986): 710–12.

14. For a description of Khomeini's *Revealing of Secrets*, see Vanessa Martin, *Creating an Islamic State: Khomeini and the Making of a New Iran* (rev. ed., London & New York: I. B. Tauris, 2003), 103–15. At this point Khomeini was not yet a fundamentalist; "fundamentalists aspire to capture political power [and] are not content to act as pressure groups, as are the [traditionalist] ulama and modernists" (Marty and Appleby, "Interim Report on a Hypothetical Family", in *Fundamentalisms Observed*, ed. Martin E. Marty and R. Scott Appleby (Chicago: University of Chicago Press, 1991), 825.

15. Brumberg, *Reinventing Khomeini*, 61. Khomeini had some association with Navvab Safavi (executed 1955), a low-ranking cleric who had contact with the brotherhood and whose pan-Islamic utopian writings show the brotherhood's influence, although his vision of a society governed by Islamic values still involves the traditional condominium with the monarchy; see Sohrab Behdad, "Islamic Utopia in Pre-Revolutionary Iran: Navvab Safavi and the Fada'ian-e Eslam," *Middle Eastern Studies* 33 (January 1997): 40–65. Both Safavi and Sayyid Qutb are celebrated in the Islamic Republic as great martyrs.

16. William E. Shepard, "Islam as a 'System' in the Later Writings of Sayyid Qutb," *Middle Eastern Studies* 25 (January 1989): 31–50. Qutb wrote in Arabic and Mawdudi in Urdu, but the originally Arabic word *nizam* is also found in Urdu and Persian.

17. Mangol Bayat, "The Iranian Revolution of 1978–79: Fundamentalist or Modern?," *Middle East Journal* 37 (Winter 1983): 40.

18. *Islamic Government*, in *Islam and Revolution. Writings and Declarations of Imam Khomeini*, trans. Hamid Algar (Berkeley, Calif.: Mizan Press, 1981), 130.

19. Marty and Appleby, "Interim Report," 825.

20. Ibid., 824.

21. *Islamic Government*, 43–44.

22. Marty and Appleby, "Interim Report," 824.

23. *Islamic Government*, 62.

24. Marty and Appleby, "Interim Report," 824.

25. Ibid., 825.

26. Gabriel A. Almond, Emmanuel Sivan, and R. Scott Appleby, "Fundamentalism: Genus and Species," in *Fundamentalisms Comprehended,* ed. Martin E. Marty and R. Scott Appleby (Chicago: University of Chicago Press, 1995), 406.

27. *Islamic Government,* 133–34.

28. Ibid., 41–42; and see also 51–54.

29. Ibid., 61.

30. See, Ibid., for example, 53–54 and passim.

31. Ibid., 60; see also 59.

32. Ibid., 60.

33. See Anoushiravan Ehteshami, *After Khomeini: The Iranian Second Republic* (New York: Taylor & Francis, 1995), 38–39; Said Amir Arjomand, *After Khomeini: Iran under His Successors* (New York: Oxford University Press, 2009), 39–40.

34. This is the part of *Islamic Government* that has received most attention from scholars, possibly because Khomeini represents the book as a continuation of this earlier material. I believe, however, that the original and crucial aspect of *Islamic Government,* as argued above, is the formulation of a theory of an ideal Islamic state using rational arguments from the doctrine of the Imamate.

35. *Islamic Government,* 124–25.

36. See Shahrough Akhavi, "Contending Discourses in Shi'i Law on the Doctrine of Wilāyat al-Faqīh," *Iranian Studies* 29 (Summer–Autumn, 1996): 229–68. Khomeini himself claims that his formulation is in line with the tradition and "nothing new" (*Islamic Government,* 125; also 124).

37. *Islamic Government,* 36: "The expounding of law did not require a successor to the Prophet. He himself, after all, had expounded the laws; it would have been enough for the laws to be written down in a book and put into people's hands to guide them in their actions." It is a most central and crucial point of traditional Shiite doctrine that the Imams succeeded to the Prophet because they were needed to supply proper interpretation of the Quran and laws, of which they alone are capable. An Internet search for "two weights" or "thaqalayn" turns up discussion of one very well known hadith used as a proof text.

38. See Ervand Abrahamian, "Why the Islamic Republic Has Survived," *Middle East Report,* no. 205 (Spring 2009), http://www.merip.org/mer/mer250/why-islamic-republic-has-survived; restating the thesis originally laid down in Abrahamian's *Khomeinism: Essays on the Islamic Republic* (Berkeley: University of California Press, 1993). See also Abrahamian, "Khomeini: A Fundamentalist?," in *Fundamentalism in Comparative Perspective,* ed. Lawrence Kaplan (Amherst: University of Massachusetts Press, 1992), 109–25.

39. Said Amir Arjomand, "Review: Fundamentalism, Religious Nationalism, or Populism?" *Contemporary Sociology* 23 (September 1994): 672.

40. Arjomand, "Unity and Diversity in Islamic Fundamentalism" in *Fundamentalisms Comprehended,* ed. Marty and Appleby, 179–98. This apparent contradiction is discussed in the previous essay.

41. Section 1, articles 1 and 2; section 2, article 1; section 1, article 5. From the official Persian-language document posted at: http://rc.majlis.ir/fa/content/iran_constitution. Accessed September 5, 2013. "Sovereignty" = *hakimiyat,* parallel to Arabic *hakimiyah,* a key concept in Sayyid Qutb's writings also spoken of by Mawdudi (Urdu: *hukumat-i ilahi*). The constitution also refers to the republic as a *nizam* (section 1).

42. Martin Riesbrodt, *Pious Passion. The Emergence of Modern Fundamentalism in the United States and Iran,* trans. Don Renau (Berkeley: University of California Press, 1993), 241.

43. Saudi Arabia is often referred to as fundamentalist. John O. Voll describes "the Saudi state and Wahhabi community" as "a concrete fundamentalist effort" providing "an important example for others" and "basic repertoire of concepts and ideas from which modern

fundamentalists draw" (Voll, "Fundamentalism in the Sunni Arab World," in *Fundamentalisms Observed*, ed. Martin E. Marty and R. Scott Appleby [Chicago: University of Chicago Press, 1991], 351). Saudi Arabia, however, is a condominium between the rulers and a clerical estate that accepts the status quo and considers its role to be advisory or supervisory, the typical position of traditional Muslim clergy. Al-Qaeda, who are proper fundamentalists, recognize this well; al-Zawahiri calls the Wahhabi shaykhs "the jurists of the [American] Marines." The similarity of Wahhabi social conservatism to that of some fundamentalists does not make Wahhabis fundamentalists themselves.

44. Ervand Abrahamian. *Radical Islam: The Iranian Mojahedin* (London: I. B. Tauris, 1989), 94–95.

45. Cited in Dilip Hiro, *Iran under the Ayatollahs* (London: Routledge and K. Paul, 1985), 100.

46. Marty and Appleby, "Interim Report," 826.

47. Section 1, article 6.

48. Quoted in Brumberg, *Reinventing Khomeini*, 134–35.

49. Arjomand, *After Khomeini*, 40–55.

50. Section 106.

51. *Islamic Government*, 81 and 55.

52. See Rainer Brunner, *Islamic Ecumenism in the 20th Century: The Azhar and Shiism between Rapprochement and Restraint* (Leiden & Boston: Brill, 2004), 379.

53. See Emmanuel Sivan, "The Enclave Culture," in *Fundamentalisms Comprehended*, ed. Marty and Appleby, 11–68.

54. Almond et al., "Fundamentalism: Genus and Species," in *Fundamentalisms Comprehended*, ed. Marty and Appleby, 415 and 407. In the later *Strong Religion: The Rise of Fundamentalisms around the World* (Chicago: University of Chicago Press, 2003), Almond, Appleby, and Sivan also speak of the "religious competition and enmity" of Shiite fundamentalism with Sunni Islam (p. 122).

55. Marvin Zonis and Brumberg, "Shiism as Interpreted by Khomeini: An Ideology of Revolutionary Violence," in *Shiism, Resistance, and Revolution*, ed. Martin Kramer (Boulder, Colo.: Westview Press, 1987), 47–66.

56. See Martin, *Creating an Islamic State*, pp. 188; Nikki R. Keddie, *Iran and the Muslim World: Resistance and Revolution* (New York: New York University Press, 1995), pp. 112.

57. Jeffrey Fleishman, "Egyptian sheik's outburst against Shiites roils Iran," *Los Angeles Times*, September 28, 2008, http://articles.latimes.com/2008/sep/28/world/fg-islamic28 (accessed September 7, 2011); Marina Eleftheriadou, "The Shia Protocols: The Iranian Project of Shiite Proselytism," *Negócios Estrangeiros* 14 (April 2009): 18–21. For other Sunni statements expressing suspicion of Iran's Shiism, see Emmanuel Sivan, "Islamic Radicalism: Sunni and Shi 'ite," in *Religious Radicalism and Politics in the Middle East*, ed. Sivan and Menachem Friedman (Albany: State University of New York Press, 1990), 39–75, and Werner Ende, "Sunni Polemical Writings on the Shi'a and the Iranian Revolution," in *The Iranian Revolution and the Muslim World*, ed. David Menashiri (Boulder, Colo.: Westview Press, 1990), 219–32.

58. The agents of the grand ayatollahs are local personalities authorized to guide believers in the ayatollahs' shariah rulings.

59. Mariam Abou Zahab, "The Politicization of the Shia Community in Pakistan," in *The Other Shiites: From the Mediterranean to Central Asia*, ed. Alessandro Monsutti, Silvia Naef, and Farian Sabahi (Bern: Peter Lang, 2007), 97–112.

60. Laurence Louër, *Transnational Shia Politics: Religious and Political Networks in the Gulf* (New York: Columbia University Press, 2008), 7.

61. Ibid., 166, 232–35; Toby Craig Jones, "Rebellion on the Saudi Periphery: Modernity, Marginalization, and the Shia Uprising of 1979," *International Journal of Middle East Studies* 38, no. 2 (2006): 213–33.

62. Ray Takeyh, "The Iran-Iraq War: A Reassessment," *Middle East Journal* 64 (Summer 2010): 365–83.

63. Henner F*Iran's Rivalry with Saudi Arabia between the Gulf Wars* (Reading, U.K.: Ithaca Press, 2002), 96–104.

64. Ghoncheh Tazmini, "The Islamic Revival in Central Asia," *Central Asian Survey* 20, no. 1 (2001): 67.

65. Fred Halliday, *Revolution and World Politics: The Rise and Fall of the Sixth Great Power* (Durham: Duke University Press, 1999), 98–99.

66. For example, pan-Islamism provides a frame for the essentially political set of relationships with Palestinians; for a recent assessment, see Elaheh Rostam-Povey, *Iran's Influence* (London & New York: Zed Books, 2010), 154–85.

67. Benedetta Berti, "The 'Rebirth' of Hizbollah: Analyzing the 2009 Manifesto," *Strategic Assessment* 12, no. 4 (2010): 91–100; Joselph Elie Alagha, *The Shifts in Hizbullah's Ideology: Religious Ideology, Political Ideology, and Political Program* (Leiden [Amsterdam]: Amsterdam University Press, 2006).

68. *Thaqafat al-Taqrib* 49 (Rajab 1432/Khurdad 1390/June 2011): caption on cover and pp. 56–57. Nasrollah was speaking at a conference in Beirut on the "dynamic legal thought" (*al-tajdid wa-al-ijtihad al-fikri*) of Khamenei.

69. Iraq with its considerable Shiite population and status as a great center of Shiite learning also produced much thought on the role of religion in politics, but this was more moderate than that of Khomeini and only became less so as a result of the example or influence of the Islamic Republic. Ayatollah Muhammad Baqir al-Sadr did move toward a radical outlook and Shiite model in the last few years of his life as he was caught up in enthusiasm for the Iranian Revolution, even issuing, a few days after Khomeini's triumphant return to Iran, a "Preliminary Legal Survey" of an Islamic constitution (Chibli Mallat, *The Renewal of Islamic Law: Muhammad Baqer as-Sadr, Najaf, and the Shi'i International* [Cambridge & New York: Cambridge University Press, 1993], 67–69). Previously, however, Sadr had spoken in terms that were essentially democratic (Faleh A. Jabar, *The Shi'ite Movement in Iraq* [London: Saqi, 2003], 281–87, and Talib Aziz, "The Political Theory of Muhammad Baqir Sadr," in *Ayatollahs, Sufis and Ideologues: State, Religion and Social Movements in Iraq*, ed. Faleh A. Jabar [London: Saqi, 2002], 231–44). Some members of the al-Shirazi group of clerics based in Karbala, Iraq, who became known for support of Khomeini's doctrine and their ties with Iran have claimed that they came up with ideas very similar to Khomeini's before he did and had created an organisation to advance them (see Louër, *Transnational Shia Politics*, 96–99; members of the Shirazi group interviewed by Louër also stated [p. 124] that Banna, Mawdudi, and Qutb were discussed in their study circles). Louër doubts that there was really an organization, and a glance at the book he was told articulated these views (Sayyid Hasan al-Shirazi, *Kalimat al-Islam* [Beirut: Mu'assasat al-Wafa, 1964]) shows that, while it does call for the rule of grand ayatollahs or ayatollahship as an institution (*marja'iyah*), it is mostly concerned with defending the prerogative of the clerics against "parties" and "individuals'' (apparently meaning intellectuals) and thus belongs to the context of struggles over authority within the Shiite community.

70. See Jabar, *Shī'ite Movement*, 235–59 .

71. See Rodger Shanahan, "Sh'ia Political Development in Iraq: The Case of the Islamic Da'wa Party," *Third World Quarterly* 25, no. 5 (2004): 946–48.

72. See Juan Cole, *The Ayatollahs and Democracy in Iraq* (Amsterdam: Amsterdam University Press, 2006), 8–9.

Fundamentalism Diluted

From Enclave to Globalism in Conservative Muslim Ecological Discourse

David L. Johnston

In this essay I argue that as religion continues to expand as a key factor related to globalization the notion of "fundamentalism" must be seen in a new light. Contrary to expectations, the world became more "religious" in the late 1970s. This phenomenon caught the attention of scholars and the Fundamentalism Project was launched. But as time passed, it became increasingly clear that facile and confident definitions of fundamentalism would fall short of the reality on the ground.

First, I look at some of the recent theory that problematizes earlier pronouncements on fundamentalism; then I offer a case study—how a growing number of mainstream Muslims have become involved in the wider environmentalist movement. If one of the characteristics of fundamentalism is a fortress mentality, an "us versus them" worldview—which I concede is part of the picture, then a focus on the potentially devastating impact of climate change and pollution seriously undermines and dilutes that group narcissism. Have we just left "fundamentalism" behind? Finally, how might "theology" be involved in this process of an expanded worldview?

Resurgence of Religion and "Fundamentalism"

The sociologist of religion Lester R. Kurtz is one of many scholars who found that the theoretical orthodoxy of his subdiscipline had become inept in explaining the dramatic revival of religion at the turn of the twenty-first century. Like his colleagues, he had been weaned on the secularization theory—modernization necessarily entails a decrease in religious observance. Though it might still be possible to defend this thesis with regard to Europe, most sociologists now conclude it is no longer adequate when it comes to the proliferation of all kinds of new religious movements, inside and outside of established, traditional religions. In his words, "Along with the creation of new religious forms, we are now witnessing some dramatic revitalizations of traditional forms of religious life. The growing interdependence of the various human cultures, along with the economic and social webs woven across thousands of former boundaries, is creating an unprecedented series of changes in the nature of human theology."[1]

In this period of feverish change and technological revolutions, with armed conflicts simmering in many places, as well as an activist civil society in the streets and in cyberspace calling for democracy, justice, and peace—in the midst of all these baffling developments, religion is never far from the center. This the first point Kurtz is making. The second one is more implicit: "revitalizations of traditional forms of religious life" and "changes in the nature of human theology" point to an explosion of religious expressions in many directions. If the media often choose to highlight "fundamentalisms," reality is much more complex and interesting. Some have left religion proper only to turn science into a new "spiritual" lifeboat. Others respond to the pressures of secular society by retreating into the private sphere. But, says Kurtz, there is much more than meets the eye in this new flowering of all things religious: "Other efforts to cope with modern and postmodern life involved the revitalization of traditional forms, the creation of new religious movements, and the formation of quasireligious systems such as civil religion and nationalism."[2]

Already this seems quite distant from the airtight definition of fundamentalism offered by Gabriel A. Almond, R. Scott Appleby, and Emmanuel Sivan in their book *Strong Religion*.[3] For them, the phenomenon of fundamentalism common to many religious traditions across the globe essentially boils down to three interrelated characteristics—"militance" in religious identity, an enclave mentality, and opposition to secular modernity: "'Fundamentalism' . . . refers to a discernible pattern of religious militance by which self-styled 'true believers' attempt to arrest the erosion of religious identity, fortify the borders of the religious community, and create viable alternatives to secular institutions and behaviors."[4]

If this is the case, then the Egyptian Muslim Brotherhood, founded in 1928 and with its stated ambition of "creating viable alternatives" to a secular society, should be their showcase example. Yet it is not, and part of the reason is that from the beginning the brotherhood dove into politics. And with political involvement comes the necessity to compromise and to cooperate with people of different ideological stripes. Enclaves get diluted.

At the same time, old, ingrained habits die hard. For the first time since its 82 year-old existence, the Muslim Brotherhood came to power in Egypt through the election of president Morsi. A few months later Khalil al-Anani wrote a piece that proved prophetic.[5] A long time student of the movement, Anani saw Mohamed

Morsi's behavior as reflecting the internal politics of the Brotherhood. As the candidate most loyal to the movement's old guard, Morsi ran the country mostly through the lens of his own party that was still structured like an opposition party hardened by years of persecution and rife with intrigue and conspiracy theories. The few efforts he did make that first year to reach out to other parties and national stakeholders were mostly rebuffed, however, and popular opposition swelled to become the "June 30 rebellion" 2013, leading to the army's coup on July 3, removing him from power, arresting its leaders and forcefully crushing any further demonstrations. Should the Muslim Brotherhood be invited to the political table one more time, it will necessarily have to shake off once and for all its ingrown victim mentality.

It is remarkable how another "fundamentalist" movement, the American "Christian Right," rose to prominence in the 1980s and waned in the 2000s. But not all "strong religious" movements venture into politics. New religious movements have appeared, Lester Kurtz observes, as well as quasi-religious fervor in the form of civil society and nationalism. His third category comes closest to fundamentalism: "the revitalization of traditional forms." So for him these three factors have led to the creation of "an unprecedented series of changes in the nature of human theology."

The word *theology* here is unusual in the sociological literature. For instance, in an important book that seeks to set new directions in the sociology of religion, the British religion specialist Grace Davie delineates the way in which sociology should proceed in the study of religion. It is not about theology, she argues, which seeks to adjudicate between "competing truth claims."[6] Rather, "the discipline of sociology is about pattern; it is concerned both with the non-random ways that individuals, communities and societies order their lives and with finding explanations for these ways of behaving." In this essay I argue for a definition of theology I have used before, which includes the "non-random" choices of individuals and communities, and which should resonate with scholars of several disciplines: "an ever-growing and evolving reflection—in the light of sacred texts and in interaction with a specific religious tradition—that leads people to better articulate their relationship to God, provides answers to the ultimate questions of human existence, and gives shape to a life-style in the world as community that best reflects that understanding."[7] In other words, people situated in particular socioeconomic, cultural, and political contexts come to the texts and the inherited norms of their religious tradition with specific questions—questions that likely did not occur to people at other times and places. Hence the tradition constantly changes shape and evolves, though certain fixed points usually do remain in place. But even the central theological focus of Islam, for instance, *tawhid* (the oneness of God), is interpreted in sometimes radically different ways, depending on which group of Muslims one has in mind. The Muslim Brotherhood's views are not those of their

Salafi allies; yet both groups' theologies and ideologies are evolving significantly. Sociology and anthropology, history, religious studies, area and cultural studies—all these disciplines help to illumine how people who see themselves as "religious" actually live out their particular worldview or common imagination. And I would add here, "and how they seek to shape the world accordingly," as is clearly the case for Muslim environmentalists.

So this essay is ostensibly about a conservative religious community—mostly Muslims in the United Kingdom—discovering the reality of a physical world damaged by human activities stemming from greed and carelessness and progressively committing themselves as people of faith to reverse the course of this nefarious impact on the environment. But first we need to consider three methodological issues, which in turn will lead us back to the concept of fundamentalism.

Important Sociological Concerns

Three theoretical concerns impinge on the data presented below. The first is about the issue of "religion"—is it a "thing" that makes people act in certain ways? This becomes a crucial issue when applied to the analysis of fundamentalism. Second, social scientists are returning to the individual, however counterintuitive that might seem. Third, we need to look at "modernity" again and recognize that, in fact, what we have today is an amalgamation of modernities.

The Issue of Essentialism and Causation

In a work attempting to peel away some of the half-truths and not-so-hidden ideological premises from the anthropological writings about Muslims and Islam, Daniel Martin Varisco is clear about one issue: as someone doing serious field work among a particular community, "it would be foolhardy to look in the field for 'Islam' in that essentialized and decontextualized sense so many scholars want to define." What he means is that some scholars seem to assume that Islam has an "essence"—a core of properties without which the "thing" being observed is or is not "Islam." And yet, any collection of ethnographic reports worth its salt will uncover "a wide variety of 'islams' and all sides of a lively debate over who is a Muslim."[8]

The anthropologist Gabriele Marranci, for his part, declares that Varisco has not gone far enough in deconstructing the problematic concept of culture, so central in the social sciences. Though I do not see Marranci providing his readers with a clear picture of what "culture" might be either, his central focus is in on the role of human emotions, both in the approach of the scholar who shows empathy for the people he or she is observing and interviewing and in the way individuals navigate the many options available to them in their own religious tradition. In fact, he claims that it is the "shared emotional experience"—affirming the common humanity of both scholar and respondent—that validates the scientific aspect of the research; and in the final analysis the only irrefutable (i.e., nonessentializing) definition of a Muslim is simply "a human being who feels he's a Muslim."[9]

While Marranci offers much theory to back up this last assertion, there is no space to go into details here. What is important, though, is the issue of causation, which, depending on the assumptions of each scholar, can be attributed to "culture" (the "culturalist" assertion that "culture shapes a person's identity as a bottle shapes the water it contains")[10] or to a particular social theory (a temptation for both anthropologists and sociologists), or to religion (a theological determinism), respectively. The sacred text does not make people act in certain ways, or even believe in certain ways. Thus, for instance, the quranic concept of the Islamic umma (the community of believers), which has become so central in Islamic discourse today, still means different things to different Muslims: "Muslims are not part of the ummah because the ummah exists in itself beyond their physical and mental realities, but because they use it, and transform it through their feelings of being Muslim. To have an ummah, you need a mind; whatever 'ummah' might mean . . . it cannot exist beyond the mental processes that we call mind."[11]

So the concept of umma is just that—an idea passed down in various forms by a religious tradition. It relates to the sacred texts of Islam, but it also means slightly different things, depending on the Muslim you ask. This is the process of theology, or envisioning what it means to be a faithful Muslim in one's own particular historical and sociopolitical context. Though all Muslims would agree that the hajj is the best symbol for the unity of the universal Muslim community, *umma* will have a different resonance for different Muslims, from the Sufi devotee in rural Pakistan to the business executive in Kuala Lumpur; from a mother of ten in a Berber village of Morocco to a young activist of the Hizb al-Tahrir in London. Besides the basic rituals of a faith (the "five pillars" of Islam), people imagine what a "good Muslim" is very differently, depending on their context; and that idea will shape in turn what the umma represents for them—a process carried out both by groups and individuals.

Return to the Individual

Already the reader probably noticed in Marranci's argument a turn to the individual. Actually, his rather complicated theory of identity is what guides his own approach to the phenomenon of fundamentalism—how it is that some people choose to embrace a religious commitment that calls for total dedication, even to the point of sacrificing one's own earthly life. In his book *Understanding Muslim Identity* the simplest definition is this: "identity is a machinery of personal imagination allowing vital coherence between the individual and his or her environment."[12]

This turn is borne out in Davie's book as well, in which she devotes a whole chapter to the enormous impact in American sociology of rational choice theory

(RCT). Drawing from both economic theory and psychology,[13] RCT follows two possible paths: first you have a purposive actor who seeks to gain a particular benefit; second, you have the existence of a religious market. This means that supply is much more important than demand: "religious activity will increase where there is an abundant supply of religious choices, offered by a wide range of 'firms' (religious organizations of various kinds); it will diminish where such supplies are limited."[14]

The French sociologist of religion Olivier Roy believes that globalization, as the acceleration of population, capital, and commodity flows, and its accompanying Westernization process, has brought about "the triumph of the self" in religion.[15] The religious market is thriving. Because traditional sources of social and religious authority have been eroded, because religion is more and more deterritorialized, and because a new global class of educated people communicates in English on the Internet, the emphasis has shifted from religion to "religiosity" (how should I be practicing my religion?). That is, the "return of the religious" has taken similar forms for Muslims, Christians, and people of many faiths and spiritualities: religiosity, or the focus on personal faith, is more important than religious orthodoxy as defined by traditional leaders.

According to Roy, then, "the self, and hence the individual, is at the core of the contemporary religiosity."[16] As in the case of Pentecostals the world over,[17] for instance, what counts is a local community of believers, truth experienced in personal faith with often-charismatic leaders, such as Pope John Paul II or Fethullah Gülen with his values-oriented, business-friendly global Islamic movement. "Revivalist movements," in Roy's view, all see society around them as irreligious—they are the true believers. And because traditional authorities are sidelined, new movements, whether New Age gurus in the West, Scientologists, Gülen, or many "neofundamentalist" Islamic groups, tend to appeal to the youth and the general feeling is that "true believers are in a minority."[18]

Hence Roy's term for the new fundamentalisms of the 1990s and 2000s is neofundamentalism. Religious tradition stays mostly as it was (a conservative mindset), but the "patterns of belief and authority are changing."[19] At the same time this neofundamentalism is not a throwback to the past—it is interacting with Westernization in a profound way. This is "because when Muslims are cut off from pristine cultures that were for them largely influenced by non-Islamic customs and traditions, an opportunity presents itself to reconstruct a Muslim community based solely on Islamic tenets." And it is individuals who in a modern context make a personal decision to "to join a new community based solely on the explicit tenets of religion.[20] Globalization, then, raises again the issue of modernity. But are these groups of "born-again" believers at core reacting against a Western-led "modernity"?

Modernity versus Modernities

Grace Davie contends that one of the flaws of the common association of fundamentalism with anti-Western modernization finds its origin in a truncated view of modernity.[21] She turns to the work of Shmuel Eisenstadt, who explicitly rejects any idea of convergence in the process of modernization. True, the process did start in eighteenth-century Europe, but now it has spun out in many directions, with often contradictory and surprising trajectories. For him the modern world is "a story of continual constitution and reconstitution of a multiplicity of cultural programs."[22] Davie agrees with Eisenstadt "that to engage with the Western understanding of modernity, or even to oppose it, is as indisputably modern as to embrace it."[23]

This means that what are commonly called fundamentalist movements are themselves bona fide expressions of modernity. As Roy puts it, "fundamentalism is both a product and an agent of globalization."[24] What is more, many new social actors, social entities, and movements have appeared on the scene in the last few decades, seeking specifically to tackle the urgent issues of our day: environmental and feminist groups, antiglobalization civil-society initiatives, as well as religious revivalist movements. Of course, here is where the disagreements arise. At what point does one label such a group fundamentalist? And is fundamentalism a useful category in the first place?

Fundamentalism and its Cognates

Marranci has convincingly pulled together some of the main strands of the vast literature on fundamentalism in his *Understanding Muslim Identity.* Other colleagues in the present volume continue the task of sorting out what is of use and what is not, whether the word itself can still be serviced, or which other term should replace it. Here I seek only to make three points, which are necessary to introduce the core of this essay: the issues of enclave, nomenclature, and, again, theology.

I said earlier that the Muslim Brotherhood should have been "exhibit A" of twentieth-century fundamentalism according to the critieria found in *Strong Religion,* yet upon examination it was not so simple. But then the multiplication of Salafi groups at the end of the last century might be a better candidate, and a recent collection of papers on the global Salafi movement raises this question in a useful interdisciplinary manner.[25] Historians, islamicists, sociologists, anthropologists, and political scientists—all came together to approach a contemporary phenomenon with the tools of their own trades and a propensity to borrow from others. The result is a fascinating kaleidoscope and a concerted effort to combine a "family resemblance" strategy with the recognition that some parts of Salafism have now fragmented to such an extent as to call into question what is "Salafi" and what has morphed into something else. But every contributor seems to agree that at its core is the "true believer" syndrome, or the "us versus them" ethos and hence the desire "to morally upstage its opponent." Notice the connection the editor, Roel Meijer, makes with Roy's analysis in his introduction:

> In a contentious age, Salafism transforms the humiliated, the downtrodden disgruntled young people, the discriminated migrant, or the politically repressed into a chosen sect (*al-firqa al-najiya*) that immediately gains privileged access to the Truth. . . . Because of its emphasis on doctrinal purity and not politics, Salafism, more than the Muslim Brotherhood or Hizb ut-Tahrir, has been able to empower individuals by providing a universal alternative model of truth and social action. . . . As Roy has pointed out, due to its universal quality and its de-territorialised, de-culturalised character it has become a highly powerful model of identification and is eminently suitable for the creation of new virtual communities.[26]

There is no doubt that Salafism fits the general type of recasting of religion under the forces of Western-led globalization as described by Roy. Most of the characteristics of this global trend of born-again believers revolve around a strong in-group consciousness or enclave ethos:

- emerging in the context of crisis, like the loss of religious authority;
- delinking of "religious and cultural patterns";[27]
- forming communities around the self-definition of individuals as "believer";
- repudiating "non-religious" elements;
- seeking to define the "true tenets of the religion";
- feeling that "our" community is a minority in the midst of a culture that is secular or even pagan.[28]

Clearly much research on fundamentalism converges on this one issue: "fundamentalist" groups form enclaves, "communities whose outside boundaries are tightly closed and where the interior division of influence and labor tends to be egalitarian."[29]

My second point relates to nomenclature. Lester Kurtz rejects *fundamentalism,* as do many others, because of its pejorative connotations. He consciously uses *traditionalism* over *fundamentalism* in the American Christian context. The modernist camp refers to the "knowledge workers," those in the mainstream American culture who shape the media, the lobbyists, writers and ideologues, community organizers and activists. Part of their challenge to religious groups comes from the "melting pot" ideal, and part of it comes from the forces of capitalism. In essence who gets to define what a family is, how much power the state can have, what the role played by women should be, and the like? For Kurtz, the Christian Right represents the orthodox position—a clash that can be seen all over the world, and particularly in Muslim circles. Yet within each religious community a wide spectrum of views are available. If *fundamentalism* is simply another word for *traditionalism* or *religious conservatism*, then dropping *fundamentalism* seems best.

Part of the reason for ditching *fundamentalism* would also be that it is not "antimodern"—exactly the point made by Davie and Roy. Many forms of religious revivalism in the twenty-first century seek to reshape the world according to the values they feel are central to their own religious worldview. Yet while they reject certain aspects of modernity, they embrace others, like the whole section of Egyptian Salafism that despite years of decrying democracy as a Western heresy nevertheless rushed to form a political party and contest the 2011 presidential elections.

It seems then that recent work in the social sciences casts some serious doubt on the kind of watertight pronouncements about fundamentalism made by the likes of Almond, Appleby, and Sivan.

Lester Kurtz describes all manner of religious revival in our day, including "some dramatic revitalizations of traditional forms of religious life"—hardly synonymous with "fundamentalism." Daniel Varisco unravels the notion that "religion," "Islam," and by implication, "fundamentalism," are "things" that make people do this or that. Gabriele Marranci's focus on the jihadist's emotions and effort to create harmony between his or her identity and context undermines the notion of a one-size-fits-all "militancy" as a key ingredient to "fundamentalism." Grace Davie, Shmuel Eisenstadt, and Olivier Roy dismiss the idea that various forms of "strong religion" are essentially antimodern. Roy shows how the enclave phenomenon is part and parcel of "neofundamentalism," along with a deculturized, deterritorialized form of "pure" religion focused on doctrine and ritual.

My own suggestion has been that, taking into account all the points above, a variety of outside factors push individuals and groups to revise their understanding of the received tradition and the way they read their sacred texts—people of faith are always "doing theology" in one way or another. Hence, the issue of environmentalism offers a useful case study on the extent to which it impinges on a conservative group's theology. Whereas the focus used to be only on otherworldly salvation and how it shaped everyday practice and rituals, a new widened perspective now includes moral values that tie the believers to humanity as a whole—believers of all kinds and unbelievers as well. The faith may not be diluted—theology is simply expanding its horizons to include more scope—but the enclave mentality is fast eroding, and, yes, in that sense the "fundamentalism" is diluted.

Ecology and the Widening of Theological Horizons of the Muslim Community

The Islamic empires and kingdoms from the tenth to the eighteenth centuries had sophisticated laws regulating the use of natural resources such as water, air, soil, plants, and animals. Part of this was a concern for justice in the distribution of precious public assets and fear of the disastrous effects of pollution for the rest of the community. Part of it was a theological concern: the earth is a gift from God to humankind, and humans will be held accountable for managing it rightly. So humanity represents God's trustees on earth, and creation is given to them as a trust. In practice, however, these laws were unevenly enforced, and the theological grounding just described has crystallized in this form only in the last few decades.[30]

With poverty and various other social and political crises gripping many Muslim-majority countries, environmentalism is not generally considered an urgent matter. Rather, as long-time observer Richard C. Foltz puts it, "not only are Muslim societies today *not* models of environmental consciousness, in many cases they provide examples of the worst sorts of environmentally-destructive lifestyles and development policies. Many of the most severely degraded environments in the world today are those in which Muslims constitute a majority of the population. While overall per capita consumption and pollution rates are generally less than in Western industrial societies, Muslim countries mostly suffer from acute environmental problems connected with poverty, overpopulation, and outmoded technologies."[31] What is more, when an awareness of ecological urgency is brought up, the crisis is usually blamed (with some justification, no doubt) on Western greed and imperialism.

Still, we are now witnessing a mounting grassroots campaign among Muslims, particularly in the West, to address issues of climate change and pollution. What is particularly noteworthy is that those leading it use verses from the Quran and the Sunna (the official collections of the Prophet's deeds and sayings) to motivate participation. This is a movement among mainstream Muslims, who, perhaps more than those of other faiths, are strongly conservative.

Before delving more into this movement and two of its foremost thinkers, it is useful to consider the writings of Nawal H. Ammar, associate dean and professor of justice studies at Kent State University, who illustrates well the issue of conservatism, theology, and yet an attitude and outlook that is anything but enclavelike. Among several chapters and essays she has written on this topic, Ammar contributed a chapter to an edited volume on population and the environment, which she began with a caveat: Muslim societies are so diverse globally and the sacred texts have been interpreted so variously over time that it would be foolhardy indeed to present "an Islamic view of the environment."[32] After all, her doctorate was in the field of cultural anthropology. On the one hand, she reasons, one finds a solid consensus both among the jurists and among the population at large that human fertility is a blessing from God and humans ought not to tamper with it.[33] As population control has been one strategy in international circles to relieve pressure on natural resources, convincing Muslims to move in this direction will require much cross-cultural sensitivity and interfaith dialogue. On the other hand, the legal tradition in Islam is rich in ethical rules for the conservation of natural resources and their equitable distribution, for treating nature with kindness and refraining from damaging or abusing it.[34]

More recently Ammar has written a more theological piece on "Islam and deep ecology," which is nicely summarized here; notice too how she "essentializes" the word *Islam*:

> Islam, in considering all God's creation as having common characteristics and divine reflections, echoes views of deep ecology. The whole universe is one single system created and united by Allah [the central notion of *tawhid*, or the unity of God]. Looking at the universe with such a perspective where all creatures are connected reveals common principles in Islam and deep ecology. . . .
>
> This unity of God's creation and the relationship of its components, however, becomes more complicated at the level of using and protecting nature as well as the role of humans in such endeavors. Although Islam's final teachings parallel the objectives of deep ecology, it nevertheless approaches the details of such objectives differently because the *Tawhid* perspective views the various components of nature as engaged in an order of interdependence for the final objective of glorification of God.[35]

My point in highlighting this quotation is not to delve into the details of her position. She had begun her essay by noting that colleagues had suggested that Muslims needed to reform their theology. This is a plausible suggestion, she avers, considering that half of the world's armed conflicts are in Muslim countries where populations have a higher than average birth rate and where cities, like Cairo, are among the most polluted in the world. Yet what is needed is not a "new theology" but rather a retrieval of "the progressive theological elements that the Prophet Muhammad brought to Arabia in the seventh century." She continues, noting that "in a progressive Islam the connection and linkage between nature and other creations of God lie at the center of the theology and social existence."[36]

In fact, Ammar is consciously "doing theology"—bringing the resources of a tradition to bear on a contemporary situation, and, in this case, on a situation loaded with moral urgency. Her essentializing of Islam and even personalizing this religious tradition (Islam believes this or teaches that) is perhaps more of a shorthand. Yet for an accomplished academic in North America to write this way, I think, signals the general conservative nature of Muslim belief with regard to the Quran (the literal word of God dictated to Muhammad).[37] One can "retrieve" principles, which, she implies, all Muslims should see (because "Islam" says so), mainly because no one questions the authority of the sacred text. Still, the texts have been read very differently over the centuries, and there is no stopping other just as devoted Muslims to read them quite differently now and in the future. That is the nature of hermeneutics, or the theory of textual interpretation.

Yet her theological construction of ecological responsibility is completely in line with other writings on the subject. The unity of God and of his creation (*tawhid*) is always the first point mentioned. The second one is most often the trusteeship of humanity. Ammar's summary is worth quoting: "In this relationship of interdependence among the created, Islam places the keeping of the earth and heavens under the hands of humans, as the *Khalifah* (vice-regents) on earth. The Qur'anic verse states, 'I am setting on the earth a vice-regent' (2:30). The *Khalifah* is a manager not a proprietor, a keeper for all generations."[38]

As most commentators have done since the classical period,[39] she ties this verse to the next one, in which God teaches Adam "the names of all things"—which in contemporary terms translates into "an independent will to know good from evil, and their ability to prevent evil."[40] This verse is almost always connected to Q. 33:72, in which the "trust" (*amana*) is offered by God to the heavens, mountains, and earth, but they refuse it. Humanity, by contrast, accepts it. Ammar comments that "the universe is given to humans as a 'trust' . . . which they accepted when they bore witness to God in their covenant of *Tawhid*." So accountability is built into the equation, which, when added to the encouragement to enjoy the earth's bounty, creates a bit of tension—a "theological test for Muslims," muses Ammar. Muslims are then exhorted to find a balance "between use and protection, namely action." This action, often described in the Quran as "enjoining the good and prohibiting evil," is all the more important in the area of protecting the environment, as two hadiths (or reports on the sayings and deeds of the Prophet) illustrate: "If anyone plants a tree or sows a field and humans, beasts or birds eat from it, he should consider it a charity on his part. Whoever plants a tree and looks after it with care until it matures and becomes productive, will be rewarded in the hereafter."[41]

I now turn to a couple of leading figures in Islamic environmentalism. The first, Mawil Izzi Dien, is a professor of Islamic studies at the University of Wales. He wrote the first book-length treatment of Islam and ecology, which combined theology, Islamic law, and contemporary concerns. *The Environmental Dimensions of Islam* devotes almost half of its content to an Islamic theology of environmentalism, which then leads to a chapter on ethics and two on sharia and ecology, with an interesting use of the legal tool of *maslaha,* or public benefit. Izzi Dien closes with a recounting of international efforts to curb pollution and biodiversity loss and promote conservation—in particular the 1983 World Charter for Nature and Agenda 21 ratified at the Rio Earth Summit in 1992. Perhaps this sentence summarizes best the purpose of the book: "The conservation of the natural environment in Islam is both an ethical and a religious imperative which should be backed with legislation and effective enforcement of an environmental law."[42]

This last statement has profound implications for the way conservative practicing Muslims view the impact of their faith on global affairs. Professor Izzi Dien's work is influential, if for no other reason than that he was chosen to participate in an international team of scholars to draft in 1983 the document "Islamic Principles for the Conservation of the Natural Environment."[43] Another reason is that he is a recognized authority on Islamic law, commonly referred to as sharia. It is not only his eagerness to write on issues of Islamic law but also some of his views that mark Izzi Dien as a conservative Muslim. One might be fooled, however, as he starts his introductory exposé of Islam, making use of the six dimensions of religion put forward by the British scholar of religion Ninian Smart. Yet that impression does not last. For instance, under the heading "The Ethical," he follows Smart in discussing the institutionalizing of religion, "which makes the theory more applicable by using the force of the institution." But then he recoils, stating that Islam is an exception to this rule: "for the Islamic religion has not been institutionalized because it rejects having any medium as intermediary between the human and the Divine." So with regard to Muslim societies, it is the opposite that takes place: "institutions became religiously orientated rather than religion becoming institutionalized,"[44] a view that no social scientist could endorse.[45]

Then too, with regard to hermeneutics, he notes that in the four schools of Sunni law "the relationship between text, ethics and social application was carefully scrutinised through the complex process of Islamic jurisprudence." What he means is that this was a textualist approach based on grammatical and lexical considerations primarily and that these were applied to real-life situations through the methodology developed gradually in Islamic legal circles. With this as a backdrop, note his following statement: "In contrast to this, there seems to be an inclination among contemporary Muslims towards experiential interpretation, which represents a new tendency distinct from the previous traditional dependency on the text and the presumption of its ability to provide answers. It is only in the future that will determine whether the consequence of these new developments will be of value or will lead to cultural and social upheaval."[46] Izzi Dien sees a new paradigm on the horizon—one of "experiential interpretation"—and he is not sure this augurs well for Muslim societies. Yet it is just this conservatism of his that most guarantees the scope of his influence. The doctrine of inspiration of the Quran as inerrant dictation from the Angel Gabriel to the Prophet is in no danger whatsoever of being displaced, and though Salafism is an extreme, the bulk of Muslims worldwide still adhere to a textualist, and even literalist, reading of the sacred texts and the body of traditional writings, whether in the Sunni or the Shii traditions.

Having pointed out Izzi Dien's influence, it is important to draw attention to the universal scope of his legal-theological interpretation. He is, in fact, widening the traditional communitarian ethos of Islamic law into one that now easily merges into a global environmental ethic. To summarize, Islamic law was traditionally seen as drawing upon four sources: the Quran, the Sunna (the perfect example of the Prophet as accessed through the major, recognized collections of hadiths), reasoning by analogy (*qiyas*), and the consensus of the jurists (*ijma'*). There were other principles also, though not attested by all the schools of law. Among these is the recourse to public interest (*maslaha*), which was mostly championed by the Maliki school, though with clear guidelines. The idea of public interest, particularly as it relates to a discussion of "sharia's objectives" (*maqasid al-sharia*) has now become a subject of intense interest in Muslim debates, especially in traditional and conservative circles, allowing in some cases a greater focus on the spirit of the law, as opposed to just the letter of the law.[47]

Izzi Dien devotes a whole chapter, "Environmental Protection and Public Interest," to this issue in his book. Drawing from the popular fourteenth-century jurist from Granada, Ibrahim b. Musa al-Shatibi, he states that there is no "absolute benefit" or no "absolute harm," except what can be discerned from a careful weighing of its relative weight in a particular situation. Thus legal provisions to protect the environment and maintain its sustainability "take precedence over individual or community interests even if the latter appear to be of an overwhelming urgency." This is because, from a long-term perspective based on the harm produced by the increased burning of fossil fuels or the destruction of the ozone layer of the atmosphere, we can say that short-term economic gains turn out to bring a greater harm and should therefore be shunned. But this also brings up the planetary scope of the debate that would never have been imagined in medieval juristic debates. The Quran says, "It is He who has created for you all things that are on earth" (2:29). In effect, argues Izzi Dien, the verse is left open for the sake of public interest. All humanity shares the earth, so this is the intended target of the pronoun *you*. This is a "global environmental interest" that concerns all humans: "the earth with all its interests and benefits was created to be shared by all creatures and by all human communities."[48] This represents a dramatic dilution of the traditional communitarian orientation of Islamic law.

Nor is Izzi Dien the only one promoting an Islamic ecological discourse with global ramifications. The British scientist and environmental activist Fazlun Khalid actually founded a movement in the United Kingdom that has impacted many Muslim communities worldwide: the Islamic Foundation for Ecology and Environmental Sciences (IFEES). In 1995 Khalid chaired an interfaith conference on religion and ecology in Japan, out of which came the Ohito Declaration for Religion, Land and Conservation. Besides its campaigns in such places as Zanzibar and Malaysia, IFEES produces literature for young and old with the aim of educating and mobilizing the Muslim public to choose a greener lifestyle and to mobilize against the ominous threats of climate change and biodiversity loss.[49]

Part of IFEES's strategy is to reach out to traditional Muslim societies and impress their religious and community leaders with the environmental values at the heart of the Islamic tradition. Thus for a two-year project of rainforest conservation in West Sumatra, Khalid and his team organized a three-day seminar for the community on Islamic principles of conservation. They taught the legal (*fiqh*) categories of *hima* (protected lands), *harim* (the protected zones around trees, rivers, wells, and springs), and *ihya al-mawat,* the revivification of land left fallow or unused—some of which even predate Islam in the Arabian Peninsula.

Importantly, this was more than just Khalid's British NGO's project. He had secured a much wider network to help with the funding and implementation of it—the U.K. Durrell Institute of Conservation and Ecology (DICE) and the British Department for Environment. Khalid is just as intentional about secular partnerships as Izzi Dien has been in his scholarly work. For instance, notice the various layers of community involvement and both local and federal government involved in a project that aims to "strengthen and integrate the religious management systems of Hima (by mapping land and forest use systems and ensuring their protection through joint community / Forestry Dept. patrols); Harim (through watershed management) and Ihya Al-Mawat (by creating nagari tree nurseries and agroforestry systems to rehabilitate and reforest degraded lands) into the traditional nagari and adat systems."[50] What is also remarkable is the seamless integration of traditional sharia terms with current conservation techniques, which remain in harmony with local Indonesian customs.

I end this case study with a quotation from a press release made by Fazlun Khalid after he was invited by the United Nations secretary general to participate in the Summit on Climate Change in September 2009 in New York. He has just alluded to the consumerist agenda of rich countries that gamble with "fictitious money" and thus only create a wider gap between them and poorer countries, while damaging our common planet and aggravating its climate change. He wraps up his one-page declaration in this way: "It would seem that in allowing to be swept away [*sic*] by forces intent on destroying the natural world in the name of economic growth faith communities have surrendered their responsibilities, Muslims, not least amongst them. Our job is to prod this group, which constitutes twenty percent of the world's population, to wake up to their teachings and join forces with other like-minded people to leave a liveable planet for our children."[51]

The task of "prodding" Muslims to take up their God-given responsibilities is a mission Khalid would like other Muslims to take up all over the world. By doing so—and he knows this very well—they will be reading their texts and putting their tradition to work in ways never imagined by their forebears. As they do so, they leave behind the narrow concerns and exclusive privileges of the past and focus on how God wants to use them to bring blessing to all humanity, by joining other forces, some religious and some not, in order to "save the planet."

Clearly one of the issues forcing people of faith in our day to take a second look at the enclavelike theology they inherited is the specter of ecological doom—issues of pollution and biodiversity loss, indeed, but even more urgently the issue of climate change. Though I have remained hesitant to endorse the word *fundamentalism* in this essay, I have acknowledged that religious resurgence is a fact, and that some varieties do fit Roy's category of neofundamentalists. Yet just as conservative Muslim movements are currently negotiating the troubled waters of a Middle East in turmoil, Muslims in many countries are beginning to see their theology expand and evolve as they tackle with others the urgent tasks of reducing their output of greenhouse gases, develop alternative energies to those based on oil, and find ways to help the poor who are most vulnerable to the onslaught of rising seas, vicious storms, and devastating droughts. Inward-looking religious communities such as the Salafis and fundamentalist Christians will continue to draw new members, but many on both sides are likely to develop a theology more focused on peace and coexistence. With that, the exclusivism or fundamentalism of these groups, in effect, is diluted.

Notes

1. Lester R. Kurtz, *Gods in the Global Village: The World Religions in Sociological Perspective*, 2nd ed. (Thousand Oaks, Calif.: Pine Forge Press, 2007), 189.

2. Ibid., 190. The phrase "quasi-religious systems such as civil religion and nationalism" was a point made long ago by Ninian Smart. See for example his *Worldviews: Cross-cultural Explorations of Human Beliefs* (New York: Scribners, 1983).

3. *Strong Religion: The Rise of Fundamentalisms around the World* (Chicago: University of Chicago Press, 2003).

4. Ibid., 17.

5. Khalil al-Anani, "Rethinking the Muslim Brotherhood," *Foreign Policy Magazine*, December 17, 2012, available online at http://mideast.foreignpolicy.com/posts/2012/12/17/rethinking_the_muslim_brotherhood (accessed December 20, 2012).

6. Grace Davie, *The Sociology of Religion* (Los Angeles & London: Sage, 2007).

7. David L. Johnston, *Earth, Empire and Sacred Text: Muslims and Christians as Trustees of Creation* (London: Equinox, 2010), 19–20. I wrote this as an activist Christian theologian attempting to construct a common theology of creation and humanity, while also building on my expertise as an Islamicist. The context, and hence tone, of the present essay is different, but the idea of "theology" is just as useful.

8. Daniel Martin Varisco, *Islam Obscured: The Rhetoric of Anthropological Representation* (New York: Palgrave Macmillan, 2005), 51.

9. Gabriele Marranci, *The Anthropology of Islam* (Oxford & New York: Berg, 2008), 78.

10. Ibid., 90.

11. Ibid., 109.

12. Gabriele Marranci, *Understanding Muslim Identity: Rethinking Fundamentalism* (New York: Palgrave Macmillan, 2009), 101.

13. RCT draws on two forms of social-scientific theorizing: first on the economic ways of thinking epitomized by Gary Becker in *The Economic Approach to Human Behavior* (1976), which in turn derive from the utilitarian individualism espoused by Adam Smith; and second on elements of exchange theory taken from psychology, an approach initiated by George Homans and Peter Blau in the 1960s, in which the actor is central to sociological thinking.

14. Davie, *The Sociology of Religion*, 70.

15. Olivier Roy, *Globalized Islam: The Search for a New Ummah* (New York: Columbia University Press, 2004).

16. Ibid., 28.

17. See the historian Philip Jenkins's classic book on the global spread of Pentecostals, *The Next Christendom: The Coming of Global Christianity*, 2nd ed. (New York & Oxford: Oxford University Press, 2007).

18. Ibid., 29. Salafis would be an example of neofundamentalists for Roy: they focus on norms and rituals of religion (their interpretation of sharia), whereas other more moderate fundamentalists are quite happy to shift the focus to values. Both, however, are of the "born-again" variety; individuals choose to join.

19. Ibid., 29.

20. Ibid., 29–30.

21. See also Marranci, *Understanding Muslim Identity*, chapters 2–3, for a detailed discussion of fundamentalism theory (see also my next section). Fundamentalism as a defense mechanism in reaction to modernity is one of the common denominators in most explanations.

22. Shmuel Eisenstadt, "Multiple Modernities," *Daedalus*, 129 (Winter 2000):2; quoted in Davie, *The Sociology of Religion*, 107.

23. Davie, *The Sociology of Religion*, 107.

24. Roy, *Globalized Islam*, 25.

25. Roel Meijer, ed., *Global Salafism: Islam's New Religious Movement* (New York: Columbia University Press, 2009). Salafis have appeared in the global press as a result of the "Arab Spring" and its impact on Egypt. As of this writing, the Salafis have entered the political fray with gusto, attempting to upstage the more "liberal" Muslim Brotherhood in the run-up to the September 2011 elections. Then in July 2013 the Salafi party Nour initially stated its approval of the army's removal of President Morsi from office, apparently out of political calculation—and likely too out of its longstanding animosity toward them.

26. Meijer, introduction to *Global Salafism*, 13.

27. Roy has deepened his analysis on this point in an ambitious work of comparative sociology, *Holy Ignorance: When Religion and Culture Part Ways* (New York: Columbia University Press, 2010).

28. Roy, *Globalized Islam*, 27.

29. Almond, Appleby, and Sivan, *Strong Religion*, 7. The notion of enclave originally came from Mary Douglas. *Strong Religion* came as a response to many criticisms of the Fundamentalism Project (of which R. Scott Appleby was coeditor). Davie's *Sociology of Religion* contains a trenchant critique of this project, particularly on the issue of its "antimodernist, antisecularist" nature. But she also wonders where all the funding came from in order to sponsor such an expensive project. It certainly tells as much about fundamentalism, she notes, as it does about American academia.

30. Richard C. Foltz has written the most about Islamic environmentalism. From 1996 to 1998 he took part in a series of conferences at Harvard University that brought together Muslim scholars on this issue. The result was the large edited volume, *Islam and Ecology: A Bestowed Trust*, ed. Richard C. Foltz, F. M. Denny, and A. Baharuddin (Cambridge: Center for the Study of World Religions, Harvard Divinity School, 2003). See also my essay, "Intra-Muslim Debates on Ecology: Is Shari'a Still Relevant?," in the issue on Islam and ecology I coedited with Anna Gade for *Worldviews: World Religions, Culture and Ecology* 11, no. 2 (2012): 218–38.

31. Richard C. Foltz, "The Globalization of Muslim Environmentalism," on the website Zëri Islam, available at http://www.zeriislam.com/artikulli.php?id=942, accessed August 30, 2013.

32. Nawal H. Ammar, "Islam, Population and the Environment: A Textual and Juristic View," in *Population, Consumption, and the Environment: Religious and Secular Responses*, ed. Harold Coward (Albany: State University of New York Press, 1995), 124. The changing nature of "the Muslim communities' conscience" over time and according to context is the first reason this task is an impossible one. The second reason she gives is that there are no popes or clergy to impose any particular interpretation of the Islamic scriptures.

33. Contraceptive methods are allowed but only under duress—only when the life of the mother is at risk. This is true also for abortion, at least before the 120th day of pregnancy (the period during which the soul of the person is considered under formation) (Ibid., 127).

34. Ibid., 130–33.

35. Nawal H. Ammar, "Islam and Deep Ecology," in *Liberating Faiths: Religious Voices for Justice, Peace and Ecological Wisdom*, ed. Roger S. Gottlieb (Lanham, Md.: Rowman & Littlefield, 2003), 551–64. This piece was originally published in an earlier volume: David Landis Barnhill and Roger S. Gottlieb, eds., *Deep Ecology and World Religions: New Essays on Sacred Ground* (Albany: State University of New York Press, 2001), 193–211.

36. Ammar, "Islam and Deep Ecology," 551.

37. She seems unaware, or unwilling to admit, that other Muslims, may read the texts differently.

38. Ibid., 554.

39. See Johnston, *Earth, Empire and Sacred Text*, for a sweeping survey of quranic commentary on this passage, classical, premodern, and contemporary.

40. Ammar, "Islam and Ecology," 555.

41. Ibid., 557.

42. Mawil Izzi Dien, *The Environmental Dimensions of Islam* (Cambridge: Lutherworth, 2000), 165.

43. This was a joint publication by the International Union for the Conservation of Nature (IUCN) and the Meteorological Protection Administration (MEPA) of the Kingdom of Saudi Arabia, published at Gland, Switzerland, 1983.

44. Izzi Dien, *The Environmental Dimensions of Islam*, 17.

45. All religious movements become institutionalized; it is simply a fact of human societies. Izzi Dien's argument here is an apologetic one—seeking to shield Islam, the true religion, from the sociological laws that likely affect other faiths, thereby revealing their corruption. Religious communities in general are conservative by nature, and this means that they espouse an exclusivist soteriology ("no salvation outside the home religion"). Hence, the enclavelike mentality among both traditionalists and the more born-again variety such as the Salafists.

46. Izzi Dien, *The Environmental Dimensions of Islam*, 17–18.

47. For more on *maslaha* and the objectives of sharia, see David L. Johnston, "An Epistemological and Hermeneutical Turn in Twentieth-Century *Usul al-Fiqh*," *Islamic Law and Society* 11, no. 2 (2004): 233–82, and "*Maqasid al-Shari'a*: Epistemology and Hermeneutics of Muslim Theologies of Human Rights," *Die Welt des Islams* 47, no. 2 (2007): 149–87; Felicitas Opwis, "The Concept of *Maslaha* in Classical and Contemporary Islamic Legal Theory," in *Shari'a: Islamic Law in the Contemporary Context*, ed. Abbas Amanat and Frank Griffel (Stanford: Stanford University Press, 2007), 62–82.

48. Izzi Dien, *The Environmental Dimensions of Islam*, 138.

49. See their magazine *EcoIslam* online, http://ecoislam.wordpress.com/ (accessed September 12, 2011).

50. Jeanne E. McKay, "Islamic Beliefs and Sumatran Forest Management," *EcoIslam* 7 (April 2010): 2.

51. This text can be found on the IFEES website: http://ifees.org.uk/index.php?option=com_content&task=view&id=40&Itemid=53 (accessed September 12, 2011).

Islamic Education and the Limitations of Fundamentalism as an Analytical Category

Florian Pohl

Past decades have seen the confident reassertion of religion in public life in many parts of the world. Seemingly defying predictions of religion's demise in modernity, religion reentered the public stage as a key player in the political and moral discourses over the public life of citizens and the state. Variously described as the "desecularization" or "deprivatization" of religions, this process has challenged the validity of earlier canons of scholarship and raised the question of how we can make sense of religion's ongoing public role in the modern world.[1] Responses have oscillated between those who welcome the resurgence of religion as a means of supplying a much-needed moral dimension to secular discourse and others who consider these developments with greater concern, describing them as a threat to democracies and civil society. One of the ways in which scholars have looked at phenomena of religious revival is to portray them as "a rejection of modernism" and as specifically antimodern, irrational responses to the unsettling uncertainties of modern life.[2] Similarly, others have configured religious revival movements as a specifically postmodern phenomenon and described them as expressions of religious fundamentalism that, in the words of Zygmunt Baumann, are part of "a wider family of totalitarian or proto-totalitarian solutions offered to all those who find the burden of individual freedom excessive and unbearable."[3] Instead of retreating from the public sphere into the private realm of individualized belief as much of sociological theory had postulated, religion has shown not only staying power but also increasing vitality in the post-Enlightenment world.

The term *fundamentalism* has become increasingly common in academic and popular usage in the comparative study of groups, movements, or individuals associated with phenomena of religious revival. To think through the heuristic value of the term *fundamentalism* for our understanding of the continuing vitality of religion in the post-Enlightenment world is the central task of this essay. A particular focus will be placed on Islamic education as an example of the ways Muslims assert the public relevance of Islam in the contemporary world. As part of the larger taxonomy of the study of the public ambitions of Muslims, fundamentalism has found its way into the contemporary debate over the persistent strength of Muslim schools and Islamic learning. Drawing on specific cases from the Indonesian Islamic educational scene, this essay demonstrates the limitations of fundamentalism as an analytical category by highlighting the term's often hidden normative dimensions that derive from its uncritical reliance on an historically contingent understanding of religion, of what it is or what it should be: namely, a distinct sphere of life kept separate from other spheres such as politics, economy, law, and education. As a result, fundamentalism fails to offer meaningful distinctions for an analysis of religious agendas in public life and heightens suspicion of religious formations that transgress the boundaries between private and public spheres.

Fundamentalism: The Emergence of an Analytical Construct

As Watt outlines in this volume, *fundamentalism* has its origins in the controversy over nineteenth-century Christian modernism. It dates back to the 1920s when it designated a particular branch of American Protestantism that reacted against the challenges posed by evolutionary theories and the development of historical critical scholarship of the Bible, popularly evidenced by the so-called Monkey Trials in Tennessee (1925). Only with the 1970s and more pervasively in the subsequent two decades was *fundamentalism* used to describe a myriad of revival movements in other religious traditions of the world. In its application to Muslims the use of *fundamentalism* accelerated in the 1980s as a key concept in a rapidly growing body of scholarly literature that set out to analyze the increasing significance of Islam in Muslim communities around the world.[4] In works on events such as the Islamic revolution in Iran, the Grand Mosque seizure in Mecca, Muslim resistance to Soviet occupation in Afghanistan, the assassination of President Anwar Sadat in Egypt, the responses by the Muslim Brotherhood and other Muslim organizations against repression by the Bashar al-Assad government in Syria, Muhammad Zia-ul-Haqq's Islamization campaign in Pakistan, and the Salman Rushdie affair at the end of the decade, *fundamentalism* became a central element in the discursive economy by which scholars sought to describe the increasing public relevance of Islam both locally and globally.[5] Despite its prevalence, the description of Muslim movements as fundamentalist was controversial. Muslim activists and thinkers rejected the term based on its negative connotations. The rejection was often supported by the observation that a cognate term did not exist in any of the Muslim languages. Its Protestant origins in the beginning of the twentieth century, moreover, disqualified it in the eyes of others to describe adequately the nature and content of contemporary activist movements in the Muslim world. Such cautionary perspectives notwithstanding, the term *fundamentalism* reached widespread recognition in the study of Islamic reform movements through the five-volume Fundamentalism Project that remains to date among the most influential works on the subject.[6]

Responding to some of the criticism over the use of fundamentalism as an analytical category, the editors of the volumes of the Fundamentalism Project, Martin E. Marty and R. Scott Appleby, and a majority of contributors, conceptualized fundamentalism as a homogeny that identifies structurally analogous phenomena of modern religion in a global and comparative perspective. Rather than defining fundamentalism as a specific set of beliefs and practices, they asserted an interrelated set of properties or "family resemblances" that identify the genus or the "family."[7] In their capstone statement in the Fundamentalism Project's fifth and final volume Gabbiel A. Almond, Emmanuel Sivan, and R. Scott Appleby appraised the "genus and species" of fundamentalism based on the contributions to the project.[8] They affirmed the analytical cogency of fundamentalism for the study of religious phenomena that emerged in the twentieth century in reaction to the intertwined processes of modernization and secularization by deducing a set of nine interacting ideological and organizational properties. Even though the authors acknowledge that some of the properties may or may not be found in some cases of fundamentalism, the first characteristic, reactivity to the marginalization of religion, constitutes for them "the basic impulse behind the other eight properties" and "the very essence of fundamentalist movements."[9]

With the essence of fundamentalism located in resistance to the erosion of religion in society as a result of modernization and secularization, a common feature of definitions of fundamentalism is that it transgresses the modern separation of private–religious and public–political spheres. In a later article on the concept for the *Encyclopedia of Politics and Religion,* Appleby reasserts: "Fundamentalism is a modern form of politicized religion by which self-styled 'true believers' resist the marginalization of religion in their respective societies. Fundamentalists identify and oppose the agents of marginalization (secularists) and seek to restructure political, social, cultural, and economic relations and institutions according to traditional religious precepts and norms. . . . The genuine fundamentalist is both religious and political."[10]

In such understanding apolitical movements of revivalism that seek to emphasize a greater role in an individual's personal life fall outside of the definition of fundamentalism, as do those revivalist groups that manipulate religious sentiment for purely political purposes and ends. Rather it is the conflation of religion and politics, the assertion of a comprehensive role of religion that transcends the boundaries between private and public spheres, that is at the heart of the fundamentalism category. These underlying assumptions about the nature of religion that pass for what is universal, normal, and thus desirable when fundamentalism is the subject of debate are what call into question the concept's heuristic value.

Operating through the category of fundamentalism as a conflation of religion and politics is a conceptualization of religion as separate and independent from other spheres of human life and social interaction. Such a view, however, is premised on the idea that there is a natural differentiation between religion and other institutions in society that fundamentalist movements violate. Such neat differentiation between religion and other social institutions, however, is anything but a natural state of affairs. The boundaries between religion and other social spheres are not straightforward but rely on a definition of religion that is the product of a particular history. The secular conceptualization of religion is, as Talal Asad has shown, the construction of European modernity in which religion is dissociated from public discourse and power and instead relegated to the newly emerging private sphere.[11] The implications of conceptualizing as fundamentalist instances in which religion is confidently affirmed in the public sphere are illustrated by John L. Esposito. He points out that "a religion which does not seem to do so (a religion that mixes religion and politics) appears necessarily retrogressive, prone to religious extremism and fanaticism, and thus a potential threat."[12] The consequences and limitations of the logic Esposito criticizes here can be seen in the debate over Islamic education.

Fundamentalism and the Revival of Islamic Education

Fundamentalism belongs to the discursive repertoire in the study of Islamic revival. Islamic education has been part of this broader trend. It is hardly surprising then that the term has found its way into the contemporary academic and popular discourses on Muslim education. Particularly after the events of 9/11 and in light of reports about madrasa institutions in Pakistan in which members of the Taliban and al-Qaeda were alleged to have acquired violent and extremist views, a general suspicion of Muslim schools as "terrorism factories" could be discerned.[13] Influenced by the perception of the role Muslim schools had played in the Afghan war against the Soviets, the madrasa system in South Asia increasingly became the focus of an international debate over a presumed link between terrorism and Islamic education.[14] In his analysis of the media portrayal of South Asian madrasas in the post–9/11 period Ali Riaz demonstrates how over time observations about specific instances of Muslim schools in Afghanistan and Pakistan developed into more generalized assessments of Islamic education as undesirable.[15] Primarily viewed through the prism of U.S. national security, Muslim educational institutions subsequently became the target of political analysts and policy makers concerned with curbing violent extremism in the Muslim world.[16]

Common targets of criticism are the religion-focused nature of the curriculum in Muslim schools, opposition to secular schooling, and instructional techniques such as memorization. In the eyes of its critics Islamic schooling is indoctrinatory and inadequately prepares students for participation in the modern world.[17] In other instances more severe accusations can be heard that charge Muslim schools with inculcating in their students a near-total rejection of Western culture, its values and lifestyle, and promoting hostility and even violent behavior toward nonbelievers.[18] Particularly concerning madrasa institutions in the border region between Afghanistan and Pakistan, some observers have alleged that these schools serve no other purpose than to incite their students to violence against non-Muslims. In a *Foreign Policy* article entitled "Islam's Medieval Outposts," Husain Haqqani characterizes Pakistan's Muslim schools as "universities of jihad" and asserts that although "the militant madrasa is a relatively new phenomenon . . . even the quietist madrasa teaches a rejection of modernity while emphasizing conformity and medieval mind-set."[19] Such perception is echoed in *The 9/11 Commission Report* that identifies the state of Pakistan's education system as "a particular concern" for the United States and its attempts to counter the threat of terrorist violence.[20] The appropriation of the fundamentalism label to describe Islamic education takes place in the context of the debate outlined above.

The persistent centrality of traditional religion in the educational routines and opposition to secular learning specifically serve as the basis for including Muslim schools in the fundamentalism category. In an article on Pakistani madrasas selected for inclusion in *The Rise of Islamic Fundamentalism*—an anthology in the Greenhaven Turning Points in World History series—the schools' focus on Islamic subjects such as Arabic, Quranic studies, and Islamic jurisprudence while excluding subjects in science and technology functions as a convenient marker of fundamentalist identity.[21] In a more nuanced manner Samuel C. Heilman's comparative essay on traditional learning in Judaism and Islam for the fifth and final volume of the Fundamentalism Project follows from a similar premise. Although he acknowledges the concept's drawbacks, Heilman defends fundamentalism as qualitatively different from traditionalism or religious conservatism. What distinguishes "fidelity to tradition" in education from fundamentalism, argues Heilman, is a defense of "the comprehensiveness of religion" in the face of the modern marginalization of religion in education and society.[22] Echoing Appleby's emphasis on "reactivity to the marginalization of religion" as essential characteristic of fundamentalism, quoted earlier, Islamic education that insists against secular demands on the central status of Islam in the educational routines of Muslim schools can be configured as "something akin to if not identical with fundamentalism."[23]

The purported fundamentalist nature of Muslim schools has given rise to policy recommendations that see in the promotion of secular education an answer to the perceived radicalizing influence of Muslim schools on their students.[24] Substantial development programs have been initiated by the Agency for International Development (USAID) and the Middle East Partnership Initiative (MEPI) aimed at improving the quality of Islamic education in different parts of the world.[25] The explicit goal of these development strategies is the expansion and improvement of secular education. Indonesia is no exception. In late August 2004 the United States announced that it would provide U.S. $157 million to Indonesia over a period of five years in order to enhance the quality of instruction in the country's religious schools.

Fundamentalism and Indonesian Islamic Education

Indonesia's system of religious schools has faced accusations similar to those encountered by the madrasa in Pakistan. In 2002 the International Crisis Group identified a network of about fifty of the country's estimated fourteen thousand Islamic boarding schools or pesantrens for which it asserted the suspicion of links to al-Qaeda.[26] On the whole, media coverage has been marked by a heightened sense that the pesantrens constitute a "problem" globally and for Indonesia's fledgling democracy and the country's transition from decades of authoritarian rule. The German magazine *Geo* brought such assessment of the problematic nature of pesantren education to a point when it declared that these schools were "die vielleicht größte Gefahr für das Land" (possibly the country's gravest danger).[27]

Similar to the criticism that their Middle Eastern and South Asian counterparts receive, the perspective on Indonesia's Islamic schools is motivated by parallel concerns about the nature of the curriculum. Following the investigations of bomb attacks on the J. W. Marriot and Ritz-Carlton hotels in Jakarta in 2009, in which links surfaced between some of the perpetrators and Islamic schools, Alexander Downer, former foreign minister of Australia, opined: "The problem with the schools is the curriculum is very narrow. . . . They focus on religious education and not much else. People come out of those schools being great experts on the Koran, but they don't have knowledge of arithmetic, geography, language and physics. It's hard for them to get jobs and they get swept into this world of fundamentalist religion."[28] Again, premised on the religion-centered nature of education, the fundamentalism label serves to heighten the suspicion of nonsecular types of religious education as dangerous and retrogressive.

Contemporary Trends in Indonesian Islamic Education

Counter to the modernizing confidence that economic realities and the growing demand for state-certified education would lead to a decline in the number and significance of traditional Islamic schools, Islamic education has continued to thrive in Indonesia. Although large numbers of privately run Islamic schools had become integrated into the national education system by the early 1980s, the Islamic revival that seized Indonesian society in the 1980s and 1990s brought with it also a resurgence of educational institutions that teach an exclusively religious curriculum. Reflecting larger societal trends toward normative Islamic piety among the Muslim public, the growing interest in religious studies and the demand for scholars trained in the classical Islamic sciences have contributed to the persistent vitality of the Islamic educational scene. Although current government statistics show that the majority of Indonesia's students are educated in the institutions of the public system, the share of schools in the private Islamic sector remains significant. Depending on the school level, from 10 to 15 percent of Indonesia's youth receive their education in Islamic schools, colleges, and universities.[29]

The overwhelming majority of religious schools cooperate with the state. State efforts at incorporating Islamic private schools into the national education system had accelerated in the 1970s. One of the strategies the government pursued was to grant degree equivalency to private religious schools that complied with government curricula and regulations. Through the incorporation of government-accredited textbooks and the alignment of their curricula with those of the state, the Muslim educational mainstream has found ways to accommodate Indonesian nationalism and the state. This process has been aided by the fact that most private Islamic schools are affiliated with one of Indonesia's two largest Muslim mass organizations—the traditionalist Nahdlatul Ulama (NU) and its modernist counterpart, the Muhammadiyah. Both organizations conceive of Islamic identity as compatible with Indonesia's pluralist nationalism and emphasize a sociomoral rather than narrowly political agenda. Although these accommodating trends have been the rule rather than the exception, Indonesia has also seen a new trend: the emergence of noncooperative and politically radical Islamic schools.

With the 1990s and in the subsequent transition to democratic rule that followed the end of President Suharto's authoritarian New Order in 1998 a small but politically assertive group of schools developed that advocated a more far-reaching Islamization of society and of the political structures of the state. These include the schools of the Prosperous Justice Party (PKS) and the Hidayatullah organization as well as politically more quietist Wahhabi-Salafi schools that receive ideological and financial support from the Middle East. Especially Pondok Pesantren Al-Mukmin in Ngruki, close to the Central Javanese city of Surakarta, is mentioned in national and international debates over the link between Islamic schools to terrorist organizations.[30] Al-Mukmin was founded by Abu Bakar Baʿasyir who is considered to have been the spiritual leader of the Southeast Asian Jemaah Islamiyah (JI). Baʿasyir's ideological proximity to JI is evident from his public statements. He has openly denounced the legitimacy of Indonesian nationalism, called for the establishment of a state based exclusively on Islamic law, and expressed harshly antipluralist views.[31] Teaching materials at the school reflect some of these positions such as the incompatibility of Islam and nationalism and the need for a state to be governed by Islamic law.[32] Although other institutions that reflect essentially noncooperative political positions may not necessarily share Al-Mukmin and Baʿasyir's politically radical outlook, what unites these schools, according to Robert W. Hefner, is their efforts to use the educational and social structures of their institutions to effect broader transformations of society and state.[33]

On the opposite end of the political spectrum, educational networks have emerged that are at the forefront of advancing and supporting the democratic political process and have shaped the public discourse on issues such as civil society, interreligious harmony, and gender equality. Particularly prominent have been efforts on the level of Islamic higher education. Progressive civic education courses have been put into place and become mandatory for all students in the state system of Islamic higher education since 2001. This state-affiliated network consists of approximately fifty institutions from State Islamic Colleges (STAIN), to State Islamic Institutes (IAIN), and State Islamic Universities (UIN) with campuses in nearly all Indonesian provinces. Building on a long history of educational openness and innovation,[34] the state system developed a civic education program that advances inclusive positions on democratic reform and multicultural citizenship within an Islamic framework.[35] Following successful implementation in the state system, a number of private Islamic colleges and universities followed suit and put into operation similar curricula. Most notable among these are the institutions affiliated with the modernist Muhammadiyah that has also begun to develop a similar program for its nationwide network of secondary schools.[36] In the same way, politically progressive energies can be detected among a section of schools in the pesantren tradition. In cooperation with nongovernmental organizations a growing number of pesantrens are involved in initiatives aimed at promoting religious diversity and the empowerment of civil society. An example of a pesantren that has achieved national recognition for its leadership in interfaith initiatives and conflict resolution is Pesantren Al-Muayyad Windan in Central Java.[37] Other schools such as Pondok Pesantren Pabelan in Magelan, Central Java, have distinguished themselves for incorporating study courses on comparative religion into their educational programs and for actively promoting interfaith harmony among their students and in their local communities.[38]

It will be helpful to keep the developments in Muslim schools on both ends of the political spectrum in perspective. Out of almost fifty thousand Islamic schools in the archipelago, Hefner puts the number of schools that exhibit noncooperative characteristics in the hundreds.[39] Schools that could be considered politically radical because they promote a violent transformation of the Indonesian state constitute an even smaller minority, perhaps not exceeding a few dozen in number.[40] Similarly, politically progressive schools such as the aforementioned Al-Muayyad Windan or Pabelan are by no means representative of the majority of Indonesia's schools. Even though moderation, compromise, and accommodation with the state are characteristic of the educational mainstream, the country's Islamic education scene is far from monolithic. It is characterized by an ongoing debate among Muslim educators over the political function of Islamic education and its relationship to the state. What developments, if any, in Indonesia's Islamic education scene could be described as fundamentalist? The complexities that emerge from even a cursory reading of the broad spectrum of Muslim schools raise questions about how feasible it is to capture the diversity of political temperaments and organizational structures with a single all-embracing term such as *fundamentalism.*

A first complication arises when the religion-centered nature of the curriculum is posited as a distinguishing feature of fundamentalist education. Religion has not been relegated to the sidelines in the educational life of politically progressive schools. It is not assigned a sequestered, privatized, or merely devotional role. Rather, support for participatory governance, social justice, and pluralism are developed precisely within a framework of Islamically derived traditions and values. Conversely, even a politically radical school such as Al-Mukmin includes formal educational programs that adhere to the government guidelines for state-certified education and has earned acclaim for high educational quality on formal subjects including English language instruction.[41] These observations challenge secularist assumptions evident in the ambitious aid programs and development strategies for the education system of Muslim countries, described earlier, that see in the promotion of secular learning effective measures against religious militancy.[42]

Another related observation concerns the activist features of Islamic schools. If those using the fundamentalism concept seek to describe the public dimension of Muslim educators, it is relevant to emphasize that the educational self-understanding of schools that promote politically progressive agendas equally extends beyond the education of individual Muslims into the public sphere. Although the quality of their engagement in the public sphere differs from that of their noncooperative and rejectionist counterparts, these schools have become part of a nationwide network of individuals and institutions that Hefner describes as "civil Islam" for their public advocacy of personal freedom and democratic pluralism based on Islamic values of justice and human dignity.[43]

Finally, complexities abound when we consider the assertion that the establishment of Islamic law is a normative political goal for Muslim fundamentalist movements. Once more, Appleby's reference article on "fundamentalism" serves to highlight this general theme: "[Fundamentalists] feel strongly that Western societies erred grievously when they replaced God, religion, and divine law with human reason and secular political principles as the basis for the legal and social order. For such people, religiously derived morality is the only acceptable framework for discerning the common good, evaluating human behavior, and governing society."[44]

The presumed tension between religious law and secular political principles poses a conceptual challenge when the Indonesian context is concerned. Surveys of both the general Muslim public and Muslim educators reveal a high level of support for the implementation of Islamic law in the country's political and legal institutions. At the same time, however, the surveys demonstrate the overwhelmingly moderate political outlook among Muslim educators and the general public alike when asked about their support for democracy and civil rights.[45] Notes Hefner: "The educators' support for democracy and civil rights should dispel any impression that the religious establishment as a whole is a reactionary drag on an otherwise pluralist public."[46] What is more, the tension between commitment to Islamic law and support for democratic governance defies easy solutions and calls into question the veracity of unifying labels such as fundamentalism for those who promote sociopolitical agendas under reference to Islam.

Converging with Simon A. Wood's eloquent assessment of the fundamentalism label for Khomeini and Mawdudi in this volume, the evaluation of the Muslim educational scene in Indonesia demonstrates that fundamentalism imposes a facile homogeneity on a broad spectrum of religious phenomena, is inattentive to difference and context-specific nuance, and unable to distinguish clearly between fundamentalist and nonfundamentalist phenomena that share presumably significant features of the category. Given these difficulties in establishing a meaningful analytical category, one needs to ask what the consequences are of calling any or all of these forms of Islamic education fundamentalist.

Consequences of the Fundamentalism Concept

In addition to its lack of definitional precision, the marking of certain types of Muslim education as fundamentalist serves to heighten the more general suspicion of religious formations that straddle the boundaries between private and public. The consequences of labeling Muslim schools as fundamentalist are twofold. First, the privileging of secular models of education expressed in the concept of fundamentalism serves to delegitimize alternative educational paradigms, especially religious ones, as it portrays these as retrogressive and unable to prepare students for the demands of modern life. It, second, fails to recognize the often progressive, pluralism-affirming, and democracy-enhancing roles that Islamic education as a public religious formation plays. These two points will be addressed in turn to demonstrate the heuristic limitations of fundamentalism that result from the concept's normative underpinnings.

Delegitimizing Alternative Paradigms

The term's delegitimizing function is connected to its ascriptive dimension. Fundamentalism rarely, if ever, constitutes an element of self-identification but is used to describe the "other." Echoing a more general criticism of comparative projects, fundamentalism exemplifies the pitfalls of colonialist map-making that confidently imposes its own categories and theories on others and in the process suppresses differences and renders mute alternative paradigms. The politically hegemonizing function of the term is a result of its normative assumptions about the nature of religion reflected in the essentialized conceptualization of fundamentalism as conflation of religion and politics. The definition of what constitutes religion, however, is an act of signification and therefore a discourse about power. Categorizing religious formations that transcend the boundaries between private and public spheres as fundamentalist is part of such discourse and therefore never only an objective description of reality. The dynamics of power inherent in the discourse on fundamentalism are pointed out by Jay Michael Harris when he writes: "The word fundamentalism . . . is applied to those whose life-style and politics are unacceptable to modern, Western eyes and, most particularly, to those who would break down the barrier we have erected between church and state. . . . Against such people we lash out with a label that immediately delegitimates them, that immediately says these people are out of the mainstream and therefore deserve to be given an ad hominem dismissal."[47] Not to conform to the discourse that defines the realm of what is normal and acceptable means that one is excluded from the discussion a priori. To question the normalizing notions about religion and its relation to the public sphere means that one runs the risk of being named a fundamentalist and one's contributions are rejected outright and bracketed from serious consideration.

Connections to the Orientalist trope about Islam's presumed inability to separate religion and politics are readily evident when Islamic fundamentalism is the subject of the debate. This conflation of the discourse on fundamentalism with Orientalist assertions about Islam is evident in Appleby's (2007) previously mentioned comparative work on fundamentalism. Having described fundamentalist movements as "both religious and political," the author singles out Islamic expressions of fundamentalism by declaring: "Muslims, however, are unique among the major monotheist traditions because they have never formally accepted and institutionalized a distinction between religion and the state, or between the 'public' and 'private' realms of society."[48] Reminiscent of Ernest Gellner's statement that Islam constitutes a "dramatic and conspicuous exception" to the presumed universal trend of secularization,[49] statements such as Appleby's not only fail to account for the vicissitudes of Christian history with its varied and changing relationships between church and state but also ignore ample precedent in Islamic history of religious institutions and organizations independent of governmental control that have functioned not to legitimize or justify state power but to set limits and hold it in check.[50] In short, by presuming a natural division between religion and state when evaluating phenomena in the Muslim world, fundamentalism retains characteristics of Orientalist knowledge production with its interpretation of other cultures solely in terms of their deviation from what passes for normality in Western history. As Bobby S. Sayyid notes: "Fundamentalism can only operate as a general category if it situates itself within the discourse of the liberal-secularist enlightenment project and considers that project to be the natural state of affairs."[51] Such normalizing strategies leave unquestioned the historically contingent cultural practices through which the differentiation of religion from the public sphere has come to pass as universal.

Beyond diminishing the legitimacy of religious paradigms, however, the discourse on fundamentalism also leads to a polarization of the debate on religion's public functions in which possibilities for gray areas are lost and the chance of an open conversation about the potential benefits and shortfalls of religion in public life narrows. It is to this second consequence of the continued reliance on the term that attention is given next.

Public Islam and Progressive Politics

How are we to account for the existence of public religious formations such as those evident in the Indonesian Islamic educational scene that affirm pluralism, support democratic governance, and promote individual rights among all citizens regardless of their religious affiliations? As a heuristic, fundamentalism fails to explain the emergence of nonsecularized public religion that supports progressive politics and strengthens the public sphere. Instead, the concept's uncritical relationship with the secularization paradigm raises suspicion of nonsecularized religious formations and can lead to the conclusion that ultimately the only alternative to a fundamentalist conflation of public and private spheres is religion's near total absence from public life. In the case of education, such uninspiring juxtaposing disregards the fact that there exists a wide range of possibilities to involve religion in the educational routines of a school. Where, for instance, the accommodation of religious pluralism is concerned, Michael Walzer has pointed out that confessional educational models have a legitimate role to play in religiously diverse societies. If and when they allow students to experience their religious tradition as a resource for tolerance, confessional educational models can help students develop "thick" motivations for tolerance that are grounded and sustained by deep confessional convictions and inoculate students against a superficial tolerance that often amounts to little more than a relativistic indifference to diversity.[52] As the case of Islamic education in Indonesia illustrates, Muslim religious schools are not inherently or essentially opposed to building confessional identities among their students that draw on and scale up Islamic values to prepare their students to live as adherents to a particular faith in diversity. In such instances religion functions as a repository for civic virtues and serves as a carrier of values that ennoble individual life and, more important, values upon which procedural democracy and civil society depend.

Recent studies such as José Casanova's work on Catholic and Protestant religious movements in different parts of the world have shown that within the sphere of civil society religion can be a counterbalancing force vis-à-vis the destructive potentials of modernity such as unchecked state power, moral relativism, and the de-culturing effects of globalization.[53] With Casanova, other scholars have emphasized that even beyond the public activism of organized religious groups the spread and diffusion of normative values in religious institutions can have civility-enhancing and democracy-promoting consequences for society as a whole. The example of Latin American Pentecostalism is among the noteworthy and well documented cases in this regard. Bernice Martin and David Martin are among those who have emphasized more recently the positive contributions of conservative forms of evangelical Protestantism in Latin America in transforming ways of behavior and thought on work, education, consumption, and the social role of women.[54] And in many cases, inadvertently or not, these evangelical movements positively influence the modernization process and the development of democratic structures in their societies. It is not surprising that these scholars have questioned how useful the term *fundamentalism* really is in their field of study.[55]

Instead of facilitating an understanding of the public role of Islam in Muslim communities, *fundamentalism* fails to offer a vocabulary that can serve to enhance an awareness of the wide spectrum of those who valorize Islam in public discourse. As a result of these and other criticisms some scholars have recommended avoiding the term altogether, whereas others have sought new, more descriptive concepts through which to capture the public dimension of Islamic expression. The term *Islamism* has emerged as a preferred alternative for many. The possibilities and challenges for this new attempt at diversifying scholarly analysis of the public role of Islam have been illustrated in the exchange between Donald K. Emmerson and Daniel M. Varisco in a recent publication on the debate about Islamism.[56] While Varisco rejects the idea that the diversity of Islamic agendas in the public sphere could be captured by one overarching concept such as Islamism that, moreover, continues to carry strong pejorative connotations similar to its predecessor fundamentalism, Emmerson seeks to enhance the descriptive qualities of Islamism by way of adjectival qualifications. These allow him to speak, among others, of "democratic Islamism" when describing public religious formations that promote Islam as a source of democratic civility and moderation. Whether or not a term such as *Islamism* can function in a nonpejorative way, transcend the normative assumptions that burden fundamentalism, and thus initiate a more qualified and descriptive discourse of the way Muslims assert the public relevance of Islam in the contemporary world remains an open question. In practice, at least, *Islamism* continues to participate in similar dynamics as *fundamentalism* as can be seen in the unreflective use of both concepts as synonymous and interchangeable.[57]

Conclusion

The discourse on fundamentalism not only inflicts a form of epistemic violence on the fundamentalist other but also shields from view the contested nature of religion's role and its relation to public life in Western societies. The effects of such uncritical assertion of Western identity are twofold. First, the normative assumption that institutions such as secular schools are better able to address modern social and epistemological changes excludes instances in which nonreligious projects, far from transcending the dynamics of power and subordination, impose their own forms of domination.[58] The ban on conspicuous religious symbols by French school authorities, primarily aimed at Muslim students wearing the headscarf, demonstrates that control over women's bodies and institutionalized forms of inequality are anything but absent from secular organization.[59] Second, more broadly, the fundamentalism concept advances a perspective on religion's role in Western societies that obscures the fact that no consensus exists on what constitutes the appropriate relationship between religion and public life. Jürgen Habermas's recent remarks about religious tolerance as "the pacemaker for multiculturalism, correctly understood, and for the equal coexistence of different cultural forms of life within a democratic polity" illustrate the contentious and shifting perspectives on the nature of religion and its relation to the public sphere in Western discourse.[60] After years of unwillingness to entertain the question of religion in his work, Habermas now advocates an "overcoming of a rigid and exclusive secularist self-understanding."[61]

There exists a wide range of possibilities to involve religion in the forum of public life, in Muslim and non-Muslim communities alike. The recognition of common questions and shared concerns among those with religious convictions who affirm that their religion has something to contribute to the public discourse on how to build a just and equitable society can foster a more imaginative exchange on the nature and role of religion in education and public life. Scholars, policy makers, and the wider public alike will benefit from moving beyond the facile distinctions and incompatibilities that the fundamentalism concept promotes toward a more enabling discourse on how to relate religion to social, ethical, and political projects.

Notes

1. José Casanova, *Public Religions in the Modern World* (Chicago: University of Chicago Press, 1994), and Peter Berger, ed., *The Desecularization of the World: Resurgent Religion and World Politics* (Grand Rapids: Ethics and Public Policy Center and Eerdmans, 1999).

2. Akbar S. Ahmed, *Postmodernism and Islam: Predicament and Promise* (New Delhi: Penguin Books India, 1993), 32.

3. Zygmunt Baumann, "Postmodern Religion?," in *Religion, Modernity, and Postmodernity*, ed. Paul Heelas, with the assistance of David Martin and Paul Morris (Oxford: Blackwell, 1998), 74.

4. See Daniel Varisco's discussion of the term's appropriation to portray Muslims in "Inventing Islamism: The Violence of Rhetoric," in *Islamism: Contested Perspectives on Political Islam*, ed. Richard C. Martin and Abbas Barzegar (Stanford: Stanford University Press, 2010), 37–41.

5. Haddad et al. estimate that the production of books in the English language on topics relating to Islamic revival averaged two hundred per year early in this decade. Yvonne Y.

Haddad et al., eds., *The Contemporary Islamic Revival: A Critical Survey and Bibliography* (New York: Greenwood, 1991), ix.

6. The great majority of articles included in the publications of the Fundamentalism Project, ed. Martin E. Marty and R. Scott Appleby (Chicago: University of Chicago Press, 1991–1995), focused on developments in the Abrahamic traditions. Among these, studies of Muslim individuals, groups, and movements outnumbered those on phenomena in the Jewish and Christian traditions.

7. Since the publications of the Fundamentalism Project many scholars have supported the validity of *fundamentalism* as an umbrella term and have outlined, with some variances, a rubric of family resemblances that include properties such as the rejection of modernism and a refusal to limit religion to the private sphere, reification of tradition, literalist interpretation of scripture, commitment to patriarchy, and an antielitist, antipluralist, and sharply dualistic stance. A noteworthy example of a work that endorses the general assumptions of the Fundamentalism Project, despite an acknowledgement of the concept's limitations, is Malise Ruthven's lucidly composed *Fundamentalism: A Very Short Introduction* (New York: Oxford University Press, 2007).

8. Gabriel A. Almond, Emmanuel Sivan, R. Scott Appleby, "Fundamentalism: Genus and Species," in *Fundamentalisms Comprehended*, ed. Martin E. Marty and R. Scott Appleby (Chicago: University of Chicago Press, 1995), 399–424.

9. Ibid., 409.

10. R. Scott Appleby, "Fundamentalism," in *Encyclopedia of Politics and Religion*, 2nd ed., ed. Robert Wuthnow, 319. (Washington, D.C.: CQ Press, 2007).

11. See Talal Asad, *Genealogies of Religion: Discipline and Reasons of Power in Christianity and Islam* (Baltimore & London: Johns Hopkins University Press, 1993), 207.

12. John L. Esposito, *The Islamic Threat: Myth or Reality?*, 3rd ed. (New York & Oxford: Oxford University Press, 1999), 260.

13. See, e.g., Jamal Malik, ed., *Madrasas in South Asia: Teaching Terror?* (New York: Routledge, 2008).

14. One of the first writers after 9/11 to single out Muslim schools as key institutions in the campaign against Islamic extremism and terror was Thomas Friedman: Friedman, "Foreign Affairs; In Pakistan, It Is Jihad 101," *New York Times*, Op-ed, November 13, 2001, http://www.nytimes.com/2001/11/13/opinion/foreign-affairs-in-pakistan-it-s-jihad-101.html (accessed October 2, 2012).

15. Ali Riaz, *Faithful Education: Madrassahs in South Asia* (New Brunswick & London: Rutgers University Press, 2008), 20–51.

16. See, e.g., the statements by Deputy Secretary of Defense Paul Wolfowitz at Georgetown University in October 2003 in which he referred to "extremist teachings that are distributed free to *millions*" in Muslim schools as "tools that turn them [poor Muslim children] into terrorists." U.S. Department of Defense, "Deputy Secretary of Defense Paul Wolfowitz Remarks at Georgetown University," news transcript, October 30, 2003 (emphasis added), http://www.defense.gov/transcripts/transcript.aspx?transcriptid=3080 (accessed October 2, 2012).

17. Andrew Coulson, "Education and Indoctrination in the Muslim World: Is There a Problem? What Can We Do about It?" *Policy Analysis* 511 (March 11, 2004), http://www.cato.org/pubs/pas/pa511.pdf (accessed October 2, 2012).

18. E.g., Anna Kuchment et al., "School by the Book," *Newsweek*, March 10, 2002, http://www.thedailybeast.com/newsweek/2002/03/10/school-by-the-book.html (accessed October 2, 2012). Similar assertions are not new to the public debate about Islamic education in Germany in which Bassam Tibi labeled attempts to institutionalize the teaching of Islam in German public schools as "Trojan Horse of Radical Muslims." Bassam Tibi, "Trojanisches Pferd

der radikalen Muslime," *Focus*, May 31, 1999, http://www.focus.de/politik/deutschland/standpunkt-trojanisches-pferd-der-radikalen-muslime_aid_175312.html (accessed October 2, 2012).

19. Husain Haqqani, "Islam's Medieval Outposts," *Foreign Policy* 133 (November–December 2002): 64.

20. National Commission on Terrorist Attacks upon the United States, *The 9/11 Commission Report: Final Report of the National Commission on Terrorist Attacks upon the United States* (New York: Norton, 2004), section 12.1, http://govinfo.library.unt.edu/911/report/911Report.pdf (accessed October 2, 2012).

21. Ajjazz Ahmed, "Madrassas Have Contributed to the Spread of Islamic Fundamentalism," in *The Rise of Islamic Fundamentalism*, ed. Phillip Margulies (Detroit: Greenhaven Press, 2006), 66–74.

22. Samuel C. Heilman, "The Vision from the Madrasa and Bes Medrash: Some Parallels between Islam and Judaism," in *Fundamentalisms Comprehended*, ed. Martin E. Marty and R. Scott Appleby (Chicago: University of Chicago Press, 1995), 72.

23. Ibid.

24. In the context of her discussion of Pakistan's education system, Jessica Stern writes: "The most important contribution the United States can make, then, is to help strengthen Pakistan's secular education system." Stern, "Pakistan's Jihad Culture," *Foreign Affairs* 79 (November–December 2000): 126.

25. For a discussion of the United States' strategies to aid education reform in Pakistan, see also K. Alan Kronstadt, *Education Reform in Pakistan*, CRS Report for Congress RS22009, December 23, 2004, http://www.fas.org/man/crs/ RS22009.pdf. On the MEPI, see Jeremy M. Sharp, *The Middle East Partnership Initiative: An Overview*, CRS Report for Congress RS21457, updated February 8, 2005, http://www.fas.org/sgp/crs/mideast/ RS21457.pdf.

26. International Crisis Group, "Al-Qaeda in Southeast Asia: The Case of the 'Ngruki' Network in Indonesia," ICG Asia Briefing 20 (Jakarta/Brussels, August 8, 2002), http://www.crisisgroup.org/en/regions/asia/south-east-asia/indonesia/B020-al-qaeda-in-southeast-asia-the-case-of-the-ngruki-network-in-indonesia-corrected-on-10-January-2003.aspx (accessed October 2, 2012).

27. Walter Saller, "Unterwegs auf Heisser Erde," *Geo* (May 2004): 165.

28. Paul Toohey, "Lesson today is hatred as Bashir cultivates bombers' breeding ground," *Australian*, July 27, 2009, http://www.theaustralian.com.au/lesson-today-is-hatred-as-bashir-cultivates-bombers-breeding-ground/story-fna7dq6e-1225754949886 (accessed October 2, 2012).

29. Azyumardi Azra, Dina Afrianty, and Robert W. Hefner, "Pesantren and Madrasa: Muslim Schools and National Ideals in Indonesia," in *Schooling Islam: The Culture and Politics of Modern Muslim Education*, ed. Robert W. Hefner and Muhammad Q. Zaman (Princeton: Princeton University Press), 173.

30. The previously mentioned report by the International Crisis Group implicated it as the center for a network of militant Muslims in Indonesia with suspected links to al-Qaeda. International Crisis Group, "Al-Qaeda in Southeast Asia."

31. Scott Atran, "The Emir: An Interview with Abu Bakar Ba'asyir, Alleged Leader of the Southeast Asian Jemaah Islamiyah Organization," *Spotlight on Terror* 3 (December 16, 2005), http://www.jamestown.org/programs/gta/single/?tx_ttnews[tt_news]=562&tx_ttnews[backPid]=26&cHash=f0e77f13a0240cad907239453f25396c (accessed October 1, 2012).

32. Charlene Tan, *Islamic Education and Indoctrination: The Case of Indonesia* (New York: Routledge, 2011), 43–61.

33. Hefner analyzes these schools through the prism of social movement theory and points to the new quality of their educational mission that aims at the Islamization of Indonesian

society and, ultimately, the institutions of the state. Robert W. Hefner, "Islamic Schools, Social Movements, and Democracy in Indonesia," in *Making Modern Muslims: The Politics of Muslim Education in Southeast Asia,* ed. Robert W. Hefner with David Martin and Paul Morris (Honolulu: University of Hawaii Press, 2009), 70–91.

34. Azra et al., "Pesantren and Madrasa," 189.

35. Elisabeth Jackson and Bahrissalim, "Crafting a New Democracy: Civic Education in Indonesian Islamic Universities," *Asia Pacific Journal of Education* 27 (March 2007): 41–54.

36. Ibid.

37. For a description of this pesantren, see Florian Pohl, "Islamic Education and Civil Society: Reflections on the *Pesantren* Tradition in Contemporary Indonesia," *Comparative Education Review* 50 (August 2006): 389–409.

38. Mark Woodward, Inayah Rohmaniyah, Ali Amin, and Diana Coleman, "Muslim Education, Celebrating Islam and Having Fun as Counter-Radicalization Strategies in Indonesia," *Perspectives on Terrorism* 4 (October 2010): 42, http://www.terrorismanalysts.com/pt/index.php/pot/article/view/114/232 (accessed October 2, 2012).

39. Hefner, "Islamic Schools," 74. The majority of these schools are associated with the educational networks of the Prosperous Justice Party (PKS) and with the smaller Hidayatullah movement.

40. Ibid., 97.

41. Ibid., 86.

42. In their assessment of counterradicalization strategies in Indonesia, Woodward et al. defend another view. They assert that the religion-centered course of study at Islamic schools, specifically in pesantrens, is working "against extremism because it provides students with knowledge of, and appreciation for, the complexities of Islamic thought" (Woodward et al., "Muslim Education," 42). Against secularist assumptions they posit that informal study circles such as "mosque-based discussion groups" that operate outside of the official curriculum of both Islamic and public schools function as "vehicles through which extremist teachings are spread" (ibid., 35).

43. Robert W. Hefner, Civil Islam: Muslims and Democratization in Indonesia (Princeton: Princeton University Press, 2000).

44. Appleby, "Fundamentalism," 320.

45. Hefner, "Islamic Schools," 91–96. Hefner draws on surveys carried out in cooperation with the Center for the Study of Islam and Society (PPIM) at the Hidayatullah National Islamic University in Jakarta in 2004 and 2006. On the question of Islamic law, 75.5 percent of the general public and 82.8 percent of Muslim educators surveyed supported state efforts to implement Islamic law (ibid., 94). In response to questions about the preference for democracy over other forms of governance 85.9 percent of Muslim educators and 71.6 percent of the Muslim public responded favorably (ibid., 92).

46. Ibid, 92.

47. Jay Michael Harris, "'Fundamentalism': Objections from a Modern Jewish Historian," in *Fundamentalism and Gender,* ed. John Stratton Hawley (Oxford: Oxford University Press, 1994), 138.

48. Appleby, "Fundamentalism," 324.

49. Ernest Gellner, *Postmodernism, Reason, and Religion* (London: Routledge, 1992), 5.

50. John Kelsay (2002) and Richard W. Bulliet (2004) both have drawn attention to extrastate religious organizations such as the *ulama* (A.; Islamic legal scholars), many of which viewed the acceptance of administrative posts as undesirable and as a danger to their religious integrity and whose decision to remain independent resulted in the ability of the state to control Islamic law. John Kelsay, "Civil Society and Government in Islam," in *Civil Society*

and Government, Ethikon Series in Comparative Ethics, ed. Nancy Rosenblum and R. Post (Princeton: Princeton University Press, 2002), 284–316; Richard W. Bulliet, *The Case for Islamo-Christian Civilization* (New York: Columbia University Press, 2004), 70.

51. Bobby S. Sayyid, *A Fundamental Fear: Eurocentrism and the Emergence of Islamism,* 2nd ed. (London: Zed Books, 2003), 16.

52. Michael Walzer, *Thick and Thin: Moral Argument at Home and Abroad* (Notre Dame: University of Notre Dame Press, 1994).

53. See Casanova, *Public Religions.*

54. See David Martin, *Tongues of Fire: Conservative Protestantism in Latin America* (Oxford: Blackwell, 1990), and Bernice Martin, "From Pre- to Postmodernity in Latin America: The Case of Pentecostalism," in *Religion, Modernity, and Postmodernity,* ed. Paul Heelas, with the assistance of David Martin and Paul Morris (Oxford: Blackwell, 1998), 102–146.

55. E.g., Bernice Martin, "From Pre- to Postmodernity in Latin America," 107.

56. Richard C. Martin and Abbas Barzegar, ed., *Islamism: Contested Perspectives on Political Islam* (Stanford: Stanford University Press, 2010).

57. Such conflation of Islamism with "Islamic fundamentalism" can been seen, for instance, in Jon Armajani's recent study of Islamist groups from the eighteenth century onward. Jon Armajani. *Modern Islamist Movements: History, Religion, and Politics* (Chichester, U.K.: Wiley-Blackwell, 2012), 1–2.

58. These have been pointed out, among others, by Talal Asad in the introduction to his *Formations of the Secular: Christianity, Islam, Modernity* (Stanford: Stanford University Press, 2003), as well as by Janet R. Jakobsen and Ann Pellegrini in "Dreaming Secularism," *Social Text* 18 (Fall 2000): 1–27.

59. John Richard Bowen, *Why the French Don't Like Headscarves: Islam, the State, and Public Space* (Princeton: Princeton University Press, 2007).

60. Jürgen Habermas, *Between Naturalism and Religion. Philosophical Essays* (Cambridge: Polity Press, 2008), 257.

61. Ibid., 138.

Conclusion

Gordon D. Newby

This is a book at war with itself over the term *fundamentalism*. This is intentional, for the definition of the term, its use, and the ability of the term to be used in comparative and transnational contexts are highly contested among scholars and the general public. At one extreme there are those who contend that the term should not be used except in a very narrow, historical way to refer to the original Protestant Americans who started a movement to return to Christian fundamentals. In common usage now, the term has gained widespread and popular use as a term of opprobrium for those who hold and strongly defend strict religious views in opposition to those of the speaker. Still others see utility in using the term in a limited and analytic way across various religious traditions to compare what appear to be similar religious and political reactions to the contemporary world. The essays in this volume are positioned to highlight the debate about fundamentalism, describe the limits and utility of the term in various contexts, and move the debate forward in pace with the changing uses of the term in scholarly discourse.

In the first essay, "Fundamentalists of the 1920s and 1930s," David Harrington Watt briefly presents the locus classicus for the term. From 1910 to 1915, A. C. Dixon, Louis Meyer, and Reuben A. Torrey edited and published twelve volumes of essays designed to set out the true and correct Protestant Christian beliefs. Their work, known as *The Fundamentals: A Testimony to the Truth,* was designed to combat the error into which the authors felt that Christianity had fallen and to oppose such threats as liberal theology, Roman Catholicism, Biblical Higher Criticism, modern philosophy, atheism, evolution, spiritualism, Mormonism, and other ideas and movements that challenged the straightforward beliefs in such doctrines as the virgin birth of Jesus Christ, the divinity of Jesus Christ, the inerrancy of the Bible, the bodily resurrection of Jesus Christ from the dead, and so on.

The publication of *The Fundamentals* led to the formation of the World's Christian Fundamentals Association (WFCA) at a meeting in 1919 in Philadelphia attended by six thousand people. As Watt states, these people did not refer to themselves as fundamentalists, nor did they see themselves as believers in a separate movement called fundamentalism. The term fundamentalists was coined by a journalist/pastor, Curtis L. Laws, in 1920 to refer to those Protestants who were committed to "the great fundamentals" and who were willing to "do battle royal" on behalf of Protestant correctness. From this beginning the notions of fundamentalism and militancy became linked, although what was meant by engaging in a "battle royal" was not clear in Laws's remarks.

As Watt points out, fundamentalism was only one of several Protestant movements in the United States. It is also clear that fundamentalists did not all believe in every "fundamental" set forth in the original publication but subscribed to a core subset, such as the divinity of Jesus Christ, the virgin birth, the reality of the miracles in the Bible, and many believed in the imminent return of Jesus Christ to earth. They believed that the revelations that God had provided in the Bible were being ignored and that it was their duty to set out an educational crusade by training "God's army" and promoting those educational and informational institutions that would train leaders to take over the main Protestant denominations. Public education in the sciences became one of their targets, and they had some success in opposing the teaching of evolution. The most famous success was the enactment of Tennessee's 1925 Butler Act, which forbade the teaching of the theory of evolution in all publicly funded schools in the state. This led to the famous Scopes Trial and set the ground for a continuing argument in the United States about the teaching of evolution.[1] In spite of the fact that the defenders of Scopes's teaching of evolution argued that the Bible and science were not in opposition, the term *fundamentalism* has acquired the additional connotation of being antiscience.

A dimension of the term *fundamentalist* is the common misperception that it should be applied to chiefly southern, un- or under-educated white male rural Americans. As Watt has shown, those who identified with the aims of the movement were as likely as not to be northern women. The movement attracted adherents across the social, educational, and economic spectrum, although in some periods women predominated over men.

Also in the popular imagination, fundamentalists are supposed to read the Bible literally. In fact, most serious fundamentalist readers of the Bible believe that there are figurative and metaphorical uses of language in the Bible. The examples that Watt gives, that God does not have a literal hand nor is Jesus, as John 15:1 says, a literal true vine, sit side by side with stricter readings of scripture that describe miracles performed by God, which they hold to be true and accurate. The reduction of fundamentalist readings of scripture as absolutely literal is meant to mock the fundamentalist hermeneutic that supports their view in the basic correctness and inerrancy of the Bible.

In the political arena fundamentalists were split on the role of government in American society. Holding that America was founded on religious freedom for

Protestants, against their view that the Roman Catholic Church was too powerful and tyrannical, they wanted government to reflect their values but not to have a large hand in controlling American lives. This was particularly the case in the economic sphere, where a kind of laissez-faire hands-off approach was preferred when confined to private and individual approaches to social ills.

The militant nature of fundamentalism was, according to Watt, a characteristic of an early phase of the movement. More important, it was more rhetorical than physical. It was "militant opposition to modernism," in the words of the historian George M. Marsden, but in words rather than violent action.[2] Nevertheless, fundamentalism and militancy, where militancy is equated with violence, has become another co-concept with fundamentalism, as we see in the book's next essay, "The Idea of Militancy in American Fundamentalism," by Dan D. Crawford. Crawford explores the reasons that a particular group, American fundamentalists, that is, the adherents of the Fundamentals mentioned above, have been singled out to be the model or prototype of a type of religious group that now includes among its denotation extremist terrorist groups bent on the violent destruction of their enemies. For Crawford, this is a mischaracterization of American fundamentalism. In the first place the word *militant* has several tiers of meaning. In its primary sense it does mean warring or fighting. However, he points out, there is a second-tier meaning of the term *militant*: someone with an aggressive, combative character, particularly in promoting or defending a cause. One example of this, he says, is the militant feminist. In this sense aggression is verbal, not violent, and the militant energies are plied, usually, within the norms of promoting causes within our society, organizing, lobbying, protests, boycotts, lawsuits, and, above all, rhetorical advocacy for the cause. It is this secondary weaker sense of *militant* that should be applied to American fundamentalists.

Another aspect of Crawford's analysis of militancy in the history of American fundamentalism is that it changes over time. At its inception there were strong words on the part of the fundamentalists against their ideological and theological enemies. However, this passionate militancy did not advance the cause of fundamentalism, and by the 1930s a group of softer-spoken leaders emerged. These more moderate fundamentalists were committed to saving souls and preaching the foundational truths. It was chiefly through this group of moderate fundamentalists that the movement changed from a fringe element to a popular mainstream movement that held the "fundamentals" firmly under their protection.

Crawford's essay raises two important issues in our analysis of the term. The first is that our current perceptions of fundamentalism rest on the analyses of previous scholars and writers. Marsden, for example, the author of *Fundamentalism and American Culture,* was among the first to argue that a militant style or attitude was a defining characteristic of the movement. By providing a contextual understanding of the movement and a clear description of its origins in the 1920s, when the major fundamentalist figures indeed possessed strident militant rhetorical stances, Marsden's views were adopted both in the American academy and more generally among the public. As we attempt to apply the term *fundamentalist* to one or another religious movement, Crawford's essay raises the caution that we need to question not only our sources but also the interpretive frames presented by the historians and critics of the movement.

The second point that Crawford raises is that fundamentalism has a history, and in that history there is both change and adaptation to cultural and sociological forces. The strident debates of the 1920s, the flamboyant preaching of the sort practiced by Billy Sunday, the separation from the power of various denominational structures proved not to work as the movement developed in the 1930s, the 1940s, and beyond. While there were, as Crawford illustrates, staunch holdouts who adhered to the militant rhetoric, the fundamentalist mission of saving souls required changes for different times. When we examine fundamentalist movements, particularly when we put them in a comparative context, we should be careful to be sure that our comparisons take into account the historical developments within the movements as well as the historical contexts surrounding them and be cautious about reifying an incomplete view of the movement.

Margaret Bendroth's essay, "Fundamentalism and Christianity," takes us beyond the confines of the fundamentalist movement, beyond the borders of the United States, and into Christianity in the wider modern world. Quoting Bruce Lawrence's *Defenders of God: The Fundamentalist Revolt against the Modern Age,* she reminds us that fundamentalists are "moderns, but not modernists, at once the consequence of modernity and the antithesis of modernism."[3] They argue for eternal truths and often yearn for a nostalgically constructed past while using the techniques and tools of the modern age to proclaim their message. Herein lies both tension and, for some, great anxiety. As Lionel Caplan wrote, "We are all of us, to some degree and in some senses, fundamentalists," uneasy about the directions of modernity and its ecological and personal incursions.[4] From Bendroth's perspective, the boundaries between fundamentalism and modernism, so sharply defined in the 1920s, and the foundation of the movement are beginning to blur as we see the fundamentalist messages being domesticated into our worldwide culture's daily thoughts. It is characteristic of the modern age for boundaries and distinctions to blur, change, and even dissolve, leaving angst and unease in their place.

Shifts in the centers of gravity are found in modern Christianities, as Bendroth points out, and in ways that make it more difficult to find fundamentalists and fundamentalism as distinct and clear. As she points out, in the last thirty years the statistical majority of the world's Christians are in Africa, Asia, and Latin America. These Christians exist in many forms and can be classified as charismatic and Pentecostal, not fundamentalist. The difference is that while fundamentalists on the one hand and charismatics and Pentecostalists on the other look alike and share some of the same beliefs about scripture and secular society, the core of the Pentecostal faith is experience and a close relationship with the Holy Spirit. Fundamentalism is grounded in text, both biblical and theological. Pentecostal and charismatic Christians feel "more at home singing their theology, or putting it in pamphlets for distribution on street corners."[5] It is not that the new churches outside of the United States and Europe were not believers in many of the foundational principles set out in fundamentalism and that they were not leery of secular modernism, but they were formed in a different environment from fundamentalism. In many places, particularly in Africa and Latin America, opposition to Enlightenment ideas was filtered through the colonial experience, or, as in China, from the underground of Christian house churches, developing a distinctively Chinese worldview. This "new" Christianity is affecting American churches through immigration and conscious globalization such that it is becoming harder to find "traditional" fundamentalism in the world's Christians, including in the United States. Bendroth asserts that "American fundamentalism is itself an unstable category, and the twentieth-century United States is an unlikely place for getting a conceptual handle on it."

One last point that Bendroth makes is about the inherent instability of text and message in the age of electronic communication. While the ease of the Web, Facebook, Twitter, and e-mail facilitates the broad dissemination of theological ideas, including those of fundamentalists, the medium itself allows for multiple transformations of that message in ways not able to be controlled by the sender. Indeed, even the canon of scripture is being challenged, as I have experienced among my students, who have presented apocryphal and pseudepigraphic material labeled "gospels" on the Web as "real" gospels, since they were regarded as gospels by someone and at some time. As we look at fundamentalism in other religious traditions, we will need to keep in mind how this modernist environment distorts the antimodernist message.

As we next include in our scope American Jewish communities that have been identified by some as fundamentalist, we have to take the term out of the American Protestant frame that was its origin. Judaism does not subscribe to the same set of theological concepts as Protestant Christianity. As a result the nature of scriptural interpretation is different in Rabbinic Judaism than it is among most Protestants. How, then, is it possible to apply the term *fundamentalism* to Judaism?

Shaul Magid, in his two essays, "America Is No Different, America Is Different," argues that the doctrine-by-doctrine approach to comparing Jewish and Christian fundamentalism unfairly constructs the argument for the use of the term *fundamentalism*. First, Magid disambiguates the term *Judaism*. A deficiency in many studies about Jewish fundamentalism, he contends, is that there is not a distinction made between American and Israeli Judaism, an important distinction for him because of the American origin of the term. Second, he identifies three distinct communities, in both the United States and Israel, to which the term *fundamentalism* has been applied: Hasidism, non-Hasidic ultra-Orthodoxy, and religious ultra-nationalists. In some circles, Hasidism and non-Hasidic ultra-Orthodox have come together under the term *haredi,* a term meaning God-fearing. Also, a portion of the ultra-nationalists have adopted the "persona" of the haredi, called *hardal* (*haredi dat leumi*), that is, God-fearing national religious. Most important, these groups do not get along, even experiencing conflict on such basic issues as the support for the current State of Israel. The example Magid cites is the Satmar Hasidic opposition to the ultra-nationalists in Israel, but he also points out that the distinctions among the major groups he cites and their subgroups, while sharp, can be seen as falling along various spectra, such as support or nonsupport for Israel, tolerance of secularism, interaction with the non-Jewish world (which, for many includes Reform, Reconstructionist, and Conservative Jews).

Another issue raised by Magid is whether fundamentalist Judaism is a post-Holocaust, postwar phenomenon. Additionally he asks whether this phenomenon exists only in Israel and in North America. If so, he adds, the differences between North America, where Jews are free to express themselves in a variety of ways, and Israel, where Jews are in the majority but where there is not the same level of religious disestablishment, mean that fundamentalism in the two places is different in kind as well as distinct in context. The distinction made by Magid speaks to the issues other authors in this volume point out, namely that religious fundamentalism is closely intertwined with the politics of the modern state and is in many ways a reaction to the state's implementation of a secular culture. Magid states: "Religious communities are not simply products of their theological convictions as much as they would like us to believe they are. They are also responding and adapting to societal conditions and are in constant states of absorbing and reframing the ethos of the world in which they live, sometimes consciously, sometimes not." With this in mind, he classifies American Jewish fundamentalism as a postwar phenomenon that responds to the Holocaust and the destruction of European Jewry, the assertion of Zionism in the form of the Jewish State of Israel, and the development of competing forms of Judaism in the forms of Reform and Conservative Judaism. Each of these factors contributes to the development of fundamentalism among some Jews who chose to live in America rather than join the Zionist state in Palestine.

One area of focus in Magid's analysis is that American Jewish fundamentalism is the combination of the fear of Jewish assimilation and/or its "distortion" in the United States through "progressive" Judaism leading to the loss of Judaism "as it was previously known." It is clear that Reform, Reconstructionist, and Conservative forms of Judaism flourish in America in part because of America's freedom of religion and partly because of America's secularism. He contrasts this with Europe, where "traditional" Judaism has a stronger foothold in the society's civil religion. America, in the imagination of many Jews, is the land of centrifugal force that is spinning Jews into a wider Christianate secular sphere. He points out, however, that in Israel the secular Jews are more alienated from the fundamentalist Jews because the society is predominantly Jewish. In the United States, he points out, most all Jews, regardless of ideology or practice, regard themselves as connected to other Jews who need to band together against the pressures of other groups. When this is combined with the fact that Europe generally is more secular than the United States, the centripetal force that keeps Jews in America Jewish in identity and practice is a more religious force than it appears to be in Europe, where Jews seem to have to remain Jews because of societal prejudice rather than because of religious choice. So Magid seems correct that fundamentalist Jews see themselves in a fight for the "soul of Judaism" in much the same way as Christian fundamentalists see themselves in the same fight for the soul of Christianity. Both groups use similar constructions of an imagined past and the role of the identified core values and/or practices in that past.

For Magid, as for many writers on the subject of fundamentalism, activism in support of one's views is one of the defining characteristics. He quotes Gabriel A. Almond, R. Scott Appleby, and Emanuel Sivan's definition: "Fundamentalism, in this usage, refers to a discernible pattern of religious militance by which self-styled 'true-believers' attempt to arrest the erosion of religious identity, fortify the borders of the religious community, and create viable alternatives to secular institutions and behaviors."[6] For American fundamentalist Judaism, I would substitute *progressive* for *secular* and see the American Jewish fundamentalist activism as aimed primarily at nonfundamentalist Jews. This is characteristic of the Hasidic sect of Judaism known as Habad, or Lubavitch, after the town where it was founded. The movement claims an unbroken chain of authority and authenticity to the founder of Hasidic Judaism, Rabbi Israel Baal Shem Tov (d. 1760). In prewar Europe it developed an active outreach to Jews living in isolated parts of Russia, but it has been in postwar America that the group has flourished and developed a strong proselytizing identity. This was coupled with a millenialist view of the impending end-time, adding to the urgency to bring about Jewish return to proper practice and assist the coming of the Messiah. The vision was more than just a mission to other Jews, however. Habad has entered into the mainstream of American religious politics by participating in lobbying for limiting public prayer in schools (to avoid exposing Jews to the dominant Christian mode of worship), the legitimacy of placing Hanukkah menorahs in public space, the establishing of Habad centers close to or connected with universities, and, in the New York area, the deployment of the Chabad Lubavitch Mitzvah Tank, designed to teach Jews how to perform various traditional Jewish practices, such as the proper ways to pray and light candles. The view is that one mitzvah will lead to another.

Magid notes that the activism of the Habad Jews is not against secularism, because for them Jewish secularism cannot exist. A Jew for the Habad necessarily has a spark of divine Judaism, pintele Yid, that is part of the essence of a Jew. According to this doctrine, the Jewish soul, no matter how occluded by lack of observance, can be helped to realize itself through education and practice and will then naturally reject a nonobservant life. Zionism is just another of the occluding forces as an ideology that distracts from the core mission. However, American Habad leaders have also supported Israel, unlike some others in the Hasidic movement.

The second of the two Hasidic groups that Magid classifies as American Jewish fundamentalists is the Satmar Hasidim, chiefly found in Williamsburg, Brooklyn, and Kiryas Joel, New York. Unlike the Lubavitcher Habad Hasidim, whom the Satmar strongly oppose, the Satmar do not believe in any interaction with the non-Satmar world except in limited, self-serving ways. Particularly, they do not believe in having anything to do with non-Satmar Jews, who have the sole utility to be a bad example and to be shunned. Magid explains their opposite view to the Habad Hasidim through a discussion of their view of the nature of the world and the necessity to observe punctiliously while waiting passively for the coming of the Messiah. They are unrelentingly anti-Zionist and prefer to live in an enclave. This world represents, for them, the final corruption that presages the arrival of the Messiah, and anything that is part of this world and this age is, of necessity, corrupt. That said, the community has also found that benefitting from America's welfare system, as well as its commercial economy in which the Satmar men find business opportunities, is within biblical commandments. The 1994 United States Supreme Court case (Kiryas Joel v. Grumer) allowed for the establishment of a public school district for Kiryas Joel in which no one other than the Satmar lived and allowed for New York State to provide public funds for the education of this separatist group's children. As the saying goes, "Only in America!" Satmar Hasidism not only exists in the United States but also thrives on the very nature of American societal values.

At the end Magid argues that both the Satmar and the Habad, though opposites in many aspects of their worldviews, are products of America, a reaction to American ideals of openness and liberalism, and are reacting to the same forces that propel Christian fundamentalists to use modern techniques and institutions to resist the pressures of the modern world. For Magid fundamentalism is bound to the American experience and can be extended beyond its Protestant Christian beginnings to limited forms of Judaism. For him the utility of the term *fundamentalism* is precisely that it points up the common American experience.

When we extend our view of Jewish fundamentalism to Israel in the essay "The Jewish Settler Movement and the Concept of Fundamentalism" by Jean Axelrad Cahan, we encounter a different environment and set of circumstances from those we saw in Magid's description of American Jewish fundamentalists. As Magid points out, the society of Israel is predominantly Jewish. Most of the Jews who can be classified as "secular" and Zionist nevertheless identify "true" Judaism as some form of Orthodox or traditional Judaism, which they do not practice. Reform and Conservative Judaism have no standing in Israel. Personal status for Jewish Israelis is under the control of the state-established Orthodox rabbinate. This does not mean that there is not tension between the secular Zionists and the Orthodox religious. The Orthodox do not serve in the Israeli Defense Force to the same extent as non-Orthodox, and unlike nonreligious Israelis, only a few Orthodox women have served. Those women were segregated from the general military population and from men in general, although, since they were married, they were allowed to bring their children to the base where they were serving. In addition the Orthodox receive monetary support from the Israeli government to run segregated schools and other institutions. As with other religious groups, it is possible, and necessary for our discussion, to distinguish various groups and subgroups among the religious Orthodox Jews in Israel. The members of *hardal,* mentioned above, are often called "Kippot Sruggot," those with knitted skullcaps, as distinguished from the Hasidim, who wear black broad-brimmed fedoras and sometimes fur hats under which are black skullcaps. But this broad-brush distinction should be further refined to make sense of applying or not applying the term *fundamentalism* to any aspect of Israeli society.

Cahan writes about the Jewish Settler movement, which has been termed fundamentalist in the popular press and by prominent scholars, such as Ian Lustick.[7] She presents a list of characteristics of fundamentalism compiled from various scholars to which she then compares various examples of Israeli Jewish fundamentalism. The list, in brief, includes:

1. Hostility to many aspects of modernity, especially reason and science as sources of authority.
2. Desire to recapture a way of life and religious practice believed to have prevailed in pre-Enlightenment times.
3. Constituting a tight "enclave" culture with a sense of "besetment."
4. "Sacralization" of the enclave.
5. Insistence on adherence to a fundamental core of religious principles, and ignoring much traditional commentary.
6. Literal readings of certain religious texts.
7. Belief in the inerrancy of sacred texts and their current "true" interpreters.
8. Treatment of women as second-class citizens.
9. Viewing the current historical conjuncture as providing a unique opportunity for activism, especially political activism.
10. Willingness to use and justify violence.
11. Rejection of the nation-state and existing political systems.

She then states that only two from the list, 6 and 9, apply substantially to religious settlers in the West Bank. Because there is only weak evidence for correspondence with the other features, if any correspondence at all, she finds the "family resemblance" model does not apply. Additionally, she points out that not all the settlers are religious, which has led some to argue that fundamentalism is only a political concept, not religious.

Cahan makes clear that, taking the totality of the settlers who have moved to the West Bank, the evidence is too mixed to lump all of these under the rubric of fundamentalism. As is well known, many Israelis have responded to government policies to populate the West Bank to produce "facts on the ground" for strategic, defensive, and negotiating purposes as well as for the opportunity to have a nicer home in a new community to raise a family. The question arises from her presentation whether it is useful to include all settlers under the rubric of Settler Movement. That is, do we mean by movement those who moved to the West Bank or should we restrict the term to the subset of those whose settlement in Judea and Samaria, the biblical terms for roughly the West Bank, are for ideological reasons based on Jewish religious reasons rather than secular and/or historical reasons? Here I am making a distinction about the use of Hebrew scriptures as a statement of "historical fact," to make claims to the biblical extent of Jewish lands, a view held by many secular as well as religious Israelis, and a chiefly religious claim that incorporates a suprahistorical spiritual, and often eschatological, claim about the actions of settlement as religiously transformative. As we see in other religious traditions where we might find fundamentalists, including American Protestant Christianity, we should expect an overlap in ideas and actions that complicate our search for fundamentalists and fundamentalism, if it exists. Some of Cahan's conclusions are telling on this point. Speaking of the Israeli demand to worship at a holy site or return to a historical spot for settlement, she says that "as historical and religious claims there is not anything distinctively 'fundamentalist' about them. But I would be inclined to agree that the claims just mentioned might be fundamentalist in the language in which they are sometimes justified and through the methods by which they may be pressed. I therefore agree that it is fair to say the following: '[Jewish] fundamentalists believe they can circumvent hermeneutic processes and gain direct access to the meaning of Scripture. They subordinate democratic values to the authority of their own leaders.' And 'A key element in Jewish fundamentalism, as in any fundamentalist movement, is the belief that its adherents possess special and direct access to transcendental truth, to a true vision of the future course of events, and to an understanding of what the future requires. For Jewish fundamentalists, history is God's means of communicating with his people. Political trends and events contain messages to Jews that provide instructions, reprimands and rewards. Political and historical analysis, properly undertaken, is equivalent to the interpretation of God's will.'"

Having said that, Cahan cites various scholars as having arrived at a view that "fundamentalism is primarily a political phenomenon utilizing religious language and resources to further essentially political ends. On this view, religion is at most a useful set of myths which serves to mobilize 'the masses' in certain extreme directions." Following the ideas of Gershom Scholem that assert that there are periodic appearances in the history of Judaism of groups that see themselves as God's agents in bringing about the Messianic Age, she says, "It seems to me that the religious settlers are just such a group: a minority of religious believers, otherwise quite traditional, who seize on the redemptive idea in Judaism and seek to actualize it in the present, challenging prevailing political authorities in the process." In terms of the project of this book, Cahan, then, rejects the use of the term *fundamentalism* as applicable to any of the groups in Israel.

There are some striking features among a small subset of Israeli settlers that seem to be not easily lumped with the traditional religious Israelis. The first of the notable examples is Yigal Amir, the assassin of Yitzhak Rabin, or, rather, the various supporters of his ideology. As part of Amir's defense, he and others cited the Law of Pursuit (*din rodef*) that allows the slaying of someone who is about to commit the murder of another person. Rabin, in the eyes of Amir, was the "pursuer" (*rodef*) because he was about to trade a portion of the land of Israel for peace with the Arabs. What is remarkable about this is that it goes beyond the usual parameters of the Law of Pursuit first to include land transfer and second that no murder of a particular individual or group of individuals was immanent. Rabbi Avigdor Neventzhal stated that "it should be known that anyone who wants to give away Israeli land is like a rodef," which prompted a debate in Israel's Knesset (parliament). Others have extended this argument to include all members of Arab groups like Hamas that threaten the existence of Jews in the land of Israel or their supporters around the world.

Another example is the case of Baruch Goldstein, who, in 1994, killed thirty-four Muslims in Hebron near the Cave of the Patriarchs, a site sacred to both Jews and Muslims. This site, cut off from Jewish visitation and worship, was made available in the 1967 war and, in 1968, Rabbi Moshe Levinger, associated with the Settler Movement, celebrated the first night of Passover there, starting a new continual settlement of Jews in Hebron. In the weeks following Goldstein's massacre, hundreds of Israelis traveled to Goldstein's grave to celebrate Goldstein's actions, some dancing and singing around his grave. They kissed and hugged his gravestone, a veneration that continued until the Israeli government removed the burial site. Even after this removal, members of the Settler movement continue to celebrate the anniversary of the massacre, dressing up and dressing their children as Baruch Goldstein. This veneration has now attracted a liturgy that has been incorporated into the Purim celebrations of some Settler Jews in Hebron and Jerusalem along with the costuming. Costuming as part of a religious celebration is particular to and characteristic of the holiday of Purim, traditionally confined to those characters mentioned in the Bible. The addition of a Baruch Goldstein costume is a significant indication of the ideological change in this celebration among the Settlers who practice this revised form of Purim.

Finally, in these examples, following Magid's contention that there needs be an American connection to Jewish fundamentalism, we can see that there is a factor of Americanization of some of the actions of the Settler religious. As Shalom Goldman has pointed out in his *Zeal for Zion,* Christian millenialist fundamentalists have long sought Jewish reclamation of the whole of the biblical landscape, the destruction of the Islamic constructions on the Temple Mount, and the rebuilding of the Temple.[8] The organizational front of this effort in Israel was founded by a Kach party rabbi, Yehuda Ariel, and, together with the American Christians, began making temple garments for priests and breeding a "red heifer," necessary to purify the Temple Mount before reestablishing Temple sacrifice. Offshoots of the Gush Emunim, known generally as the Jewish Underground, plotted unsuccessfully to destroy the Arab monuments on the Temple Mount but were thwarted by Israeli Intelligence. These acts were designed to sacralize, or, rather, resacralize the Temple area to bring about the messianic era, displacing the secular State of Israel.

Such groups and actions, and more particularly, their ideologies, reflect a millennialist fundamentalism comparable to those we have seen in the essays on American Judaism, albeit taken to a violent extreme. The view that their reading of scripture is too influenced by traditional metaphoric exegesis to fit within fundamentalist strictures misconstrues, I feel, the way that those whom we term fundamentalists actually have read scripture. I feel that it would be a useful study for someone to do a thorough-going rhetorical analysis across various traditions to ascertain the degree to which there might be a fundamentalist way of reading, a project that would revisit the work done in the Fundamentalism Project and that lies outside the scope of this essay and this volume.

In "The Concept of Global Fundamentalism: A Short Critique," Simon A. Wood offers a view that would largely restrict the use of the term *fundamentalism* to American Protestant contexts. For him the use of the term *fundamentalism* outside American Protestantism is vague and problematic. He rejects the family-resemblance arguments put forth by Almond, Appleby, Sivan, and others in *Strong Religion: The Rise of Fundamentalisms around the World;* joins with critics who hold that the "signifier lacks a concrete signified"; and suggests that the term is too tied up with Christian tradition to be applicable to other religious traditions. In discussing the term he raises various problems and difficulties with it. He suggests that some of the term's proponents have noted some of these difficulties but have effectively proposed—unsatisfactorily in Wood's view—that their resolution lies in the future: "the juncture at which difficulties raised by critics are fully resolved lies at an unspecified future point." In his challenge to the use of the term he cites the examples from Islam of Mawlana Abul-Ala Mawdudi and Ayatollah

Ruhollah Khomeini and their followers. Of them he says that "their movements in no way circumscribe what is viewed as Islamic fundamentalism, [but] they may certainly be taken as seminal representatives of it." "If the two," he argues, "cannot be shown to fit a paradigm indicative of family resemblance with other fundamentalists the concept of Islamic fundamentalism is called into question. This, in turn, undermines the concept of global fundamentalism as a broad signifier or umbrella term."

In the cases of the two Islamic figures, Wood points out that both reject scriptural literalism. He also emphasizes the ways in which the two figures are products of specific local conditions and argues that "they do not embody Sunni and Shiite manifestations of global fundamentalism. The distinctive features of their movements, I find, originate more in the distinctive environments of the subcontinent and Iran than in the rejection of ideas originating in Europe's enlightened cafes." On a more general note he contends that the term has been applied to so many different groups that it has lost any specific analytic force. After an examination of both Khomeini and Mawdudi, finding them not to fit within the fundamentalist definition, he concludes that "efforts to construct and deploy broad umbrella terms that capture structurally similar developments within different global settings are integral to the study of culture. The argument outlined above is framed by the suggestion that some umbrella terms work better than others. Of the criteria that must be satisfied for such terms to be useful, the most important is their capacity to identify and differentiate. I have suggested that in the case of fundamentalism this criterion has not been fulfilled. . . . While advocates of the concept have noted differences between Christian, Jewish, and Muslim engagements with modernity, they have insufficiently theorized the ways in which these differences bear on and undermine the concept of a genuinely global phenomenon." Wood's argument to remove two prominent Islamic figures from under the term *fundamentalism* parallels Cahan's argument to remove Israelis from under the term, and his critical stance may be seen together with that adopted by Khalid Yahya Blankinship in the next essay.

In "Muslim 'Fundamentalism:' Salafism, Sufism, and Other Trends," Blankinship argues on the side of those who would entirely avoid the use of the term *fundamentalism.* After showing that Salafism and Wahhabism share with those who have been termed fundamentalist in drawing sharp boundaries to distinguish themselves from others and sometimes denouncing other Muslims as unbelievers who do not share their particular views, he states that "to do so is not a crime in a land that offers freedom of religion, but it may be necessary for group coherence." Additionally, he agrees with John L. Esposito, who says, "I regard 'fundamentalism' as too laden with Christian presuppositions and Western stereotypes, as well as implying a monolithic threat that does not exist." Esposito then suggests less value-laden terms deriving from the Islamic tradition. Blankinship concludes:

"Thus it would be desirable for the field of Muslim studies to distance itself from broad claims about the unified identity of diverse groups, each of which deserves consideration separately and on its own. At the same time it would be desirable to abandon the term *fundamentalism* altogether, since it is being used primarily as a term of abuse."

In making his arguments Blankinship chooses to advance two lines of argument. One is that academic works on fundamentalism and Islam are not sympathetic to or neutral to groups that are identified by the scholars writing about them. The second line of argument is that groups so identified as fundamentalist exhibit behaviors and ideas in common with other Islamic groups in the present and in the history of Islam. As we shall see, Blankinship's arguments, as well as those of others in this volume, raise issues of the hermeneutics of the part to the whole.

Lynda Clarke's article "Fundamentalism and Shiism" offers a set of nuanced arguments about the complexity of analyzing Islamic fundamentalism. Her first argument is that the differences between Shiism and Sunnism are important to keep in mind when looking at fundamentalism among Shiites. Allied with that is her observation that Shiite Islam, as a minority in the Muslim world, is affected by fundamentalism through Sunni Islamic societies, where it appeared first. Next she distinguishes three "waves" of fundamentalism: 1) mass-based organizations such as the Muslim Brotherhood; 2) the "utopian schemes of the Indo-Pakistani Abu al-Ala Mawdudi (d. 1979) and Sayyid Qutb (d. 1966) from Egypt;" 3) clandestine extremist groups, including the "grouplets" active in Egypt in the 1970s and al-Qaeda. What she sees in common with these waves is their desire to establish the absolute rule of Islam.

An additional aspect of her argument about the minority status of Shiism follows James Piscatori's notion that fundamentalism in Islam is a "second-order reaction" not directly to "modernism" but to the religious and political leaders who had to deal with the failure of modernism. This, both Clarke and Piscatori contend, places the actions of Islamic fundamentalism within a political realm, with the problem defined as a lack of Islamic rule and the solution thought to lie in militant action. This explains why fundamentalism is blended with nationalism and pan-Islamism. Also, she advances,

> The editors of the Fundamentalism Project see fundamentalism arising in situations in which believers feel "beleaguered" by a "syncretistic, areligious, or irreligious cultural milieu"; but this does not fit the Muslim case. Muslims in Muslim-majority countries are not in reality faced by any serious "irreligious cultural milieu"; what they feel "beleaguered" by is rather foreign culture as a symbol of foreign dominance associated with "ethnoreligiously alien, imperialistic, and exploitative forces." Islamic fundamentalism is not a direct

> reaction to Enlightenment values or so-called modernity but to the perception that these are a part of a political assault; that the West is engaged in a plot to penetrate Muslim lands culturally in order to take them over is something emphasized by all fundamentalists and believed by many others.

For Clarke, Islamic fundamentalism is a second-order reaction to Western ideologies, which ideologies are comingled with a stronger dose of politicization because of the imperialist colonial filter through which they are apprehended. Having said all the above, however, Clarke is reluctant to see fundamentalism generally among Twelver-Shiites because of the nature of Shiite authority dispersed among independent ayatollahs. Individuals, like Khomeini, however, exhibit enough characteristics in common with this second-order fundamentalism for the term to be applied within limits.

In the final two essays on Islam and fundamentalism, both authors offer interesting case studies that examine Islamic activities by Muslims labeled as conservative by some that do not fit one definition of fundamentalism or another. For their studies they do not find the term *fundamentalism* to be useful as an analytic term. In this, they raise the question that is at the heart of this volume: "What is achieved by calling a phenomenon 'fundamentalist' and what is concealed?"[9] I would add to that the question of to what purpose is the term, or any term, invoked. The use of terms as labels or pointers presupposes not only an anticipated outcome from the act of pointing but marshals as well the semantic range of the pointer-word, which range extends beyond the scope of a dictionary entry, which itself is a pointer toward the term's semantic range at a point in time and for a particular purpose.

A number of the authors in this volume and many outside of it start from the assumption that the term is an American Protestant term from its original usage and choose not to use the term in their scholarship because of its original meaning and, for them, ongoing association. As we know, and as has been mentioned in this volume's essays, terms can change over time and become domesticated into general (and accepted) usage. Many scholars are now using the various corpora of the languages in which terms are used in order to gauge current usage and its change over time. These language databases are, of course, limited by the sources they mine but give a wider range than the standard dictionary and are less subject to accidental bias than using an Internet search. From one database as an example (http://corpus.byu.edu/coha/), a database of American English usage, it is possible to see the application of the term *fundamentalism* from its beginnings in the 1920s to the present and its shift from Protestant American Christianity to Islam, with occasional applications to "liberal fundamentalists" and the "sephardization" of Israeli politics. From this range of usage, one can make arguments about the utility or nonutility of the term *fundamentalism*.

Several authors have dismissed the use of the term *fundamentalism* because the parts of the definition of the term, as they have set them forth, have features in common with those whom they would label nonfundamentalists. While this approach to the term allows for certain types of comparison among the investigated groups, the argument that the word *fundamentalism* has no meaning or is too general because there are too many features in common with the features of other terms, *fundamentalism* and *conservatism* or *fundamentalism* and *evangelicalism*, for example, raises an issue that is at least as old as Aristotle, the issue of the part and the whole. In the *Metaphysics* he says, "In the case of all things which have several parts and in which the totality is not, as it were, a mere heap, but the whole is something beside the parts, there is a cause."[10] He is arguing about a totality, such as a man or wine, in which something is lost if by the term *man* or *wine* we mean only its parts are together as a heap rather than as a whole. If we look at the oft-quoted misattribution to Ovid, *adde parvum parvo magnus acervus erit,* where *acervus* is translated as heap (add a little to a little and it will become a heap), we see echoes of an ancient type of sophistical argument called in Greek *sorites* (*soros* = Latin *acervus,* "heap"), a logical sophism formed by an accumulation of arguments. It is discussed, for example, in Cicero's *Academica* 2.49: "the method of proceeding by minute steps of gradual addition or withdrawal. They call this class of arguments soritae because by adding a single grain at a time they make a heap. It is certainly an erroneous and captious kind of argument!" (translated by H. Rackham in the Loeb Classical Library edition). Horace mentions this type of sophism at *Epistles* 2.1.47—*elusus ratione ruentis acervi*—"foiled by the argument of the dwindling pile."[11] Thus we can talk about a forest or we can talk about trees, as a type or individually, as all oaks or pines, or as a particular oak or pine in the larger forest environment. The questions we pose depend, obviously, on what kind of information we seek. Do we wish to talk about all old-growth forests or about a particular feature of certain trees in a particular old growth forest? In the case of the term *fundamentalism,* we are, of course, not referring to an actual object but a concatenating of abstract metaphoric ideas under a "suprametaphor," as it were, that gathers other metaphors together. It is similar to other like terms, *socialism, democracy, liberalism, fascism, modernism,* each of which has a positive, neutral, or negative valence depending on its context and possesses residual semantic baggage from its original use.

A second issue raised by some authors is whether or not one needs to find an indigenous term in the language of those being examined as fundamentalists to use the term. The Arabic word *salafî* is one example that comes to mind. As a movement among Sunni Muslims, it can have one of several meanings. It can refer to the act of following the actions of the first three Islamic generations of followers of Muhammad, or it can refer to following the figures of Muhammad Abduh, Jamal ad-Din al-Afghani, and Rashid Rida, or, third, following the more literalist injunctions of Ibn Taymiyyah. The aptness of using the term *fundamentalist* for the third meaning, for example, will depend on how the author frames the argument for its aptness, keeping in mind the intended audience. Using the term *salafî* untranslated in an English-language work is a choice that implies that the author feels that this term is untranslatable. Such a choice limits comparison but enhances and emphasizes the distinctive characteristics associated with the use of the term among Arabic-speaking peoples. In Hebrew, for example, the word פונדמנטליסט (fundamentalist) is used as a calque for the English word fundamentalist.[12] For those authors who advocate abolishing the use of the term, it is, in my opinion, too late. Not only is it in general use across the various registers of English; the Library of Congress has also designated a special classification for books on the subject. As many have done, it is possible to invoke the term and then explain how the term has been used and will then be used by the author. Then the term can be used or avoided, but educating, thereby, the reader to the possibilities and limitations of the term, strengthening the author's own argument about the material under investigation.

In sum, the contestation over the term *fundamentalism* in this volume and in previous academic work shows that in any situation where terms are used to describe and compare actions and ideas, the author must decide whether the "yield" from using the term will outweigh the limitations of using the term. As Florian Pohl states, "What is achieved by calling a phenomenon 'fundamentalist' and what is concealed?" Solving that equation and then stating the solution clearly for the reader is an important part of the pedagogic function of academic writing.

Notes

1. The Butler Act was repealed only on May 18, 1967.

2. George M. Marsden, *Fundamentalism and American Culture: The Shaping of Twentieth-Century Evangelicalism, 1870–1925* (New York: Oxford University Press, 1980), 4.

3. Bruce Lawrence, *Defenders of God: The Fundamentalist Revolt against the Modern Age* (San Francisco: Harper & Row, 1989), 2.

4. Lionel Caplan, introduction to *Studies of Religious Fundamentalism* (Albany: State University of New York Press, 1987), 22.

5. Harvey Cox, *Fire from Heaven: The Rise of Pentecostal Spirituality and the Reshaping of Religion in the Twenty-First Century* (Reading, Mass.: Addison-Wesley, 1995), 15.

6. Gabriel A. Almond, R. Scott Appleby, and Emmanuel Sivan, eds., *Strong Religion: The Rise of Fundamentalisms around the World* (Chicago: University of Chicago Press, 2003), 17.

7. Ian Lustick. *For the Land and the Lord: Jewish Fundamentalism in Israel.* New York: Council of Foreign Relations Press, 1988. See also http://www.sas.upenn.edu/penncip/lustick/ (accessed October 2, 2012).

8. Shalom Goldman, *Zeal for Zion* (Chapel Hill: University of North Carolina Press, 2009).

9. Florian Pohl, "Islamic Education and the Limits of Fundamentalism as an Analytical Category," this volume. The second essay is by David L. Johnston, "Fundamentalism Diluted: From Enclave to Globalism in Conservative Muslim Ecological Discourse."

10. *Metaphysics,* 1045a.

11. I owe this this to my colleague, Professor Garth Tissol of Emory University's Department of Classics.

12. As a cultural note, the close connection of Israeli Hebrew speakers to English usages and ideas is likely the reason that the Hebrew academy has not invented a Hebrew neologism to replace the calque.

Afterword

Simon A. Wood and David Harrington Watt

Clearly, this book has not resolved the question of whether or not comprehending certain modern forms of Christianity, Judaism, and Islam is facilitated by labeling them examples of "fundamentalism." But it has, in our view, presented some of the major current arguments on both sides of this debate. The views of Shaul Magid and Lynda Clarke, who cogently argue that *fundamentalism* captures important features of certain non-Christian movements, are directly contrary to those of David Harrington Watt, Jean Axelrad Cahan, Simon A. Wood, Khalid Yahya Blankinship, and Florian Pohl. Gordon D. Newby suggests that the latter group is seeking to close the gate after a horse has bolted: it is too late in the conversation to discard the term. We acknowledge the point. Indeed, several books on fundamentalism were published during the period of this book's gestation and production. But we stand by our view that the term's currency in various registers of English, such as it is, has in no way brought us to a point of no return. Nor do we feel that a Library of Congress classification for books on fundamentalism points toward a definitive resolution of the debate. We do not see that the Library holds a mortgage on the matter. Further, we find plenty of precedent for once popular terms subsequently falling into disuse and likewise for their revision or replacement in the Library's classifications list. The largely discarded "primitive religion," removed from the list in 1993, is one of numerous examples that might be cited.[1]

Overall, this project has deepened our suspicions about the unanchoring move from historic American fundamentalism to global fundamentalism. By no means have we seen the last word on American fundamentalism. In this book Dan D. Crawford suggests that its extremist character has frequently been exaggerated, while Shaul Magid suggests that it takes Jewish as well as Protestant forms. And we have no doubt that the discourse on American fundamentalism will continue to grow and move in new directions. But—and this is the crux of the matter—while its precise character remains open to debate and contestation, we feel that the great majority of scholars, including ourselves, can agree that "American fundamentalism" labels *something*. In the case of so-called global fundamentalism, we do not see that this is the case. We remain unconvinced that the concept of global fundamentalism is useful. To revisit a point mentioned in the introduction, in no way are we saying that unanchoring moves from one context to another—Western to non-Western; Christian to non-Christian; specific to general—are always unhelpful. To the contrary, these moves are often very helpful, and in such cases Bruce B. Lawrence's description of those who would reject them as overly rigid "originists" is apt. But we are saying that sometimes these moves are unhelpful, fundamentalism being a case in point. We appreciate that many, including three contributors to this book, will take a different view. We would like to end our discussion by briefly addressing a couple of issues raised by the preceding essays.

Fundamentalism Is As Good a Term As Any

The debate here recalls the proverbial "rose by any other name still being a rose," to which critics of the term respond, "that's fine and well, but we are not talking about a rose." And many critics further find the "so what should we call it?" question badly formed: there is no "it" here. This stance is neatly captured by Gabriele Marranci's suggestion that those who identify examples of global "fundamentalism" in a remarkably diverse set of contexts are "mistakenly seeing a smiley face where there are only dots, a line, and a semicircle."[2] Several scholars have plausibly suggested that, depending on the case, other terms better capture what is at issue. Without rehearsing a complete list, we note Khalid Yahya Blankinship's suggestion that frequently what is discussed under the rubric of fundamentalism is effectively separatism or exclusivism. Why not refer to these cases as such? What payoff results from labeling them fundamentalism? We struggle to find one. Additionally, some might consider following Laurence Iannaccone and moving away from *fundamentalism* and toward *sectarianism*.[3] Or if what we are really trying to conjure up is a category of religious people who are prone to violence or militancy then it might make sense for us to focus on comparing "militant forms of religion" or "violent forms of religion." Similarly, if the object is effectively politicized religion—a reaction to political situations that draws on the resources of religious tradition—why not refer to it as such? That label would apply to some but certainly not all movements identified as fundamentalist. To be sure, terms such as *Political Islam* bring their own sets of complications and controversies, but these are by our reading less problematical than those associated with fundamentalism. Or if we want to talk more broadly about "religious movements that resist modernity" then we are going to have to recognize the fact that since modernity has many different meanings resisting modernity has many different meanings, too. Scholars such as Pauline C. Westerman have pointed out the difficulties connected with defining one vague and contested concept through its relationship to another vague and highly contested concept.[4] Much of the literature on fundamentalism does not deal with those difficulties successfully. We will need to be as explicit as possible regarding what we mean by modernity and what we think it means to resist it.

Perhaps the general point we are trying to make could also be expressed as follows. When people say we are going to have to call it something, so we might as well call it fundamentalism, we are tempted to respond, but you still have not told us what the "it" that you want to talk about really is. We know that you are referring to a set of religious movements. But we find the argument that there is no simple way to separate religious movements from nonreligious or secular ones quite persuasive.[5] It seems clear to us that what counts as religious and what counts as nonreligious or secular changes from place to place and time to time, while numerous movements are informed by both religious and secular concerns. To be sure, scholars invested in the concept of global fundamentalism have noted that fundamentalism often integrates an eclectic combination of the religious and the secular. Yet beyond noting that the two categories are less easily separated than much of the literature on fundamentalism allows, the critical point is that fundamentalism's sine qua non is said to be its essentially or ultimately religious character (hence, nationalism, bolshevism, and so on are not fundamentalisms). This is sometimes explicated in terms of fundamentalism's orientation towards an "ultimate reward" that nonfundamentalist ideologies do not offer. We simply do not find this line of thought productive. How is the concept adding to our understanding here? We already know that notions of ultimate reward are integral to Christian and Islamic teaching. If here the concept merely enables a distinction between a "fundamentalist" activist who is motivated by an ultimate reward and a "nonfundamentalist" activist who is motivated by something else, it is not enabling much, to say nothing of the rather narrow understanding of ultimate reward that it rests upon. And here again the concept seems to break down completely when set against Asian examples, as some of its proponents implicitly or explicitly acknowledge.[6] Are Hindu or Buddhist activists and militants motivated by something that could reasonably be labeled an "ultimate reward"? That seems unlikely.

Finally, we are doubtful that fundamentalism can be adequately defined as something disagreeable or dangerous. That definition again leads us down the path of defining something contested by something else that is contested: to what or whom is fundamentalism dangerous? People invested in something called liberal religion or the broad assumptions of neo-liberalism? To be sure, some scholars committed to the concept of global fundamentalism have attempted to address these questions. Some have attempted to specify to whom or to what fundamentalism is disagreeable or dangerous, and, more generally, commented on how their own commitments might have influenced their scholarship.[7] In our view these efforts have not been fully successful and still leave us with the conundrum of defining a vague concept through its relationship to others that are not terribly specific. There are, for instance, multiple ways of envisioning or practicing "liberal religion." In sum, we do not see that there is an Archimedean point from which we can make confident pronouncements about which religious and social movements are good and which are bad or dangerous.

Where Do We Go from Here?

We are under no illusion that we have said the last word about fundamentalism. We know that there are many issues related to the various phenomena that are said to be a part of fundamentalism that we do not know as much about as we should. We do not know as much as we should, to pick but one example, about the sort of American fundamentalists—the ones who might well be described as moderates rather than extremists—to which Dan D. Crawford's essay points our attention. Nor do we know, to name as second example, as much as we would like to about how Christian movements in Africa, Asia, and Latin America that have strong ties to Christian fundamentalism in the United States are similar to and different from the American fundamentalist movements of the 1920s and 1930s. And we do not know nearly as much as we would like to about the lives of women who are associated with Jewish and Muslim movements that are labeled fundamentalist. To be sure, thanks to the work of scholars such as Tamar El Or and Saba Mahmood we know far more about the lives that those women lead than we did just a decade ago. But there is still much work to be done. When people talk about movements labeled as fundamentalist they sometimes speak as if the label refers to a set of movements that are made up exclusively of men. That is simply not a helpful approach.

But empirical studies of the movements that have been described as examples of global fundamentalism will not, by themselves, tell us all that we need to know about the subject. We also need to know more about the development of the concept of fundamentalism. In particular we need to achieve a better understanding of how it was that the concept became unanchored from Protestantism. Clearly things that happened from 1975 to 1985 played a crucial role in that process. But there are also a few instances in the 1920s, 1930s, 1940s, 1950s, and 1960s of the term *fundamentalism* being applied to Jews and Muslims.[8] And it seems clear that Talcott Parsons's ideas about fundamentalism—ideas that were quite fully developed by 1940—played an important role in shaping Martin E. Marty's understanding of fundamentalism.[9] Marty himself has made that clear. It would be good to know more about why scholars such as Marty turned to Parsons when they were trying to work out a way of analyzing events such as the Iranian Revolution. It is quite clear that Parsons interpreted fundamentalism as a rebellion against modernization. But theories of modernization are far less widely accepted now than they were in Parsons's heyday. It would be useful to explore the reasons why scholars came to embrace the concept of fundamentalism in an era when so many scholars were turning away from the concept of modernization.

In this book we have been chiefly concerned with the way in which the concept of fundamentalism has been used by scholars. But the scholarly use of fundamentalism is perhaps only half the story. Or even less than half. For more than three decades the concept has been deployed by activists, journalists, and governmental officials. And Americans are not, by any means, the only people who invoke fundamentalism. When, for example, Jews in Israel or Muslims in Egypt are trying to label their opponents they often invoke *fundamentalist* and its cognates, some of which are effectively appropriations of the English word into other languages. We still know far less than we should about how the concept of fundamentalism works in international popular—as opposed to scholarly—discourse. We know very little indeed about how the popular use of fundamentalism has influenced the way that scholars think about fundamentalism and about the way that scholars' ideas about fundamentalism have affected popular discourse.

It is difficult, we realize, to give compelling accounts of topics such as these. But, in principle at least, it is not impossible to do so. Our hope is that other scholars will go on to explore with enthusiasm and creativity. There is still a great deal to be said about fundamentalism. We will not get the last word on this subject. Which is all to the good.

Notes

1. On this point, see Steven A. Knowlton, "Three Decades since *Prejudices and Antipathies*: A Study of Changes in the Library of Congress Subject Headings," *Cataloging & Classification Quarterly* 40, no. 2 (2005): 123–45.

2. Gabriele Marranci, *Understanding Muslim Identity: Rethinking Fundamentalism* (New York: Palgrave Macmillan, 2009), 48.

3. Laurence R. Iannaccone, "Toward an Economic Theory of 'Fundamentalism,'" *Journal of Institutional and Theoretical Economics* 153 (March 1997): 103–5.

4. Pauline C. Westerman, "The Modernity of Fundamentalism," *Journal of Religion* 74 (January 1994): 80.

5. See for example Michael W. Kaufmann, "The Religious, the Secular, and Literary Studies: Rethinking the Secularization Narrative in Histories of the Profession," *New Literary History* 38 (Autumn 2007): 607–28.

6. See for instance Gabriel A. Almond, R. Scott Appleby, and Emmanuel Sivan, *Strong Religion: The Rise of Fundamentalisms around the World* (Chicago: University of Chicago Press, 2003), 15.

7. See, for instance, Almond et al., *Strong Religion,* 15.

8. Hamilton A. R. Gibb, *Mohammedanism: A Historical Survey* (New York: New American Library, 1955), 134–38.

9. Martin E. Marty, "Fundamentalism Reborn: Faith and Fanaticism," *Saturday* Review 7 (May 1980) 37–42; Talcott Parsons, "Memorandum: The Development of Groups and Organizations Amenable to Use Against American Institutions and Foreign Policy," in *Talcott Parsons on National Socialism*, ed. Uta Gerhardt (New York: Aldine De Gruyter, 1993), 101–30.

Selected Bibliography

Abdul-Wahhab, Muhammad bin. *Kitab at-Tauhid.* Riyadh: Dar-us-Salam Publications, 1416 [1996].

Abrahamian, Ervand. *Khomeinism: Essays on the Islamic Republic.* Berkeley: University of California Press, 1993.

——. *Radical Islam: The Iranian Mojahedin.* London: I. B. Tauris, 1989.

——. *Tortured Confessions: Prisons and Public Recantations in Modern Iran.* Berkeley: University of California Press, 1999.

——. "Why the Islamic Republic Has Survived." *Middle East Report* no. 205 (Spring 2009).

AbuKhalil, As'ad. *The Battle for Saudi Arabia: Royalty, Fundamentalism, and Global Power.* New York: Seven Stories Press, 2004.

Ahmed, Akbar S. *Postmodernism and Islam: Predicament and Promise.* New Delhi: Penguin Books India, 1993.

Akbarzadeh, Shahram, and Abdullah Saeed, eds. *Islam and Political Legitimacy.* London & New York: Routledge Curzon, 2003.

Akhavi, Shahrough. "Contending Discourses in Shi'i Law on the Doctrine of Wilāyat al-Faqīh," *Iranian Studies* 29 (Summer–Autumn 1996): 229–68.

——. "Elite Factionalism in the Islamic Republic of Iran," *Middle East Journal* 41 (Spring 1987): 181–201.

——. *Religion and Politics in Contemporary Iran: Clergy-State Relations in the Pahlavī Period.* Albany: State University of New York Press, 1980.

Akram, Ejaz. "The Muslim World and Globalization: Modernity and the Roots of Conflict." In *Islam, Fundamentalism, and the Betrayal of Tradition: Essays by Western Muslim Scholars,* revised edition, ed. Joseph E. B. Lumbard, 255–97. Bloomington, Ind.: World Wisdom, 2009.

Alagha, Joseph Elie. *The Shifts in Hizbullah's Ideology: Religious Ideology, Political Ideology and Political Program.* Amsterdam: Amsterdam University Press, 2006.

Algar, Hamid. *Wahhabism: A Critical Essay.* Oneonta, N.Y.: Islamic Publications International, 2002.

Allen, Charles. *God's Terrorists: The Wahhabi Cult and Hidden Roots of Modern Jihad.* Cambridge, Mass.: Da Capo Press, 2007.

Almond, Gabriel A., R. Scott Appleby, and Emmanuel Sivan. *Strong Religion: The Rise of Fundamentalisms around the World.* Chicago: University of Chicago Press, 2003.

Amanat, Abbas. *Apocalyptic Islam and Iranian Shi'ism.* London: I. B. Tauris, 2009.

Amanat, Abbas, and Frank Griffel, eds. *Shari'a: Islamic Law in the Contemporary Context.* Stanford: Stanford University Press, 2007.

Antoun, Richard T. *Understanding Fundamentalism: Christian, Islamic and Jewish Movements.* 2nd ed. Lanham, Md.: Rowman & Littlefield, 2008.

Appleby, R. Scott. "Fundamentalism." In *Encyclopedia of Politics and Religion.* 2nd ed. Edited by Robert Wuthnow. Washington, D.C.: CQ Press, 2007.

Arato, Andrew. *Constitution Making under Occupation: The Politics of Imposed Revolution in Iraq.* New York: Columbia University Press, 2009.

Arjomand, Said Amir. *After Khomeini: Iran under His Successors.* New York: Oxford University Press, 2009.

——, ed. *The Political Dimensions of Religion.* Albany: State University of New York Press, 1993.

——. "Review: Fundamentalism, Religious Nationalism, or Populism?" *Contemporary Sociology* 23 (September 1994): 671–75.

——. *The Shadow of God and the Hidden Imam.* Chicago: University of Chicago Press, 1984.

Armajani, Jon. *Modern Islamist Movements: History, Religion, and Politics.* Chichester, U.K.: Wiley-Blackwell, 2012.

Armstrong, Karen. *The Battle for God: A History of Fundamentalism.* New York: Ballantine Books, 2001.

Asad, Talal. *Formations of the Secular: Christianity, Islam, Modernity.* Stanford: Stanford University Press, 2003.

——. *Genealogies of Religion: Discipline and Reasons of Power in Christianity and Islam.* Baltimore & London: Johns Hopkins University Press, 1993.

——. *On Suicide Bombing.* New York: Columbia University Press, 2007.

Auerbach, Jerold S. *Hebron Jews: Memory and Conflict in the Land of Israel.* Lanham, Md.: Rowman & Littlefield, 2009.

Banna, Hasan al-, "Toward the Light," Translated into English at http://web.youngmuslims.ca/online_library/books/towards_the_light/index.htm#preface.

Bartholomeusz, Tessa J., and Chandra R. De Silva, eds. *Buddhist Fundamentalism and Minority Identities in Sri Lanka.* Albany: State University of New York Press, 1998.

Bayat, Asef. *Making Islam Democratic: Social Movements and the Post-Islamist Turn.* Stanford: Stanford University Press, 2007.

Bayat, Mangol. "The Iranian Revolution of 1978–79: Fundamentalist or Modern?" *Middle East Journal* 37 (Winter 1983): 30–42.

Behdad, Sohrab. "Islamic Utopia in Pre-Revolutionary Iran: Navvab Safavi and the Fada'ian-e Eslam," *Middle Eastern Studies* 33 (January 1997): 40–65.

Bendroth, Margaret Lamberts. *Fundamentalists in the City: Conflict and Division in Boston's Churches, 1885–1950.* New York: Oxford University Press, 2005.

Berger, Peter, ed. *The Desecularization of the World: Resurgent Religion and World Politics.* Grand Rapids: Ethics and Public Policy Center and Eerdmans, 1999.

——. *Homeless Mind: Modernization and Consciousness.* New York: Vintage Books, 1974.

Bowie, Fiona. *The Anthropology of Religion.* 2nd ed. Oxford: Blackwell, 2006.

Brereton, Virginia Lieson. *Training God's Army: The American Bible School, 1880–1940.* Bloomington: Indiana University Press, 1990.

Brumberg, Daniel. *Reinventing Khomeini: The Struggle for Reform in Iran.* Chicago: University of Chicago Press, 2001.

Brunner, Rainer. *Islamic Ecumenism in the 20th century: The Azhar and Shiism between Rapprochement and Restraint.* Leiden & Boston: Brill, 2004.

Bulliet, Richard W. *The Case for Islamo-Christian Civilization.* New York: Columbia University Press, 2004.

Campo, Juan Eduardo. "Hegemonic Discourse and the Islamic Question in Egypt." *Contention* 4 (Spring 1995): 167–94.

Caplan, Lionel, ed. *Studies of Religious Fundamentalism.* Albany: State University of New York Press, 1987.

Carpenter, Joel A. "Fundamentalist Institutions and the Rise of Evangelical Protestantism, 1929–1942." *Church History* 49 (March 1980): 62–75

——, ed. *The Fundamentalist–Modernist Conflict: Opposing Views on Three Major Issues.* New York: Garland, 1988.

——. *Revive Us Again: The Reawakening of American Fundamentalism.* New York: Oxford University Press, 1997.

Casanova, José. *Public Religions in the Modern World.* Chicago: University of Chicago Press, 1994.

Chalfant, H. Paul, Ted Jelen, and William H. Swatos Jr. "Book Review Symposium on Fundamentalisms Observed." *Review of Religious Research* 35 (September 1993): 63–75.

Choueiri, Youssef M. *Islamic Fundamentalism: The Story of Islamist Movements.* 3rd ed. London: Continuum, 2010.

Clarke, Lynda, ed. *Shiite Heritage: Essays on Classical and Modern Traditions.* Binghamton, N.Y.: Global Publications, 2001.

Cohen, Erik. "The Changing Legitimations of the State of Israel." In *Israel: State and Society, 1948–1988,* edited by Peter Y. Medding. Oxford: Oxford University Press, 1989.

Cohen, Norman, ed. *The Fundamentalist Phenomenon: A View from Within, A Response from Without.* Grand Rapids: Eerdmans, 1990.

Cole, Juan. *The Ayatollahs and Democracy in Iraq, ISIM Paper 7.* Amsterdam: Amsterdam University Press, 2006.

——. *Sacred Space and Holy War: The Politics, Culture and History of Shi'ite Islam.* London: I. B. Tauris, 2002.

——. "The United States and Shi'ite Religious Factions in Post-Ba'thist Iraq," *Middle East Journal* 57 (Autumn 2003): 543–66.

Cole, Stewart. *History of Fundamentalism.* New York: Richard R. Smith, 1931.

Commins, David Dean. *Islamic Reform: Politics and Social Change in Late Ottoman Syria.* Oxford: Oxford University Press, 1990.

——. *The Wahhabi Mission and Saudi Arabia.* London: I. B. Tauris, 2006.

Cook, David. "Messianism in the Shiite Crescent." *Current Trends in Islamist Ideology* 11 (April 8, 2011).

Cox, Harvey. *Fire from Heaven: The Rise of Pentecostal Spirituality and the Reshaping of Religion in the Twenty-First Century.* Reading, Mass.: Addison-Wesley, 1995.

Crawford, Dan. *A Thirst for Souls: The Life of Evangelist Percy B. Crawford* (1902–1960). Selinsgrove, Penn.: Susquehanna University Press, 2010.

Davie, Grace. *The Sociology of Religion.* Los Angeles & London: Sage, 2007.

Dayton, Donald, and Robert K. Johnston, eds. *The Variety of American Evangelicalism.* Downers Grove, Ill.: InterVarsity Press, 1991.

DeBerg, Betty A. *Ungodly Women: Gender and the First Wave of American Fundamentalism.* Minneapolis: Fortress, 1990.

Deeb, Marius. "Shia Movements in Lebanon: Their Formation, Ideology, Social Basis, and Links with Iran and Syria," *Third World Quarterly* 10 (April 1988): 683–98.

DeLong-Bas, Natana J. *Wahhabi Islam: From Revival and Reform to Global Jihad.* Oxford: Oxford University Press, 2004.

Dollar, George W. *A History of Fundamentalism in America.* Greenville, S.C.: Bob Jones University Press, 1973. Reprint, Orlando: Daniels Publishing Company, 1983.

Don-Yehiya, Eliezer. "The Book and the Sword: The Nationalist Yeshivot and Political Radicalism in Israel." In *Accounting for Fundamentalisms,* edited by Martin E. Marty and R. Scott Appleby. Chicago: University of Chicago Press, 1994.

Draney, Daniel W. *When Streams Diverge: John Murdoch MacInnis and the Origins of Protestant Fundamentalism in Los Angeles.* Colorado Springs: Paternoster, 2008.

Ehteshami, Anoushiravan. *After Khomeini: The Iranian Second Republic.* New York: Taylor & Francis, 1995.

Enayat, Hamid. *Modern Islamic Political Thought.* London: I. B. Tauris, 2005.

Esposito, John L. *The Islamic Threat: Myth or Reality?* 3rd ed. New York & Oxford: Oxford University Press, 1999.

——, and Dalia Mogahed. *Who Speaks for Islam? What a Billion Muslims Really Think.* New York: Gallup Press, 2007.

Feiglin, Moshe. *Where There Are No Men: Zo Artzeinu's Struggle against the Post-Zionism Collapse.* Jerusalem: Published by Jewish Leadership, 1999.

Filiu, Jean-Pierre. "The Return of Political Mahdism." *Current Trends in Islamist Ideology* 8 (2009): 26–38.

Frey, Rebecca Joyce. *Fundamentalism.* New York: Facts on File, 2007.

Friedman, Menachem. "Habad as Messianic Fundamentalism: From Local Particularlism to Universal Jewish Mission." In *Accounting for Fundamentalism,* edited Martin E. Marty and R. Scott Appleby. Chicago: Chicago University Press, 1994.

Furnish, Timothy R. "Islamic Fundamentalism." In *Encyclopedia of Fundamentalism,* edited Brenda E. Brasher. New York: Routledge, 2001.

Furniss, Norman F. *The Fundamentalist Controversy, 1918–1931.* New Haven: Yale University Press 1954.

Gellner, Ernest. *Postmodernism, Reason, and Religion.* London: Routledge, 1992.

Goble, Paul. "Uzbekistan: Analysis From Washington—Fighting Fundamentalism With Sufism." *Radio Free Europe Radio Liberty* (September 9, 2000).

Goldberg, Ellis. "Smashing Idols and the State: The Protestant Ethic and Egyptian Sunni Radicalism." *Comparative Studies in Society and History* 33 (January 1991): 3–35.

Goldberg, Jeffery. "Among the Settlers: Will They Destroy Israel?" *New Yorker,* May 31, 2004.

Haddad, Yvonne Y., John Obert Voll, and John L. Esposito. *The Contemporary Islamic Revival: A Critical Survey and Bibliography.* New York: Greenwood, 1991.

Harding, Susan F. *The Book of Jerry Falwell: Fundamentalist Language and Politics.* Princeton: Princeton University Press, 2000.

Harris, Jay Michael. "'Fundamentalism': Objections from a Modern Jewish Historian." In *Fundamentalism and Gender,* edited by John Stratton Hawley, 137–73. New York: Oxford University Press, 1994.

Hart, D. G. *Defending the Faith: J. Gresham Machen and the Crisis of Conservative Protestantism in Modern America.* Baltimore: Johns Hopkins University Press, 1994.

Hawley, John Stratton, ed. *Fundamentalism and Gender.* New York: Oxford University Press, 1994.

Heelas, Paul, ed., with the assistance of David Martin and Paul Morris. *Religion, Modernity, and Postmodernity.* Oxford: Blackwell, 1998.

Hefner, Robert W., ed., with David Martin and Paul Morris. *Making Modern Muslims: The Politics of Islamic Education in Southeast Asia.* Honolulu: University of Hawaii Press, 2009.

Hiro, Dilip. *Iran under the Ayatollahs.* London: Routledge and K. Paul, 1985.

Hofstadter, Richard. *Anti-Intellectualism in American Life.* New York: Knopf, 1963.

Iannaccone, Laurence R. "Toward an Economic Theory of 'Fundamentalism.'" *Journal of Institutional and Theoretical Economics* 153 (March 1997): 100–116.

Israeli, Raphael. *Muslim Fundamentalism in Israel.* London: Brassey's UK, 1993.

Jabar, Faleh A. *The Shī'ite Movement in Iraq.* London: Saqi, 2003.

Jansen, Johannes J. *G. The Dual Nature of Islamic Fundamentalism.* Ithaca: Cornell University Press, 1997.

Jenkins, Philip. *The Next Christendom: The Coming of Global Christianity.* 2nd ed. New York & Oxford: Oxford University Press, 2007.

Johnston, David L. *Earth, Empire and Sacred Text: Muslims and Christians as Trustees of Creation.* London: Equinox, 2010.

Juergensmeyer, Mark. "Thinking about Religion after September 11." *Journal of the American Academy of Religion* 72 (March 2004): 221–34.

Kabbani, Muhammad Hisham. *Islamic Beliefs & Doctrine According to Ahl al-Sunna: A Repudiation of "Salafi" Innovations.* 2nd ed. Mountain View, Calif.: As-Sunna Foundation of America, 1993.

Kaplan, Lawrence, ed. *Fundamentalism in Comparative Perspective.* Amherst: University of Massachusetts Press, 1992.

Keddie, Nikki R. *Iran and the Muslim World: Resistance and Revolution.* New York: New York University Press, 1995.

Kepel, Gilles. *The Revenge of God: The Resurgence of Islam, Christianity, and Judaism in the Modern World.* University Park: Penn State University Press, 1995.

Khomeini, Ruhollah. "Islamic Government." In *Islam and Revolution: Writings and Declarations of Imam Khomeini.* Translated by Hamid Algar, 25–166. Berkeley, Calif.: Mizan Press, 1981.

——. *Islamic Government: Governance of the Jurist (Velayat-e Faqeeh).* Tehran: Institute for Compilation and Publication of Imam Khomeini's Works, 2002.

——. *al-Rasá'il.* Edited by Mujtabá al-Tihrání. Qum: Mu'assasah-i Matbú'átí Ismá'ílíyán, 1385/1965.

Knauss, Elizabeth. *The Conflict: A Narrative Based on the Fundamentalist Movement.* Los Angeles: Bible Institute of Los Angeles, 1923.

Knysh, Alexander. "A Clear and Present Danger: 'Wahhabism' as a Rhetorical Foil." *Die Welt des Islams* n.s. 44, no. 1 (2004): 3–26.

Kramer, Martin, ed. *Shiism, Resistance, and Revolution.* Boulder, Colo.: Westview Press, 1987.

Kurtz, Lester R. *Gods in the Global Village: The World Religions in Sociological Perspective,* 2nd ed. Thousand Oaks, Calif.: Pine Forge Press, 2007.

Lapidus, Ira M. *A History of Islamic Societies.* 2nd ed. Cambridge: Cambridge University Press, 2002.

Larson, Edward J. *Summer for the Gods: The Scopes Trial and America's Continuing Debate over Science and Religion.* New York: Basic Books, 1997.

Larson, Mel. *Youth for Christ.* Grand Rapids: Zondervan, 1947.

Lawrence, Bruce B. *Defenders of God: The Fundamentalist Revolt against the Modern Age.* San Francisco: Harper & Row, 1989.

——. *Shattering the Myth: Islam beyond Violence.* Princeton: Princeton University Press, 1998.

Lawrence, Bruce B., Azim Nanji, and William Shepard. "Discussion," *Religion* 19 (July 1989): 275–92.

Laws, Curtis Lee. "Convention Side Lights." *Watchman-Examiner,* July 1, 1920, 834.

Lawson, Todd, ed. *Reason and Inspiration in Islam: Theology, Philosophy and Mysticism in Muslim Thought.* London & New York: I. B. Tauris, 2005.

Lazaru-Yafeh, Hava. "Contemporary Fundamentalism in Judaism, Christianity and Islam." *Jerusalem Quarterly* 47 (1988): 27–39.

Liebman, Charles. *Deceptive Images: Toward a Redefinition of American Judaism.* New Brunswick: Transaction Books, 1988.

——. "Jewish Fundamentalism and the Israeli Polity." In *Fundamentalisms and the State,* edited by Martin E. Marty and R. Scott Appleby. Chicago: University of Chicago Press, 1993.

Lincoln, Bruce. *Holy Terrors: Thinking about Religion after September 11.* Chicago: University of Chicago Press, 2003.

Lippy, Charles H., and Peter W. Williams, eds. *Encyclopedia of the American Religious Experience: Studies of Traditions and Movements.* 3 vols. New York: Scribners, 1988.

Louër, Laurence. *Transnational Shia Politics: Religious and Political Networks in the Gulf.* New York: Columbia University Press, 2008.

Lustick, Ian. *For the Land and the Lord: Jewish Fundamentalism in Israel.* New York: Council on Foreign Relations, 1988.

MacClancy, Jeremy, ed. *Anthropology for the Real World.* Chicago: University of Chicago Press, 2001.

MacEoin, Denis. "Anwar al-Awlaki: 'I Pray that Allah Destroys America,'" *Middle East Quarterly* (Spring 2010): 13–19.

Machen, J. *Gresham. Christianity and Liberalism.* New York: Macmillan, 1924.

——. *What is Faith?* New York: Macmillan, 1925.

Mahmood, Saba. "Islamism and Fundamentalism." *Middle East Report* 24 (November–December 1994): 29–30.

Mallat, Chibli. *Shi'i Thought from the South of Lebanon.* Oxford: Centre for Lebanese Studies, 1988.

Mamdani, Mahmood. *Good Muslim, Bad Muslim: America, the Cold War, and the Roots of Terror.* New York: Pantheon Books, 2004.

Margulies, Phillip, ed. *The Rise of Islamic Fundamentalism.* Detroit: Greenhaven Press, 2006.

Marranci, Gabriele. *The Anthropology of Islam.* Oxford & New York: Berg, 2008.

——. *Understanding Muslim Identity: Rethinking Fundamentalism.* New York: Palgrave Macmillan, 2009.

Marsden, George M. "Defining Fundamentalism," *Christian Scholar's Review* 1 (Winter 1971): 141–51.

——. "Fundamentalism." In *Encyclopedia of the American Religious Experience*, edited by Charles H. Lippy and Peter W. Williams. (New York: Scribners, 1988), 956.

——. *Fundamentalism and American Culture: The Shaping of Twentieth-Century Evangelicalism, 1870–1925.* 2nd ed. New York: Oxford University Press, 2006.

——, ed. *The Fundamentals: A Testimony to the Truth.* New York: Garland, 1988. First edition, 1910–1915.

——. *Reforming Fundamentalism: Fuller Seminary and the New Evangelicalism.* Grand Rapids: Eerdmans, 1987.

——. *Understanding Fundamentalism and Evangelicalism.* Grand Rapids: Eerdmans, 1991.

Martin, David. *Tongues of Fire: Conservative Protestantism in Latin America.* Oxford: Blackwell, 1990.

Martin, Richard C., and Abbas Barzegar, eds. *Islamism: Contested Perspectives on Political Islam.* Stanford: Stanford University Press, 2010.

Martin, Vanessa. *Creating an Islamic State: Khomeini and the Making of a New Iran.* Rev. ed. London: I. B. Tauris, 2008.

Marty, Martin E. "Fundamentalism Reborn: Faith and Fanaticism," *Saturday Review* (May 1980): 37–42.

Marty, Martin E., and R. Scott Appleby, eds. *Accounting for Fundamentalisms: The Dynamic Character of Movements.* Chicago: University of Chicago Press, 1994.

Marty, Martin E., and R. Scott Appleby, eds. *Fundamentalisms and Society: Reclaiming the Sciences, the Family, and Education.* Chicago: University of Chicago Press, 1993.

——, eds. *Fundamentalisms Comprehended.* Chicago: University of Chicago Press, 1995.

——, eds. *Fundamentalisms Observed.* Chicago: University of Chicago Press, 1991.

Mawdudi, Abul-Ala. *Towards Understanding the Qur'an.* Vol. 1. Leicester: Islamic Foundation, 1988.

McIntire, Carl. *Twentieth-Century Reformation.* 2nd ed. Collingswood, N.J.: Christian Beacon Press, 1945.

Meijer, Roel, ed. *Global Salafism: Islam's New Religious Movement.* New York: Columbia University Press, 2009.

Menashiri, David, ed. *The Iranian Revolution and the Muslim World.* Boulder, Colo.: Westview Press, 1990.

Milani, Abbas. *Eminent Persians: The Men and Women Who Made Modern Iran, 1941–1979.* 2 vols. Syracuse: Syracuse University Press, 2008.

Misztal, Bronislaw, and Anson Shupe. "Making Sense of the Global Revival of Fundamentalism." In *Religion and Politics in Comparative Perspective: Revival of Religious Fundamentalism in East and West,* edited by Bronislaw Misztal and Anson Shupe. Westport, Conn.: Praeger, 1992.

Moaddel, Mansoor, and Karam Talattof, eds. *Modernist and Fundamentalist Debates in Islam: A Reader.* New York: Palgrave Macmillan, 2000.

Monsutti, Alessandro, Silvia Naef, and Farian Sabahi, eds. *The Other Shiites. From the Mediterranean to Central Asia.* Bern: Peter Lang, 2007.

Moran, Jeffrey P. "Reading Race into the Scopes Trial: African American Elites, Science, and Fundamentalism." *Journal of American History* 90 (December 2003): 891–911.

———. "The Scopes Trial and Southern Fundamentalism in Black and White: Race, Region, and Religion." *Journal of Southern History* 70 (February 2004): 95–120.

Muhammad ibn Sa'îd al-Qahtânî. *al-Walâ' wa-al-barâ' fî al-Islâm.* Cairo: al-Fath li-al-I'lâm al-'Arabî, 1402 [1982].

Muslih, 'Abd Allâh al-, and Salâh al-Sâwî. *Mâ la yasa'u al-Muslim jahluhu.* Cairo: Islamic Foundation of America, 1416 [1995].

Nakash, Yitzhak. *Reaching for Power: The Shi'a in the Modern Arab World.* Princeton: Princeton University Press, 2006.

Nasr, Sayyid Vali Reza. "Communalism and Fundamentalism: A Reexamination of the Origins of Islamic Fundamentalism." *Contention* 4 (Winter 1995): 122–23.

———. *Mawdudi and the Making of Islamic Revivalism.* New York: Oxford University Press, 1996.

———. "Regional Implications of Shi'a Revival in Iraq." *Washington Quarterly* 27 (Summer 2004): 7–24.

———. "When the Shiites Rise." *Foreign Affairs* 85 (July/August 2006): 58–74.

Niebuhr, H. Richard. "Fundamentalism." In *Encyclopedia of the Social Sciences.* Vol. 6. New York, 1937.

Nielsen, Kenneth Bo, ed. *Trysts with Democracy: Political Practice in South Asia.* London & New York: Anthem Press, 2011.

Olivetti, Vincenzo. *Terror's Source: The Ideology of Wahhabi-Salafism and Its Consequences.* Birmingham, U.K.: Amadeus Books, 2002.

Plantinga, Alvin. *Warranted Christian Belief.* New York: Oxford University Press, 2000.

Riesbrodt, Martin. *Pious Passion. The Emergence of Modern Fundamentalism in the United States and Iran.* Translated by Don Renau. Berkeley: University of California Press, 1993.

Riley, W. *B. Inspiration or Evolution.* 2nd ed. Cleveland, Ohio: Union Gospel Press, 1926.

Roy, Olivier. *Globalized Islam: The Search for a New Ummah.* New York: Columbia University Press, 2004.

———. *Holy Ignorance: When Religion and Culture Part Way.* New York: Columbia University Press, 2010.

Russell, C. Allyn. *Voices of American Fundamentalism: Seven Biographical Studies.* Philadelphia: Westminster, 1976.

Ruthven, Malise. *Fundamentalism: A Very Short Introduction.* New York: Oxford University Press, 2007.

——. *Fundamentalism: The Search for Meaning.* New York: Oxford University Press, 2004.

——. *The Search for Meaning.* Oxford: Oxford University Press, 2001.

Saad-Ghorayeb, Amal. *Hizbu'llah: Politics and Religion.* London & Sterling, Va.: Pluto Press, 2002.

Sandeen, Ernest R. "Defining Fundamentalism: A Reply." *Christian Scholar's Review* 1 (Spring 1971): 227–33.

——. *The Roots of Fundamentalism: British and American Millenarianism, 1800–1930.* Chicago: University of Chicago Press, 1970.

Sayyid, Bobby S. *A Fundamental Fear: Eurocentrism and the Emergence of Islamism.* 2nd ed. London: Zed Books, 2003.

Schulze, Reinhard. *Islamischer Internationalismus im 20. Jahrhundert: Untersuchungen zur Geschichte der Islamischen Weltliga.* Leiden: Brill, 1990.

——. *A Modern History of the Islamic World.* Translated by Azizeh Azodi. New York: New York University Press, 2002.

Segal, Haggai. *Dear Brothers: The West Bank Jewish Underground.* Woodmere, N.Y.: Beit Shamai Publications, 1998.

Shapira, Anita. *Land and Power: The Zionist Resort to Force, 1881–1948.* Oxford: Oxford University Press, 1992.

Shepard, William E. "Islam as a 'System' in the Later Writings of Sayyid Qutb." *Middle Eastern Studies* 25 (January 1989): 31–50.

Sidahmed, Abdel Salam, and Anoushirvan Ehteshami. *Islamic Fundamentalism.* Boulder, Colo.: Westview Press, 1996.

Silber, Michael. *"The Emergence of Ultra-Orthodoxy: The Invention of a Tradition."* In *The Uses of Tradition: Jewish Continuity since Emancipation*, edited by Jack Wertheimer, 23–84. New York & Jerusalem: JTS distributed by Harvard University Press, 1992.

Silberstein, Laurence, ed. *Jewish Fundamentalism in Comparative Perspective: Religion, Ideology and the Crisis of Modernity.* New York: New York University Press, 1993.

Sivan, Emmanuel, and Menachem Friedman, eds. *Religious Radicalism and Politics in the Middle East.* Albany: State University of New York Press, 1990.

Sprinzak, Ehud. *The Ascendance of Israel's Radical Right.* Oxford: Oxford University Press, 1991.

Stadler, Nurit. *Yeshiva Fundamentalism.* New York & London: New York University Press, 2009.

Strozier, Charles B., David M. Terman, and James W. Jones, with Katherine A. Boyd. *The Fundamentalist Mindset: Psychological Perspectives on Religion, Violence, and History.* Oxford: Oxford University Press, 2010.

Swatos, William H., and Kevin Christiano. "Secularization Theory: The Course of a Concept." *Sociology of Religion* 60 (Fall 1999): 209–28.

Taji-Farouki, Suha. "Islamic State Theories and Contemporary Realities." In *Islamic Fundamentalism*, edited by Abdel Salam Sidahmed and Anoushirvan Ehteshami. Boulder, Colo.: Westview Press, 1996.

Tavger, Ben Zion. *My Hebron.* Translated by Pnina Tadmor. Hebron, 2009.

Terhalle, Maximilian. "Are the Shia Rising?" *Middle East Policy* 14 (Summer 2007): 69–83.

Torrey, Reuben. "Will Christ Come Again? An Exposure of the Foolishness, Fallacies and Falsehoods of Shailer Mathews." In *The Fundamentalist–Modernist Conflict: Opposing Views on Three Major Issues*, edited by Joel Carpenter. New York: Garland, 1988.

Trollinger, William Vance. *God's Empire: William Bell Riley and Midwestern Fundamentalism.* Madison: University of Wisconsin Press, 1990.

'Uthaymîn, 'Abd Allâh Sâlih al-. *Muhammad ibn 'Abd al-Wahhâb: The Man and His Works.* London: I. B. Tauris, 2009.

Varisco, Daniel Martin. *Islam Obscured: The Rhetoric of Anthropological Representation.* New York: Palgrave Macmillan, 2005.

——. "The Tragedy of a Comic: Fundamentalists Crusading against Fundamentalists." *Contemporary Islam* 1 (October 2007): 207–30.

Visser, Reidar. "Basra, the Reluctant Seat of 'Shiastan.'" *Middle East Report* 242 (Spring 2007).

Watt, David Harrington. "Meaning and End of Fundamentalism." *Religious Studies Review* 30 (October 2004): 271–74.

——. "The Private Hopes of American Fundamentalist and Evangelicals, 1925–1975." *Religion and American Culture* 1 (Summer 1991): 155–75.

——. *A Transforming Faith: Explorations of Twentieth-Century American Evangelicalism.* New Brunswick: Rutgers University Press, 1991.

——. "What's in a Name? The Meaning of 'Muslim Fundamentalist.'" *Origins* 1 (June 2008): 1–5.

Waugh, Earle H. "Fundamentalism: Harbinger of Academic Revisionism." *Journal of the American Academy of Religion* 65 (Spring 1997): 161–68.

Wood, Simon A. *Christian Criticisms, Islamic Proofs: Rashid Rida's Modernist Defense of Islam.* Oxford: Oneworld, 2008.

——. "Rethinking Fundamentalism: Ruhollah Khomeini, Mawlana Mawdudi, and the Fundamentalist Model." *Journal for Cultural and Religious Theory* 11 (Spring 2011): 171–98.

Contributors

MARGARET BENDROTH is author of *Fundamentalism and Gender, 1875 to the Present* (1993) and most recently contributed the essay "Fundamentalism" to the *Cambridge History of Religion in America* (2012). She is the director of the Congregational Library in Boston, Massachusetts.

KHALID YAHYA BLANKINSHIP is associate professor in the Department of Religion at Temple University. He writes on Muslim history and Muslim law. His books include *The End of the Jihad State: The Reign of Hisham ibn 'Abd al-Malik (724–743) and the Collapse of the Umayyads* (1994), *The History of al-Tabari,* vol. 11; *The Challenge to the Empires: A.D. 633–635/A.H. 12–13* (1993), and *The History of al-Tabari,* vol. 25, *The End of Expansion: The Caliphate of Hisham A.D. 724–738 / A.H. 105–120* (1989).

JEAN AXELRAD CAHAN is senior lecturer in philosophy and director of the Harris Center for Judaic Studies at the University of Nebraska–Lincoln. Her research interests include the philosophy of Spinoza and modern Jewish thought. A co-edited volume, *Returning to Babel: Jewish Latin American Experiences, Representations and Identity,* was published in 2011.

LYNDA CLARKE writes on Shiism, gender, law, and Islam in the West. She is professor of religion and Islam at Concordia University, Montreal.

DAN D. CRAWFORD is senior lecturer in religious studies at University of Nebraska–Lincoln and works on the history of evangelicalism in America. He is the author of *A Thirst for Souls: The Life of Evangelist Percy B. Crawford (1902–1960)* (2010).

DAVID L. JOHNSTON is the author of *Earth, Empire and Sacred Text: Muslims and Christians as Trustees of Creation* (2010). His website is humantrustees.org, and he is a visiting scholar at the Department of Near Eastern Languages and Civilizations at the University of Pennsylvania.

SHAUL MAGID is the Jay and Jeannie Schottenstein Professor of Modern Judaism at Indiana University. He is the author of *Hasidism on the Margin: Reconciliation, Antinomianism, and Messianism in Izbica/Radzin Hasidism* (2003), *From Metaphysics to Midrash: Myth, History and the Interpretation of Scripture in Lurianic Kabbalah* (2008), and *American Post-Judaism: Identity and Renewal in a Postethnic Society* (2013).

GORDON D. NEWBY is the Goodrich C. White Professor of Middle Eastern and South Asian Studies in the Department of Middle Eastern and South Asian Studies and a professor in the Graduate Program of West and South Asian Religions at Emory University. His research specialties include early Islam, Muslim relations with Jews and Christians, and comparative sacred texts. Among his scholarly works are *A History of the Jews of Arabia* (2009), *The Making of the Last Prophet* (2009), and *A Concise Encyclopedia of Islam* (2002). He was the founding editor of the journal *Medieval Encounters* and is currently working on a multivolume encyclopedia of the Middle East as well as a monograph on apocalypse and apocalypticism among Jews, Christians, and Muslims at the time of the rise of Islam.

FLORIAN POHL is the author of *Islamic Education and the Public Sphere: Today's Pesantren in Indonesia* (2009). He is associate professor of religion at Oxford College of Emory University.

DAVID HARRINGTON WATT is the author of *A Transforming Faith: Explorations of Twentieth-Century American Evangelicalism* (1991) and *Bible-Carrying Christians: Conservative Protestants and Social Power* (2003). He is a professor of history at Temple University.

SIMON A. WOOD is the author of *Christian Criticisms, Islamic Proofs: Rashid Rida's Modernist Defence of Islam* (2008). He is an associate professor of religious studies at the University of Nebraska–Lincoln.

Index